CORPORATE
ROCK
SUCKS

Also by Jim Ruland

Forest of Fortune

Big Lonesome: Stories

Cowritten by Jim Ruland

Do What You Want: The Story of Bad Religion
    (with Bad Religion)

My Damage: The Story of a Punk Rock Survivor
    (with Keith Morris)

Giving the Finger: Risking It All to Fish the World's Deadliest
    Sea (with Captain Scott Campbell Jr.)

CORPORATE

ROCK

SUCKS

The Rise and Fall of

SST RECORDS

Jim Ruland

hachette
BOOKS

New York

Hachette Books
Hachette Book Group
1290 Avenue of the Americas
New York, NY 10104
HachetteBooks.com
Twitter.com/HachetteBooks
Instagram.com/HachetteBooks

First Edition: April 2022

Published by Hachette Books, an imprint of Perseus Books, LLC, a subsidiary of Hachette Book Group, Inc. The Hachette Books name and logo is a trademark of the Hachette Book Group.

The Hachette Speakers Bureau provides a wide range of authors for speaking events.

To find out more, go to www.hachettespeakersbureau.com or call (866) 376-6591.

The publisher is not responsible for websites (or their content) that are not owned by the publisher.

Print book interior design by Amy Quinn

Library of Congress Control Number: 2021952121

ISBNs: 9780306925481 (hardcover); 9780306925474 (ebook)

Printed in the United States of America

LSC-C

Printing 1, 2022

For my mother,
Kate Flanagan,
the first in the family
to fall in love with Hermosa Beach

While art is not always trash, it is always disposable; and while it may have relevance, it also just takes up space. People seem to get attached to things destined to pass—flowers, orgasm, friendship, life. The monuments that mark our graves will one day disappear. As much as we want to think so, art is not immortal. Only the fearless spirit it takes to invent an act of creation from nothing is ageless, and knows no death.

—M. Segal of Paper Bag

CONTENTS

Greg Ginn during the recording of *Nervous Breakdown* at Media Art Studio in Hermosa Beach, California, in early 1978. (Photo by SPOT.)

CHAPTER 1
SST vs. Bomp!

The end of the '70s

1

Greg Ginn was frustrated.

The Hermosa Beach guitarist had spent the better part of two years pouring his heart and soul into his band—a noisy quartet called Panic!—and had nothing to show for it. Panic! was faster than the Stooges and heavier than Black Sabbath. The band had its own gear, rehearsed in its own practice space, and wrote its own material, which was part of the problem because venues wouldn't book new bands that played original music. From the clubs in Hollywood to the bars along Pacific Coast Highway, bookers were looking for musicians who could play Top 40 hits. "I thought of music as kind of a scam," Ginn said.[1]

Ginn didn't get into music until he checked out the action at the Lighthouse—a nightclub down the street from his parents' house that happened to be the most important venue for jazz music on the West Coast. Ginn played guitar during breaks from his studies at UCLA, but after seeing the Ramones play at the Roxy Theatre in the summer of '76, all he wanted to do was make his own noise.

Ginn started writing songs—both the music and the lyrics. It took him a while to find people who were as serious about being in a band as he was. His younger brother Raymond struggled through the songs on bass guitar, but he wasn't a musician. He had his own ambitions as a visual artist and christened himself with the pen name Raymond Pettibon. Ginn's abrasive yet commanding style developed from not being able to rely on other players. "I was doing songs that could be held down by lead guitar," Ginn said.[2]

Ginn found his singer, Keith Morris, at the local record store. Morris knew a rock and roll drummer named Bryan Migdol, the younger brother of a close friend who'd died in a car accident. They started jamming in Ginn's garage. Things began to click when Gary McDaniel of Würm took over on bass. McDaniel, who would change his name to Chuck Dukowski, let them use his band's practice space in an abandoned bathhouse on the Strand dubbed "the Würmhole."

The Hermosa Beach police decided this was too much excitement and kicked everyone out. Ginn rented a space in a strip mall on Aviation Boulevard, not far from one of the bait and tackle shops Morris's father owned and operated. The band went back to work, conducting marathon practice sessions that lasted late into the night and occasionally attracted crowds of friends. When the calendar flipped from 1977 to 1978, Panic! still hadn't played a single show, which was becoming a source of frustration.

Panic! participated in the burgeoning punk scene that had taken root in Hollywood and was spreading to every corner of Southern California. Morris even made the drive up to San Francisco to see Johnny Rotten detonate the Sex Pistols at Winterland. Despite the band's engagement in the scene, Panic! was spurned by Hollywood punks. "They considered us to be nothing more than beach rats," Morris said. "If they were competing in the Sid Vicious lookalike contest, we were competing in the Peter Frampton lookalike contest. That didn't sit well with a lot of those people."[3]

The band's appearance defied fashion-conscious Hollywood insiders and helped define its own aesthetic. The members of Panic! didn't dress up to go to punk rock shows or to play gigs. They wore the same clothes on stage as they wore when rehearsing or going to work. This translated to a lack of opportunities in Hollywood. "There was a kind of anti-suburban vibe in the early LA punk culture," Dukowski said.[4] Ginn believed the best way to get people to take his band seriously was to put out a record. Panic! couldn't get a gig because it didn't have a record, but how do you get a record deal when you've never played a show?

Glen "Spot" Lockett, a recent transplant to Hermosa Beach who worked at the Garden of Eden vegetarian restaurant where Ginn frequently ate lunch, offered a solution. "I was writing for the *Easy Reader* and doing music reviews," Spot said, "and one day he was eating there and he kind of called me out on one of the reviews I wrote. So we got into a discussion, talking about this stuff."[5]

Ginn and Spot learned they had a great deal in common. They were passionate guitar players, and both of their fathers were military aviators who'd flown combat missions overseas during World War II. Ginn's father, Regis, served as a navigator with the US Eighth Army Air Corps in England. Spot's father was a member of the famed Tuskegee Airmen: the first Black aviators of the US Army Air Corps.

Spot suggested that Ginn record at Media Art, an art complex with a darkroom where Spot developed his photos and a recording studio where he recently started working as a sound engineer. Best of all, it was right down the street. Ginn said he would look into it. Spot didn't know how serious Ginn was, but he would soon find out.

Panic! assembled at the studio late one night (when the rates were cheapest) and recorded eight songs—all originals. Because the songs were so short, it wasn't nearly enough material for an album, but more than enough for an EP. The record was engineered by Dave Tarling with assistance from Spot. It was the first of many projects Spot would have a hand in making with Ginn. Panic! sent a tape of the recording to Bomp! Records and received a favorable response: Greg Shaw was interested in signing the band and offered to put out the EP.

Things were finally moving forward, but the band was in a near-constant state of flux. Bryan Migdol parted company with Panic!, and Ginn put an ad in the paper for a new drummer. Roberto "Robo" Valverde responded and immediately started rehearsing. In September, Bomp! sent Panic! a recording contract for the eight songs. Ginn crossed off four of them—"No Values," "White Minority," "I Don't Care," and "Gimme Gimme Gimme"—and in an accompanying letter indicated his preference for "Nervous Breakdown" to appear on Side A with "Fix Me," "I've Had It," and "Wasted" on the flip side.[6] Ginn wasn't worried about the brevity of the songs. "I was rebelling against these people who try to establish their manhood by composing prog rock opuses," Ginn said. "My goal was to create a concise listening experience."[7]

Ginn promised to send photographs to help promote the record, which he did the following month. Ginn's correspondence with Shaw was typed on stationery for SST Electronics, his mail-order company, and signed "Gregory Ginn."

More changes were afoot, this time involving the band's name. Pettibon caught wind of another band with the same handle. "I remember telling my brother, 'There's already this band named Panic from England,'" Pettibon said. "'Maybe it's not a good idea to have the same name as some other band.'"[8]

This created an opportunity to rename the band. Morris recalled Ginn wanted to call the band Rope, which he wasn't too thrilled about. Pettibon had another idea. He suggested Black Flag, which conjured up a number of associations: It was both a symbol of anarchy and of piracy on the high seas. Black Flag was also the name of a popular insecticide. But it was Pettibon's simple but innovative logo that sealed the deal: four staggered vertical bars forming a stylized flag rippling in the wind; individually, they resembled the pistons of an engine. Ginn took it and ran with it.

With a new drummer, a new name, and a new logo, Black Flag was ready to go, but Bomp! was slow to respond. Pettibon suspected Shaw wasn't in favor of the name change. After months of delays, Ginn considered putting out the EP himself, but he didn't know anything about making records. He did, however, know of another band in Hermosa Beach—a pop-infused garage band called the Last—and he decided to give them a call.

Black Flag with Ginn, Robo, Dukowski, and Morris at Mabuhay Gardens in San Francisco, California. (Photo by SPOT.)

2

The early punk rock records made in Los Angeles were few and far between, pebbles cast into an ocean of corporate-controlled rock and roll, but even the smallest stone creates a ripple.

In July 1977, the Germs released what many regard as the first LA punk record. The band recorded the single "Forming" in Pat Smear's garage on a reel-to-reel recorder. Chris Ashford, a friend of the band, volunteered to help the Germs put out the record. As the night manager at Peaches Records and Tapes on Hollywood Boulevard, Ashford knew a lot of people in—or at least adjacent to—the music industry, but he didn't know anything about pressing a record. Through his experience at Peaches, Ashford knew that Rhino Records released novelty and compilation records under its own imprint, so he went to Richard Foos at Rhino for advice. Foos recommended that Ashford take his project to Monarch Record Manufacturing Company on West Jefferson Boulevard in West LA.

Ashford was in business. He chose the name What Records? for his label and pressed one thousand copies of the Germs' debut at Monarch. "Forming" was backed with a live recording of "Sex Boy" at the Roxy Theatre from the night the Germs auditioned for the Battle of the Bands sequence in Cheech and Chong's *Up in Smoke*.[9] "We never had any idea that it would ever amount to anything," Ashford said. "We got onto this thing the universe put us into and it kind of took off."[10]

Through his contacts at Peaches, Ashford got the record to new fanzines, like *Slash* and *Flipside*, cropping up around town. Despite the crude quality of both the recording and the musicianship—or perhaps because of it— "Forming" caught the attention of the underground punk press. The bemused review by Claude Bessy (a.k.a. Kickboy Face) in *Slash* helped spread the word about this noisy, rambunctious band. "First of the hard-core LA groups to come up with a single, the Germs have recorded (I think that's the word) one of the most mind-boggling songs I've ever heard. They take monotony to new heights and push the absurdity factor further than almost any other group."[11]

Not everyone liked the record. "We gave the single to *Back Door Man*," Ashford recalled, "and they hated it. We just took that as, 'This is great. We're getting bad reviews here, bad reviews there. It's selling the record.'"[12] *Back Door Man* was an influential rock zine run by Phast Phreddie Patterson and Don Waller out of Torrance in LA's South Bay. *Back Door Man*'s writers took a hard stance against soft rock and roll with screeds from the first generation of LA music writers. Although *Back Door Man* wasn't a punk zine, the editors covered it with cautious enthusiasm and even included a centerfold poster of Johnny Rotten of the Sex Pistols in the March/April 1978 issue.

Despite its mixed reviews, Greg Shaw of Bomp! Records took an interest in "Forming." Bomp! had its roots in the spirited underground music zine *Who Put the Bomp*, which he and his wife Suzy founded in 1970. *Who Put the Bomp* helped launch the writing careers of Lester Bangs of San Diego, Greil Marcus of San Francisco, and Richard Meltzer of New York, and it ran until November 1979.

Who Put the Bomp reflected Greg and Suzy Shaw's passion for rock and roll: how it was made, played, written about, and celebrated. They sought to start a conversation about the music they loved that had little to do with access to the musicians or even the industry itself. The Shaws viewed punk as the latest manifestation of '60s garage rock and psychedelic music, and they were early champions of the LA punk scene. Bomp! distributed the Germs' debut single along with the Dils' "I Hate the Rich," which was issued in September 1977. Both singles hit *Record World*'s New Wave Chart. Although What? would go on to release records by other early LA punk bands like the Eyes, the Skulls, and the Controllers, Ashford didn't regard it as a proper business. He had been inspired to make records the way others were motivated to pick up instruments, take photographs, or create zines. It was his way of participating in the scene. The notion of creating a commercial enterprise came after the fact, if it came at all.

Still, that a crudely recorded single by a band many didn't take all that seriously could catch the attention of fringe elements of the media and register a minor blip in the music industry demonstrates how ready LA was to shake up the status quo. For Ashford, it was a matter of being at the right place at the right time. The Masque, the practice and performance space in the basement of the Pussycat Theatre that served as ground zero for the early LA punk scene, was right next door to Peaches.

Hyperbolic descriptions of punk rock shows in *Slash* lent a mirage-like quality to the scene, another overhyped manifestation of the LA dream machine. But watching the Germs play at the Masque and then seeing the band's single in the bins at Peaches alongside records by the Sex Pistols and the Ramones galvanized scores of people to start their own bands and create their own labels. The release of "Forming" in the summer of '77 sent a message that a local band could make a record and be recognized for it—and you didn't even have to know how to play your instruments.

As bands proliferated like bacteria in a petri dish, it didn't take long for indie labels to start popping up around LA. Dangerhouse Records and Posh Boy Records issued releases the following year. *Slash* got into the game with the first EP from Slash Records: *Lexicon Devil*, also by the Germs. In 1977, Bomp! released *Destroy All Music*, the first EP by the Weirdos, who were arguably LA's most popular punk rock band at the time.

These labels bolstered the fractious scene and proved that punk rock was more than fucked-up kids with blue hair playing dress-up with the dregs of

Hollywood's faded grandeur. They provided the oxygen the scene needed to breathe and enabled bands to break through the barriers imposed by the record industry. Without these labels, there'd be scores of bands like the Screamers who flamed out without leaving a proper, band-sanctioned release as vinyl proof of its white-hot existence. These labels operated for reasons that had nothing to do with the rock and roll fantasy of getting rich and famous: to make art, to document the scene, to create something new and in doing so prove that anyone could do it.

3

It was a bad time for rock and roll. If the government wanted to ban kids from forming rock bands, it couldn't have gone about it any more effectively than the music industry did in the 1970s.

After World War II forced big bands to downsize, rhythm and blues began to flourish. While New York and Memphis both claim to be the cradle of rock and roll, no city had more record labels than LA, where R&B, gospel, and Latin bands played to packed houses, often sharing the same stage.

In postwar America, the radio disc jockeys who brought these new sounds to the public had an enormous influence. In cities big and small, the most popular DJs were bona fide celebrities. They were personalities who made regular appearances at dance halls and nightclubs and were frequent guests on local television shows. In the song-based music industry, if a DJ liked your single, they'd play it on the radio and listeners would buy it. Sometimes these DJs had a hand in getting bands booked for a showcase or a matinee performance sponsored by the station. In this culture, hundreds of bands thrived in cities across the country, and the best of them broke through to the national stage. It was a flawed system that often exploited songwriters, but with a mix of luck, pluck, talent, and perseverance, bands could make the leap from garages to the airwaves.

Then everything changed. When the dust settled after the payola scandal—the practice of rewarding disc jockeys with cash, gifts, and even royalties in exchange for airplay—radio stations took the power away from their DJs and started negotiating with the labels themselves. The record labels worked with program managers to ensure that only predetermined "hits" were broadcast. People in suits dictated the songs that would get the most airplay and inserted commercials at regular intervals, which also generated income from corporations that wanted to reach their target audiences. Gone were the days of DJs spinning whatever records they wanted, whenever they wanted, for as long as they wanted. Welcome to corporate rock and roll.

Naturally, the commercialization of radio favored national touring acts over regional bands. It no longer mattered what was happening in New York, Chicago, Miami, or Los Angeles. All across the country, everyone was listening to the same thing. This environment eschewed risks and put a premium on appealing to the greatest number of people, dumbing down the music and paving the way for easy listening, a genre of music so innocuous that no one could possibly be offended by it.

As the public's listening habits changed, the venues that featured live music acted accordingly. They stopped booking local bands that played original music. For musicians in the '70s, there were plenty of opportunities to perform—as long as they played other people's music. For artists with something to say, there were far fewer outlets for creative expression than there had been just a decade before.

This shift was felt in the large sprawling exurbs of major American cities. Bars and nightclub owners who featured live music insisted their acts play covers of Top 40 hits. Sometimes a booker would give a local band a chance, only to get cold feet when the audience complained. It was a frustrating time for musicians, and the South Bay was an archetype of this dynamic.

The South Bay wasn't your typical suburb but a densely packed network of sub-cities that stretched from Los Angeles International Airport to the Palos Verdes Peninsula. Suburbs, by definition, are urban-adjacent bedroom communities where people live but don't work. The post-suburban "edge cities" of the South Bay were entirely self-contained, with jobs, schools, stores, industry, and clusters of single-family residences all packed together.[13] The suburbs of the twentieth century were defined by movement from place to place, but in post-suburban America you could find everything you needed within a few square miles. Nowhere was this truer than in LA, a city without a center and with more single-family residences than anywhere else in the country.[14]

The southwest corner of Los Angeles County sits on parts of Santa Monica Bay, the Pacific Ocean, and San Pedro Bay, and is home to the Port of Los Angeles, which is still the busiest port in the country. After World War II, the South Bay became headquarters for the burgeoning aerospace industry with its many links to the military and defense. The Beach Cities were also the playground of world-class surfers like Dewey Weber and Greg Noll and played an important role in the popularization of skateboarding and roller skating. Yet this same region was once home to a dynamic music scene.

In the '60s, the South Bay was known for its jazz clubs, coffee shops, and bars where one could hear the latest sounds in bebop, folk, and psychedelic rock. But by the mid-1970s, this was no longer the case. The sounds coming out of the clubs were as uniform as those on the FM dial. This was especially frustrating for songwriters and musicians in the South Bay because of its proximity to Hollywood, the heart of the music business. These were dark days for musicians who wanted to play their own material. Either you fell in line or found something else do. For Joe Nolte, neither option was acceptable.

4

Joe Nolte wrote songs, sang, and played guitar with his brothers Mike and David in a Hermosa Beach band called the Last.[15] They played an unclassifiable blend of neo-psychedelic pop and up-tempo garage rock to create a sound as all-American as the Beach Boys—who, despite revolutionizing surf music, were actually from Hawthorne, several miles inland. Unfortunately, there was nowhere to play. "It was a closed circuit," Joe explained. "There was no way in, especially if you wanted to play rock and roll because you'd be dead. We'd let this rebellious music roll over and die with a whimper."[16]

Joe was no stranger to the Hollywood punk experiment. After reading about New York bands like Television, Blondie, and the Ramones, he sought out this new genre of music and liked what he found. Like Shaw, he saw punk as rock and roll's best hope, and he was determined to be part of it. Joe and his brothers regularly attended shows at the Masque and badgered the proprietor, Brendan Mullen, to book them, but they weren't having much luck.

Joe decided to do what other independent-minded bands were doing and put out a record. He didn't have to look to Hollywood for insight; he found inspiration much closer to home. *Back Door Man* was now putting out records through its own imprint. Earlier that year *Back Door Man* had released a seven-inch single of "He's a Rebel" backed with "You're So Strange" by the Zippers, a power pop band with big hooks and a jagged sound whose members were from all over the South Bay.[17]

When it was time to make a record, Joe turned to his bandmate Vitus Mataré, who played keyboards and the flute but also had a passion for recording. Mataré's mother was a classical harpsichordist who had a two-track recorder and a pair of microphones. Mataré had recorded the Last once before: a song called "Light Another Candle" at Randy Neece's house in Brentwood. Neece, an acquaintance of Mataré's, had performed in the Young Americans, an internationally acclaimed show choir whose image was as wholesome as its name. Neece was always encouraging Mataré and his bandmates to write and record their own music.

Mataré asked Neece to sing on a song and help them record. Neece agreed, but when they realized they needed another guitar, they turned for help to Neece's neighbor, who happened to be the Eagles' guitarist Joe Walsh. Not only did Walsh lend them a Les Paul guitar and a combo amp for the recording, but he also offered to run a mic cable from his house to Neece's. "The coolest dude ever," Mataré recalled.[18]

In the fall of 1977, the members of the Last gathered at the band's practice space at Scream Studios in the Valley to record the backing tracks. Then they convened at Mataré's mother's house in Brentwood, where he'd set up a home recording studio in the pool house. The Last recorded eight songs before Joe's amp caught fire. "His amp shorted out and was smoldering," Mataré said. "I carried it out to the backyard and dropped it into my mother's pool."[19]

For its first single, the Last settled on "She Don't Know Why I'm Here" backed with the Clash-inspired "Bombing of London." Mataré consulted with Neece, who suggested they get the recordings mastered by Hank Waring at Quad Teck and pressed at Alberti Record Manufacturing Company in Monterey Park. Mataré took heed of Neece's advice, and on November 7, 1977, three hundred copies of the Last's debut single were ready to be picked up. They called the label Backlash.

Joe dropped off personalized copies of "She Don't Know Why I'm Here" with Kim Fowley, who organized a series of New Wave Nights at the Whisky; Mullen at the Masque; Patterson and Waller at *Back Door Man*; and Shaw at Bomp! Records. Lisa Fancher, who worked at Bomp! and went on to start Frontier Records, loved the single: "I still think it's one of the greatest LA songs ever," Fancher said. "It gives you a feeling like the Modern Lovers when they sing about Massachusetts. 'She Don't Know Why I'm Here' is just an absolute classic."[20]

The Nolte brothers had written enough songs for an LP, and they hoped their single would catch the eye of someone willing to put it out. Joe and David were at the Masque one night when a triumvirate of tastemakers—Patterson, Mullen, and Shaw—told Joe they'd listened to the record and liked it. In his enthusiasm, Shaw expressed interest in releasing it. Joe was overjoyed. "It was the culmination of what I wanted for so long," he said. "It was insane!"[21] David was a bit more circumspect: "Greg might have said, 'Yeah, I want to put out a record by you,' but I think he said that to a lot of people."[22]

The Last's fusion of '60s garage rock and '70s pop was perfectly suited to the label's psychedelic sensibilities. On paper, Bomp! was the ideal home for the Last, but Shaw lacked the financial capital to follow through with his plans. "I think that was his nature," David said, "not just with us, but with everybody he worked with back then. That was part of what he did. Just Greg being Greg."[23]

Shaw wanted to re-press "She Don't Know Why I'm Here" on the Bomp! label and bought out all of the remaining copies of the single. What had seemed like a demonstration of the label's good intentions struck the band as a bad move once Bomp! began to drag its feet. As the days turned into weeks and the weeks turned into months, the Last was playing more shows but didn't have any records to sell.

In June, the Last went back to Alberti to press the band's second release: "Every Summer Day," an homage to the Beach Boys that name-checks Hermosa Beach in the lyrics. The Last's new record helped get the band noticed around Los Angeles, including in its hometown. In the fall of 1978, David answered the phone and Ginn was on the line. He wanted to talk to Joe about the Last, but Joe was at work, so he spoke with David instead.

David had heard about Panic! from Bill Stevenson, his classmate at Mira Costa High School. Although Bill was a grade lower than David, they were enrolled in the same Spanish class. Stevenson was an avid fisherman, and he knew the band's singer through the Hermosa Tackle Box, Morris's father's shop on Pier Avenue, which Stevenson had been going to since he was eight years old. "Within a few weeks of Bill telling me about Panic!," David said, "Greg called the house to ask about the Last and how we put out our record. He said he had a thing going with Greg Shaw and was maybe going to do a deal with him to put out the *Nervous Breakdown* EP."[24]

David recalled they had a good conversation, and he shared his band's experiences with Ginn: gigs they'd played, record stores that carried their music, and—most importantly—where they pressed their records. Although Ginn hadn't completely soured on Shaw, he was exploring his options. "He was starting to get the sense that Shaw was promising the sky and couldn't deliver," David said.[25]

The news that there was another punk rock band in town came as a welcome surprise to Joe, who believed Hermosa Beach's "entire punk rock contingency could fit in my car."[26] David was trying to do something about that by turning his classmate on to punk rock. He made Stevenson tapes and finally had a breakthrough with Devo's "Mongoloid." David took Ginn up on his offer to come by the practice space on Aviation, and Stevenson and the Nolte brothers joined in on a jam session that included the Devo song, KISS's "Love Gun," and riffs that would eventually coalesce into Black Flag's "Room 13." For Stevenson, it was an earth-shattering experience: "That was when I realized, 'Oh, you don't have to play covers, you can play your own things that you come up with?'"[27]

Over the course of this impromptu session, Greg Ginn and Joe Nolte discovered they had a lot in common. They shared their frustrations with the lack of opportunities to play in LA and the limitations imposed by the music industry, which now included Bomp! Both musicians were concerned that it was taking too long for the label to put out their records. "We needed to capitalize on the momentum of 'She Don't Know Why I'm Here' by getting a record out," Joe recalled. "Panic! is supposed to have their record released on

Bomp! That didn't come out either. So we're both in a holding pattern. We're frustrated as hell."[28]

Joe wasn't going to let his opportunity to put out a record with Bomp! slip away. He was determined to hold Shaw's feet to the fire, even if it meant some unpleasantness. His patience was rewarded when Bomp! Records finally released the Last's debut, *L.A. Explosion!*, the following year.

Ginn's situation was different. Black Flag, which still hadn't played its first show, didn't have the Last's track record. In addition, the Last's pop-infused melodies on songs like "Every Summer Day" were at least palatable to bookers and promoters; Black Flag's frenzied, ear-bashing chaos was not. In 1978, Black Flag was virtually unknown outside its small circle of friends in the Beach Cities. Joe briefly discussed with Ginn putting *Nervous Breakdown* out on Backlash. Ultimately, Ginn decided to follow the example of his Hermosa Beach neighbors and do it himself.

This was a crucial step for the growth of the band. It also proved to be a pivotal connection for countless Southern California punk and hardcore bands that followed Black Flag's example and pressed their own records for decades to come—all thanks to an unlikely string of connections between the Last and Black Flag that went back to a forward-thinking song and dance man named Randy Neece.

SST Electronics ad in *Ham Radio* magazine, May 1978.

CHAPTER 2
SST vs. Hollywood

1979–1980

1

Greg Ginn was uniquely equipped to launch an independent record label. Despite knowing very little about the music industry, he had the infrastructure, education, capital, and—perhaps most importantly—experience in running a successful mail order operation.

Like many young men of his generation, Ginn was fascinated with amateur radio. By flipping a few switches, amateur radio operators were able to communicate with each other all over the world. Amateur radio was a subculture with its own language, tools, and means of communication. Ginn's call sign—the handle ham radio operators use to identify one another—was WB6ZNM.

Amateur radio enthusiasts were not unlike early adopters of the internet. They combined technical know-how with a curiosity about the way things worked. These enthusiasts shared information with each other simply because they could, and they corresponded with one another in ways that were so baffling and mysterious to outsiders that it might as well have been its own secret language. It was a culture that encouraged participation and rewarded experimentation, especially if you shared your findings. As with the internet, what you looked like or where you were from mattered less than what you knew and how you conducted yourself.

From an early age, Ginn displayed a remarkable aptitude for under-standing the culture's codes and technical jargon. In the April 1969 edition of *Popular Electronics*, the following appeared in the News and Views section of the magazine: "Gregory Ginn, WB6ZNM, 1240 21st St. Hermosa Beach, Calif. 90254 encloses the following note when he sends his QSL card. 'Ur QSL will be much appreciated and will be displayed in my shack for all to see and envy.' Greg has worked 95 countries and the 50 states, running 100 watts into a 10-, 15-, and 20-meter triband beam with a Hallicrafters SX-111 receiver doing the huffing and a Gonset GSB-100 doing the puffing. Twenty meter DX chasing is Greg's favorite facet of amateur radio: his big ambition is to become a QSL manager for a DX station."[1]

Amateur radio operators sent QSL cards to one another to verify contact between stations. In the early part of the twentieth century, radio stations used these cards to gauge the reach of its broadcasts, but by the '60s, they were mostly sought after as collectibles. They included the station's call sign, loca-tion, and a photograph or design that reflected the user's personality. Hobbyists used them like calling cards. The more remote the station, the move coveted the card. The note that ran in *Popular Electronics*, which was provided by Ginn himself, demonstrates his mastery of the emerging technology and his desire to do more. When this news item was published, he was just fourteen years old.

Ginn also started a ham radio zine called the *Novice*, the purpose of which was to flatten the learning curve for those interested in pursuing amateur radio as a hobby. Other enthusiasts noted Ginn's efforts and spread the word on their networks. The August 1971 edition of *Radio Amateur* ran the following notice: "There is a newsletter being put out just for Novices and beginners. Appropriately named THE NOVICE, it is put out by Greg Ginn (WB6ZNM) and appears monthly with news of Novice traffic handling, Novice nets, FCC actions as related to the Notice [sic], contests, awards, let-ters, product reviews, and dozens of simple but handy construction projects.

It is a big job that Greg is trying to do in putting out THE NOVICE and he would like to get more Novices involved in both reading and writing for THE NOVICE."[2]

The Novice's scope demonstrates Ginn's enthusiasm not only for amateur radio but for sharing information and nurturing a community. Amateur radio is all about making connections with like-minded people; the Novice was a way to turn those connections into a network. Those looking for the roots of Ginn's do-it-yourself ethos—sharing knowledge, building communities, creating new modes of self-expression—can find it in his passion for amateur radio.

Ginn, however, was no novice. He was an astute study who wasn't deterred by the technical aspects of his hobby. Ginn sought out amateur radio magazines and electronics periodicals the way other teenagers craved information about their favorite bands. These publications were full of ads for equipment from small electronics companies. The Novice ran similar ads, and it wasn't long before Ginn started promoting his own company, SST Electronics, which stood for solid state transmitters.

It was an exciting time in the electronics business. Just as digital technology started phasing out analog equipment in the late '90s, solid-state electronics were replacing bulky vacuum tubes in the early '60s. There were plenty of opportunities for an entrepreneur to develop new products or enhance old ones such as tuners, transformers, and amplifier kits. Ginn threw himself into this enterprise. He developed his own line of products, printed up catalogs describing his merchandise, and mailed them out to past and potential clients on an ever-expanding mailing list.[3]

Ginn received a great deal of mail from customers and other amateur radio enthusiasts. Ginn's mentor provided him with a post office box, a mailing address that indie music fans from all over the world would come to know intimately: PO Box 1, Lawndale, Calif. 90260.[4]

After Ginn graduated from Mira Costa High School, his business continued to grow while he pursued his studies at UCLA. He earned a degree in economics, which had a direct impact on SST's day-to-day operations.

How big was SST Electronics? Ginn's catalog offered an extensive line of branded equipment. In the early days of Panic! and Black Flag, Ginn's bandmates became accustomed to sharing space with his inventory. On occasion, Ginn would hire his friends to help alter or assemble the equipment. Some of Ginn's modifications were unique, and he held the patent to multiple products that generated significant income.

While far from wealthy, Ginn had discretionary income that many of his peers in the punk rock community lacked. For instance, the space Panic! shared with Würm was essentially a squat. Being evicted by the police spelled the end for many bands without the financial resources to secure another place to practice. But Ginn had the wherewithal to immediately rent a commercial space a few blocks away on Aviation Boulevard. He and his bandmates soundproofed the room with carpets they found in a dumpster and practiced at night when the noise wouldn't interfere with other businesses in the strip mall. Crisis averted.

For many young artists, the confluence of art and commerce can be difficult to navigate, but for Ginn making a record was no more mysterious than manufacturing a tuner or applying for a patent. The success of SST Electronics was built on Ginn's ability to leverage his networks. Ginn understood that if he started a record label, he would need all the help he could get. Luckily for him, he had a secret weapon living under his own roof.

2

Regis Ginn could be forgiven if he believed his son Raymond was destined to be a great artist. After all, he was born on the most auspicious day in modern literature: June 16, Bloomsday, the day on which the Irish author James Joyce set his novel *Ulysses*, a groundbreaking work that many regard as the pinnacle of twentieth-century literature.

Regis also desired to make his mark in the world of letters, but then life got in the way. He attended—oddly enough—Regis College, a private Jesuit school in Denver, Colorado, where he played both football and baseball for the Brown and Gold and cultivated a lifelong love of literature.

By the time he graduated, the United States had entered the Second World War, and Regis was commissioned as an officer in the air force. Regis shipped overseas and was serving as a navigator with the US Eighth Army Air Corps in London when he met Oie Peters, a refugee of Russian-occupied Estonia.[5]

After the war, Regis returned to the States with Oie, and the couple had five children: Linda, Gregory, Erika, Raymond, and Adrian. According to Pettibon, Regis was fond of making up "nonsensical nicknames for his kids. Greg was Kierkegaard. My young brother was Kafka. My sister was Rodriguez."[6]

Regis gave his son Raymond the nickname "Petit bon." This would assume many forms: for example, he signed early works "Raymond Pettibone" and "St. Pettibone" before finally settling on his nom de plume.

When Regis exited the military, he went back to school. His two eldest sons, Gregory and Raymond, were born in Tucson, Arizona, where Regis received his master of arts in English literature from the University of Arizona in 1960. Regis wrote his thesis about "the imaginary world created by Graham Greene," and this novelist's work would exert a strong influence on the literature-loving pilot.

Like Regis, Greene was a Roman Catholic, and although the English author wrote extensively about his faith, he was best known for his novels of espionage and intrigue. His stories, set in Europe during the aftermath of World War II, won him accolades for their lean storytelling and literary merit. Though Greene primarily wrote popular fiction, he was shortlisted for the Nobel Prize in 1966 and again in 1967.

In his thesis, Regis refers to Greene's imaginary world as "Greeneland." In the novels, Regis writes, "there constantly is a sense of the jungle, either the green jungle of witchdoctors who can make lightning or of the concrete and chrome lair of teenage boys with bottles of vitriol."[7]

The Ginns made their way to the South Bay, where Regis put his master's degree to use and taught English at the community college level, but he spent his evenings working on his own literary project: a spy novel called *Tyger! Tyger!* Regis completed the book and sold it to the Macmillan Publishing Company, which published it in 1968. Regis chose the unusual handle "R. C. K. Ginn." *Tyger! Tyger!* tells the story of recently retired air force colonel named Roger Widsmith who is recalled to military service by the CIA for a special operation abroad: to find the mysterious Peter Kraelenbuehermann.

Set many years after World War II, the novel indulges the kind of sexual hijinks that made James Bond a household name but aspires to the caliber of a Graham Greene story—a page-turner underpinned by complex moral issues. Of all Greene's books, *Tyger! Tyger!* corresponds most closely to *The Third Man.* Like Greene's protagonist Harry Lime, Kraelenbuehermann doesn't appear in the story until the final pages, yet his presence hangs over every scene.

Regis borrows details of Widsmith's backstory from his own career as an air force pilot. For instance, Widsmith falls hard for a spy who is half Estonian. Throughout the novel, Regis is unusually sympathetic to the plight of the Baltic states—Estonia in particular—lending *Tyger! Tyger!* more nuance than is typical for a spy-versus-spy thriller.

The publication did not launch Regis's career as a novelist. Although he wrote several novels, he would publish just one more spy thriller, *The Cold Warrior,* with the Marron Corporation in 1975. Regis continued to teach at schools throughout the South Bay before finally settling down as an instructor at Harbor College in Wilmington, where he stayed for almost twenty years. Former students recall him as a spirited instructor who often included anecdotes about his sons in his lectures.[8]

It wasn't easy raising five children on a teacher's salary, and Regis was legendarily frugal. To help make ends meet, Regis would purchase clothing from thrift stores in bulk. Naturally, Regis stressed the importance of education, but he didn't discourage his children from their own pursuits or push them out of the house. Even as adults, some of the kids continued to live at home, comfortable in the quasi-Bohemian environment their parents had created.

"The home environment there was rather unique," Spot said. "It was almost on the order of *The Addams Family* where everybody there was different from everybody outside of that environment."[9] The Ginn home may not have been the most conventional household in Hermosa Beach, but their children's friends were always welcome, and when his sons got into trouble, Regis was there to bail them out.

3

That Regis's two eldest sons chose to study economics, despite their interest in art and technology, speaks to their pragmatic natures. Both were influenced by their father's Jesuit education and military service, which served them well in their chosen fields. Both autodidacts possessed restless imaginations and enjoyed a wide range of interests to which they brought their legendary work ethic to bear. Artists are made, not born, and they require an environment where they have the freedom to pursue their passions, whether amateur radio, art, or music. It was a household in which the Ginns, particularly Raymond, thrived.

Pettibon started out as a substitute high school teacher and even considered becoming an economics instructor, but quickly abandoned a career in education. Nor was he interested in being a musician, despite his brother's best efforts to rope him into Black Flag. "That's not the life for me," Pettibon said of being in a band. "It's not what I wanted. To be a musician just consumes too much time."[10]

Pettibon spent his days at his parents' house reading, writing, drawing, and listening to baseball games on the radio. Entirely self-taught, Pettibon embarked on a self-guided course of study that involved combing through his father's extensive library, which was so large that it spilled into the garage. Regis had even built a free-standing study, whose shelves were lined with books, in the backyard. Pettibon wrote out ideas for his illustrations and then executed them with ink and brush. From the very beginning of his career, Pettibon was extremely prolific, creating image after image that he piled on the floor.

Pettibon's work as a writer has been overshadowed by his eye-catching illustrations and prodigious output, but his prose is just as important to what he was trying to achieve. Nowhere is Pettibon's writing more prominent in his work than in his first zine, *Captive Chains*, which he published in November 1978—many weeks before the release of *Nervous Breakdown*.

Captive Chains opens with a manifesto that seeks to define the work by what it is not: "IN THIS ISSUE: no bronze-skinned barbarians, their wonderful muscles rippling, a strip of hide hiding—; no lush science fiction, art nouveau, mythology (pick 1) pieces to hang next to your McDonald's Nieman; no art as therapy for devotees of de Sade and Sacher-Masoch; no stories about peace-loving hippies vs. heartless authorities set in the summer of love…2067; no superheroes for your kid brother."[11]

"No superheroes for your kid brother" is a curious way to warn readers

Raymond Pettibon in his studio in 1983. (Photo by Edward Colver.)

about the comic's abundance of graphic sex and explicit violence, including allusions to incest, depictions of rape, and descriptions of widespread carnage. References to the Marquis de Sade and Leopold von Sacher-Masoch, writers whose names gave us the terms "sadism" and "masochism," are clues that *Captive Chains* is not your typical comic book. It never would have been approved by the Comics Code Authority. Nevertheless, its preface is one of the few times Pettibon deigned to explain his work.

Pettibon introduces his large cast of characters on the cover of *Captive Chains* with a composite of twenty of the miscreants in its pages. With names like Sid Sawyer, Nap Wahooey, and Joanie Bombshell, these characters suggest a story out of the pages of a lurid pulp novel, and *Captive Chains* doesn't disappoint. The cover features a scene of street violence where local toughs face off in an alleyway with knives and broken bottles. This image mashes together many of its intertwining story lines.

The opening page establishes a scene right out of Graham Greene's jungles of "concrete and chrome": "King Kicks ruled the streets and the law of the asphalt jungle was the only law he knew."[12] Thus begins a loosely linked series of vignettes about the members of a gang called the Damned Ones. Pettibon deploys his large cast of characters in short scenes that, taken together, constitute a braided narrative. The action switches every page or so, creating a disorienting diorama of their chaotic lives.

Pettibon is less interested in creating a cohesive, easy-to-follow story than conveying a feeling of debauched desperation. Like Alex and his ultraviolent droogs in *A Clockwork Orange*, the young antiheroes of the Damned Ones pursue mindless sex, are easily led astray, and find redemption in violence that mirrors the chaos they're trying to escape at home.

Pettibon's disjointed panels and imaginative leaps echo the confusion his characters feel as they navigate their nameless city. His kaleidoscopic narrative marries sex and violence with little distinction between aggressors and their victims. Each character has a separate, sordid life, but their fates are yoked together, like links in a chain.

In the narrative sections of *Captive Chains*, which constitute the first half of the comic, Pettibon exposes the underbelly of Southern California: its fascination with cults, blatant misogyny, and unchecked violence. Pettibon's milieu is populated with degenerates of every stripe who make no secret of their predilections and act on their desires in public. In Pettibon's world, no one is innocent.

Pettibon's figures are coarse and crude not only in terms of their content but in their execution as well. Representations of beauty, physical or otherwise, are not part of Pettibon's aesthetic. Some figures are oddly proportioned. Many of his thick-waisted brutes and bullnecked toughs look the same. In several scenes, the characters seem trapped by the frame.

The second half of the comic features standalone images that take up an entire page: a mad scientist shows off a two-headed Doberman pinscher, a crazed gunman holds a pistol to a baby's head, and Leatherface from the horror movie *Texas Chainsaw Massacre* wields his weapon of choice in horrifying ecstasy. Without the limits of panels or text crowding his images, the illustrations burst off the page. It's not surprising that many of these images were used as flyers for Black Flag shows.

Captive Chains is a remarkable document. At sixty-eight pages, it's an astonishing achievement for an artist's first published work. It's also the longest zine Pettibon ever made. The split between narrative-driven comics and standalone images represents the yin and yang of Pettibon's work. The first half reveals a writer unshackled by the restraints that inhibited other comic artists; the second half demonstrates that, while he doesn't need text to captivate an audience, the images lack something without it. By blending the two styles together—pairing "lowbrow" black-and-white images with text culled from his many literary influences—Pettibon established a unique place in arts and letters. *Captive Chains* showed him the way forward.

Pettibon printed five thousand copies of *Captive Chains*, but demand was less than expected, and most of the copies eventually found their way into the trash. "If you have a box full of zines you're giving out on the street," Pettibon explained, "most motherfuckers will cross the street."[13]

Although the release of *Captive Chains* was far from a success, Pettibon was undaunted. He continued to produce work at a breakneck pace, experimenting with ink in much the same way that his older brother was experimenting with sound. However, two images from *Captive Chains* were about to find a wider audience.

4

While Ginn was writing songs, playing guitar, and rehearsing with Black Flag, he couldn't help but notice that his younger brother was also hard at work. Ginn requested some of his brother's artwork for the cover of SST Record's first release: *Nervous Breakdown* (SST 001). In exchange, Greg would promote *Captive Chains* through SST. Pettibon agreed with a caveat: he wasn't going to create something specifically for the record.

This established a precedent for how Pettibon's art would be used in the future by Black Flag and other bands. Pettibon generously allowed his friends and family to make use of his illustrations as long as they selected pieces from the deep and seemingly endless trove of work he'd already created and to which he was constantly adding.

This arrangement worked out well for both Pettibon and the bands. Pettibon could keep to his own rigorous schedule without worrying about other people's deadlines, and the bands benefitted from Pettibon's unique vision. Even though he wasn't making "punk" art, the themes he returned to again and again in his work—sexual taboos, toxic masculinity, police oppression, random violence, and so on—lent a hard, dark, violent edge to records and flyers. This was certainly the case with *Nervous Breakdown*.

The front cover depicts a young boy backed into a corner and raising his fists at a male teacher brandishing a chair—like a lion tamer punishing an unruly beast. The image is a subliminal reenactment of a specific type of pulp novel cover showing criminals at the moment of their last stand, outgunned and outnumbered by police. Pettibon's image of a frustrated schoolboy captures the moment when the tables have turned and the boy defies the teacher's bogus authority. It's a quintessential "We're not gonna take it anymore" statement that articulated punk rock's relationship to the status quo.

The back cover features an illustration of five women in a police lineup. It's a scene straight out of a sexploitation film like Jonathan Demme's *Caged Heat*, which was released a few years earlier in 1974. Pettibon's illustrations aren't related to one another, but their juxtaposition under the banner of "Nervous Breakdown" heightens his subjects' emotional distress.

Pettibon's images raise the question "What's going on here?" There's a narrative at work but the plot is faint, its meaning shrouded in mystery. In comic art, image and text work in tandem to explain what is happening. This is almost never the case with a Pettibon piece. As the brain struggles to construct a narrative out of the information available, the gap between image and text creates unresolved tension that Black Flag was primed to exploit with an onslaught of distortion from Ginn's guitar. When Morris delivers the song's iconic first line, the sounds, words, and images all come together in a sonic apotheosis. Four songs. Five minutes and thirteen seconds. Rock and roll would never be the same.

The back cover of *Nervous Breakdown* contains a bounty of information, not all of it accurate. Ginn was still going by Gregory, and Gary McDaniel hadn't made the switch to Chuck Dukowski. Robo is listed as the drummer even though he didn't play on the record; Bryan Migdol did. This would cause hard feelings between Migdol and the band for years to come.

SST's transformation was complete. In a matter of months, SST Electronics had expanded into a record label and publishing company and released a pair of ambitious products. Although SST Electronics would continue for several years, the release of *Nervous Breakdown* marked a turning point.

5

Black Flag played its first show a few weeks after the record's release. So what if Ginn had to book the hall at the Moose Lodge in Redondo Beach himself? A show was a show.

Ginn circulated flyers and asked two other LA bands to play: the Alley Cats from Lomita and Rhino 39 from Long Beach. The choice was strategic. While the Alley Cats and Rhino 39 had made a splash in the Hollywood punk scene, both bands were from South LA. Ginn was less concerned about fitting in with the cliquish Hollywood crowd than playing with people who were steadfast in their determination to do their own thing.

Although the Alley Cats were given top billing on the flyer, the gig was a showcase for Black Flag. The band played two sets—one at the beginning of the show and another at the end. While it was fairly common for punk bands to play two sets, one for the kids and another for the twenty-one-and-over crowd, it was unusual for just one of the bands to play twice.

After the first set, a drunken Keith Morris was accused of disrespecting the American flag by lodge members and was given the boot, but he put on a wig to play the second set. It shouldn't have worked, but it did. "Part of the genius of Black Flag," recalled Joe Nolte, who attended the show with his brothers, "was their ability to do the impossible."[14]

The Moose Lodge show also drew Stiv Bators of the Dead Boys and KROQ's Rodney Bingenheimer. Both left with a copy of *Nervous Breakdown*, which Bingenheimer promptly played on his influential radio show. Like

Greg Shaw, Bingenheimer was a holdover from the previous generation of rock and roll tastemakers who understood what punk rock was all about. He more than did his part to get LA punk bands exposure on the radio. Kids would make tapes of Rodney's show and exchange them with friends. As the music spread throughout the Southland, bands that had recorded a handful of songs on a seven-inch available only in local record stores would play gigs for kids who—thanks to Rodney's show—knew all the words to their songs. "If one person deserves credit for helping open things up in Los Angeles," Dukowski said, "that person is Rodney Bingenheimer."[15]

Black Flag's second show was also arranged by Ginn. He was passing out flyers at a show when he met D. Boon and Mike Watt, who told Ginn about their band the Reactionaries. Ginn offered the opening slot, and the two musicians, who were new to the punk scene, agreed to play.

The gig was held at a teen center in San Pedro and featured the Alley Cats, the Plugz, Black Flag, the Descendents, and the Reactionaries. Morris, who was a talented visual artist in his own right, created the flyer. Even though it was Black Flag's second show and the Reactionaries and the Descendents hadn't played before, the show was well attended. Ginn's strategy of playing in the South Bay with like-minded musicians—even if they were just starting out—was working. Show by show, he created his own scene that was separate and distinct from the one that was stymied in Hollywood after the Masque's frequent closures.[16] This success wasn't measured in records sold or income earned but in the connections Ginn made with other artists and bands. Although the Reactionaries were new and inexperienced, before the year was over, Boon would replace Martin Tamburovich on vocals and the band would re-form as the Minutemen.

Black Flag continued to practice, but Ginn was on the lookout for a new space so the band could rehearse during the day. Ginn found what he was looking for at the Creative Craft Center, a multipurpose facility at 1215 Manhattan Avenue in Hermosa Beach, which was just up the hill from Pier Avenue. The new space had a number of advantages. Not only was it closer to the beach and the Strand, but it was near Media Art and the Garden of Eden.

The Creative Craft Center inhabited a large, sprawling building with walls so thick that when the band rehearsed in the basement no one could hear a sound from the street. There were multiple rooms available, and they were all cheap. Not only did Ginn rent a room there, but so did Dukowski. Even Morris rented a space so that he'd have a place to crash on nights he didn't want to go to home. These rooms often doubled as work spaces. "Greg modified attenuators and shipped them off to ham radio operators around the country and he hired me to help out," Morris said. "We did all the soldering and distribution in a rented room inside a community art space on Manhattan Avenue that used to be a church, so that's what everyone called it: The Church."[17]

There was plenty of room at the Church for both Black Flag and SST Electronics, and it served as a gathering point. "He was building those tuners in the back room of the Church," Spot recalled. "That's when I started going over there and listening to records and visiting with these people. There were all these new lives that were presenting themselves to me."[18]

It didn't take long for the Church to become the unofficial headquarters of the South Bay scene. Punks from all over would come to watch Black Flag rehearse—and they rehearsed a lot—so the atmosphere was often festive. There were impromptu parties after Hollywood shows. The back door was never locked, and a parade of punks came in and out at all hours of the day and night.

Most of Black Flag's gigs were glorified parties around the South Bay, and the band wasn't always well received. "We were a brutal ball of energetic noise," Morris said, "and they wanted Led Zeppelin covers. But I was on booze and cocaine and didn't give a fuck what people screamed or what they threw at us."[19]

Black Flag got its first big break by scoring a gig at the Hong Kong Café—thanks to the Last. The Hong Kong Café was a new restaurant and bar in Chinatown that followed the lead of its neighbor across the plaza, Madame Wong's. Kim Turner, along with his business partners Suzy Frank and Barry Seidel, booked bands in the café's upstairs banquet hall. Shows were all ages, and tickets cost between three and four dollars. The Hong Kong Café was committed to new wave, "the music of the 1980s," Turner said in an article in *Billboard* magazine about the "rebel" club's success. "We book no disco acts, no jazz bands, and no blues shouters."[20]

The Last, who could pass as new wave, was invited to play. When the other band on the bill backed out, Joe urged Turner to let him pick the opening band, and the new club agreed. "The fools," Joe said. "We got Black Flag."[21]

On a Monday afternoon in June, members of both bands drove up from Hermosa Beach to do a sound check at the Hong Kong Café. When they went upstairs to the banquet hall, it was still set up for meal service. Joe remembered Morris not being happy about that. "Keith ran over to the nearest table and grabbed a tablecloth and jerked it off. Waiters were running around, it was still daylight outside, and there was already a sense of chaos taking hold of the place."[22]

Esther Wong, the proprietor of Madame Wong's, was so incensed with the competition from the Hong Kong Café, which was located a short walk across the tourist plaza, she banned any band that performed at the rival club. Although many bands flouted this edict, Wong remained suspicious of punk rock bands. Some bands, like the Last, were able to blend in at both venues. Black Flag wasn't one of those bands.

That summer and fall, Black Flag became a Chinatown fixture and played the Hong Kong Café a dozen times. With two venues hosting shows with local bands most nights of the week, the Chinatown tourist plaza became a popular punk hangout.

Things were finally starting to happen for Black Flag. "When our EP came out," Ginn explained, "we got some good reviews and people basically had to start giving us some gigs, but the scene in LA was really closed."[23]

The summer of '79 was particularly eventful for the band. On July 22, Ginn secured a spot on a bill for a summer concert at Polliwog Park in Manhattan Beach with Eddie & the Subtitles, Big Wow, and the Tourists, an early incarnation of Red Cross. Steve McDonald, who was just twelve years old at the time, had seen Black Flag play at Moose Lodge and was impressed that they had a record. When he saw the Lawndale mailing address on the back cover, the Hawthorne native realized they'd made it themselves. For musicians like McDonald, the music industry was an impenetrable wall, but bands like Black Flag hammered a crack just wide enough to slip through. When other bands followed their example, as they did again and again, first in the

South Bay and then throughout the country, that crack in the wall became a door to a new kind of creative freedom.

But the door had a tendency to slam shut, and Ginn had to use every trick in the book to keep it open. To get on the bill for the show at Polliwog Park, Ginn told the promoter that Black Flag was a Fleetwood Mac cover band. Black Flag was many things, but no one would characterize their music as a variety of the easy listening format that was dominating the airwaves.

Morris downed several beers before he took the stage. With a Budweiser can in his hand, Morris stirred up the crowd with calls for "audience

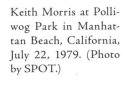

Keith Morris at Polliwog Park in Manhattan Beach, California, July 22, 1979. (Photo by SPOT.)

participation." They responded by pelting the band with the dregs of their picnic lunches: empty cans, half-eaten sandwiches, chicken bones, and watermelon rinds. "It was an entirely fun time," Joe Nolte said. "The families got into the spirit of things and started giving their children things to throw at the band."[24]

But trouble was brewing. In the next edition of the *Easy Reader*, the local paper that served the Beach Cities, an article about the show stated that the organizers were "angered and embarrassed" by Black Flag's performance.[25]

The article included a photo, taken by Spot, of a sneering Keith Morris with two of the band's biggest fans, Ron Reyes and Dez Cadena, wrestling in front of the trash-strewn stage. "I'd never seen anything like that happen before," Spot said. "This was definitely an unprecedented cultural event in California."[26]

The most damning part of the article singled out Morris: "Lead singer Keith spewed obscenities while challenging many of the crowd to a fight. Parents quickly collected their children and fled the park."[27] This unflattering description fed the rumors that Black Flag had brought punk rockers to Manhattan Beach to start a riot, which wasn't the case. Those who came to see Black Flag gathered around the band and enjoyed the show, while those who were caught off guard by the band's abrasive performance kept their distance and threw food. The show at Polliwog Park initiated a dangerous precedent: people who had nothing to do with the band would cause trouble, and Black Flag would get blamed for it.

On the last day of the month, Black Flag hosted another show at the Church with the Last, the Urinals, the Gears, and the Tourists, but this time Ginn extended the invitation beyond his expanding circle of punk rock friends in the South Bay. Patterson and Jeffrey Lee Pierce attended the party. Both were now writing for *Slash*. Joe was in their ear all night and encouraged them to write about what was happening in the South Bay. "No one took Black Flag seriously in the beginning," Joe said, but he was determined to change that.[28]

Shortly afterward, Pierce interviewed Black Flag for *Slash*, and that month *Flipside* ran a short piece about the band that was printed across from a full-page ad Ginn bought to advertise the *Nervous Breakdown* EP. Ginn understood that purchasing ads in zines was a shrewd way to develop a relationship with publications. In an environment where the people securing ads were also making editorial decisions, an ad buy was more cost effective than a press release. Ginn knew from experience that journalistic standards were considerably more relaxed at fanzines, and advertising could lead to favorable reviews and consideration for editorial content in future issues.

Although Black Flag strove to create its own space where Ginn and his bandmates could develop and grow, recognition from the established scene was crucial to its success. Even though SST Records had just one release, it was behaving like a record label. Advertisements for *Nervous Breakdown* were clear, compelling, and professional looking. The ad featured Pettibon's cover art, but the rest of the information was typeset. Ginn had experience creating ads and assembling catalogs for SST Electronics. He saw no reason to take a different approach with his label. Just because the product was "punk" didn't mean the ad should be.

However, not everything Black Flag did was part of a master plan to increase the band's visibility and move units. Ginn had his own reasons for what he did and how he did it, and he didn't care if he ruffled a few feathers along the way. He wasn't going against the grain for the sake of being contrarian; he believed there was value in exposing people to new things.

In an interview in *Flipside* #22, Ginn was asked why he was in a band. Ginn was very clear about his feelings: "The motivation is to express something," he said. "We do want to get our material out as widely as possible, but we don't want to change to do that.... What we try to do is create a situation that opens people's minds up to something new and possibilities of something different." When he was asked about the show at Polliwog Park, Ginn responded that people always asked him why they played for those "hippies" at the beach. Again, his answer was remarkably straightforward: "You've gotta threaten people sometimes. Sometimes it's more effective than somebody who already accepts what you're doing."[29]

Ginn wasn't trying to convey a particular message—he was adamant about that—but he wanted his music to serve as a shock to the system. Even if the audience didn't get what Black Flag was doing, there were always one or two people at every show who responded positively to the music. If they thought, *This is for me*, then that was a win as far as Ginn was concerned.

Ginn was already thinking about Black Flag's next record. Although he had another four songs in the can, the band was a lot tighter than when it recorded in early '78, and Ginn thought it could do better. Not everyone had the same priorities. Morris loved to play shows, which Black Flag sporadically continued to do, but they didn't always go as planned. In August, Black Flag was finally invited to play a fundraiser for the Masque at the original location, but the show was shut down by the fire marshal before the band could play.

Morris was less than enthusiastic about rehearsing. Black Flag's rehearsals, led by Ginn and Dukowski, were often just as intense as a show but lasted much longer. Morris was already putting in long hours at his father's bait shop, which required that he get up early. He also worked at local record stores. Rehearsals were starting to feel like another job. Morris liked to blow off steam after work and would rather go to Hollywood to see live music than practice in the bunker at the Church. "We rehearsed every night," Morris complained, "sometimes for six hours. Sometimes I wouldn't be getting home until, like, four in the morning."[30]

While Morris thought Black Flag was rehearsing for the sake of rehearsing, Ginn had his own reasons. He wanted to record the new material he'd been working on and booked another recording session at Media Art in early October. This time Spot manned the board. "Most of the stuff I was doing in the studio was with people trying to be complex and sophisticated with lots of overdubs," Spot said. "When I heard the Ramones I thought, 'Now this is what I want to hear!'"[31]

Spot's sensibilities meshed well with Black Flag's aesthetic, but in the studio, the creative differences between Ginn and Morris came to a head, and the vocalist abruptly quit the band. Black Flag was left in the lurch, and Ginn's plans to release another record were put on hold.

Music incites the savage beast at Polliwog Park Sunday. More than 1000 people attended the evening of punk rock. Photo by Spot

Manhattan meets punks

by Kerry Welsh

Manhattan Beach unexpectedly got its first — and definitely its last — taste of punk rock music Sunday at Polliwog Park.

The caustic new wave/punk sounds of The Tourists and Big Wow had caused many of the families in attendance to leave even before the featured act, a group called Black Flag, took the stage. As it turned out, the first two acts were like the Vienna Boys' Choir in comparison to the Hermosa-based Black Flag.

Their ardent fans, with hair in every conceivable (and inconceivable) color, jumped up and down in the traditional punk "pogo," pelting the band and the nearby crowd with oranges, tomatoes, watermelons, cans, rocks, and bottles as the band played their brand of frenetic, anarchistic rock.

Lead singer Keith, meanwhile, spewed obscenities while challenging many of the crowd to fight. Parents quickly collected their children and fled the park.

A punk rock concert at the Fleet-wood Club in Redondo Beach in June had a similar result, ending with considerable plumbing, furniture, and structural damage to the club. "Never again," said Fleetwood owners Svend Holm and Craig Lindstrom.

The organizers of the Polliwog Park concert expressed a similar sentiment.

"The recreation department was as angered and embarrassed as the audience," said Ric Morton, special events supervisor who organized the concert. "We plan to screen and audition every act from now on that wants to perform at Polliwog Park, so nothing like this will ever happen again."

According to a statement released by parks and recreation director James Stecklein, Black Flag was "erroneously scheduled to perform."

Stecklein further noted, "With the exception of this last concert, the 22 concerts held thus far have been extremely successful and enjoyed by over 20,000 people."

Black Flag at Polliwog Park in the *Easy Reader*, July 1979. (Photo in article by SPOT.)

CHAPTER 3
SST vs. the Media

1979–1980

1

Keith Morris reached out to his former bandmates in Black Flag with an unusual request. Penelope Spheeris was making a documentary about the LA punk scene and hoped to include Black Flag in her movie, but with one critical caveat: she wanted Morris to perform as the vocalist. Was Black Flag interested?

Ginn's response was unequivocal: absolutely not. Morris had not endeared himself to the band since his departure from Black Flag. He immediately started a new group called the Circle Jerks with Roger Rogerson, Lucky Lehrer, and Red Cross guitarist and South Bay native Greg Hetson. When the Circle Jerks started playing live, its set included songs its members had worked up with their previous bands, including two from Black Flag: "I Don't Care" and "Wasted," the Hermosa Beach tribute to inebriation, both of which Morris had written with Ginn.

Ginn and Dukowski weren't happy about this and replied that Black Flag would like to be a part of Spheeris's project, but with its new vocalist, Ron

Reyes. The nineteen-year-old was passionate about the band's music, knew the songs, and was already living at the Church. He was on such good terms with the band that he sat in for Robo during Black Flag's interview with *Slash*.

Reyes wasn't a stranger to the punk scene. After a brief flirtation with glam rock, he became a devotee of the Ramones. He made the trip to San Francisco to witness the Sex Pistols' last show and was a regular at the Masque. Shortly after the gig at Polliwog Park, Reyes joined the Tourists, replacing John Stielow on drums. The band immediately changed its name to Red Cross (and later to Redd Kross) and signed with Posh Boy Records, which included six of the band's songs on *The Siren*.

Although Reyes was in the mix, his first Black Flag show was a paradigm-shifting experience for him. "Everything that I'd heard up until then was connected to what I had known before, and Black Flag just completely blew that connection apart. They obliterated it. It was like nothing that I had ever seen or heard before."[1]

Reyes was born in Puerto Rico and lived in the Bronx before his father relocated to the South Bay. Unlike his bandmates Ginn and Dukowski, who both graduated from college, Reyes dropped out of Mira Costa High School in Manhattan Beach his senior year, but his connection to the South Bay mattered more than a diploma.

To participate in *The Decline of Western Civilization*, Reyes needed to get up to speed in a hurry. Black Flag played a handful of shows in LA and Orange County with Reyes handling the vocal duties, including a raucous gig at Blackie's in January 1980. The police broke up the show and arrested everyone on stage for disturbing the peace. "That was just at the time when the police started to harass the band incessantly," Dukowski said. "They impounded our gear a few nights before at a club called Blackie's. I spent the whole night before the filming wondering if my gear was going to be available to do the shoot."[2]

Spheeris's film was dogged with problems. She was married to Bob Biggs, who had acquired *Slash* from Steve Samiof and had helped launch Slash Records. As a result of this relationship, many of the participants in *The Decline of Western Civilization* were connected to the label: the Germs, X,

Fear, and Catholic Discipline, which was something of a joke band fronted by
Slash writer and editor Claude Bessy. These were the bands that Spheeris had
access to, and she needed help pulling together the rest of the lineup because
she wasn't part of the community.

Morris agreed to help Spheeris and played an important role behind the
scenes by securing a small rehearsal studio across the street from the original
Masque where Spheeris filmed performances by Black Flag and the Germs.
Ultimately, three of Black Flag's songs were used in *The Decline of Western
Civilization*: "Depression," "White Minority," and "Revenge," which Reyes
dedicated to the LAPD, referencing the band's recent arrest at Blackie's. "They
called us a nuisance in public or something like that," Reyes complained from
the stage, "and they put us in jail!"[3]

Despite being a relative newcomer to the band, Reyes turned in an exuberant performance that reflected the way the songs seesaw between anxiety
and animosity. The irony of a Hispanic singer performing "White Minority"
was buried under an avalanche of blatant racism and misogyny, from Darby
Crash referring to a deceased Mexican as a "beaner" to Lee Ving taunting
the crowd at the Fleetwood with homophobic epithets. "Contempt for and a
wish to exterminate the other," said rock critic Greil Marcus about the film,
"is presented here as a rebellion against the smooth surface of American life,
but it may be more truly a violent, spectacular accommodation to America's
worst instincts."[4]

Even the label "documentary" is problematic. Spheeris's connection to
Slash is a clear conflict of interest, making *The Decline of Western Civilization* more of a showcase for the label. "Basically, it's a commercial for Slash
Records and not a real true representation of the scene in any way," said Lisa
Fancher of Frontier Records. "And it felt very artificial that they had slapped
in the Circle Jerks and Black Flag to be cool because Slash didn't have anything to do with hardcore."[5]

Some of the most radical scenes in *The Decline of Western Civilization* are
the short interviews with LA punks, real kids giving real answers to questions they mostly aren't equipped to answer. But expressions of honesty and
pain, like Eugene Tatu and Michael Miller, a punk from Pasadena known

Penelope Spheeris with Reyes, Dukowski, and Ginn at the Church during filming of *The Decline of Western Civilization*. (Photo by SPOT.)

as X-Head, admitting they don't know who their fathers are, are negated by casual racism and bigotry. It's a confusing double standard that contradicts the film's intentions and sensationalizes its subjects. In spite of its many problems, the film proved massively influential in providing audiences with a set of instructions for navigating LA punk and, with its emphasis on "real people," giving America a foretaste of reality TV.

2

Black Flag was finally ready for its first gigs outside of the state of California. The band headed up to Canada for a pair of shows at Smilin' Buddha in Vancouver where the band was interviewed by the zine *Skitzoid*. Perhaps being out of the country made Ginn less guarded because he was remarkably candid about SST's plans for the future, which included the release of a full-length album with Reyes as vocalist.

However, as much as Reyes was a natural on the stage—bristling with energy and herky-jerky enthusiasm—that energy didn't always transfer to the studio, where he really struggled. "It was brutal," Reyes explained. "I hated it and I think everybody knew that." Although Reyes enjoyed listening to the album come together, when it was his turn to contribute, he panicked. "It was a nerve-racking, horrible experience."[6]

Although Ginn intended to release a Black Flag LP in March to be available when the band returned to Canada in April, those plans were scuttled when he realized Reyes wasn't ready. Ginn decided to release another EP until he had enough quality material for a full-length record. Reyes, however, played his last show on May 23 at the Fleetwood in Redondo Beach. The venue had a large concrete dance floor and could hold up to twelve hundred people, making it the largest concert hall in the South Bay. The Fleetwood didn't serve alcohol and welcomed kids age sixteen and up. The club's size and location made it an attractive venue for bored teenagers from beach cities on both sides of the LA–Orange County border. The venue featured Orange County bands like the Adolescents, Middle Class, and Vicious Circle—Jack Grisham's band before forming T.S.O.L.—but it was also attractive to LA bands who had trouble booking gigs at Hollywood clubs, such as the Germs and Black Flag.

The Fleetwood quickly became a mecca for hardcore shows and with that came a reputation for violence. Morris recalled a Circle Jerks show where he watched from the stage as a fan got jumped. "This guy, he was bleeding from both of his eyes. He's standing there, right in the middle of the floor and all of a sudden like ten guys just pound on him. They dragged the guy out. And this guy was back there by the next song, standing there! And it was like he was crying blood."[7]

One of the Germs' final performances ended with violence spilling out of the Fleetwood and Pat Smear urging the crowd to mellow out. Reyes was in the audience that night and got in a physical confrontation with the bouncers. Bill Bartell of White Flag remembered, "The whole crowd turned against the security; the bouncers took off running, with hundreds of punk rockers chasing them out the doors, and into the streets!"[8]

Reyes had every reason to be leery when he returned to the Fleetwood a month later. He'd met a woman while Black Flag was up in Vancouver, and she was in the crowd at the Fleetwood the night of the show. Perturbed by the violence unfolding all around him, Reyes refused to sing until the fighting stopped, a tactic that other bands had employed with mixed results. The crowd ignored Reyes and he walked off the stage. Reyes claimed it was a spur-of-the-moment decision; something clicked when he saw his bandmates continue to play without him. "If they don't care, then maybe I shouldn't care either," he recalled, "and that's when I started thinking maybe it was time to move on."[9]

Ginn and Dukowski were undoubtedly aware that Reyes had also quit Red Cross in the middle of a performance. Reyes returned to the stage that night but walked off again, this time for good, as the band played on.

3

The beginning of the '80s was a time of tumult both inside and outside the band. With Black Flag once again without a singer, Ginn turned his attention to a band from San Pedro he believed had its act together: the Minutemen.

After the Reactionaries broke up, drummer George Hurley moved on from the band. Mike Watt and D. Boon asked Frank Tonche to take over on drums, and they re-formed as the Minutemen. Although Tonche had never been to a punk show before, he accepted the offer. The band's first gig was at Harbor College with the Plugz, the Gears, and Red Cross on Friday, May 30, 1980. Jack Brewer of Saccharine Trust was also at the show, and he planted the seed in Ginn's ear to sign the Minutemen to SST. Afterward, Ginn approached Watt and asked him if he wanted to put out a single.

The Minutemen's second gig was with Black Flag; the Orange County bands Middle Class, the Adolescents, and the Crowd; and Canada's Subhumans at an art gallery in downtown LA. Even though the show was on a Monday, it was early summer and school was out. Numerous fights erupted during the Minutemen's performance, including an ugly scene where Spot, the only black man at the gig, was sucker-punched by X-Head.[10] Tonche was appalled by the violence and promptly quit the band. "He had a freak out over this whole scene like a lot of dudes did in those days," Watt said of the ugly confrontation, "because nobody liked it, hardly—it was heavy."[11]

Ginn, however, had already booked a recording session for the Minutemen at Media Art in July. Boon and Watt needed to find a drummer—and fast. They reached out to the Reactionaries' former drummer George Hurley, who had just three weeks to learn the songs. The EP was recorded and mixed in one night for three hundred bucks.

The six-and-a-half-minute-long EP was called *Paranoid Time* (SST 002) and featured cover art by Raymond Pettibon depicting a cowboy fondling a cowgirl while a film crew records the scene. Was this surreal scenario plucked from Pettibon's imagination or was the artist channeling Ronald Reagan's ascent from screen actor to the highest office in the country?

The Minutemen were one of the most original punk rock bands to emerge from the LA scene. The seven short songs on *Paranoid Time* reflect working-class concerns at a time when the escalating tensions of the Cold War made communist-sympathizing rhetoric verboten in public discourse. In the song "Paranoid Chant," Boon gives voice to fears that the world was racing toward annihilation.

Right when hardcore bands were ramping up the intensity by getting faster and louder, the Minutemen moved in a different direction. Boon's jangly guitar provided a counterpoint to Watt's ruminative bass lines. Watt referred to the songs as "tunes." Punk rock had been called many things, but "tuneful" generally wasn't one of them. The Minutemen seldom played on top of each other, preferring to showcase instruments like arguments in a debate. Both Watt and Boon wrote material that made use of unconventional song structures. Played one after the other, the songs blended together. Sometimes the endings were so abrupt it wasn't always clear to people in the audience if the conclusion was intentional.

All of that was fine with Ginn. He wasn't interested in releasing records by Black Flag clones. Black Flag had an evolving sound. The Minutemen had ideas. Both bands were relentless in their own unique way, and *Paranoid Time* marked the beginning of a long and tumultuous collaboration between the Minutemen and SST.

4

When Black Flag returned to the stage after Reyes's departure, Ginn and Dukowski reached out to Morris to fill in for an upcoming show at the Fleetwood. Morris was game and also traveled with Black Flag and Geza X and the Mommymen to San Francisco for a gig at Mabuhay Gardens. The fact that this show went on as planned despite the band not having a full-time singer and the venue being nearly four hundred miles away demonstrates Black Flag's commitment to playing anytime anywhere. Most bands would have canceled.[12]

Brendan Mullen, who was then drumming for the Mommymen, was impressed with the hardcore band from Hermosa Beach. When Black Flag played at Vanguard, he nervously took over the vocal duties, and Morris was there to heckle him. But for Mullen it was a grim and gruesome scene. "One guy was lying at my feet, face covered in blood, looking up at me with bug eyes, screaming something at me," he recalled. "I couldn't hear, because the band was playing incredibly loud behind me and I was screaming the lyrics as loud as possible into the mike. There was blood all over my shoes and all over the monitors."[13]

Joe Nolte was the next performer invited to take part in the carnage with Ginn, Dukowski, and Robo, but the long rehearsals left his voice ragged. Given a choice between playing with Black Flag and an important gig with the Last, the singer chose his own band.

These performances by former members, acquaintances, and friends suggest that Ginn and Dukowski viewed the other members of the band as replaceable parts. Singers weren't the focal point of the band but rather were vocal instruments that were no more important than drums or guitar. This wasn't how most bands operated. A charismatic singer-songwriter was considered by most of the rock and roll establishment as essential to a band's success, but for Black Flag the singer was just another cog in the machine.

Ginn and Dukowski found their next vocalist by poaching another player from Red Cross: guitarist Dez Cadena, who moved into Greg Hetson's spot when he left to play with the Circle Jerks. Like Reyes, Cadena was a transplant from the East Coast whose father had settled in Hermosa Beach when

Cadena was in his early teens. Cadena's father, Ozzie, was acquainted with Morris's father, Jerry, long before their sons met. Ozzie had been involved in jazz music for most of his professional life and even ran a record label. He booked bands for the Lighthouse, which stood almost directly across the street from the Hermosa Tackle Box. That was how he got to know Jerry, who was a jazz aficionado.

Cadena differed from prior Black Flag vocalists in that he was a talented musician in his own right. Music was in his blood, and he'd been playing guitar since he was twelve years old. Ginn understood and appreciated Cadena's talent and immediately went to work on how to make use of it. "We have some ideas for using songs that would be better with two guitars," Ginn said. "We've been working on it, but as far as playing that way, we haven't yet, but we're going to. I think it's gonna fit in real good. It'll just give us more to work with. More freedom for doing some stuff that I've always wanted to do. I always really wanted to have two guitar players, but when the band started, it was hard enough finding a drummer and a bass player that would play this kind of music."[14]

Black Flag was finally ready to go, but as the summer of 1980 unfolded, the scene was wracked with turmoil. With school out, more kids from suburbs across the Southland were attending punk shows and causing problems at the venues. The LAPD was making a habit out of pulling the plug on shows and hassling the punks in attendance. Black Flag, along with the Germs and the Circle Jerks, were banned from the Hong Kong Café, the Hermosa quartet's most reliable venue. The club also gave a half-dozen bands from Orange County the boot, including Agent Orange, Middle Class, and Eddie and the Subtitles, and refused to admit anyone under the age of twenty-one. So much for "the music of the '80s."

In an article that appeared in the Sunday *Los Angeles Times* on June 29, 1980, Patrick Goldstein declared that punk rockers "don't just dance anymore. They mug each other." The story cited examples of violent physical confrontations that included the stabbing of a young woman during an X show at the Whisky. According to Goldstein, "Accounts of violence, vandalism and mutilation at some area rock clubs read like reports from a war zone." He even gave a name to the style of dance that went on at these clubs: "the Slam," a term that he claimed to have picked up at the Fleetwood.[15]

The much-ridiculed article became notorious in the punk community, which had never witnessed a mutilation nor heard of "the Slam" before. When Black Flag played a show with D.O.A. in Santa Cruz in the fall, the zine *Ripper* asked Ginn about it. Ginn asserted that not only had he never heard of slam dancing before Goldstein's article but no one had.[16] In other words, the term was Goldstein's invention. Nevertheless, the name caught on and gained cultural currency outside of the scene—much to the irritation of punk rockers in LA.

Although the article conceded that only "a small minority of punks" were responsible for the violence, it pointed a finger at specific bands. Goldstein spoke with Turner, the manager of the Hong Kong Café, who said, "No one's saying these groups encourage violence, but they do attract it and they do tolerate it."[17] The article started a debate about punk rock: Were bands responsible for the violence that took place at shows?

"We don't want to get on stage and be authority figures and tell people what to do, we feel that that's wrong," Ginn told *Flipside*. "We want to get up on stage to create an atmosphere where people can think for themselves. They're not always gonna do the right thing. It would be real easy for us to get up there to control the audience so we'd have nice places to play all the time, but that contradicts our whole way of thinking. If we have to be authority figures we might as well not be there at all."[18]

As far as Ginn was concerned, telling the crowd how to behave was antithetical to punk rock. Punk rock was a form of creative expression, not a tool for inhibiting it. Ginn didn't form a band so that he could police its fans.

For Black Flag, Goldstein's article, which mentioned the band by name, was both a turning point and an omen. Craig Lee and Danny Weizmann (a.k.a. Shredder) believed Goldstein's piece "freely exploited and made media meat out of the suburban punk scene; citing that punks (especially OC kids) were criminal, vicious, and dangerous....It was a disaster for such bands as Black Flag, the Circle Jerks, Fear, China White, etc."[19]

Ever since Black Flag was lambasted for turning a family event at Polliwog

Park into an unpleasant affair, the Hermosa Beach Police Department had been making life miserable for the band. Black Flag was routinely followed every time the van left for a gig, and the Hermosa cops were not happy about all the activity at the Church. "The police would pull me over every time they saw me," Dukowski said. "I had to sneak into town on side streets. Every time I drove down Pier Avenue, I got pulled over. The Hermosa police were fucking assholes."[20]

Some of the people who lived at the Church were souring on the place as well. The Church didn't have a shower, which meant residents had to rely on family and friends for basic hygiene. Ginn moved into a house a few doors down, which he shared with his girlfriend Medea Jones. "She came out of the shadows," Morris said. "We didn't know her until she showed up with Ginn."[21]

Medea was an enthusiastic supporter of the band and served as Ginn's muse and cocreator on the songs "Room 13," which was Medea's apartment number in the building where she lived on Pier Avenue, and "Thirsty and Miserable."[22] Robo credited Medea for her guerrilla marketing tactics. "Greg's girlfriend Medea used to go to Hollywood with a spray can," Robo recalled, "and every wall that she saw, she put up the four bars. The police were like, 'Who the fuck is doing all this?' "[23]

Although the Church was an ideal practice space and base of operations for SST Electronics, which was still going strong, and SST Records, which was gearing up to release two more records, it wasn't a comfortable place to live. Black Flag shared the space with several other tenants, and residents never knew who might be coming through the back door. Nolte walked in one day and found himself looking down the barrel of a police officer's shotgun. Apparently, a burglar had ducked inside to elude the police, and while this incident didn't have anything to do with Black Flag, it certainly didn't help the Church's reputation as a hub of criminal activity with local law enforcement.

Ginn could see the writing on the wall. The police wanted Black Flag out of Hermosa Beach and were not above intimidation and threats of violence. So he decided to go out in style. Using SST's mailing list, he invited five

Robo, Morris, Ginn, Dukowski, and Medea pose for photographer Chris D. of the Flesh Eaters in West LA in late 1980. (Photo by SPOT.)

hundred hardcore kids to a free show at the Church to see the new singer of Black Flag. "They wrecked the place," Cadena said, "and broke some of the windows of some of the businesses around the place."[24] A police officer told Dukowski, "Don't come back ever. If you come back you'll wind up first in the hospital then in jail."[25]

The local paper ran headlines like "Police Kick Black Flag Out of Town," making it seem like the Hermosa Beach authorities had rounded up the band members and escorted them to the edge of town like a scene in a western.[26] With Goldstein's article in the *Los Angeles Times* sounding the drumbeat against "violent" bands like Black Flag, it was only a matter of time before others piled on.

5

Black Flag moved SST's operations into a new location in Redondo Beach but didn't stay long, a practice that occurred with such frequency it became a pattern. However, the release of *Jealous Again* (SST 003) signaled the label was back in business. For most of the summer, Ginn had focused his attention on getting Cadena ready to play, preparing for the release of Black Flag's second EP, and laying the groundwork for the band's first extended tour, which was scheduled to kick off toward the end of the year. SST had sold out of both the initial pressing of two thousand copies of *Nervous Breakdown* as well as a subsequent run of one thousand. While *Jealous Again* and the Minutemen's *Paranoid Time* were being pressed up, Black Flag played a handful of West Coast shows.

Although Morris had helped the band out while Black Flag was between singers, all was not well between the two camps. Ginn was still upset that Morris had reworked Black Flag songs the two had collaborated on for the Circle Jerks. The most egregious was "I Don't Care," which the Circle Jerks were releasing as "Don't Care" on its debut album *Group Sex* with Frontier Records. Ginn sent an angry letter to Fancher, demanding that he receive credit for the song. Fancher made the change on the next pressing, but she wondered why Ginn went to the trouble when he simply could have picked up the phone. "That's just dumb," Fancher said, "but it gets your attention."[27]

This didn't settle the band's beef with Morris. When *Jealous Again* was finally released, it included an attack against the former vocalist. Dukowski rewrote the lyrics to "I Don't Care," calling Morris a liar and a thief. The diss track "You Bet We've Got Something Personal Against You" doesn't name Morris, but the song makes its grievances clear.

Not everyone in the SST camp was upset with Morris. Right up until the release of *Group Sex*, Pettibon continued to provide the Circle Jerks with his distinctive black-and-white artwork for the band's flyers. Although punk—hardcore in particular—was growing in popularity, at the center of the action was a relatively small group of people. Black Flag and the Circle Jerks played with the same bands, performed at the same clubs, and worked with the same artists, promoters, photographers, and writers. Sometimes the bands even played together. Although Ginn and Dukowski may have had something personal against Morris, Pettibon clearly didn't.

Morris wasn't the only former Black Flag vocalist to come under fire on *Jealous Again*. The band also took shots at Reyes. On the back of the record's jacket, the vocals were credited to Chavo Pederast (Kid Pedophile). This was not a playful punk nickname that Reyes embraced or even understood. The first time Reyes saw *Jealous Again* in a record shop in Vancouver, where he'd moved after leaving Black Flag, he assumed "Chavo Pederast" was the band's new singer. It wasn't until he played the record at home and heard his own voice that he realized the name referred to him. The nickname made it awkward for Reyes when explaining his contribution to the record to friends and family. He laughed it off at first, but eventually bitterness set in.

Ginn likely felt betrayed by Reyes's sudden departure. From a business standpoint, it sabotaged his plans to release a full-length record, which had been SST's mission from day one. The anger wasn't limited to the frustration Ginn felt as an artist; it was baked into everything Black Flag did.

Ginn and Dukowski made it clear that they were not above airing the band's dirty laundry. The anger that could be heard on Black Flag's records and seen at the band's shows was not a pose, and neither Ginn nor Dukowski was the least bit reticent about lashing out at those who earned their enmity. Although these tactics could be juvenile and mean spirited, they came from a place of indignation that was at times incongruous with other positions (e.g., bad-mouthing Morris for not giving Ginn credit on the Circle Jerks' record while leaving Migdol off of *Nervous Breakdown*). Ginn and Dukowski attacked their enemies with a righteous fury that often caught its recipients off guard. They held themselves to a high standard, and when others didn't meet those standards, they lashed out. That their retaliation was out of proportion to the original grievance was beside the point.

Nor was their anger reserved for former members of the band. Ginn took umbrage with *Flipside* over an interview with the Circle Jerks. When asked about his departure from Black Flag, Morris made statements that Ginn regarded as outright lies. It bothered Ginn that the fanzine would print Morris's remarks as fact without verifying them with him.[28]

Ginn's anger led to the creation of a typewritten document on SST letterhead called "The Creepy Crawler," which was published in the zine *Outcry*. It begins with a rant that has an interesting preface: "The following is not a song lyric, but an attack directed at people whom we consider to be 'yellow journalists' or assholes." It's an odd screed that reads like the wounded response of a jilted lover. While the author takes pains not to name the "yellow journalists," the rant is clearly directed at *Flipside*, though Ginn's catalog of "assholes" was growing by the day.[29]

Ginn and Dukowski finally got a chance to clear the air when they sat down with Al Kowalewski, *Flipside*'s publisher, for an interview at SST's new base of operations in the heart of Torrance. Ginn asked Kowalewski about *Flipside*'s editorial standards: "Have you seen discrepancies about things that have been written about us, not opinion but matter of fact?" After rehashing the band's issues with Morris's statements, Dukowski admitted that "Greg resents the fact that you guys didn't ask us." A bewildered Kowalewski tried to explain that it would be impossible to corroborate every statement that each band member made in an interview.[30]

Although SST and *Flipside* were underground organizations without a whiff of corporate sponsorship, both emulated the institutions they hoped to subvert. *Flipside* was clearly a magazine, SST a record label. Ginn and Dukowski took great pride in creating, promoting, and distributing a professional product, as did Kowalewski and *Flipside*'s army of writers and contributors.[31]

Flipside, like other zines that documented and celebrated the punk scene, wasn't staffed by trained journalists any more than the bands they covered were composed of trained musicians. Nor did these zinesters necessarily think of themselves as journalists. They were people with a passion for the music they covered. Many of the contributors who penned reviews, wrote up scene reports, or conducted interviews had never been published before; ergo, errors abounded, both human and typographical.

Ginn's resentment was the main issue. To his way of thinking, neither independence nor exuberance was an excuse for a lack of professionalism, and when the so-called pros in the scene conducted themselves in a manner that he deemed less than professional, he took it personally. Then—even if it took months or years to get back at whomever slighted him—he let them have it.

There was a bit of a double standard at work here because Black Flag wasn't above using insults, innuendos, and falsehoods to take shots at people in interviews. It's one thing to refer to Reyes as "the overcooked Keith" but quite another for Dukowski to call him "that kind of half-Mexican, half-black guy," which is both inaccurate and racist.[32]

Uncalled for or not, these attacks sent a strong message to the punk community that came across loud and clear: don't mess with Black Flag.

6

As the summer of 1980 drew to a close, SST set its sights on a much larger target: the LAPD. In "The Creepy Crawler" Black Flag also published the lyrics to "Police Story," a song with one of the most incendiary opening lines in hardcore history. The song was written before Black Flag started playing outside of its hometown and refers to its many run-ins with the Hermosa Beach Police Department. When asked whether "Police Story" was a political song, Ginn emphasized that it was based on his own experiences and frustrations. "'Police Story' deals with police in a very personal way."[33]

Every punk in the LA scene had stories about being physically assaulted by the police. Many had multiple run-ins with violent cops. "They would come in with the billy clubs swinging and you couldn't get away from them," said Bill Stevenson. "They're like cockroaches."[34] Pettibon was also clubbed in the head. Morris was roughed up by a cadre of cops after foolishly slashing the tires of an unmarked police car. Joe Nolte was thrown down a flight of stairs and felt like he got off easy because the assault occurred at the Elks Lodge Hall on March 17, 1979, the night of a massive police operation that resulted in numerous injuries and arrests.

For many white middle-class punks, it was the first time they'd experienced this kind of treatment, and it was shocking for them. Being unfairly arrested, jailed, or roughed up by the police accomplishes one of two things: either it curbs the behavior that attracted the unwanted attention, or it inspires the recipient to fight back. The Hermosa Beach Police Department's campaign to force Black Flag out of town was a radicalizing experience for Ginn. As a white man from a middle-class family, he'd never been mistreated by the police before. His mother's immigrant status, his father's suspicion of institutions, and the brutality they'd both witnessed overseas during the war

Robert Becerra of the Stains. (Photo by Edward Colver.)

conditioned their children to be suspicious of institutional overreach, particularly when the goal of the greater good was achieved with threats of violence. In other words, Ginn knew a fascist operation when he saw one.

Although "Police Story" wasn't on either of Black Flag's first two releases, its defiance found a receptive audience in the throngs of punks who'd been mistreated by the LAPD. The song's us-versus-them narrative articulated the peril that punks found themselves in every time they went to a show. But if there was a single event that marked a point of no return for the embattled punk scene, it was an all-ages show at the Hideaway on September 19, 1980, in downtown LA.

The Hideaway wasn't a club per se but a small warehouse that had been modified into a performance space. The lineup featured groups that would become part of the SST family of bands, and it had all the makings of an epic night. However, the inexperienced promoters oversold the show, the event started late, and ventilation inside the club was nonexistent. As temperatures inside the venue climbed, so did the mood outside as ticketed guests learned they wouldn't be getting in. The security guards the promoters hired were over-aggressive and had little experience dealing with punks, of whom there were between one thousand and fifteen hundred hoping to get into the tiny space.

Jack Rivera of the Stains got a sense there would be problems with the show during sound check. "I remember we got there early to load in," Rivera said. "It was like four o'clock in the afternoon, the sun was still out, and there were already kids waiting outside."[35]

The Stains took the stage after Mad Society. During the set, vocalist Jerry "Atric" Castellanos took out a butcher knife he'd taped to his leg and buried it in the stage floor. Bassist Ceasar Viscarra swung his bass to keep people from climbing on stage, which was covered with beer. Guitarist Robert Becerra also got in on the act. "Someone threw water on me," Becerra said, "and I jumped off stage and started going after him. My homeboys were like, 'Keep playing. We'll take care of it.' They pushed me back on stage. Then they took care of it."[36]

Fights broke out. Glass was smashed. One frustrated punk commandeered a custom car parked outside the club. "The promoter parked his Cadillac in front of one of the large garage doors," Morris said, "and some punker dunker came up with the brilliant idea of hot-wiring the car and ramming it into the door. Of course this was due to all the people standing out front who couldn't get in."[37]

Inside the Hideaway, punks were just as destructive, kicking holes in the walls and knocking down barriers inside the club that limited their movement. They broke down the door to get in and tore the place apart to get out. Naturally, the police were called, and they cordoned off the streets around the Hideaway and arrived in full force to break up the show.

"It all went to shit the second I walked in," remembered photographer Edward Colver, who didn't even have time to snap a photograph. "Then the power went off and people were throwing vinyl records through the air and running out of there with chairs over their heads. It was nuts!"[38]

Even though Black Flag never got to play, the events at the Hideaway set the stage for a showdown at the Whisky a few weeks later. Black Flag's association with Brendan Mullen, who booked shows at the club, resulted in an invitation to play with D.O.A. The bands were scheduled to play two sets, but after the first one, the LAPD moved in. The police didn't just stop the show; they put on a show of their own with a chaotic display of force that brought back memories of the curfew riots on the Sunset Strip in 1966. Two dozen squad cars came screaming down the boulevard and descended on the club. The LAPD blocked off Sunset and San Vicente, rerouting traffic and trapping concertgoers whose only crime was waiting in line for an event for which they had purchased tickets. In some instances, police took the tickets out of fans' hands and ripped them up in their faces. "If that happened to me," Ginn said, "I'd start looking for bottles."[39]

That's exactly what Reid Campbell, bass player in the band Modern Industry, did.[40] He tossed an empty bottle at the cops, who responded by swarming the scene and chasing punks down side streets before tossing them into police cruisers.

Black Flag watched the action unfold from the dressing room on the second floor. "This one Hardcore Punk kid threw a beer bottle at this line of riot police," Cadena said, "and it hit one guy in the helmet and it was chaos."[41] Injuries were widespread as punks were beaten and knocked to the ground. Many were clubbed in the head. One woman had her leg broken by an especially overzealous cop. Some officers were armed with shotguns. The police weren't there to "restore order"; order wasn't on the menu that night. What they did was disrupt the show and deliver a beatdown.

Ginn had had enough. Frustrated by the LAPD's harassment, he made the unusual move of contacting media outlets before Black Flag's next show, at Baces Hall in East Hollywood, in the hope of demonstrating the band wasn't responsible for the violence at its gigs. By now everyone accepted that punk shows were synonymous with violence. Black Flag wanted proof that police were the instigators.

LAPD on the Sunset Strip outside the Whisky on October 9, 1980. (Photo by Edward Colver.)

This was something of a gamble. While the LAPD showed its true colors at the Whisky, the punks at the Hideaway were wildly destructive; if something similar went down at Baces Hall, the stunt would blow up in their faces. But Ginn believed the violence marring Black Flag's gigs started with the people who ran the venues. The kids only got agitated when shows were oversold, started late, or shut down early. In other words, if promoters acted as professionally as the bands they booked, these incidents wouldn't occur, and the police wouldn't need to get involved. "Generally people think the authorities are correct," Ginn said. "If there is a riot, it's always, 'What are these people doing to cause it?' My perspective is quite different. We didn't go out to cause anything, we were a rock band. We had an implicit politics. The police started the riots, then at a certain point, a riot became the thing to do."[42]

On November 10, 1980, Rona Barrett produced a segment for *The*

Tomorrow Show with Tom Snyder. While the episode is best remembered for a Mohawked Dukowski calling the LAPD Nazis, the segment opens in explosive fashion with footage of Wendy O. Williams of the Plasmatics literally blowing up a car with a stick of dynamite on stage at Perkins Palace in Pasadena. Over a montage of Gary Leonard's photographs of punks from Huntington Beach doing "the Slam," Barrett describes in contradictory terms how punk transcends "age, sex, and color" but is still somehow made up of mostly "young WASPS who masquerade at night in leather and chains." Barrett's sensational spiel winds down as Black Flag takes the stage at Baces Hall: "A band from Hermosa Beach, California, called Black Flag has earned a reputation as a group with a particularly violent following."[43]

A chaotic mix of concert footage, punks loitering outside the hall, and mustached cops in riot gear unfolds. A police officer from the Rampart Division explains that the venue's owner asked police to stop the show because of property damage, but no such damage—or any unruly behavior—was caught by the camera crew. Once the punks were kicked out of the venue and banished to the other side of the street, the cops rushed them. On screen the scene played out exactly like Ginn anticipated it would.

But that hardly seemed to matter to Barrett. In a talk-show style roundtable conversation with Dukowski, Leonard, and Mad Society's manager Daphne Vendetta, Barrett repeatedly returns to the violent nature of punk rock itself, never once acknowledging the violence the police inflicted on kids at the shows, despite repeated attempts by her guests to steer the conversation that way.

The following Sunday, Patrick Goldstein, who was still stirring the pot in the *Los Angeles Times*, poked fun at Barrett's segment and referred to disturbances at Black Flag shows as "skirmishes with the police," as if the band were responsible for instigating them.[44] No matter what Ginn and Dukowski did to set the story straight, the media stuck to its own skewed version of the truth.

7

If for no other reason, punk rock will be remembered as a successful art movement because of its power to agitate, and few entities were more agitated by punk rock than the news media.

Punk was a subject that news outlets returned to again and again because stories about punk rockers smashing up music venues or rioting in the streets reliably provoked moral outrage from the audience. Pundits laid the blame for society's failings at the feet of a poorly understood pursuit that provided sensational headlines and sound bites. In these stories, the news media minimized punk rock as expressions of anger and animosity accompanied by an ear-splitting soundtrack. In many reports, the music was treated as a humorous sideline to the violence that took place at shows. "Until Black Flag figures out what to do with the enormous rage implicit in both their music and their fans," decried the *Los Angeles Herald-Examiner*, "all of their elegant anarcho-nihilist philosophizing will remain the worst sort of dilettante bunk."[45]

There were plenty of hucksters who were quick to cash in on the punk panic. Serena Dank, founder of the Parents of Punkers family therapy organization, published a pamphlet with "everything a parent would want to know about the punk movement and their child." Dank appeared on news networks to tell stories of children led astray by punk as if it were a cult or a highly addictive drug. She even sat for an interview with filmmaker Penelope Spheeris and talked about being harassed by a prank caller who threatened to blow her away. "Sounds like he might listen to Black Flag," Spheeris quipped.[46]

The media's inability to comprehend the most basic aspects of punk rock led to the amplification of its ugliness. This proved to be a self-fulfilling prophecy. Instead of discouraging people from attending these so-called orgies of violence, their portrayal of shows as an outlet for mindless aggression resulted in an influx of new "fans" for whom violence was the chief attraction and everything else was ancillary. When you tell people there's going to be violence, violent people are going to come.

Stories like Rona Barrett's segment served as recruitment tools for the worst kind of fans: jocks, racists, homophobes, and actual psychopaths were drawn to punk shows. While these stories served as free advertising, the bands were often made to look foolish and were denigrated as brainless barbarians. This discouraged many open-minded kids from going to shows, particularly women, who were curious about punk but not enough to risk getting harassed and beaten up for it.

With the violence at punk shows getting so much attention, those at the heart of the punk rock community blamed fans at the fringes for ruining "their" scene. Those who'd been punks since the '70s resented that the scene was no longer theirs to control. Many of the early LA punks had elevated style into a kind of identity and would mark newcomers by their derivative fashion sense as poseurs. But the influx of hardcore kids did not share these values. Either they embraced a different style (as they did in Huntington Beach) or rejected it altogether (as they did in Hermosa Beach).[47]

The worst of the violence was often attributed to outside agitators from the Beach Cities. By shifting the blame, the media helped drive a wedge within the punk community between the "original" Hollywood punks and the younger, more aggressive hardcore fans from the suburbs. The debate as to who was at fault for ruining the scene raged in all the zines.

It was a strange time for punk. Even though the movement was more popular than ever before, it was ignored by record companies, banned by Hollywood clubs, abused by a police force with little or no oversight, and decried by the news media, whose embrace of the talk-show format was beginning its slide into infotainment. What could possibly go wrong?

8

SST stood at the vanguard of a new and exciting style of music, but Black Flag entered the American consciousness at a time when it was dangerous for a punk band to do so.

Because the band wasn't directly involved in the violence that took place at its shows, Black Flag refused to take responsibility for it. The band didn't urge fans to attack each other or destroy property; nor, obviously, did Black Flag call the police. Nevertheless, it was blamed for the vandalism and violence that went down at shows. In an article titled "The Black Flag Violence Must Stop!" the author ranted, "Although Black Flag don't encourage the violence, they don't discourage it, much less really acknowledge it on stage. Which is not only wrong but profoundly evil."[48]

The media did its part to foster the impression that Black Flag fans were bad people, but good business practice also helped put a target on the band's back. Black Flag's easy-to-spray-paint logo, bold flyers, consistent branding, and relentless marketing made it stand apart from other bands, many of which blatantly imitated its approach.[49] If a fight broke out, if property was damaged, or if the police ended a show, Black Flag was to blame. It was like Polliwog Park all over again, but the consequences were much more severe.

However, it would be a mistake to call Black Flag a victim. Ginn and Dukowski understood that, from a marketing perspective, the controversy benefited both the band and the label. Throughout this period SST did everything in its power to attract more young people to Black Flag shows, even targeting high schools in Huntington Beach for flyer drops. While Ginn and Dukowski would prefer to play shows without being interrupted or anyone getting hurt, if the media was determined to make Black Flag its punching bag with a consistency that constituted a campaign, then the band would fight back. Anyone who thought differently didn't know Black Flag very well.

One way that SST responded was through advertising. Ginn and Dukowski took the novel step of buying airtime on local radio stations to advertise upcoming shows. This was a bold move for an indie record label, but the way they went about it was audacious. For example, to advertise a show at the Fleetwood, SST embedded the details in a monologue from a distraught punk threatening to kill himself at the show. In another inspired advertisement, Spot plays the role of an on-scene reporter broadcasting from inside the Starwood, and the cryptic commercial makes reference to "creepy crawl" a half-dozen times. In SST's most provocative spot, which ran in early 1981, a pair of cops en route to the Stardust Ballroom to break up a Black Flag show where a "major disturbance" is underway bemoan the fact that Police Chief Daryl Gates "is in a real uproar."[50]

While it's easy to dismiss these commercials as stunts to enflame the general public, by mentioning Gates in these psyops, Ginn wasn't just thumbing his nose at the top cop in the LAPD, he was giving voice to a widely held belief in the punk community that Gates had a personal vendetta against them. Many believed this was because Gates's son, Lowell, who was the black sheep of the family, was a punk.

Was Lowell a punk rocker? He certainly had a long and colorful arrest record, but many of his crimes were tied to drugs. Gates wrote in his own autobiography that Lowell was high on heroin at his swearing in ceremony as chief of the Los Angeles Police Department in 1978. That's a startling admission from someone who had a long history of blaming others for problems the LAPD routinely exacerbated.[51]

Gates's unofficial war on punk suggests he saw punks as part of the criminal class. Punk's lack of rules and rejection of dogma attracted people whose so-called lifestyle choices pushed them to the margins of society: drug users, sex workers, petty criminals, and the like. Before widespread acceptance of LGBTQ communities, those who sought to make a life for themselves outside the paradigm of the nuclear family were regarded as sexual deviants, and their behavior was criminalized. Punk provided a community where people could find their place, reinvent themselves, or at the very least blend in while they figured things out.

Police were threatened by all of it. But by accusing LAPD officers of being Nazis on television and calling out Chief Gates on the radio, SST staged a counterattack on the LAPD through the media, though Ginn knew better than anyone it was a war they couldn't win.

9

After Black Flag's notoriety made it all but impossible to play shows in LA, Ginn and Dukowski planned its first nationwide tour. While punk rock was old news in places like New York and LA, in much of the United States it was still something of a novelty. Although most major cities and college towns had music scenes with a range of punk and post-punk performers, these communities tended to be idiosyncratic and self-contained. What if SST took the message to them?

It was a gamble Ginn was willing to take. He had already enjoyed some success exploring the West Coast, where he found receptive audiences in San Francisco, Seattle, and Vancouver. "Gigs in LA are much harder for us to set up," Ginn said, "just because of the problems with the police department trying to put a stop to them. Playing out of town is much easier in comparison."[52]

Ginn and Dukowski leveraged these out-of-town shows for all they were worth. They bought ads in the zines, resulting in coverage for their records and shows. The San Francisco zine *Damage* reviewed *Nervous Breakdown* eight months after it came out. "All four tracks on this EP boast a raw, densely-textured guitar, frenetic bass playing, jackhammer drumming and shrieking maniacal vocals."[53]

Dukowski had some experience booking shows for an arts organization. The gregarious bass player was good on the telephone and had become Black Flag's de facto spokesperson, a role Ginn was all too happy to hand off to him. More importantly, Dukowski had traveled the country with his friend Ed Danky, his bandmate in Würm. "That road trip was the seed experience for Black Flag's early touring," Dukowski said. "I knew how to travel the country, roughing it, on very little money."[54]

Ginn grafted a concept onto Dukowski's know-how for this bare-bones adventure. A tour conjured up images of bloated rock stars in luxury tour buses. Black Flag's operation was much more stripped down: a used passenger van modified to hold the band's gear. Ginn and Dukowski weren't just planning a tour; they were messengers on a mission.

They adopted the term "creepy crawl," which had been used by members of the Manson family to describe the practice of breaking into a home and rearranging the furniture to create a subtle but noticeable disturbance. The effect wasn't just to shock the members of these households but to unnerve them. Black Flag had a similar ambition. Not everyone would understand what they were experiencing when they came to see the band play, but something of Black Flag's essence would linger like a bad vibration long after the band left town.

Ginn understood there was no point in giving creative direction to Pettibon for flyers and record covers, but he also knew that his brother was obsessed with images of countercultural figures from the '60s. Manson-like figures—naked, bearded men, often armed with knives in terrifying poses—appeared in Pettibon's work with the frequency of a recurring nightmare. Paired with Back Flag's anarcho-pirate iconography, the band's flyers were like a bad acid flashback, a sinister reminder of the dark and demented side of the California dream. Armed with a van, the band's gear, and some merchandise, Black Flag left LA to creepy crawl America.

Ginn, Cadena, and Dukowski at *New Wave Theatre* taping. (Photo by SPOT.)

CHAPTER 4
SST vs. MCA

1980–1981

1

On December 7, 1980, Darby Crash slipped into the static forever when he intentionally overdosed. Darby's fifteen seconds of infamy were cut brutally short by John Lennon's assassination the following afternoon. For many, the sad and pointless death of the man who'd helped supercharge the LA punk scene with his live-wire personality on and off the stage didn't so much spell the end of punk as expose it for what it was: a dead end. This feeling was underscored by Slash Records' release of the soundtrack to *The Decline of Western Civilization* later that month. The cover, which had been designed long before Darby's death, featured the drug-addled singer lying on the stage with his eyes closed.

On the night of Darby's demise, Black Flag was playing at Jimmy's Music Club in New Orleans, laying the foundation for the future of indie rock by establishing a network of clubs, crash pads, punk houses, and halls for hire across America where bands with the courage to leave home could play. It would be months before the kids at Jimmy's would hear Black Flag tear up the opening tracks of *The Decline of Western Civilization*, but that was okay; the boys from Hermosa Beach would be back at Jimmy's in a few months and would return to New Orleans many times after that.

While on the road, Black Flag was asked again and again about the state of punk in LA. To outsiders, Darby's death suggested the scene itself was dying, but Ginn wasn't having it. He wasn't interested in clubs, cliques, or classifications. On the contrary, Ginn was looking for "a place without an age limit that anybody can go to. No restrictions, you don't have to look a certain way. Open to any kind of taste which means putting up with some assholes."[1]

Ginn believed it was his duty to bring his message to the masses—whether they wanted to hear it or not. If that meant dealing with people who punk provocateur Black Randy described as "off-duty Marines, meth-crazed jocks, and other extremely weird and sick people showing up at punk concerts," so be it.[2]

Ginn was an unlikely ambassador for this movement because he preferred to let his guitar speak for him. But just as he'd discovered open-minded people in California, the Northwest, and Canada, he found them in the heartland too. It wasn't the most efficient tour, but the band, which routinely traveled to San Francisco and Vancouver for one-off gigs, was up for it. Ginn made crucial connections during Black Flag's swing through Texas, and he found a thriving scene in Chicago.

In 1981, a new nemesis rose to the fore who would become as much a part of the legacy of '80s hardcore as the bands themselves. On January 20, Ronald Reagan, the former governor of California, was sworn in as president of the United States. Prior to his political career, Reagan was famous for his work in film and television, where he was best known for his roles in war movies and westerns. For conservatives, he was a symbol of an uncomplicated time when conflicts had good guys and bad guys. Even if victory was elusive, the good guys always came out on top.

Of course, it was all a sham. Under Reagan the income gap widened, debt skyrocketed, and social services were gutted. The presidency of Jimmy Carter, a former naval officer who pardoned draft dodgers and supported the civil rights movement, was effectively over when he took responsibility for the botched mission to rescue the hostages in Iran in April 1980. The age of the Gipper had begun and with it a culture of rapacious greed and crass commercialism that defined the decade.

The Reagan years were awful for America's underclass, but they provided hardcore fans with a target. The enemy was no longer your hippie mom, your alcoholic stepfather, or that annoying Eagles song that was always on the radio. The enemy was the cartoonishly evil Ronald Reagan and everything he stood for. It was the cloying Christianity of the Moral Majority and its gospel of intolerance. It was the terror of knowing with every molecule in your body that you were going to die in a nuclear war.

2

Black Flag spent much of the period between the presidential election and the inauguration on the road, but in San Pedro, the Minutemen stayed busy.

With SST now based in Torrance, Watt and Boon spent more time there, occasionally working for Ginn soldering antenna tuners. Along with former Reactionaries front man Martin Tamburovich, they had formed their own label: New Alliance Records. The label's first release was a madcap compilation called *Cracks in the Sidewalk*, which featured friends from San Pedro and Hermosa Beach, including a musical project by Spot called Artless Entanglements. "You gotta do something," Spot explained. "You're in a studio. Nothing's going on. No one's there. It's part of how you learn how to use some of the equipment when no one else is around. You just do what you do, and it's more fun to do it when you don't know what you're doing."[3]

Because *Cracks in the Sidewalk* came out a month before *Paranoid Time*, which was finally released in December, it had the very first Minutemen track made available for public consumption. The Minutemen's "9:30 May 2" is followed by the howling fury of Black Flag's "Clocked In," with Cadena singing Ginn's ode to punching a clock. "Hearts & Barbarians" is a death rock romp through Cold War themes by Saccharine Trust, a band led by Jack Brewer and Joey Baiza, who had a delightfully deranging influence on their creative cohorts in the South Bay.

Side B of the twelve-inch EP comprises three songs by bands that can be charitably called experimental, featuring George Hurley's brother Greg, Spot, and Tamburovich. Illustrated with a half-dozen panels by Raymond Pettibon, including a portrait of a half-dead-looking Ronald Reagan in a cowboy hat, the final product resembled an SST record—all that was missing was the logo. *Cracks in the Sidewalk* sold well and was promptly re-pressed, building the foundation for the next release from New Alliance. While SST had paved the way for New Alliance, the ease with which *Cracks in the Sidewalk* came together caused Watt and Boon to wonder what took SST so long to put out the Minutemen's record. "The Flag guys had to get their record out first, for their tour," Watt said. "You know, the resources, there was always a delay."[4]

The Minutemen were eager to make things happen. While waiting for *Paranoid Time* to come out, the Minutemen recorded *The Punch Line* (SST 004) at Media Art with Spot, who also mixed the album, over the course of two or three nights. Watt referred to the sessions as "a gig in front of microphones," and the band's energy shines through on Boon's jagged guitar riffs and Watt's tumbling bass lines.[5]

Of the nine songs on Side B, not a single one is over a minute. Although *The Punch Line*'s eighteen songs come in at just under fifteen minutes, roughly the same length as the Circle Jerks' *Group Sex*, it doesn't feel like a short record. The album is packed with ideas and delivered at a pace that's impossible to digest all at once. It's as if the songwriters were taking lessons learned from British post-punk bands like Wire to their extreme conclusion.

The Punch Line features a preponderance of songs with one-word titles. Hurley, whose creative contribution was limited on the previous record, wrote lyrics for seven of the songs. He worked at a machine shop, and he composed them in the early predawn hours. They were untitled, so when Watt set them to music, he gave them heavy-sounding names to ground the abstract lyrics. The drummer introduced an ethereal counterpoint to Boon's political commentary. Watt balanced out the two with stream-of-consciousness lyrics, like a TV that had been left on at night.

It wasn't unusual for Watt or Boon to sing on a song the other had written. They didn't hoard their own material for themselves. For instance, if a song Watt composed had a complicated bass line, he'd hand off the vocal duties to

Boon—whatever worked for the greater good of the band. Although there were times when all three members wanted to steer the ship, there were no rock stars in the Minutemen.

Hurley also created the artwork on the back cover. For the front, Boon provided an abstract painting in red, yellow, and blue, with each color representing a different member of the band. This made *The Punch Line* the first SST release that didn't feature Pettibon's artwork, but the artist's influence can be felt in the title, which is taken from one of his illustrations. A skeleton stands at the microphone in front of a packed house. "Life is a joke!" the skeleton exclaims. The cryptic caption reads, "THIS IS THE PUNCH LINE."[6] *The Punch Line* was SST's first studio album, but a year would pass before it was finally released.

3

When Black Flag went out on the road, Ginn and Dukowski brought an acolyte from the Church with them, and after the crew returned to Torrance, he became a permanent fixture among SST's growing coterie of misfits. Steve "Mugger" Corbin dropped out of school his freshman year of high school. He grew up in a Latino neighborhood in Artesia—his mother was Mexican—twenty miles east of Hermosa Beach. Mugger roamed all over LA and Orange County with punks like Rob Henley and Eugene Tatu and would crash wherever he could.[7] One of those places was the Church, where Mugger knew he could always find a sleeping bag in the basement.

"One time, maybe when I was fifteen, we didn't have any place to go," Mugger recalled. "So me, Rob, and Darby actually crashed at my mother's house in the hood. I was walking to the bus stop on Crenshaw Boulevard with Darby and Rob and we had Mohawks or blue hair and all these vatos started throwing fucking rocks and shit at us. 'You fucking homos! Pinche homos!'"[8]

Mugger earned Ginn's respect by putting in long hours assembling, packaging, and shipping equipment for SST Electronics. Impressed with his work ethic and can-do attitude, Ginn asked him to roadie for Black Flag. "I'm not as creative as Greg," Mugger said, "but I'm very resourceful. We bonded because I could work. And so at that point they said 'Hey, Mugger, you want to be a roadie and help tune guitars?'"[9] Despite his youth—he was just seventeen—Mugger's effusive personality made him an enthusiastic and energetic traveling companion.

The atmosphere at SST headquarters in Torrance was very different from the Church, which was cavernous and compartmentalized. In Torrance there was nowhere to hide. Everything was out in the open. There was a ton of work to do, and no one had any job titles. You might be asked to roadie one day, paste flyers the next, and ship orders the day after that. Either you contributed to the cause or you were out. There was no middle ground. "We were working seven days a week, ten hours a day," Mugger recalled. He was a quick study at whatever he put his mind to, an essential trait for working in an operation that had to adjust on the fly when things went wrong, which was often. "I was the worker," Mugger said. "I drove their truck, I fixed their guitars, and I put their shit together. I fixed things for them."[10]

Mugger fit the mold of what SST required of its "employees": he was a young adult who lived at the margins of society, lacked strong family ties, and supported the cause. Commitment was key to making it work; otherwise, sleeping under a desk in a shabby office with a bunch of other dudes would quickly lose its charm. But the situation in Torrance was strange by any measure, and the local police thought so too. What were these people up to in that old dentistry office? Where did they go and—even more concerning—what did they do at night? Did these weirdos not have homes to go to?

The SST crew didn't, but they had plenty of gigs to play. Encouraged by the success of Black Flag's first nationwide tour, Ginn and Dukowski immediately started planning the next one, along with more trips up to San Francisco and Vancouver. Not only did they want to play as many shows as possible, but they also wanted to take other SST acts with them.

4

"The Stains are the best band in the world," Dukowski said when asked about some of his favorite bands from LA.[11] Ginn, too, was taken with the LA punk band, especially Robert Becerra, whose electrifying guitar playing was unique in the Southern California scene. Becerra had a wild style influenced by heavy metal bands of the early '70s. He would frequently break away from the song's melody to unleash a squall of noise. Becerra's onstage antics—like playing his guitar behind his back—and passion for guitar solos drew criticism from punk purists, but Becerra was one of the first musicians in LA, if not *the* first, to bridge punk and heavy metal in service of something new. What's more, he had the chops to pull it off.[12]

Ginn recognized in Becerra someone who was not only a supremely talented player but a kindred spirit who used punk as a vehicle of expression. There were numerous parallels between the two bands. Like Black Flag, the Stains came from a part of the city that had its own identity distinct from the rest of LA. The members of the Stains were mostly from Boyle Heights, which outsiders, especially white outsiders, tended to lump together with East LA.

Like Black Flag, the Stains formed in 1976. Initially, the band had trouble finding gigs—too loud, too obnoxious—so they resorted to playing backyard parties. The Stains did not shy away from controversy; rather, they embraced it. The band started out calling itself the Young Nazis. The name change came about after one of the members had an accident in bed. "We're the little brown stain on a white sheet," said Jesse "Fixx" Amezquita, the band's original bass player. "Get it? White society, stains, okay? That's where that came from."[13]

Their rehearsal space was infamous: a ramshackle garage known as the Dungeon, which was located behind an elementary school on Third Street in Boyle Heights. When the neighbors complained about the noise, Becerra moved rehearsals into his bedroom at his mother's house, where it was not unusual for members of Black Flag or X to join in for a jam session and the walls were covered with graffiti.

The Stains went through numerous lineup changes, with different singers, drummers, and bass players. But in spite of the near-constant upheaval, the Stains would play anywhere, anytime. The one constant was Becerra. "So many people were in and out that band," Becerra said.[14]

Becerra was tall, intense, and a wizard with a guitar in his hands. Is there any wonder Ginn was drawn to the Stains? "There was a real brotherhood between the bands," Rivera said of the Stains' relationship with Black Flag.[15] Ginn even sold Becerra one of his precious guitars. "He said he had a guitar for sale," Becerra recalled. "I asked him, 'How much?' He said, 'Two hundred bucks.' That was cheap. 'With the case and everything?' I asked. 'Yeah.' The case is worth two hundred bucks alone. So I bought it." This wasn't an ordinary guitar but the Ibanez Flying V that Ginn used to record the *Nervous Breakdown* EP.[16]

Although regarded as the first punk band on the Eastside, the Stains struggled to gain acceptance in its own neighborhood. The Stains brought a lot of attention to Eastside punk by dint of being from there, but that's where the association ended. "We were a band that just happened to be from Boyle Heights," said Ceasar Viscarra, who replaced Amezquita on bass. "We didn't sing any songs in Spanish. We didn't do any traditional Mexican music. There's nothing traditional or Mexican about the Stains other than, perhaps, the families that we came from."[17]

The Stains preferred to play with its punk rock peers from the Masque, where the band briefly had a studio, and with bands like X, the Germs, Fear, and especially Black Flag. "There was nothing like a Black Flag gig," said Rivera, who took over from Tony Romero on drums. "You'd get the flyers, like, three months in advance. That's how organized they were."[18]

Despite the mutual appreciation between the two bands, the Stains did things its own way. The Stains had a well-earned reputation as hell-raisers who drank beer, smoked PCP, and dropped acid until all hours of the night. After rehearsal, the band might head down to the Hong Kong Café. One night, a member of the Stains allegedly set Rodney Bingenheimer's hair on fire. "He still played our demos," Rivera said. When Rivera joined the band, he was still attending high school, and many Eastside musicians warned him about the Stains' hard-partying ways.[19]

Ultimately, what set the Stains apart from its punk rock peers was the musical skill of its members: they all knew how to play their instruments. They were musicians versed in a range of styles, from jazz fusion to Spanish classical. They had played in numerous outfits, from soul acts to Santana cover bands. What other LA punk band could cite Django Reinhardt, Andrés Segovia, John McLaughlin, and Jimi Hendrix as influences?

Jack Rivera of the Stains in Robert Becerra's bedroom in Boyle Heights on October 10, 1980. Note the graffiti. (Photo by Wild Don Lewis.)

In this regard, the Stains were like another in-your-face and out-of-step musical act that discovered punk as the perfect vehicle for expression: Bad Brains. "I want to express my feelings and I never really found a place to express them," Amezquita said. "When I would try to express them in school, I got punished. When I tried to tell my parents about my feelings, I got punished. When I played in a punk rock band, I got paid. You think I'm fuckin' stupid?"[20]

Ginn's desire to incorporate another guitar player was inspired in part by Becerra's high-wire act on stage. Most of the songs in Black Flag's set were several years old, and Ginn longed to express himself more fully with his instrument, but to do that he needed another guitarist in the band.

In February 1981, Black Flag played two nights at Mabuhay Gardens in San Francisco and brought the Stains and the Minutemen with them. The Stains' singer had left the band, and Rudy Navarro took his place. Navarro was seemingly an odd choice: he was younger than everyone else in the band, he wasn't from the neighborhood, and he was a fan of musicians like Devo and Elvis Costello.

The Black Flag gig at the Mab was Navarro's first show with the Stains. The band was so broke its members had to sleep in the van and eat at a mission, but it was a memorable show for the young singer from Temple City. After the gig, Jello Biafra came up to shake his hand and congratulate him for scaring all the San Francisco punks away from the stage.

Ginn was eager to get the Stains in the studio and make a record for SST, and the money the band made from opening for the Dead Kennedys at the Whisky in March went toward the cost of recording an album with Spot. The session took place late at night at Media Art in Hermosa Beach and was fueled not with alcohol and angel dust but with donuts and caffeine, to which some members attribute to the record's warp-speed attack. Instead of using his own guitar, Becerra recorded the album with Spot's 1969 Fender Stratocaster. "He wasn't known for using a tremolo bar," Spot said of Becerra's performance, "and he just went for it."[21]

Like most sessions with Spot, it was quick and efficient, with the added pressure of knowing that the studio was shutting down. The Stains wrapped up the recording session as the sun was coming up, and Navarro went to school the next day with a tape in his pocket. Unfortunately, this didn't translate into a quick release. The Stains had to get in line behind the Minutemen and another band from San Pedro, the incomparable Saccharine Trust.

5

In the universe of SST, if Black Flag was the sun and the Minutemen was Mars, then Saccharine Trust was a comet streaking toward the farthest reaches of the galaxy.

How to describe Saccharine Trust? The quartet looked like a punk band and had a fairly traditional makeup but sounded like no one else. Saccharine Trust is what happens when someone who dreams of becoming a rock star joins forces with someone who wants to make a splash in the arts. One wanted to get famous and meet girls; the other was after something far more conceptual. Two dreams, one musical project.

Joe Baiza was an art student who was drawn to the extreme and the offbeat. He was taking art classes at Harbor College in Wilmington, a city whose predominant feature was heavy industry. There were no art scholarships at Harbor College. Jack Brewer was born in Havana, Cuba, and his family bounced around the southeastern corner of the South Bay with stops in Harbor City, Wilmington, and San Pedro. Brewer had a band called the Obstacles that he'd formed with his friend Marshall Mellow. Baiza joined the Obstacles and—like a virus taking over its host—slowly steered Brewer toward punk rock and pushed the band in a new direction.

When all was said and done, Mellow quit, Baiza took over on guitar—an instrument he was still learning how to play—and Brewer became the singer. The duo recruited a series of bass players and drummers who thought they were joining a punk or hardcore outfit only to learn after a few rehearsals they'd taken up with something far more experimental. "I was trying to do something new," Baiza said of his unorthodox approach, "something that

Earl Liberty, Jack Brewer, Rob Holzman, and Joe Baiza of Saccharine Trust at Cathay de Grande. (Photo by Edward Colver.)

hadn't been done before—which is not always successful. . . . I would create my own melodies or chords just by the shapes on the fretboard or the way they sounded."[22]

The band's first gig came about when Mike Watt offered a spot at a backyard barbecue in Wilmington, which forced the band to come up with a name to put on the flyer. Saccharine Trust came from a line in the David Bowie song "The Bewlay Brothers." The band embraced the manifesto of "make it new" at a time when "fast and loud" was the emerging dogma of the hardcore bands popping up around the country. Saccharine Trust did both. In September 1980, the band went into the studio with Luis Maldonado on bass and Richie Wilder on drums to record "Disillusioned Fool" and "Hearts & Barbarians." The latter song appeared on New Alliance's compilation *Cracks in the Sidewalk*, but Wilder would leave the band shortly afterward.

Rob Holzman, another graduate of Mira Costa High School, heard about the opening. "I was hanging around the guys in Toxic Shock," Holzman said. "They told me that Saccharine Trust was looking for a drummer. I got introduced to Joe and Jack at a gig at the Polish Hall. I don't really remember the conversation because I was drinking but they asked me to join."[23]

Baiza had moved into a dance studio in San Pedro called Star Theatre, which became the hub for the band's parties and rehearsals. Holzman brought his friend Mark Vidal to band practice, and when Maldonado left he took over on bass. Vidal (a.k.a. Earl Liberty) was a tall Cuban American who got his nickname when Boon compared him to the Statue of Liberty. Not only did Holzman and Liberty attend Mira Costa High School together, they'd played in a band called the Jetsons.[24]

Ginn and Dukowski came to a rehearsal at the Star Theatre, were impressed with what they heard, and invited the band to record an album with SST. Four months later, in April 1981, Saccharine Trust recorded *Paganicons* (SST 006) at Media Art in a single session with Spot and Watt. "We also recorded the single 'A Christmas Cry,' during the *Paganicons* session," Holzman recalled. "That was like an improv jam."[25] But the eight-song, almost eighteen-minute-long LP wouldn't be mixed for several months and wasn't released until the following year.

The albums were stacking up, but Black Flag was on the road, and the other bands on the roster would have to wait until Ginn and Dukowski came back to California.

6

Black Flag returned from its second national tour motivated to get back in the studio and record new material. Although *Jealous Again* had only been out for a little over six months, the EP featured a singer who hadn't been in the band for almost a year. Cadena had recorded songs with Black Flag for *Chunks*, a second compilation from New Alliance that would be released that summer. Ginn had also made the unusual move of allowing Posh Boy Records to put out a Black Flag single with Cadena singing "Louie Louie" and backed with an early version of "Damaged I."[26] Black Flag often ended its set with a thrashy, trashy version of "Louie Louie," a song so brainlessly repetitive that it became the perfect vehicle for Ginn's murderous guitar solos and a staple of the band's live shows.

The original "Louie Louie" was born in Anaheim, California, in 1956 when R&B singer and songwriter Richard Berry heard the Rhythm Rockers perform Rene Touzet's "El Loco Cha Cha Cha" to a packed house of lowrider afficionados and car club enthusiasts. Berry, whose father worked in the South Bay's shipyards, was spellbound and quickly crafted a song around the hypnotic riff that would make the song a sensation. "Louie Louie" took an infamous turn in 1963. A cover recorded by the Kingsmen, a group of teenage garage rockers from the Northwest, became an unexpected hit after it was featured on Boston DJ Arnie "Woo-Woo" Ginsberg's Worst Song of the Week. After rumors circulated that the song contained obscene lyrics, J. Edgar Hoover opened a ridiculous investigation into the song, which only made it more popular.[27]

The origins of Black Flag's version go all the way back to Morris's tenure in the band. Both he and Ginn were fans of the colorful interpretation of the song on Iggy and the Stooges' *Metallic K.O.* Best of all, everyone already knew the song. "It was just like you'd snapped your fingers," Morris recalled of the first time the band played the song, "and here we are bashing away on 'Louie Louie.'"[28]

Whoever was singing often ad-libbed lyrics to put his own spin on the song, and in Black Flag's deconstructed version, one can hear the rudimentary elements of Nirvana's "Smells like Teen Spirit," the ghost of a pop song holding together all that smash and clatter. But sometimes a song is more than a song.

On the night Ron Reyes walked off the stage at the Fleetwood, Black Flag played "Louie Louie" over and over again as various members of the audience took the mic, including Richard "Snickers" Scott, the vocalist of the Simpletones and the Klan. "It was kind of a disgusting performance," Spot recalled, "but it was a hell of a performance."[29]

At Baces Hall, when the promoter begged the band to wrap up its set because the cops had arrived, Ginn ripped into "Louie Louie" and then refused to stop playing, setting the stage for the events that followed. The band used "Louie Louie" as a weapon, grinding out an extended version that kept going long after the joke stopped being funny. Promoters learned the hard way not to let Black Flag perform "just one more song."[30]

Black Flag was already planning its summer tour. Because the band was returning to cities and venues it had already played, it was imperative to release a new single. Unfortunately, Media Art had shut down, and the Stains were the last SST band to record there.

For *Six Pack* (SST 005) the band decamped for Hollywood to record at Golden Age Recording with Spot and Geza X, a punk performer and producer. Geza X produced "Lexicon Devil" by the Germs and "Holiday in Cambodia" by the Dead Kennedys. The record was a return to a seven-inch format and a striking black-and-white illustration by Pettibon. The boy crouching on the floor and grinning like a loon after painting himself into a corner could be the same kid on the cover of *Nervous Breakdown*.

The single, with its upbeat attitude and ironic lyrics, was something of a departure for the band. It's one of Black Flag's most accessible songs, with a rousing, repetitive chorus. What seems like a celebration of alcoholic excess is a scathing diatribe against those who make partying a priority. While there were plenty of intelligent fans who understood the song's intent, many of the band's new admirers missed the message, and the song became an anthem for jocks winding up for a night of drunken shenanigans.

Ginn's goal hadn't changed since he'd formed the band five years earlier: to put out a full-length album. Black Flag had released four singles and EPs in different formats, with different labels, and with different singers, and while demand for these records was high, Ginn wanted an album. Did Cadena's performance in the studio raise doubts that the vocalist was up to the task? Or did Ginn and Dukowski have someone else in mind for the job?

7

Black Flag's short but momentous summer tour got off to a disastrous start. The day after the band departed, the Torrance police department raided SST's headquarters. Spot and Watt, who were in the office at the time, could only watch helplessly while the cops tore the place apart searching for drugs that weren't there.

The police refused to believe the office was home to a legitimate business and were convinced that something shady was afoot. Everyone at SST knew they were being watched. The surveillance was laughingly obvious, but they were surprised to learn the police had seized packages SST had shipped to local distributors in the hope of finding drugs. The intoxicating sounds of Black Flag weren't what the cops had in mind. "Anything that we were doing was considered suspect by the general public," Spot explained.[31]

Although the police didn't find what they were looking for, the message was clear: get out of Torrance. Spot shut down the office, wrapped up some loose ends with the many bands he'd recorded that spring, and flew out to the East Coast to catch up with Black Flag. Watt, however, was hauled into court. Because the Minutemen used the SST office as a rehearsal space, Watt was on the hook. The police had put a lot of time, money, and manpower into its undercover operation and were determined to prosecute, but the judge wasn't impressed and threw the case out. Watt was fined for some zoning violations, which Regis Ginn paid for, and was released.

There were big changes afoot on the road too. Ginn and Dukowski were searching for someone to replace Cadena as vocalist, and they found their man in Washington, DC. The story of how Henry Garfield became Black Flag's fourth singer is the stuff of hardcore legend. Garfield, the singer of

S.O.A., was invited to New York, auditioned for the band, and was offered the gig. But while the decision to invite Garfield to join Black Flag feels foreordained, it was hardly written in stone.

Earlier that year, Torrance native Merrill Ward was offered the job. Ward was at the Black Flag performance at Polliwog Park and had seen several Black Flag vocalists come and go. He declined the invitation and joined Overkill instead. There were no hard feelings, and SST supported Ward's endeavors by putting out the band's single, "Hell's Getting Hotter" (SST 008) backed with "Our War" and "Burn the School," which Spot recorded at the Music Lab in Silverlake.[32]

But Ward wasn't the only local in the mix. Mugger believed that if he'd had the chops, he would have been offered the gig. "I probably would have been the singer of Black Flag if I had any musical capabilities," Mugger said, "because I was there before Rollins, and I have more of an outgoing personality than Rollins."[33] Like Ward, Mugger had the moxie to get up on stage and command—or infuriate—an audience, which he would do before the year was out with his offensively named heavy-metal gag band the Nig-Heist.

The Sluts front man Dave Turgeon (a.k.a. Dee Slut) was also considered for the role. The Sluts was a satirical punk band from New Orleans that Black Flag had seen play on a previous tour in Louisiana. Ginn and Dukowski thought highly enough of the singer that they invited him up to New York for an audition.

"I was back in New Orleans working on a Sluts tour," Turgeon said, "when Chuck and Greg called me and said they wanted to put their singer Dezo back on rhythm guitar—so Greg could kinda go crazy on his—and have just a frontman singer. So they flew me up to New York and we recorded the album that was 'Damaged.'"[34]

According to Turgeon, the recording sounded nothing like Black Flag, and he surmised Ginn and Dukowski went with Garfield because "he was the sound that they wanted."[35] But his drug use also may have played a role. Turgeon accompanied Black Flag to Pittsburgh for a Fourth of July show at the infamous Electric Banana. Turgeon was announced as the next singer of Black Flack and sang "Clocked In" as well as a few other songs. On the way

Ginn and Dee Slut in New York, summer of 1981. (Photo by SPOT.)

back to New York, Turgeon surprised Ginn and Dukowski by smoking marijuana in the van, which may have been the deciding factor. When Ginn and Dukowski announced their decision at a diner in New York, both Turgeon and Garfield were present, albeit in different booths.

Garfield returned home to quit his job and his band. He detonated his life in DC and joined Black Flag on the road. On tour, Garfield served as a roadie and sang during encores while learning the ropes from Cadena and Dukowski. The first thing Garfield did when he got to California was change his name to Rollins. "When I joined Black Flag, they said to me, 'You'd better get a different name. Because within 24 hours, the LAPD is gonna open a file on you.'" He chose the name Rollins because his best friend's older sister, Susannah MacKaye, was attending Rollins College in Winter Park, Florida. The name was an inside joke but also served as a secret link to his past.[36]

With Henry rechristened, the Rollins era was officially underway, but in Chicago, someone else would join the SST crew, someone whose impact would be every bit as far reaching as Rollins's.

8

Every time the band went out on the road, not only did its fan base grow but so did SST's network of venues to play and places to crash. In addition to these critical logistics were the creative connections with like-minded bands, some of whom would be invited to join SST. The grueling and inefficient way Black Flag toured meant that the business of running a label had to wait until Ginn and Dukowski returned to LA. This small window of time was chewed up by rehearsals and recording sessions. If only Ginn had someone who could stay behind and run the label while Black Flag pummeled audiences across America.

Enter Carducci. Joe Carducci's passion for writing spurred him to leave Illinois to follow his dreams out West. He yo-yoed up and down the West Coast looking for the right opportunity. In LA he worked at a restaurant and a movie theater before moving north to Portland, Oregon, where he found his niche as one of the cofounders of Systematic Record Distribution.[37] After two years in Portland, the distributor moved its base of operations to Berkeley, California, where Carducci got involved with the punk rock scene by starting up Thermidor Records with Jon Boshard, a local disc jockey at KALX.[38] One of the last things Carducci did before leaving the Bay Area was to assist with the release of Flipper's "Love Canal" single. Both Systematic and Thermidor were small-scale operations, and there wasn't enough for someone of Carducci's intelligence and ambition to do. "I wanted to get out of Berkeley—there were no pressing plants up there," Carducci said, "and great bands like Flipper and the Sleepers, they didn't tour....I wasn't looking to have a career in the record business, but I didn't want to waste my time."[39]

Carducci was looking for a way to get back to LA. At a Black Flag show at

Tuts in Chicago, he approached Ginn and Dukowski and offered his services to SST. They accepted Carducci's offer on the spot but warned him that not only did they lack the funds to pay him—they didn't even have an office. But Carducci had done his homework. As an independent record distributor, he knew which underground bands were moving units at record stores around the country. He understood that SST's records were in high demand but that product was hard to come by due to Black Flag's erratic and unpredictable touring schedule.

Coincidentally, Carducci had phoned the SST office in Torrance during the police raid, and Watt answered. Black Flag's reputation was such that Carducci didn't suspect the band had done anything illegal. On the contrary, because of Carducci's affiliation with Flipper, Ginn and Dukowski believed Carducci smoked dope; he didn't.

Carducci was willing to gamble that he could shore up SST's operations and make Black Flack's long-awaited debut album an indie success. He went back to Berkeley and prepared to move down the coast in September. After a few more shows in the Midwest, Black Flag returned to LA with its new vocalist to begin work on the new album.

Without an office to return to, the SST crew crashed in Hollywood at the Oxford House, where a group of punks who identified themselves as TC (the Connected) stayed. Residents included Emil McKown, drummer for the Oziehares, and his girlfriend Maggie Ehrig, who would go on to sing in Twisted Roots. Ginn and Dukowski offered fifty dollars toward rent to Aimee Cooper, whose name was on the lease. Cooper jokingly asked for a percentage of Black Flag's sales. Ginn quipped she'd be better off taking the money.[40]

Ginn and Dukowski ran SST's operations out of a bank of pay phones between the post office and a liquor store near the intersection of Western Avenue and Beverly Boulevard.[41] Despite being essentially homeless, SST was thinking big. They knew they had an audience for Black Flag's first full-length album and looked into teaming up with a major label to help with distribution.

One intriguing possibility was Unicorn Records, a subsidiary of MCA.

Tony Adolescent, Rollins, and Cadena at the Oxford House in Hollywood, California. (Photo by SPOT.)

Ginn and Dukowski targeted Unicorn because it had a large studio with vacant offices on Santa Monica Boulevard in West Hollywood. Not only could Black Flag record there but SST could make use of the ample office space, which had a bathroom, a shower, and plenty of room for the SST crew. Carducci was skeptical. With his experience in record distribution, he believed SST could handle the demand, but Ginn and Dukowski considered the perks too good to pass up.

SST moved into its new digs and turned Unicorn Studios into SST's latest all-purpose office, rehearsal space, and living quarters. For Rollins the experience was more than a little unsettling: "When I first joined Black Flag, I thought I was ready. Greg Ginn taught me otherwise."[42]

While Rollins fit the mold of an SST apprentice—young, intense, and up for anything—he was an outsider. This was nothing new for Rollins. He had been an outsider at the private school for boys he attended in southern Maryland. He was outsider in the DC hardcore scene. And now as an East Coast transplant in Southern California, he was more of an outsider than ever before. "Joining Black Flag was a very abrupt lifestyle change for me,"

Rollins said, "going from a bank account, car, stereo, job—to a duffel bag, shoplifting food, getting rousted by cops, no money, living on people's floors, getting fleas, living in the same clothes for weeks."[43]

Rollins was a city kid who liked to explore his surroundings on foot, but LA was a whole other animal. The city's smoggy sprawl made DC seem tiny in comparison, and the view outside Rollins's front door was grim. SST's new headquarters was situated in the heart of the sex trade on Santa Monica Boulevard. Men and women, as well as teens, worked the streets at all hours of the day and night. "When I first walked around that neighborhood," Rollins said, "I was like, *Whoa, this place is intense.*"[44]

Santa Monica Boulevard was a long way from the South Bay, but the SST crew brought its surfer-bohemian, quasi-Krishna style to West Hollywood. Working, rehearsing, sleeping on the floor, and foraging for food—they did everything together. "The band, and the label, seemed to have a weird, almost cultish vibe," said Baiza, who was a frequent visitor at Unicorn.[45]

Some of the weirdness came from the label itself. Founded by Daphna Edwards in 1979, Unicorn lacked bankable stars and failed to produce any hits. Edwards had very little experience in the music business but was enamored with the lifestyle that came with running a label, hosting parties at her mansion on Mulholland Drive. "Maybe they thought they could control this woman to their liking," Spot said of Ginn and Dukowski's decision to work with Edwards, "and it turned out to be exactly the opposite."[46]

Edward Colver's photo of Edwards with the five members of Black Flag signing their contract at Unicorn Records captures the strangeness of the situation. "A fateful day," Colver recalled. "You can tell nobody looks happy, which is really weird. Daphna looks like, 'What am I doing sitting here with these cats?'"[47]

Black Flag went to work. During epic practice sessions, Ginn and Dukowski exhorted Rollins to meet their exacting standards. When Black Flag wasn't practicing or recording, Rollins was enlisted to help fulfill orders, distribute flyers, and answer mail. They never let Rollins forget he was the new guy and had to earn the respect not only of the band but of its crew as well. "I wasn't his favorite person," Mugger said. "Because I bossed him around and

Black Flag with Daphna Edwards at Unicorn Studios in West Hollywood. (Photo by Edward Colver.)

told him what to do. 'Clean up your fucking mess.' 'Help out.' And my famous line, 'This ain't no Van Halen dream.' I don't think he took that too kindly."[48]

Rollins was exposed to rigorous discipline at an early age. He'd graduated from the Bullis School, a private academy founded to prepare young men for military service and whose pupils are required to wear uniforms. Rollins and his peers were subject to a host of rules and restrictions that would have been unthinkable to those who'd attended public high school in Southern California. Whether by necessity or desire, Rollins bought into the unorthodox and sometimes grueling situation at SST. "Black Flag had this attitude," Cadena said, "and it was true at times, that it was us—our little handful of people— against the world. And I think Henry took a lot of that to heart."[49]

Though an intensely private and introspective person, Rollins didn't back down from a challenge. After Ginn, Dukowski, Robo, and Cadena (on second guitar) recorded, or rerecorded, the songs that would appear on *Damaged* (SST 007), Rollins was summoned for the vocals. Like drill sergeants berating a new recruit to build him up into a better version of himself, Ginn and Dukowski put him through his paces. Rollins responded. He stepped into the studio a screamer, uncertain about his place both in the band and in the world, and emerged as the future of Black Flag.

At just under thirty-five minutes, *Damaged* was SST's longest record to date. *Damaged* is a tale of two halves. The front side is loaded with up-tempo songs. Ginn's skittering guitar work on "Rise Above" and Dukowski's epic bass line in "Six Pack" are seductively slick. While the message of "TV Party" condemns the passive brainlessness of the TV-watching experience, it's still a party and a welcoming one at that. While "Police Story" and "Gimme Gimme Gimme" were fan favorites the band had been playing for years, *Damaged* introduced material designed to appeal to listeners new to the Black Flag experience. Side 2 is another story. After the shock treatment of "Room 13," the tempo begins to slow. Ginn's grinding guitar serves up moments of dark beauty and heavy collisions that provide space for the vocalist.

This is where Rollins emerges, raw but bold. The slower speed left plenty of room for the guitar work that Ginn wanted to explore, but it also opened a door for Rollins to step through and assert himself like no Black Flag vocalist had done before. The second half of Side 2 heralds the beginning of something new, meaning something old. On "No More" and "Life of Pain," Ginn and Dukowski reach back to the clank and clamor of the dawn of heavy metal. With "Damaged II" Black Flag created something distinctly its own. The song's tempo doesn't speed up and slow down but flexes in a way that scrambles the senses, as if the rules that govern time are different inside the song.

Out of the droning chaos of "Damaged I," Rollins bares his soul with a story of subjugation. Rollins brings his special talent for imbuing the present moment with the intensity of his lived experience. It feels traumatic because it is. At twenty years old he was no longer a child but not yet a man, and his childhood cast a long shadow over his psyche. His parents' divorce, physical and sexual abuse by one of his mother's boyfriends, beatings by older kids in his neighborhood, and his biological father's glacial indifference worked their way into his performance. As a child he was prescribed Ritalin for hyperactivity, but they didn't diagnose children with PTSD back then.

"Damaged I" wasn't the first time a songwriter laid their soul bare—that's what songs are for—but it was equal parts arresting and unsettling to hear someone perform the process like an exorcism. Incredibly, Rollins recorded the vocals in just two takes, but Spot believed the first take was "the one."[50] Garfield's transformation from the straightedge kid from DC into Henry Rollins the singer for Black Flag was complete. With *Damaged*, Ginn found the perfect vehicle for expressing the angst and anxiety he poured into his lyrics and ignited with his guitar.

Perhaps it was too perfect. At the end of the day, they were Ginn's songs— not Henry's. "*Damaged* was a description of *my* internal life," Ginn said. But it was Rollins who would suck up the spotlight.[51]

9

It wasn't all work and no play for the SST crew in West Hollywood. The Whisky, Tower Records, Licorice Pizza, and the infamous Tropicana Motel were all nearby. Rehearsals attracted friends and musicians, many of whom Ginn had promised to sign and were hoping the new relationship with Unicorn would speed the release of their records. Rollins befriended Earl Liberty, who took him to see Saccharine Trust's rehearsal space. The gang often went to shows together, particularly at venues where they would soon appear, to distribute flyers and support bands that had a relationship with SST.

In late July, Black Flag played the Cuckoo's Nest in Costa Mesa with two bands that had same name: the Stains from LA and the Stains from Texas. The venue shared a parking lot with a cowboy bar called Zubie's, which had an actual mechanical bull inside, and the patrons of the two establishments were prone to antagonizing each other, to put it mildly.

Everywhere it went, Black Flag talked up the Stains. Cadena sent his friends from the Eastside a postcard informing them of the imposters from Texas. Black Flag was so enthusiastic about the Eastside Stains' exploits that the band from Texas changed its name to MDC before arriving in LA, and a crisis between the two bands was averted.

The following month, Rollins returned to the Cuckoo's Nest to make his debut as the lead vocalist for Black Flag with a pair of shows. The first was a 3:00 p.m. all-ages matinee with Wasted Youth and Circle One. The second show went down several hours later with Saccharine Trust and Overkill. The gigs drew a large crowd and a slew of photographers (Alison Braun, Edward Colver, and Glen E. Friedman) as well as a videographer (Dave Markey) to document the historic event. Rollins's shaved head and shirtless torso made an immediate impact on the kids at the Cuckoo's Nest. Rollins stalking the stage instantly made Black Flag sound angrier and more damaged. The scene had come full circle. One of the DC punks who'd brought West Coast punk back to the nation's capital was the new face of the heaviest hardcore band on the planet.

10

With *Damaged* in the can, Ginn and Dukowski ordered twenty-five thousand copies, a number that far exceeded the combined total of all of SST's previous releases. Thanks to MCA's distribution, *Damaged* would be one of the few punk rock records on the shelf at record stores across the country. Ginn was willing to bet that fans would snap it up. This gamble was not without risk. Many of the songs on *Damaged* were several years old, and some had been recorded by each of the band's three previous vocalists.

Ginn and Dukowski came up with a concept for the cover: an angry young man shattering a mirror with his fist, but Pettibon refused to illustrate it, calling the idea "sophomoric" and "beneath what we were doing."[52] SST turned to Edward Colver, who'd photographed Cadena for the "Louie Louie" single in an alley behind Duke's Coffee Shop next to the Tropicana. Colver had worked with a number of LA punks, including the Circle Jerks, Exene Cervenka of X, and Saccharine Trust, and his work regularly appeared in *Slash*, *Flipside*, and *NO MAG*.

The self-taught photographer from Covina was something of a character himself. He went out almost every night to shoot bands, and his custom hearse tipped people off to his presence at punk rock shows across the Southland. Dressed all in black with boots and a bolo tie, he resembled an undertaker in an offbeat western or an understudy for Robert Mitchum in *The Night of the Hunter*. The *Damaged* photo shoot took place at the Oxford House in Hollywood. To get the shot SST wanted, the scene had to be

Henry Rollins and Edward Colver shooting the cover for *Damaged* at the Oxford House in Hollywood. (Photo by SPOT.)

carefully staged. "They wanted Henry smacking a mirror," Colver recalled, "and I came up with how to make it happen."[53]

To make the shot look authentic, Colver prepped the mirror by covering the back with duct tape and whacking it with a hammer. For the blood on Rollins's fist, he mixed up a concoction of red India ink, dishwashing soap, and instant coffee. Colver also came up with the idea to shoot the mirror by itself for the back cover.

Damaged was ready to go, but at the eleventh hour, MCA Records announced it would not be distributing Black Flag's debut. The label did this neither quietly nor discreetly. Instead, Al Bergamo, MCA's head of distribution, announced his decision to the *Los Angeles Times*: "I'm not the kind of guy who believes in burning books, but this record bothered me. As a parent with two children, I found it an anti-parent record, past the point of good taste. I listened to it all last weekend and it just didn't seem to have any redeeming social value."[54]

There was no need for Bergamo to make a public statement. Black Flag was a lightning rod for criticism, but outside of LA the band was an underground phenomenon. Bergamo may or may not have listened to the record all weekend, but SST thought Bergamo's statement was cover for MCA's lack of confidence in Unicorn and belief that *Damaged* was destined to fail.

The timing could not have been worse. The records were all pressed up and ready to go with the MCA logo displayed on the back cover. The SST crew sprang into action, printing up a sticker that used Bergamo's words as an endorsement: "AS A PARENT . . . , I FOUND IT AN ANTI-PARENT RECORD . . ." They slapped this sticker over the MCA logo and shipped *Damaged* through an independent distributor. Undaunted, Ginn and Dukowski turned the tables on their critics.

Bergamo's decision to drop Black Flag would prove to be an enormous miscalculation. Ginn and Dukowski were incensed when they learned that, prior to making his statement to the *Los Angeles Times*, Bergamo had phoned *Rolling Stone* to make sure it wouldn't be a hit. Although the Parents Music Resource Center (PMRC) was still a few years away, a new conservatism was taking hold in Reagan's America. "They're trying to stabilize something that was never meant to be stable," Ginn said of MCA's actions.[55]

In Ginn's view Bergamo's public statement was more than a personal attack, it was a conspiracy fomented by corporate media to keep Black Flag out of the mainstream. There was little that SST could do about it: its contract was with Unicorn, not MCA. While the SST crew worked feverishly to get *Damaged* to the masses, a trio of drug-addled wild men showed up at Unicorn Studios to record their debut album.

Cris Kirkwood of the Meat Puppets. (Photo by Linda Aronow.)

CHAPTER 5
SST vs. Unicorn

1981–1983

1

Cloaked in mystery, the Meat Puppets, a three-piece band from Phoenix, Arizona, first made a splash with the song "H-Elenore" on the *Keats Rides a Harley* compilation released by Happy Squid. Led by Curt Kirkwood on vocals and guitar with his younger brother Cris on bass and Derrick Bostrom behind the drum kit, the Meat Puppets unleashed a caterwauling catastrophe of noise that retained a twang of Americana. At a time when hardcore was hardening into doctrine, the Meat Puppets was like a blast of hot desert air announcing the arrival of something sinister and strange.

Monitor, an LA art rock collective, asked the Meat Puppets to record the song "Hair" for its self-titled album to be released on its own label, World Imitation. While in the studio, producer Ed Barger invited the Meat Puppets to record another five tracks, which World Imitation released as an untitled EP. This EP, which featured an illustration by Bostrom's younger brother, Damon, helped establish the Meat Puppets' reputation among punk rock enthusiasts around the country, none of whom could agree what the band sounded like. "It was so not aimed at anything other than us amusing our-selves," Cris said of the record, which didn't have a title but came to be known by the opening track, "In a Car."[1]

The Meat Puppets didn't look or sound punk, but the band didn't look or sound like anything else either. It had seemingly leapfrogged over hard-core and into a genre of music that hadn't been invented yet. The shaggy but good-looking front man performed as if someone had given a deranged sideman from the '50s unlimited access to amplifiers and acid. There was no logical explanation for the Meat Puppets' sound. Intrigued by what seemed like a cacophonous eruption of noise, listeners gradually came to understand the Kirkwoods were playing actual songs—unconventional songs but songs nonetheless. What baffled some and intrigued those who got to know the band was its deep musical knowledge. The Meat Puppets knew hundreds of covers, and its shows were tinged with a touch of madness.

Everyone had a story about seeing the Meat Puppets for the first time and hearing a bizarre cover song. For Mike Watt it was "96 Tears" at the LA Press Club. For Gregg Turkington (a.k.a. Neil Hamburger) it was "Battle Hymn of the Republic" at Madison Square Garden in Arizona. For Dez Cadena it was Led Zeppelin's "No Quarter."

A Meat Puppets live show was loose to the point of chaotic, and to the casual observer it wasn't always clear that the musicians knew what they were doing. That was just fine with the Meat Puppets. "We got into music believ-ing that we were supposed to stay out of the way," Bostrom said, "and let the music go where it wanted to go."[2]

Naturally, SST was interested. The Meat Puppets played several shows with Black Flag in San Francisco and Phoenix, including an infamous gig in the boxing ring at Madison Square Garden where Feederz singer Frank Dis-cussion killed a lab rat on stage, which infuriated Rollins, who had a fondness for all creatures that crept and crawled.

How the Meat Puppets found its way to SST was as mysterious as the band itself. Watt claimed he saw the band first, but Black Flag had been hearing about the Meat Puppets since it passed through Phoenix. But it was Carducci who officially brought the band to SST. He heard about the Meat

Cris, Curt, and Derrick of the Meat Puppets outside the LA Press Club, September 20, 1981. (Photo by Edward Colver.)

Puppets through Laurie O'Connell, a member of Monitor. Carducci saw the Meat Puppets perform at Mabuhay Gardens with Flipper, and Thermidor bought "In a Car" from Monitor's label, World Imitation, for distribution.

"We did not join SST because we were huge fans of Black Flag per se," Bostrom explained. "We got in because Joe Carducci was working with us and had already approached us about doing a record. We weren't looking to join their scene, we had our own thing. So we always felt a little bit separate from that."[3] While at SST, Carducci convinced his partner at Thermidor to pony up $400 for a downtime recording session with the Meat Puppets at Unicorn Studios for a record that would be co-released by Thermidor and SST.

The Meat Puppets tumbled into West Hollywood in late November for recording sessions that were spread out over several days. Black Flag was busy making last-minute preparations for its winter tour. Around the time the Meat Puppets was in the studio, Black Flag did an interview with Rodney

Bingenheimer for his radio show and jokingly made fun of the band. "They were being sarcastic," Bostrom said. "But they singled us out as having a bad name, bad music, and a bad look. The only reason that they were working with us is because they were obliged by contract."[4]

The subtleties of Black Flag's humor were lost on its fans, and there were a lot of them hanging around Unicorn. They didn't quite know what to make of the Meat Puppets with their long hair and overalls. Thankfully, the studio at Unicorn was housed in a separate building, and the Meat Puppets took advantage of the distance from Ginn and Dukowski by getting high. This was nothing new for the Kirkwoods. They had recorded the *In a Car* EP stoned. "Weed wasn't 'drugs' to us," Cris explained. "And neither were psychedelics really—it was more like a place you could get to."[5]

The band put this theory to the test by taking psychedelics prior to the recording session with Spot, who did not participate. "I learned a long time ago," Spot said, "that engineering was not a drug-related activity."[6] O'Connell served as liaison between the Meat Puppets and SST, and she told Spot the band wasn't comfortable with the setup. To create a more intimate space, the band turned the amps so that they faced each other. This produced a muddier sound that presented problems when it was time to mix the record.[7]

Despite its blistering speed and nearly indecipherable lyrics, the Meat Puppets' debut is weirdly lush. "Saturday Morning" skewers punk rock pontificating and "Our Friends" makes an unexpected swerve into jam band territory with an extended guitar solo. The record also contains a pair of covers, "Walking Boss," a Depression-era working song, and "Tumblin' Tumbleweeds," which kicks off Side 2. Written in the 1930s by Bob Nolan, it was made famous by the Sons of the Pioneers, featuring Roy Rogers, and showcased in a Gene Autry film of the same name. It was a fitting cover for the Meat Puppets. While the lyrics evoke the Wild West, Nolan wrote the song when he was a working stiff in LA. The Meat Puppets get to the core of the song and render it weirdly psychedelic. The lyrics "I know when night is gone / That a new world's born at dawn!" take on a whole new meaning with the Meat Puppets' pharmacological spin.

Curt Kirkwood of the Meat Puppets at the LA Press Club, September 20, 1981. (Photo by Wild Don Lewis.)

Before the Meat Puppets left town, the band was interviewed by some new fans for *Flipside*. When asked to name their influences, Bostrom replied, "Our main influence is the desert," and to the desert they returned.[8]

O'Connell went back to the studio at Unicorn with Barger for some remixes, but there was not much that could be done. "You just couldn't mix the album," Carducci explained, "since it had complete bleed through of all instruments on all tracks."[9]

Later, Carducci met with O'Connell, Barger, and the SST crew, which included Ginn, Dukowski, and Mugger, to discuss the label's plans for the band. O'Connell didn't want the Meat Puppets to appear in ads with other SST bands. "They didn't get SST or Black Flag," Carducci said, "and thought of the Meat Puppets as spiritual shamans." Carducci recalled that Ginn was in a light mood after the meeting. "Now I remember why we used to beat up hippies," Ginn said.[10]

2

SST closed out 1981 with two more releases. Carducci put up the money to press the Minutemen's *The Punch Line* in November and Saccharine Trust's *Paganicons* in December. In true Minutemen fashion, the band had already written, recorded, and released another record: the seven-inch EP *Joy* on New Alliance Records. *The Punch Line* received a favorable review in the *Los Angeles Times* by Craig Lee, a former member of the Bags, which helped the band get gigs in and around LA. Both Black Flag and the Minutemen were included in the compilation *Rodney on the ROQ—Volume 2*, which Posh Boy put out around the same time. Ginn had been considering releasing "Rise Above" as a single but let Posh Boy include it on the comp instead.

The release of *Damaged*, *The Punch Line*, and *Paganicons* served notice to punk enthusiasts both in LA and beyond that SST was not just a label that put out EPs and singles. SST was home to an idiosyncratic community of artists committed to exploring new ideas in music. SST refused to contribute to the orthodoxy that was taking hold of punk, hardcore in particular. Willingness to tour determined a band's place in the SST pecking order and was also a contributing factor in how long a band had to wait for its record to be released. The only requirement was the desire to get in the van and do some damage. While there wasn't a hierarchy per se, Black Flag sat at the top of the heap.

"Because the Minutemen, Descendents, the Stains, Overkill, couldn't or wouldn't tour," Carducci said, "Black Flag took Saccharine Trust on all of their 1981–1982 touring for the *Damaged* LP."[11] Saccharine Trust's first nationwide tour coincided with Rollins's first trek across America as the vocalist for Black Flag. A few weeks before the tour, Liberty was at a party with Black Flag when the police showed up. Everyone ran, and Liberty knocked out his front teeth and broke a leg leaping over a fence. Holzman wasn't at the party, but he went to see his friend in the hospital. "I couldn't believe how messed up he looked," Holzman said.[12]

The tour took Black Flag and Saccharine Trust across the Southland to Texas and on to Washington, DC, where Rollins reunited with his old friend Ian MacKaye. Rollins had complicated feelings about his hometown, nostalgia mixed with rejection, which intensified when friends from the DC hardcore scene called him a rock star and a sellout. Immediately after the show at the 9:30 Club, Black Flag flew across the Atlantic for a tour of the United Kingdom with the Exploited. Rollins was no stranger to cold weather, but the band did not come prepared for freezing temperatures. Black Flag was also given the cold shoulder by its peers across the pond. Wattie Buchan from the Exploited and Gene October of Chelsea went out of their way to insult the band. To make matters worse, Dukowski gashed his head open in an onstage collision with Rollins and required several stitches.

Worse than the weather, hostile punks, indifferent audiences, and trips to the hospital was the boredom that came with being trapped in a foreign country with little money and nothing to do but watch Ginn practice his guitar. At least Rollins had MacKaye, who'd come along for the tour, to keep him company.

In Wales, audiences were treated to a performance by the Nig-Heist, Mugger's project to offend and annoy as many people as humanly possible. "We had all these crappy punk bands opening for us," Mugger explained. "So we just got people from the band or the road crew to play, but they wouldn't play the instruments that they played in Black Flag." Mugger sang songs such as "Love in Your Mouth" and "Walking Down the Street," and MacKaye, Spot, and Cadena all joined in.[13]

The final show of the UK leg of the tour was a festival in Leeds headlined by the Damned and U.K. Subs, whose members offered a belated welcome to Black Flag. Unfortunately, the customs agents at Heathrow weren't as gracious, and Robo, who was a citizen of Colombia, was detained because of irregularities with his paperwork, forcing Black Flag to return to America without him. The drummer had played his last show with the band.

Meanwhile in Washington, DC, the members of Saccharine Trust cooled their heels at the Dischord House until Black Flag returned. To pass the time, drummer Rob Holzman shaved his head and watched television with the straightedgers, but when he rolled a joint and cracked open a forty-ounce bottle of beer, he started getting dirty looks. "I didn't even really have that thought in my head about them being straightedge," Holzman said. "I didn't even really think about it. I thought, Fuck it, I don't care, I'm just gonna do what I'm gonna do. If they get mad, they get mad." But at least one resident of Dischord House was sympathetic, and he showed off his secret stash of marijuana to Holzman.[14]

Saccharine Trust did more than sit around and watch TV. Holzman recalled a handful of shows, including opening for Bad Brains with an early version of the Beastie Boys at Max's Kansas City. "I was nervous being in New York," Holzman said. "I didn't know how we were going to be received. And then when the Bad Brains hit the stage the place just erupted. It was insane. I'd never been to a more insane gig at that point in my life. It was quite a heavy experience."[15]

When Black Flag returned from overseas, both bands were eager to get on with the tour, and they called Bill Stevenson of the Descendents two days before Christmas to ask him to fill in for Robo on drums. "I was sitting in the living room with my dad," Stevenson recalled of the phone call that changed his life. "And I don't even remember if it was Chuck or Greg that called me. I think it was probably Chuck and he said, 'You have to come. Robo got stuck. You have to come play.' And I go, 'Well, let me ask my dad.' And I asked my dad and he took me to the airport ten minutes later."[16]

For Stevenson, it was even more eye opening than his first experience jamming with the band. "I was still in high school and I didn't even have long pants or a jacket because you don't need long pants and a jacket in Hermosa," Stevenson said. "But when I landed in New York in December, I needed an overcoat. I remember Dezo and I looked around behind the club and I found a packing blanket to sleep on. And then at the thrift store I got a trench coat. It was like three bucks."[17]

Stevenson was ready for his first show with Black Flag at the legendary Mudd Club in Manhattan. He knew the songs, and the only hiccup was "TV Party," which he played too fast. Black Flag was a last-minute addition to a Christmas show at Hitsville in Passaic, New Jersey, with the Necros and the Misfits, and the band finished out the year with gigs in New York, Boston, and Chicago.

Black Flag and Saccharine Trust were scheduled to play a New Year's Eve gig at the Olympic Auditorium with Fear, the Blasters, and Suburban Lawns, which meant somehow driving from Chicago to LA in two days. Black Flag raced across the country, stopping for food and gas and nothing else, and made it to the gig on time, but the show got off to an unusual start.

Black Flag opened with "Depression," and "right when we kick into the fast part of the song," Stevenson recalled, "Henry knees himself in the head and knocks himself out. Can you imagine headbutting down and kicking your knee up so hard that you knock yourself out? I didn't see it happen. I was like, 'What happened to Henry?' Nobody knew. I think Dezo tried to sing a little bit until we figured out what was going on. In those days you didn't stop. Well, Henry's unconscious. We got to stop for a minute. Right? No. You just didn't stop. It's like skinheads were gonna beat you up if you stopped."[18]

Eventually, Rollins pulled himself together and finished the gig, but this show-must-go-on mentality was a metaphor for how Black Flag conducted its business. Our drummer's been deported? We'll get another one. Our singer's unconscious? Someone else will take the mike. They only thing that mattered was to push forward and never give up. So when Stevenson decamped for San Francisco to play a gig with the Descendents the following day, Black Flag immediately started looking for a new drummer.

3

The beer-swilling punk rockers stuffed into mass-produced bondage gear who came to see Black Flag in the UK provided Ginn and Dukowski with a glimpse of the future, and they didn't like what they saw. With a few notable exceptions, their English peers were churning out derivative hardcore to crowds that cared more about conformity than creativity. The English fans hated Black Flag not just because it was American, although that was part of it, but because it looked and sounded different. Ginn and Dukowski understood that the situation in the UK would spread to the United States. To avoid this fate, or at least forestall it, they kept pushing themselves to experiment and explore, to rekindle the spark that seemingly had gone out in England.

But when Black Flag returned to California, nothing had changed. The mainstream press ignored *Damaged*. The only way people were going to find out about Black Flag's new album and other SST releases was to bring its bands to the audience. The key was to connect with like-minded communities and start new ones. It was no different from the mission Ginn had given himself when he started his amateur radio fanzine. His message was simple: for those willing to take a leap of faith and put in the work, there's a rich community to explore. The reward for this labor was making something yourself and sharing it with others. And if people thought it was too difficult or too strange, then it wasn't for them and never would be.

Black Flag and Saccharine Trust had driven across the United States and back but played only a handful of shows. The tour was marked by long, uncomfortable drives for very little money. If SST was going to justify the enormous effort it took to move bands across the country, it needed to find a more sustainable model.

When Black Flag returned to LA in 1982, it immediately went to work on planning its spring tour. SST had amassed an impressive mailing list and routinely mailed flyers to fans around the country who'd ordered records from its catalog. Carducci contributed data from Systematic and Thermidor, and Dukowski worked the phones, reaching out to club bookers across the country. Using clipboards, calculators, and road atlases, they were determined to find a way to play more shows and drive shorter distances. This, of course, meant longer tours, but SST was up for the challenge.

Dukowski was also busy recording a new single with his old band Würm, with Ed Danky on vocals and Loud Lou Hinzo on drums. "We're Off" and "I'm Dead," which Dukowski sings, hew close to the Detroit-influenced "Sewer Rock" sound that Danky and Dukowski cranked out at the Würmhole. The flip side features a faithful cover of a song whose message never goes out of style: "Time Has Come Today," by the Chambers Brothers.

Unicorn wanted Black Flag to record a new version of "TV Party" (SST 012) to release as a single. The result was one of Black Flag's more unusual recordings, with a cavalcade of producers, including Unicorn's Daphna Edwards; Edward Barton, who'd worked on many of War's hits; Glenn Feit, who'd served as engineer on the Würm single recorded at Unicorn; and Black Flag.

First, Ginn and Dukowski had to find a drummer. They enlisted Emil McKown, who adopted the last name Johnson. After his band the Oziehares broke up, Johnson played in Twisted Roots with his girlfriend Maggie Ehrig, Germs guitarist Pat Smear, Screamers keyboardist Paul Roessler, and Paul's sister Kira on bass, all of whom would eventually factor into the SST story. The first thing Johnson did was spray-paint the clear plastic on Robo's drum set. Next, the lyrics were updated to reflect popular television shows of the day. "TV Party" is backed with a pair of Ginn's songs—"I've Got to Run" and "My Rules"—that were recorded the previous year with Rollins providing the vocals and Bill Stevenson on drums.

When the single was released, *We Got Power* asked Black Flag what it thought about those who called "TV Party" a "sellout." "I think TV Party is hilarious," Ginn replied. "And if we would not do it because we might think we might get some criticism, that would be selling out, rather than saying, 'Well, we're gonna do what we like.' For us, it's a great break in our set to have some kind of humor in some of the songs because…that's part of our thing, the zany-ness, I guess. What are we supposed to do, suppress that because somebody might think it's not right?"[19]

Although Spot wasn't involved in recording the new "TV Party," he was very much in SST's plans. Ginn and Dukowski had been thinking about how to make use of the many recording sessions Black Flag had done with Spot at Media Art. They envisioned a massive compilation featuring songs, some of which had never been released, recorded during the tenure of each of the three previous singers. SST ran the idea past Edwards and got the green light from Unicorn to proceed.

But something was rotten in the studio on Santa Monica. Unicorn was required to issue a statement reporting the sales for *Damaged*. When Unicorn failed to do so, the SST brain trust became uneasy. After all, they knew exactly how many records they'd pressed. Ginn, Dukowski, Mugger, and Carducci put their heads together. It was clear that none of Unicorn's other artists were making money. Was Unicorn using Black Flag to keep the lights on?

As he'd done with Bomp! and Frontier, Ginn drafted a letter to Edwards stating that, since Unicorn wasn't holding up its end, Black Flag was no longer bound to the contract. Perhaps Ginn underestimated Edwards; maybe Edwards underestimated Ginn. Either way the letter triggered a lawsuit from Unicorn and a countersuit from SST.

Because Unicorn knew of SST's plans to release another record, it obtained an injunction against Black Flag from putting out any new material. This was a disaster for SST. Black Flag was at the peak of its popularity, and not only was the band not making money from the sales of *Damaged*, but it was prohibited from capitalizing on Black Flag's rising fame by making more records.

SST hired a pair of lawyers, Walter E. Hurst and Max Abrams, to help out with its case against Unicorn. This was an unprecedented move for an independent record label. The majors were notorious for screwing over musicians. They blatantly ignored the contracts they signed with artists, and by the time the treachery was discovered, the damage was done and mounting a defense against an army of corporate lawyers often cost more than what was owed. SST, however, refused to back down. Ginn and Dukowski used Hurst and Abrams as consultants, and in true do-it-yourself fashion did as much of the legal work as they could themselves. Both men had college degrees and weren't intimidated by the mountain of paperwork the lawyers threw at them.

For SST, Unicorn's skullduggery was yet another example of the music industry's unreliability and unprofessionalism. Black Flag did its part. It delivered a groundbreaking record and busted its ass to sell it. Unicorn was at fault, not Black Flag. Ginn and Dukowski were justifiably angry; for them this was personal.

The situation at Unicorn quickly deteriorated. It became obvious that SST wasn't the only enterprise the label was screwing over. Not only was Unicorn not paying SST, it wasn't paying *any* of its bills, including the company that pressed SST's records and the people who owned the building that Unicorn occupied. Unicorn was going bankrupt, but its lawyers continued to fight SST. Ginn and Dukowski worked out an arrangement with the building's landlord until they moved into new headquarters, which they did that spring.

With little to keep them in LA, Black Flag set out on its most ambitious

SST vs. Unicorn   105

tour to date with a new game plan. It started with a show in Texas on May 8, 1982, and that month Black Flag played twenty shows with just three nights off and even more gigs booked for June. Spot didn't accompany Black Flag on this trip, so Mugger added soundman to his duties.

Black Flag looked and sounded different from the crew that toured the country the previous year. It was now a five-man unit with a two-guitar attack, and Rollins was firmly established as the vocalist. The only thing holding the band back was the inexperience of the new drummer, which limited the scope of the set list. Ginn had new material he was eager to play, but he didn't want to overwhelm Johnson on his first tour. Initially, Holzman thought Johnson was an odd choice to replace Robo. "I figured they'd get a bigger, heavier, power-hitter guy," Holzman said. "But Emil was good. He held his own. In fact I learned some stuff from him."[20]

One of the ways the members of Black Flag fought back against the conformity that was creeping into the punk scene was by growing out their hair. By taking the stage with longer hair, Black Flag served notice that it was willing to rattle perceptions and oppose the status quo. In the late '70s, short hair put a target on your back from intolerant squares who felt threatened by punk, but by the early '80s short hair had become part of the punk rock uniform. There was nothing uniform about Black Flag. While no one would mistake the members of Black Flag for the Manson-like figures that haunted Pettibon's flyers, they looked *heavier*. So radical was their change in appearance that some fans didn't recognize them, and bouncers repeatedly blocked Rollins from taking the stage. "We're trying to always make a statement that it doesn't matter what you're wearing," Ginn said. "It's how you feel and how you think."[21]

Another way the band messed with expectations was by disrupting the flow of the show with an extended version of "Damaged I." This howling dirge-like theater of pain could last as long as fifteen minutes. Many fans were flummoxed by this. The performance was especially irritating to the type of suburban consumer that "TV Party" was orchestrated to attract. They'd come to see kick-ass hardcore punk, not some arty bullshit. A big part of the band's energizing animus was to repel those who were attracted to its noise. This was the conundrum that was Black Flag. Why would a band that had worked so hard for acceptance go to such lengths to antagonize its own fan base?

4

The law of averages dictated that playing more shows meant more problems. Problems with cops. Problems with bouncers. Problems with the crowd. More gigs also meant more breakdowns on the road. The van caught fire in Kansas, and in California Black Flag almost lost the trailer that carried its gear when it detached during a rainstorm.

Being on the road so much took a heavy toll on the band. The rhythm section came down with walking pneumonia, and Dukowski had to seek medical attention. "The Black Flag tours were punishing," Holzman recalled, "especially when you're only making $5 a day."[22]

Johnson was so homesick his new bandmates began to question his commitment. Everyone but Johnson knew that Mugger had slept with Johnson's girlfriend. Ginn and Dukowski believed that if Mugger told Johnson, he would break up with her and focus on Black Flag. Unfortunately, Mugger's revelation had the opposite effect, and Johnson quit the band.

The timing of Johnson's departure, however, worked to Black Flag's advantage. The legendary Chuck Biscuits had just left D.O.A. At a Fourth of July show in Vancouver, Ginn and Dukowski seized the opportunity to invite him to play with Black Flag. Johnson finished the remainder of the dates on the West Coast, and Biscuits joined Black Flag in time for a raucous gig with Circle One, Dr. Know, and Minor Threat at Dancing Waters in San Pedro.

Johnson, however, had the last laugh. After the tour, he got his hands on some of Black Flag's original recordings and refused to give them up. "I had to go over there and buy them from him," Mugger said, "and he had ten of his friends there."[23]

The Minutemen had its own struggles. Despite some high-profile shows with Fear at the Whisky and X at the Roxy, the band was heckled and harassed at a gig in its hometown of San Pedro. Boon had moved to Culver City and was spending more time in Hollywood and less time in the South

Bay. Watt had surgery on both of his knees—first one, then the other. The casts he had to wear hampered his movement and forced him to play gigs sitting down. The band wasn't practicing as much, and its members spent more time apart than usual, which was reflected on what Watt described as "the most different Minutemen record."[24]

For *What Makes a Man Start Fires?* (SST 014), Watt wrote all the music, and Boon sang all of the songs. The album is also twice as long as *The Punch Line*, and its eighteen songs show a more eclectic range of influences. On standouts such as "The Anchor," the Minutemen express the duality of the human experience: beautiful minds housed in decaying bodies destined for a life of pain. Watt could certainly relate.

After Watt's second surgery, Boon moved in with him at his mother's house, and the two musicians hammered out the songs. The Minutemen spent the summer rehearsing at the band's practice space in Long Beach for a no-frills recording session with Spot at the Music Lab. *What Makes a Man Start Fires?* was mixed the following month and was ready to go by the end of the summer, but—once again—the Minutemen would have to wait for the record to be released.

This was particularly exasperating for Watt and Boon, who'd released five records on New Alliance in 1981 and would release five more in 1982, including future classics by Hüsker Dü (the debut album *Land Speed Record* and the EP *In a Free Land*) and the Descendents' first album, *Milo Goes to College*. Watt suspected that if SST wanted to put out the Minutemen's records in a timely fashion, it would. "What was trippy about SST," Watt reflected, "was it was always Greg's thing, the band and the label. I think I had a better understanding than a lot of the dudes around him. I always knew. I wasn't thinking Greg was a dog or anything, I just knew it was his dealio. So you gotta defer to him."[25]

The Minutemen also wanted to put out an anthology of songs from various recording sessions going all the way back to Media Art in Hermosa Beach. Carducci came up with a solution by releasing *Bean-Spill* on Thermidor, after which he cut ties with the label. The EP looked nothing like an SST release—it didn't even have cover art—and to the members of the Minutemen, it must have felt as if they'd been demoted to junior varsity.

SST-by-the-beach. (Photo by Naomi Petersen Photography.)

There was friendly competition between Black Flag, the Minutemen, and Saccharine Trust, such as when Baiza jokingly challenged Boon to a guitar duel. But simmering beneath it were feelings of frustration and professional jealousy compounded by Black Flag's growing notoriety and the rate new releases trickled out of SST. "We could have done so much more," Carducci lamented, "but we never had enough cash."[26]

5

Black Flag's exploits on the road were as legendary as they were well documented. Rollins compulsively recorded where the band played, who it played with, and what happened along the way. Rollins's habitual note-taking inspired others on tour to do the same, and taken together these journals provide an intimate look at the physical and psychological toll Black Flag's tours took on its members.

But as hard as the conditions were on the road, they weren't much better at the series of decrepit, rat-infested office spaces that SST called home.

The next stop on SST's journey around the Southland was Phelan Lane in Redondo Beach. "SST-by-the-beach" was familiar territory for much for the crew, and it relished being back in the South Bay, just a mile and a half from the ocean. For Rollins and Carducci, it was a new experience.

Ginn used the office on Phelan Lane as a storage space for SST Electronics, but he no longer had the time or resources to run the operation. The one-room office was very small, but it had a shower and was dirt cheap. SST installed the coffee machine it had purloined from Unicorn and hooked up the telephone. The record label was back in business.

The Phelan office was too small to rehearse in, so Black Flag briefly rented out a space at Pax in nearby Carson where Overkill rehearsed. Spot learned that the people who had run Media Art opened a new space called Total Access Recording. Owner Wyn Davis was eager to resume his relationship with SST. "I signed a bulk recording deal with Greg Ginn, the founder of SST Records, at a very low rate for some guaranteed work."[27] SST no longer had to wait until it had the capital to pay for a recording session, and Total Access could keep its engineers busy and the studio booked. Ostensibly, this meant SST could record more artists, release records at a quicker pace, and pay the studio with funds from sales.

Black Flag wasted no time and recorded a demo with its new drummer at Total Access. Although the injunction from Unicorn prevented Black Flag from releasing new material, the band continued to experiment, developing a more muscular sound that made full use of the new lineup's talents. The eleven-song demo opens with a pair of tracks written by Dez Cadena, "What Can You Believe" and "Yes I Know." In the former, Ginn's monstrous guitar plays *behind* Cadena's blues-driven leads, but on songs such as "Slip It In," the roles are reversed with Cadena bolstering Ginn's out-on-a-limb riffing. These songs would all eventually appear on Black Flag albums with different arrangements by different players. Although some tracks, like the wildly cacophonous "My War," are superior to the versions that would appear on studio albums, the demo was never released. Tapes of the session spread throughout the underground, and many fans consider the "1982 Demos," as it came to be known, the best Black Flag record that never was.

For those in SST's inner circle, it must have felt as if Black Flag was cursed. Ever since the band became entangled with Unicorn, it couldn't catch a break. In August, Black Flag departed on another tour, but the band had to cancel after just three weeks when Rollins's knee gave out in Montreal and required surgery to repair. On the way back to the United States, the tour van suffered a catastrophic breakdown and had to be replaced. SST purchased a new van and rented a U-Haul for the gear, but en route to California the trailer hitch broke, and most of the band's equipment was demolished, scattered in broken heaps along the side of the road.

Throughout these difficulties, Ginn and Dukowski kept looking for creative ways to work around the injunction from Unicorn. "At one point, Black Flag was going to change their name," Mugger said. "And so we were all coming up with ideas." Brazil and Jakarta were discussed as possible alternatives.[28] Carducci recalled that October Faction, which was Dukowski's suggestion, was also floated as a possibility.

Another alternative was putting out a record by Black Flag comprising members who weren't actually in the band, but they decided against moving forward with this plan. SST was hemorrhaging cash, and little money was coming in. This was particularly frustrating because *Damaged* was selling well. Ginn estimated that by the end of the year between fifty-five thousand and sixty thousand units had sold.[29] But where was the money?

Ginn and Dukowski had had enough. While poring over legal documents with their lawyers, they found what they believed was a loophole. While the injunction prohibited Black Flag from releasing new material, they believed there was nothing to stop them from putting out a record of old material under their own names. The anthology that Edwards had approved was the perfect test for this theory.

Spot and Ginn went to Total Access to mix the tracks that Morris, Reyes, and Cadena had recorded between 1978 and 1981 and sent them off to be mastered. They already planned on calling the compilation *Everything Went Black* (SST 015), but now the title took on a double meaning. SST had to black out all references to Black Flag on the front and back of the jacket. The names Greg Ginn, Chuck Dukowski, Dez Cadena, Robo, Chavo Pederast, and Johnny "Bob" Goldstein appeared instead.[30]

This was supposed to be Black Flag's year. Instead, everything that possibly could go wrong did, ending with yet another demoralizing setback. Whether it was because of Black Flag's new direction or the primitive conditions at SST-at-the-Beach, Biscuits quit the band. Ginn and Dukowski looked forward to putting 1982 in the books and getting a fresh start the following year, but things would get worse—much worse—before they got better.

6

While the courts barred Black Flag from releasing the new material it was working on, Ginn and Dukowski turned their attention to the other artists on SST's roster, many of whom had been waiting months or even years for their records to be released. Overkill's "Hell's Getting Hotter," the Meat Puppets' debut (SST 009), and Würm's "I'm Dead" (SST 011) came out at the end of 1982. SST also released the Minutemen's *What Makes a Man Start Fires?* at the beginning of 1983, right as the band went into the studio to begin recording its sixth release, *Buzz or Howl Under the Influence of Heat* (SST 016).

SST issued a poster-sized flyer featuring its new releases, including an image of *Everything Went Black* with Black Flag's name prominently displayed, which might have been a mistake. Under "SOON TO COME" the flyer touted six new LPs by Black Flag, the Subhumans, the Stains, the Dicks, Saint Vitus, and Overkill. The back side of the flyer was devoted to Black Flag merchandise and "Pettibone's stuff": a library of zines that Pettibon had been working on since the release of *Captive Chains*. Black Flag may have been muzzled, but Pettibon continued cranking out art at a prolific pace. The flyer served as a potent reminder of everything they had created.

Black Flag invited the Minutemen on its second European tour. Although Black Flag's previous visit to the UK was disappointing, the Minutemen had never left the country before and were excited about the opportunity to explore Europe. For Ginn and Dukowski it was a good time to get out of the country. SST was still entangled with its lawsuit against Unicorn, and the billable hours from their legal team accrued each week the case dragged on. Ginn and Dukowski had been working on new material but were reluctant to play it in front of American audiences. Everywhere Black Flag went it inspired people to make their own records and book their own tours; Ginn worried about bands copying their sound at a time when the band was prohibited from releasing new material.

There was no fear of that happening in Europe, where audiences were generally hostile to Black Flag. For many Europeans, punk had morphed from an art movement to an identity, to which adherents displayed their allegiance with fashion accessories that they embraced with deadly seriousness. Punk was more political in Europe than in the United States, and to many European punks, Reagan's arms race with the Soviet Union put the planet in peril. Neither Black Flag nor the Minutemen met their criteria for what a punk band looked or sounded like, and the Americans encountered scorn and derision at every stop along the tour.

Everyone handled it differently. Boon and Watt bickered constantly. Mugger and Dave "Davo" Claassen, a friend of Cadena's who was taking classes at UCLA before he dropped out to become a full-time member of the SST road crew, taunted audiences with scabrous performances as Nig-Heist. Ginn, Dukowski, and Cadena tried to avoid the missiles hurled at them from the crowd, which included batteries, cans of beer, and even cups of urine.

One of the highlights of the tour was opening for Richard Hell in Osnabrück, Germany. Watt wrote, "We didn't get a sound check and half the p.a. went out but we had a lot of fun. I mean we got to play with richard hell!"[31] Rollins also had a remarkable night, which he, too, recorded in his journal: "I bit a skinhead on the mouth and he started to bleed real bad. His blood was all over my face."[32] Same show, two very different experiences.

Rollins became the focal point for all the abuse the Europeans hurled at the band, and he embraced it. With few exceptions, Ginn's and Dukowski's lyrics were angry, dark, and extremely personal. The new material was all this but slower, requiring a different kind of performance from Rollins. Black Flag unleashed long, grinding freak-outs such as "Scream" and "Nothing Left Inside," which featured Rollins's own lyrics. When Rollins rolled around on

Henry Rollins and a fan at the Vex in Boyle Heights April 30, 1983. (Photo by Wild Don Lewis).

stage, audiences lashed out at the vocalist, kicking, punching, and burning him with cigarettes. Rollins embraced the abuse, but it took a toll. He was no longer just a singer in a punk band but a weirdly polarizing, yet extremely vulnerable, endurance artist.

After a month overseas Black Flag and the Minutemen returned to the United States and continued the tour with assistance from Chris Gremsky, SST's booking agent on the East Coast. In New York, the Minutemen got a brief write-up in the *New York Times*, a newspaper more accustomed to writing about Minuteman missiles than a "hardcore" band from San Pedro.[33] At a club in the Bowery, Beat poet Allen Ginsberg immediately grasped that Black Flag, Rollins in particular, was doing something that fell outside the parameters of punk rock.

"What really inspired me to start a band," Ginn said, "was reading about what was happening in New York. I used to read in *The Village Voice* about CBGB's and Max's Kansas City and the scene, and it sounded real exciting and open. It was all kinds of different bands playing all kinds of different music. And that's what a lot of people don't realize about punk rock. When it started it wasn't a certain style of music. It was an environment where people that made any kind of music that was outcast from the formulaic rock of the time had a venue to play."[34]

Ginn was interested in punk rock as a concept—a creative call to arms— not as a specific style of music. Black Flag's evolution reflected this anarchic spirit of expression. Black Flag had helped establish American hardcore, but instead of locking into that style of music, it continued to experiment, slowing the tempo at a time when other hardcore bands were playing faster and faster. While American audiences were more receptive to Black Flag's new material than European audiences, there were always a few knuckleheads in the crowd who came to hear a version of the band that existed only in their imagination, and they took out their frustrations on the man in front.

In Chicago, Rollins broke down. He experienced what Davo described as "an emotional event" that left him shaking and sobbing uncontrollably.[35] Rollins continued the tour, but it was clear that if he was going to let Black Flag take him to the darkest places in his mind, he was going to have to take steps to protect himself.

The 1983 tour marked several turning points. When Black Flag started out, the band was ridiculed by Hollywood punks for looking like a bunch of surf rats. To experience that same mindset again five years later in Europe, where so many punks dressed like it was still 1977, made the band realize it had less in common with many punk rockers than ever before, hardening its view of those on the outside and making it more insular.

When Black Flag returned to the South Bay, things continued to unravel. Cadena quit the band in April, telling Ginn that he wanted to start his own project. His departure had a domino effect on Black Flag's dynamics. Without Cadena's guitar to bolster the sound, Ginn complained during rehearsals about the flaws in Dukowski's technique. Dukowski's aggressive bass playing was more theatrical than technical, and it set the tone for Black Flag's approach both on and off stage. The frenzied pace of early Black Flag allowed the songs to breathe like a living organism. Ginn, however, believed the new material called for greater precision and a deeper commitment to the musicianship.

No quitter, Dukowski worked on his craft, but in the hyperintense and ultra-claustrophobic atmosphere at Phelan Lane, every mistake was magnified. Locked in an ego-driven battle of wills, neither Ginn nor Dukowski would back down. Eventually, Dukowski came to understand that Ginn didn't want him to improve; Ginn wanted him out of the band.

Black Flag celebrated the release of *Everything Went Black* with a reunion show at Santa Monica Civic with the Misfits and the Vandals. Ginn invited Reyes and Cadena to participate in the show, which helped ease some of the bitterness Reyes had been feeling. Morris was on tour with the Circle Jerks and never got the message. Mugger, who was getting plenty of practice at it,

Ginn, Rollins, and Dukowski of Black Flag at Santa Monica Civic, June 1, 1983. (Photo by Wild Don Lewis.)

donned a wig and filled in for Black Flag's founding vocalist, and a host of special guests joined the band onstage.

But the sword of Damocles that had been hanging over SST's head finally dropped. A complaint was brought before the court that, with the release of *Everything Went Black*, Black Flag had violated the injunction against issuing new material. The Honorable Bruce R. Geernaert agreed with this assessment. "I deem this to be a very, very significant proceeding," the judge declared. "The fine here would approach $5 million, the number of jail days would be 5,000 days, if the contempt is proved."[36]

Ginn and Dukowski were charged with contempt of court. Both men were sentenced to five days in jail, and Ginn was fined $1,500. Their lawyers filed an appeal, arguing that the injunction was void once Unicorn filed for bankruptcy, but the judge didn't see it that way. "The judge treated us like scum and still said we had violated the injunction," Ginn said. "Chuck and I spent five days in LA county jail—which is a long time to spend there."[37]

It was a demeaning and humiliating experience for them both. "I went through some things in jail," Dukowski said.[38] It marked a new phase in the war between SST and Unicorn. In fact, Ginn nearly went to jail for an additional fifteen days over the $1,500 fine. Ginn, who had filed for bankruptcy in July, argued he was unable to pay.

The case took a dramatic turn when SST learned that Unicorn was in violation of bankruptcy laws. "We found out they were taking checks that were supposed to go into the Chapter 11 account," Carducci said, "and putting them into one of their non-bankrupt corporations. When they did that, the judge threw them into Chapter 7 and foreclosed on 'em, and that freed us— much to the judge's consternation, 'cause he fucking hated us. He looked at those Raymond Pettibon drawings on *Everything Went Black*, and wanted to lock us up."[39]

SST dug up this information by checking in with distributors that SST and Unicorn shared. This shrewd maneuver effectively put an end to Unicorn and its lawsuit with SST. "Game over," Carducci declared.[40]

The label emerged from its dispute with Unicorn and the courts battered but not broken, but it was a Pyrrhic victory. Although Hurst and Ward had agreed to defer their legal expenses until after the matter was settled and SST could ramp up its operations, the label now owed approximately $200,000, and Ginn was destitute.[41]

No matter how steep the bill was, the opportunity cost of signing a contract with Unicorn proved much higher. "There is no dollar figure for that," Carducci said, "the tours you couldn't do, the push you couldn't give to records, the titles you couldn't keep in print, the music videos you couldn't make when MTV was new and wide open, the natural follow-up record to *Damaged*." Carducci believed that if Ginn hadn't borrowed money from his parents to keep the label afloat, he would have dissolved SST.[42]

During the long dispute with Unicorn, Black Flag went through three drummers—Robo, Johnson, and Biscuits—and lost the services of Cadena. But there was one final casualty in the Unicorn war. Dukowski finally quit Black Flag. Carducci called the way Ginn froze Dukowski out of the band "the most brutal thing I ever witnessed that didn't involve bloodshed or lawyers."[43]

Perhaps the most damaging aspect of SST's legal victory over Unicorn was a shift in attitude. From the moment Dukowski joined Black Flag, he had inspired an "us-against-the-world" mindset that unified the band and its crew and turned them into true believers willing to endure individual deprivation for the good of the cause. The long and bloody battle with Unicorn intensified this perspective. A battle line was drawn, with winners on one side and losers on the other. Only it wasn't just the enemy that was out to get SST, but everyone outside the circle. A culture of paranoia seeped into all levels of the organization.

Emboldened by its victory over Unicorn, SST's worldview shifted to "global domination," which could be unpleasant for those who drew SST's ire. In its war against corporate rock, the label had achieved an improbable yet crucial victory—but at what cost?

Scott Reagers of Saint Vitus at Club Lingerie. (Photo by Wild Don Lewis.)

CHAPTER 6
SST vs. Hardcore

1983–1984

1

When the members of Hüsker Dü took the stage at Oz, an infamous after-hours club in Chicago, they knew Black Flag was in the house. The punk rock trio from Saint Paul, Minnesota, played their guts out to win the approval of their hardcore heroes. At the end of the show, Grant Hart—Hüsker Dü's drummer—tossed a bucket of blue paint onto the dance floor, splattering the crowd. "The crowd liked them a lot," Dem Hopkins, who booked the show, said. "He was just fucked up and was looking for a big finish."[1] Hart went along with this assessment. "It was the kind of gig that impressed Black Flag and impressed Greg Ginn," Hart said.[2]

Hüsker Dü's efforts to attract SST's attention worked. After the show, Ginn expressed an interest in the band, but when Hüsker Dü reached out to the label, SST balked because of cash flow problems. Carducci recommended the band get in touch with Watt at New Alliance Records. But because he liked the band, he reached out to Watt himself. "Watt told me he would release it without even hearing it," Carducci said.[3]

New Alliance was a good fit because the Minutemen and Hüsker Dü had a great deal in common. Like the Minutemen, Hüsker Dü paid its dues in a blue-collar scene in the shadow of a larger city. Like the Minutemen, none of Hüsker Dü's members looked or dressed like they were in a punk band. And like the Minutemen, all three members of Hüsker Dü made significant creative contributions to their records—from the songwriting and lyrics to the artwork on the jackets.

Bob Mould, Grant Hart, and Greg Norton combined an enthusiasm for all things punk with a rigorous technical proficiency that allowed them to play at blazing speeds. While Hart and Norton were St. Paul natives, Mould came from upstate New York to attend Macalester College in the Twin Cities. He fell in with Hart after hearing music blasting out of the tiny record shop on campus where Hart worked.

The trio started playing locally and quickly established a reputation as a relentless hardcore band. Prince may have made First Avenue famous, but Hüsker Dü, amped up on trucker speed and cigarettes, honed its craft in the club's much smaller side room: 7th Street Entry.

"I'd never seen anybody play so fast," said First Avenue's soundman and occasional writer Terry Katzman.[4] In his column for *Sweet Potato*, the local alternative newspaper, Katzman described a Hüsker Dü performance as "tension, speed, timing and aggressiveness all working in perfect harmony."[5] Mould and Hart were as prolific as they were intense. By late 1980 Hüsker Dü had already written fifty songs, and Katzman predicted great things for the band.

The band's name came from a symbol-matching memory game of the same name, derived from the Danish and Norwegian phrase "Do you remember?" Mould characterized it as "a kid's game where the child can outwit the adult."[6] Hüsker Dü replaced the macrons (ū) with umlauts (ü), which the rock community has decreed is the toughest-looking diacritic.

Hüsker Dü set its sights on signing with the local independent label Twin/Tone Records because of its affiliation with hometown heroes the Suicide Commandos, but the label rejected the band's demo. Twin/Tone's subsequent signing of the Replacements, who were relative newcomers to the scene, made the rejection that much harder to take. The band responded by starting its own record label to prove it didn't need Twin/Tone. "We named our label Reflex Records," said Norton, "because that was our reflex to being rejected."[7]

Because all of the members of Hüsker Dü had worked at various record shops around town, they had connections who were in bands and owned recording equipment. The fledgling label's first release was the single "Statues" backed with "Amusement," a song about the band's frustration with Twin/Tone. Throughout the summer of 1981, Hüsker Dü dialed in its sound with a tour that took the band from Calgary to Vancouver and down the West Coast to San Francisco, where Carducci saw them play at Mabuhay Gardens. The tour, which the band referred to as the Children's Crusade, was sandwiched between a series of frenzied hometown shows.

When Hüsker Dü returned to the Twin Cities, they played faster than ever. "All of us were really excited to see them," recalled Tom Hazelmyer, a local musician who would go on to form Amphetamine Reptile Records, "and it was in the big room at First Avenue. With the chops they picked up on the road, they fucking sheared everybody's head off. The other guys in my hardcore band looked at each other with their jaws literally open."[8]

Mould and Hart split the vocals, each singing the songs he had written. Hüsker Dü performed at a blistering pace with the only respite between songs a breathless "1-2-3-4!" Mould slashed away at a heavily duct-taped Ibanez Flying V guitar, and Hart battered his kick drum with bare feet. Hüsker Dü delivered songs about suburban teenage ennui like "I'm Not Interested," "Don't Have a Life," and "I'm Tired of Doing Things" with the ferocity of a kick in the teeth. "We were copy cat killers," Hart said. "We were applying that hardcore ethic to the songs that we had composed, and then we brought that ethic to Minneapolis."[9]

Hüsker Dü sent a live recording of its show on August 15, 1981, to New Alliance, who pressed up six thousand copies. The band called it *Land Speed Record*—a tribute to the drugs the band consumed on its first national tour. By the time the record was released in January 1982, the band was getting ready to record another single for New Alliance, "In a Free Land," at Blackberry Way in Minneapolis, where Hüsker Dü had recorded its first demo.

Hüsker Dü and a Minutemen set list. (Photo by Edward Colver.)

New Alliance released the EP in time for the band's arrival in LA a few months later, in the summer of 1982.

Hüsker Dü cruised down to Redondo Beach to record twelve songs at Total Access with Spot, where the Descendents were also recording *Milo Goes to College*. Drawing inspiration from the bands they were playing with during the Children's Crusade, all of the songs were written and rehearsed on the road. Everyone at SST loved Hüsker Dü but the label was very much in disarray and had a backlog of material to release. Carducci summed up the label's reluctance to sign the band: "We also had the early Black Flag singles to keep in print, and the ill-fated *Everything Went Black* vault comp, plus we'd already recorded the first Meat Puppets album, the basic tracks for the Over-kill album, and we still had the Stains album and an earlier Overkill 45 to get released."[10]

Other than putting the band on the bill with Black Flag, 45 Grave, D.O.A., and the Descendents for a massive show at the Olympic Auditorium, SST was in no position to help Hüsker Dü out. The show at the Olympic was put on by Goldenvoice, and the promoter, Gary Tovar, wanted Pettibon to design a flyer. "Because the Olympic Auditorium used to do wrestling and roller derby," Pettibon explained, "he had this fabulous idea to have them in roller derby outfits....I tried to talk him out of it. 'This is a bad idea. They won't like it!'"[11]

In the end, Pettibon relented. He created the flyer to Tovar's specification, illustrating the members of Black Flag in leotards and roller skates. Pettibon got the last laugh by signing it "Tovar/Money/Pettibon" and including information about his zines available for mail order.

Hüsker Dü went back up the California coast before returning home, where the trio wasted no time preparing for the release of their first studio album, *Everything Falls Apart*, which takes aim at hardcore. "Blah, Blah, Blah," "Target," and "Obnoxious" all skewer scene politics. *Land Speed Record* moves in a straight line, but *Everything Falls Apart* possesses a pronounced groove, particularly on the songs performed at less than breakneck speed, like the cover of Donovan's "Sunshine Superman." "Signals from Above" breaks hardcore convention by opening with a noisy guitar solo before tumbling into fuzzed-out thrash. But it's the title track that shows the way forward. Mould powers through the verses with chugging riffs, but in the chorus the guitar shifts into something moodier that reveals the song's quiet power. While Black Flag was retreating from hardcore to something heavier, Hüsker Dü was in the process of transforming into a more melodic version of itself.

Whether it was Hüsker Dü's artistic progression, the band's growing popularity, its willingness to tour, or the fact that New Alliance burned through its stock of *Land Speed Record* and "In a Free Land," SST could no longer put off bringing the band into the fold. In the fall of 1982, SST invited Hüsker Dü to record its new album at Total Access. The following January, the band arrived in Redondo Beach with copies of *Everything Falls Apart*. The session took two days and of the twelve tracks that were recorded, seven made it on to Hüsker Dü's SST debut, *Metal Circus* (SST 020).

Metal Circus is Mould's record, having written five of the songs himself, but Hart's songs "It's Not Funny Anymore" and "Diane" stand out because of their slower tempo and tuneful melodies. While Mould's guitar on the former is sharp and angular, "Diane" has a fuller sound that could almost be

Clash of the Titans: Saint Vitus at the Vex in 1983. (Photo by Wild Don Lewis.)

called lush in this haunting portrait of the rape and murder of a waitress that Hart knew. *Metal Circus* culminates with "Out on a Limb," a spare song with few lyrics and plenty of room for Mould's noisy solos.

Before returning to Minneapolis, Hüsker Dü took the stage with Black Flag, Redd Kross, and the Descendents as part of a legal benefit billed "BLACK FLAG VS. UNICORN." Tickets were six dollars, and the local zinesters complained that nobody got in for free. The opening band that night was Saint Vitus, a band few people in the crowd had ever heard of, but that would not be the case for long.

2

After Biscuits hit the skids and Milo went to college, Ginn formally invited Bill Stevenson to join Black Flag. "I was committed to the Descendents," Stevenson said. "But Black Flag was my favorite band. So I always tried to make myself available to them, and there were lots of instances where I filled in. I played more shows, and it just kind of seemed like it would solve a lot of problems for me to be in the band."[12] Although Black Flag didn't rehearse at Pax for long, another band working in the studio caught its attention: a weirdly compelling heavy metal band from the South Bay called Saint Vitus.

"Vitus was in the next practice room over and we could hear them," Stevenson remembered, "but we kind of started spying outside the door and listening to how heavy they were playing. That definitely was an interesting thing. We were kind of slowing our stuff down because we were going through a really big Sabbath kick. When you go through a Sabbath kick it just consumes you. Then we heard Vitus and it was like, 'Whoa, they're *really* going through a Sabbath kick!'"[13]

To most, Saint Vitus sounded like a slower, heavier version of Black Sabbath.[14] To Ginn, Saint Vitus sounded like the future. Intrigued by the band's blend of ferocious riffs over a wrecking-ball rhythm section, Ginn asked Carducci to check the band out. Carducci was impressed, but the label's legal woes made the timing terrible. He considered a single, but Saint Vitus's songs were too long and too heavy for a seven-inch. Saint Vitus required the grooves of a twelve-inch slab.

Saint Vitus started out as a band called Tyrant. Guitarist Dave Chandler and bassist Mark Adams were high school friends from Lomita, a densely packed patch of exurbs between Torrance and San Pedro. Drummer Armando Acosta was from Venice and had moved to San Pedro after serving in the air force. The name change came when vocalist Scott Reagers joined the band. Saint Vitus recorded its first record, the five-song self-titled EP (SST 022), during a late-night session at Total Access in August 1983.

At the time, Ginn wanted to make a record that was, in Spot's words, "dark and sludgy—i.e., anti-punk."[15] In Spot's estimation, Saint Vitus was the real deal. There was no one darker or sludgier. "They were the kind of band that shouldn't have been popular with anyone at that time," Spot said, "but there was something about them."[16]

The album opens with the eponymous "Saint Vitus" followed by "White Magic / Black Magic"—classic heavy metal songs in the Black Sabbath mold with epic riffs. On "Zombie Hunger" the tempo slows and the droning guitars pulverize the senses. The darkly psychedelic songs on Side B are even slower and longer, with "The Psychopath" coming in at 9:24 and the turgid

"Burial at Sea" at 8:37. This arrangement set the template for Black Flag's next album, which would follow a similar pattern of back-loading the album with the gloomiest, doom-laden tracks. The longest song from the Saint Vitus recording session, the epic twelve-minute-long "The Walking Dead," didn't make it on to the album, but it would be released as an EP a few years later (SST 042).

Black Flag's new drummer was particularly impressed with Saint Vitus's debut. By his own admission, he was a fast drummer adept at playing the kind of live wire pop-punk songs that he and his bandmates in the Descendents perfected, but he struggled with heavier beats. "I wasn't designed to play slowly," Stevenson said. "It's just not in my DNA, but that's what the guys were writing and that's what they wanted, kind of a heavier sound, so I did my best."[17]

Saint Vitus started playing shows with Black Flag and other SST bands, and it developed a small but dedicated following in Los Angeles. Unfortunately, a year would pass before the album was even mixed, which meant Saint Vitus missed out on the cavalcade of compilations that SST released in the second half of 1983.

3

For a band that devoted so much energy to the making and selling of records, Black Flag was obsessed with tapes. When Black Flag returned from its European tour with the Minutemen and Nig-Heist in 1983, the band listened to a tape of Dio's *Holy Diver* over and over again while traveling up and down the West Coast. Ginn's obsession with Dio was so intense that when Dukowski left the band, Rollins, thinking Ginn wanted to replace him with someone who sounded like Scott Reagers or Ronnie James Dio, asked Dukowski if he should go with him.

Rollins, too, was obsessed with collecting, making, and trading tapes and had even bought an Aiwa dual cassette recorder. To offset the cost, Rollins made tapes for friends and fans, whom he'd invite to the SST office for a dubbing session, and the singer wasn't shy about asking people to buy him lunch as payment for his services. It was only a matter of time before SST hit on the idea to release a tape.

The First Four Years (SST 021) wasn't SST's first cassette, but it was the first time an SST product was issued exclusively in the format. The compilation collects all of the songs Black Flag put out before Rollins joined the band. This includes the tracks on the first four records as well as the songs from the New Alliance compilations *Cracks in the Sidewalk* and *Chunks*. The project had a similar ambition as *Everything Went Black*: to bring together songs from Black Flag's catalog. The difference was that all of the tracks on *The First Four Years* had been previously released.

SST followed up *The First Four Years* with *The Blasting Concept* (SST 013), a compilation of fourteen cuts from eight of the artists the label had recorded. Pettibon's artwork for the album features a man choking a woman in what appears to be a brutal rape while a mushroom cloud from a nuclear blast rises into the sky. Even by Pettibon's standards, the artwork is extreme.

Compilations tend to be retrospective catalogs or an attempt to capture the current moment. *The Blasting Concept* is a curious mixture of both. The album arranges SST's experimental arty bands on Side 1 (the Minutemen, the Meat Puppets, and Saccharine Trust) and the heavier bands on Side 2 (Black Flag, Overkill, the Stains, Würm, and Hüsker Dü). Half the songs on the record are by the Minutemen and Black Flag. While both bands were extremely active at the time, SST opted to include older material, which was unusual considering the label had just released a pair of comps that accomplished the same thing.

This preoccupation with the past extends to the liner notes from Harvey Kubernik, a well-connected journalist who started a label called Freeway Records to promote LA poets and performers of "spoken word," a term he claims to have coined.[18] Kubernik's notes read like a manifesto, declaring, "Listen to this artifact" and referencing SST as a "record label and house of freedom."[19] Kubernik casts the release of *The Blasting Concept* as something of a corrective of the limited distribution SST's output suffered during its first five years of operation. However, he overstates the case with wooden

remarks like "SST music has always reflected social and political consciousness," which certainly wasn't true.[20]

Kubernik was a cultural force in LA and would prove to be an influential
figure in SST circles for many years to come. Freeway Record's first release
in 1982, *Voices of the Angels (Spoken Words)*, is an eclectic compendium of
tracks recorded between 1975 and 1980 by a raft of cultural figures, including
poets Charles Bukowski, Dennis Cooper, and Wanda Coleman; musicians
and producers Kim Fowley, Dave Alvin (of the Blasters), and Ethan James (a
former member of Blue Cheer and founder of Radio Tokyo recording studio);
as well as a number of artists from the LA punk community, such as Chris
D., Geza X, Phast Phreddie, and Pleasant Gehman. The double album also
includes a piece by Charles Dukowski called "SWA Manifesto (a Work in
Progress)," which provides a glimpse of the bass player's creativity beyond the
scope of Black Flag.[21]

Rollins's literary ambitions were still in their infancy, and Dukowski
provided the vocalist with guidance and encouragement. The previous year,
Dukowski had penned his "History of L.A. Punk Rock" for the LA fanzine
NO MAG. The piece thoroughly documents LA's punk experiment. Dukowski's mentorship of Rollins extended beyond Black Flag and into the literary
arts. Rollins accompanied Dukowski to his recording session for the *Voices
of the Angels* compilation, and the following year Kubernik invited Rollins to
participate in Freeway Records' second release, *English as a Second Language
(Talking Package)*. This compilation featured an even more impressive roster
of performers and included a second, more fleshed-out version of Dukowski's "SWA Manifesto," a track by Rollins called "Henry," and a collaboration
between the two called "D.S.Y."

What was SWA? What began as a mishmash of slogans morphed into
something stranger during trips up the coast. On May 22, 1982, during the
opening slot for Throbbing Gristle, Dukowski staged an "SWA Orientation
Rally." When Dukowski was joined on stage by members of the SWA elite
such as Pettibon, Spot, Boon, Ward, and Liberty with their arms raised in
salute, the scene resembled a satirical Nuremberg rally.

English as a Second Language also featured many of the same punk

SWA Rally at Veterans Auditorium in Culver City on May 22, 1982. (Photo by Edward Colver.)

personalities who had appeared on the previous record, plus additional artists from SST's circle of friends. Kubernik organized and hosted events around town, and it was at the Lhasa Club in Hollywood that Rollins got his start as a spoken word performer. This opportunity couldn't have come at a better time for Rollins, and he started performing at other venues around town, including Bebop Records in Reseda. He was growing as an artist, and while Black Flag afforded opportunities to express himself, there were limitations.

Rollins was becoming increasingly frustrated with interviews. Punk fanzines mostly printed the interviews as they occurred, with little context or editorial oversight. The articles the mainstream media produced about Black Flag, and Rollins in particular, cherry-picked information to fit the editor's slant. It's not that these stories were inaccurate, but they typically presented the singer in a way that he disagreed with or found embarrassing. "I feel that when I do them," he said, "I'm selling out and it makes me feel very bad about myself."[22]

Rollins returned to this idea often in his journals, complaining that doing interviews left him feeling "fist-fucked."[23] With spoken word, Rollins discovered, he could tell his stories *and* control the narrative. This combination was immensely appealing to him. Kubernik booked Rollins for more shows, and an unlikely friendship sprang up between the two. Kubernik was a connector, and he introduced Rollins to another side of LA's counterculture, which led to collaborations with artists who operated outside of the claustrophobic confines of the SST universe.

One of these early influences was the New York performance artist and musician Lydia Lunch, who'd recently crash-landed in LA. The two began collaborating, and Lunch exposed Rollins to a wide range of artists who would inform his work and expand his circle of friends for years to come. "Lydia Lunch loaned *Black Spring* to me and said read this," Rollins said. "I was twenty-two years and seven months old. I read that book and I've never recovered. That was like the first Clash album for me."[24]

Thanks to Lunch, Rollins was reading books by Henry Miller and Hubert Selby Jr. and listening to music by Diamanda Galás, Einstürzende Neubauten, Nick Cave, Sonic Youth, and Swans. Rollins wasn't just gazing in admiration at this new constellation of artists; he was corresponding with them as well, including an exchange of letters and tapes with Charles Manson, the dark star of Southern California subculture. If Black Flag gave Rollins a hands-on education in the performing arts, Lydia Lunch was his graduate school.

4

Just as musicians typically don't record songs in the sequence they appear on the album, record labels don't always release albums in the order of the catalog numbers they're assigned. For instance, although the Meat Puppets' debut in 1982 (SST 009) preceded the release of the Stains' in 1983 (SST 010), the Stains had recorded its LP long before the Meat Puppets went into the studio, and the Eastside punks waited years for their record to come out. New Alliance beat SST to the punch by including "Sick and Crazy," arguably the album's best track, on the *Chunks* compilation all the way back in 1981.

For the cover of the Stains album, Viscarra reached out to Wild Don Lewis, a photographer from Pasadena who had taken several photos of the band for an interview that ran in *Youth Party*, a publication of the Mau Maus'

Rick Wilder. After that session, Lewis became enamored with the band. Viscarra knew he was one of the only photographers in LA—with the exception of Edward Colver—who had photos of the band, and asked Lewis to design the album cover.

Lewis began with a group shot that he'd taken in front of the Vex and then he got creative. "I went down to their neighborhood in Boyle Heights and walked around the alleys at midnight alone," Lewis explained. "I shot photos of alleys in their hood so it'd be authentic. Then I cut out their group shot at the Vex and juxtaposed them against the alley. So if you look at the cover, you'll see it's cut out."[25]

Sadly, by the time SST finally released the Stains debut, the band had more or less broken up and would never record another album. Becerra wasn't too upset about it. "We didn't sell very much because the band broke up," Becerra said. "When a record comes out, you got to go on tour to promote the record. I was doing something else. That's how it goes."[26]

Rivera, Becerra, Navarro, and Viscarra of the Stains at the Vex in East LA, March 1981. (Photo by Wild Don Lewis.)

Nevertheless, SST sat on the album for so long, it was inevitable that the band's disappointment would turn to resentment. On the Eastside, rumors circulated that Black Flag didn't want the competition. Although the Stains reunited for a gig at On Broadway in San Francisco with the Minutemen, Hüsker Dü, and the Dicks, Becerra had moved on from the Stains and formed the heavy metal outfit called the Nightmare.

The Stains' legacy as one of the sickest and craziest LA bands of the early punk scene stems not from its outsized reputation as Eastside bad boys but from Robert Becerra's incandescent guitar playing. His skittering riffs and howling solos were unmatched in the LA scene and inspired a long list of guitar players, on which Greg Ginn sits at the top.

5

When courting controversy, sometimes it's best to spell out one's position up front so that no one gets the wrong idea. This was exactly what the Dicks did with its first single, "Dicks Hate the Police."

Fronted by the large, loud, and outspokenly gay Gary Floyd, there was little chance that anyone who saw the Dicks perform would mistake the singer for the murderous, racist cop portrayed in the song. Floyd's long journey to the hardcore stages of Austin, Texas, began in the dusty little town of Gurdon, Arkansas, which he described as a place where a pair of "railroad tracks full of dead men still spooking people with lanterns ran like rough zippers through town."[27] Floyd's father and both his grandfathers were railroad men. His father's job as a car knocker for the Missouri Pacific Railroad took the family to Palestine, Texas. After Floyd was drafted to fight in Vietnam, he registered as a conscientious objector and worked as a janitor at the Jefferson Davis Hospital in Houston, Texas.

When Floyd finally made it to Austin, he posted flyers around town announcing upcoming shows by the Dicks, an outfit that existed only in his imagination. It took a year to pull a band together, but once he did, Floyd quickly established himself as a provocative presence in the Austin punk scene. Floyd dressed in drag and mesmerized crowds with his in-your-face anti-fascist, anti-racist, anti-homophobic performances. Floyd "was brazen and truly formidable, a portly cross-dressed madhouse of a man," wrote David Yow of Scratch Acid. "He was such a cool, mean nightmare to watch, but his growl had all the soulful rasp of Donna Summer."[28]

Everything about the Dicks was unconventional—except its sound. Unlike many of his hardcore contemporaries, Floyd could actually sing, and his songs about racial intolerance and government oppression meshed well with the band's blues-based rock riffs. With its stridently anti-police messaging, the band was destined to catch SST's attention. The Dicks hit SST up for a spot on its roster, and the label made the unusual move of flying Spot to Austin. Spot was familiar with both Austin and the Dicks from his work recording the Big Boys. Spot met the band at Earth & Sky to record the album, and after forty-eight hours and a lot of beer, *Kill from the Heart* was in the can.[29]

When Spot returned to LA and listened to some rough mixes, he nearly had a heart attack. "Everything got recorded way, way, way too hot and it was distorted as hell," Spot said. "Somehow I figured out a way to make it sound good. I was really lucky with that."[30]

Following MDC's lead, the Dicks moved to San Francisco and success-fully lobbied to join the Rock Against Reagan Tour. When the band passed through Austin at the end of the tour, *Kill from the Heart* (SST 017) was ready and waiting, but the jackets had been packaged with the wrong vinyl. The issue was corrected, and the Dicks celebrated with a record release party in December at Raul's, where the band had recorded a live album with the Big Boys three years earlier.

After the release of *Kill from the Heart*, the rest of the band decided they wanted to stay in Austin, but Floyd was adamant about returning to San Francisco, where he re-formed the Dicks with new players before pursuing other projects. The Dicks wouldn't make another record with SST, but Floyd would. In 1988, his new band released the self-titled album *Sister Double Happiness* (SST 162).

The Subhumans—not to be confused with the British band of the same name—found itself in a similar situation. Black Flag had crossed paths with the Canadian outfit on several occasions, and the two bands developed a rela-tionship. The Subhumans played with Black Flag at the Fleetwood all the way back in 1980, and Black Flag played multiple shows with the Subhumans in Vancouver in 1982.

The Vancouver band, which was closely associated with D.O.A., had a fascinating history that involved multiple lineup changes, a string of influential singles and records, and a former member of the band going to jail. (He was involved in an underground political activist group called Direct Action, which was responsible for the bombing of an industrial plant that made parts for missiles.) Despite these stories, only a small portion of the Subhumans' saga intersected with SST.

The Subhumans mixed catchy songs with irreverent political takes exemplified by the band's highly danceable yet uncompromising 1979 single "Fuck You." The Subhumans toured all over Canada and the United States and built up a following on the West Coast, but the constant touring took its toll. When the Subhumans recorded *No Wishes, No Prayers* (SST 018) with Spot at a studio in Santa Monica, there was just one founding member left in the band, vocalist Brian Goble.[31]

The record combines early '77-style punk with political hardcore and was favorably received, but by the time it was finally released in the summer of 1983, Goble had left the band to play bass in D.O.A. Same old punk rock story: it was fun while it lasted, but it seldom lasted for long.

SST's relationships with the Stains, the Dicks, and the Subhumans illustrate the challenges the label faced. The punk scene was in a constant state of upheaval, with bands struggling to keep lineups intact. By the end of 1983, some of the biggest names in the Southern California hardcore scene, such as the Adolescents and T.S.O.L., had already broken up, with prominent members forming new bands. Extreme music attracted extreme personalities that didn't always mesh well with others, making it difficult to maintain working relationships over long periods of time.

People joined bands for different reasons. Some relished the opportunity to express themselves creatively, while others were simply looking for an emotional outlet for their anger and frustration. Many musicians learned the hard way that the lives they desired as creative artists were incompatible with the realities of touring. Bands embraced the example of Black Flag, the

Minutemen, Minor Threat, and Hüsker Dü only to discover that the DIY ethos required a tremendous amount of work. Those who chose this path eventually discovered that the satisfaction one took in doing the work was the only reliable reward.

There was a reason most musicians didn't make their own flyers, book their own shows, and put out their own records. Not only did these tasks take hours of labor, but after the flyers were made and the records were pressed, the artists had to find ways to distribute them, which required yet another set of skills. It took a special kind of performer to leave it all on the stage every night and still have the wherewithal to participate in the running of a small business—all while traveling hundreds and thousands of miles in the company of people with whom you spend all your waking hours. As the saying goes, if it was easy, everyone would do it.

But as far as bands like the Subhumans, the Dicks, and the Stains were concerned, SST wasn't holding up its end. A record is a snapshot of a band at a particular moment in time. In a climate where clubs were constantly closing and people were falling in and out of the scene, it was essential that those "round vinyl documents," to quote Kubernik, get out as quickly as possible before the band, its supporting scene, or even the world itself was blasted to smithereens.

No one understood this better than Ginn, whose efforts to record a proper full-length record with Black Flag were beset by years of frustrating setbacks. Its long dispute with Unicorn finally over, SST urged its artists to embrace Black Flag's road dog mentality. The label believed the best way to spread the word about a new record was to play its songs in front of a live audience. Not all bands, however, could afford to tour. Financial obligations and family responsibilities kept many musicians at home.

For the Minutemen, playing shows was the number one priority. Watt broke down all of the band's activities into two categories: gigs and flyers. Anything that wasn't a gig fell under the category of flyer and was thus secondary to the joy of playing songs in front of a live audience. But SST didn't sell gigs; it sold records. This illustrates how bands and labels often found themselves at odds, with both sides arguing that the other wasn't doing enough.

Obviously, a band can't tour after it has broken up. That's why SST didn't include the Dicks or the Subhumans on *The Blasting Concept* and featured a band whose album wasn't out yet instead. Because in 1983, no one was burning up the miles or writing more material than Hüsker Dü.

6

When Hüsker Dü returned to Total Access to make a new record in October 1983, Black Flag bore little resemblance to the outfit they had played with earlier that year. Dukowski and Cadena were gone, and no one had taken their places. But while Black Flag was regrouping, Hüsker Dü was flying high. Reviews of *Everything Falls Apart* were still being published in fanzines when *Metal Circus* came out, and the band was generating lots of buzz. When the members of Hüsker Dü sat down for interviews, they were questioned about everything, from the band's sound to its image.

Like Black Flag, Hüsker Dü had its own one-man art department: Grant Hart, who credited his elaborate sleeve designs to Fake Name Graphx. Because the records didn't include images of the band members, fans who were new to Hüsker Dü had no idea what they looked like. Shortly before departing for LA, the band was featured in a profile penned by Steve Albini, who commented at length on the band's appearance: "Greg looks like he stepped out of GQ, with cropped hair, trimmed mustache and muscular build; Grant could replace anybody in Motorhead (maybe *two* people in Motorhead); and Bob looks like a St. Paul gas station attendant after a hard day's work."

"The way we look isn't important," Mould quipped.[32]

While the album art cultivated an air of mystery around the band's image, Mould and Hart were upfront about how they crafted their songs, what the lyrics were about, how they felt about the punk scene, and where they were headed musically. Writers from fanzines to slick music magazines were obsessed with pinning down Hüsker Dü's sound, which was next to impossible. The band never stopped writing and recording new songs and was in a state of constant evolution. Hüsker Dü made no secret of the fact that it was growing tired of hardcore. "We don't just listen to Black Flag, and then that's it," Mould said. "I like listening to a lot of sixties stuff."[33]

Many fans thought the cover of Donovan's "Sunshine Superman" was a tongue-in-cheek inclusion on *Everything Falls Apart*, but Hüsker Dü disabused them of this notion with the soaring psychedelic sound of fuzzed-out guitars on "Diane." This was the direction the band wanted to go. Hüsker Dü had come a long way from *Land Speed Record*, and Hart acknowledged that playing with so many hardcore bands had a dispiriting effect. "When you go on tour and you see a hundred, two hundred bands, and 90% of them sound alike," Hart explained, "it just kind of burns you on listening to any hardcore."[34]

The trio had more than just another record in mind. Again, Mould, Hart, and Norton made no secret of its intention to shake things up. "I think that this summer and this fall, things are really going to change," Mould predicted. "I think people are going to be in for a big surprise."[35]

Hüsker Dü went into the studio at Total Access with loads of new songs, intent on recording a double album. This decision was based on more than just an abundance of material; Hüsker Dü had worked out a narrative that would take the listener on an emotional journey that spanned two discs. In other words, the band had composed a double *concept* album.

Although some punk bands had written records with hard-bitten themes (X's *Los Angeles*) and many hardcore bands espoused ideologies that came across as blunt-force manifestos (Minor Threat's *Out of Step*), no one had pulled off a punk rock concept album, much less a double album full of linked songs that, taken together, told a rich and compelling story.

Zen Arcade (SST 027) is a big, noisy, ambitious album about a young man who sets out on a journey. Each song can be viewed as a chapter of this story, which is divided into three acts. Each act corresponds with the first three sides, with the final side constituting a dramatic and controversial epilogue. Although Hüsker Dü has dropped clues about the album's meaning over the years, those looking for a line-by-line exegesis of this tale won't find one in the lyrics, which were often the most elusive part of the songwriting process for Hüsker Dü. "If we had an easier time with lyrics," Mould confided, "we'd have twenty songs a month, no problem."[36]

No one leaves home without a reason. The opening tracks on Side 1 focus on the courage it takes to put a bad situation behind ("Broken Home, Broken Heart") and how empowering it can be to make a clean break with the past ("Never Talking to You Again"). But things get more challenging for the young protagonist after he leaves home, and he entertains thoughts of joining the military ("Chartered Trips") or a cult ("Hare Krsna")—systems of control that provide the comfort of structure but risk leading him away from his dreams.

Side 2 explores the wild world outside the safety of home ("Beyond the Threshold"), which tries to lure him back with promises of security ("Pride"). He has a very particular dream to create a video game. He lands a dream job developing this project in Silicon Valley, but he can't escape the pull of the past ("The Biggest Lie").

Although Side 2 is far from mellow, on Side 3 things take a chaotic turn for our hero. He throws himself into developing a game called *Search*. The game's title implies that its creator still hasn't found what he's looking for, and his journey continues on a deeper level ("Somewhere"). After his girlfriend overdoses ("Pink Turns to Blue"), he ends up in a sanitarium and questions everything from the state of the world ("Newest Industry") to his own tumultuous past ("Whatever").

Zen Arcade concludes with just two "songs" on Side 4: the galloping "Turn on the News" and "Reocurring Dreams," a sprawling fourteen-minute-long instrumental that returns to motifs expressed on Side 2 in "Dreams Reocurring." While "Turn on the News" suggests a mental patient's interest in returning to the concerns of the world, the shimmering guitars of "Reocurring Dreams" signifies a return to consciousness. Our hero's search was all a dream. Hüsker Dü preferred "to leave things up to people's imaginations instead of making concrete definitions," Mould said. "We didn't want it to be a rock opera."[37]

In interviews the band insisted that what the listener takes away from the song is more important than the songwriter's intentions. *Zen Arcade* is about the games people play in their minds, fantasizing about what their lives might be like if they choose one path over another; then, after summoning the courage to stumble into the unknown, looking back and wondering whether they made the right decision. It's a spin on the old saw that it's the journey that matters, not the destination.

Ultimately, the album functions as an inspiration to those who leave home not because they want to but because it will kill them if they stay. This message comes with a warning: forging your own path will put some distance between you and your past, but you'll never truly leave it behind. *Zen Arcade* isn't asking you to remember your roots or anything so didactically numbskull—that's for the hardcore hooligans who find safety in staying with the herd. Rather, *Zen Arcade* pays tribute to the sacrifice it takes to leave without scorning those who stay. To put it another way, the problem every young person faces is to leave childhood behind and embrace the challenges of navigating the adult world; the realization that comes with adulthood is the impossibility of truly breaking with the past. The genius of *Zen Arcade* is it allows the listener to experience both extremes—yearning for the future and longing for the past—in an intensely realized present.

For an album recorded at the dawn of personal computing, Hüsker Dü's message is weirdly prescient and has never been more relevant than it is today. For the hero of *Zen Arcade*, the wake-up call at the end of the album is a reprieve from a life of staring at screens. Now he, and by default the listener, can choose a different path.

Zen Arcade's power lies in its provocation: you never really escape where you came from, and "waking up" to this reality will put you back on the path to fulfilling your dreams. It's an oddly optimistic message from a band that sounds incredibly angry for much of the album. "People have misconstrued the pessimism and anger in our songs," Mould said. "We're really the opposite of all that; we're not callous, insensitive people. But we're frustrated by the fact that most people seem to end up that way—hopeless, defeated. We're afraid of ending up that way ourselves, and that fear comes out in our songs."[38]

Hüsker Dü recorded and mixed *Zen Arcade* in eighty-five hours over the course of two weeks, with the last forty hours being one marathon mixing session. Spot recalled that the studio's availability was very limited. "After we got the basic tracks," Spot said, "we had to do overdubs in these three- to four-hour blocks that might not have come to us until that day. 'Okay, you've got four hours after midnight.'"[39]

During down time from these sessions, Hüsker Dü hung out in SST's cramped quarters, where the band quickly got on Rollins's nerves. A young musician named David O. Jones, who played in the band Magnolia Thunderpussy and frequently traded tapes with Rollins, received a call from the aggrieved vocalist. "Do you want to come down to SST? Hüsker Dü is here and they're kind of driving me crazy. All they do is play their own live tapes and talk about it." Rollins knew Jones and his friends would appreciate this—and get Hüsker Dü out of his hair—and invited them down to SST. "We were in heaven," Jones said of the experience.[40]

Most of the songs on *Zen Arcade* were recorded in one take, and the ferocious instrumental track that ends the album was recorded live with "no overdubs or funny stuff."[41] Because of the challenges that went into recording *Zen Arcade*, Spot had a different view of the album. "It's a very imperfect record," Spot said. "We had to kind of go with what we knew."[42]

7

With Dukowski no longer in the picture, Black Flag recorded *My War* (SST 023) with Ginn, Rollins, and Stevenson. Ginn played both guitar and bass, crediting "Dale Nixon" as the bass player. This change had a domino effect in the studio. While Ginn's bass lines are clean and precise, Stevenson's sturdy drumming feels almost tentative as he follows Ginn's lead. There's little of the inspired chaos that animated the studio when Dukowski was playing bass. The opening tracks of *My War* were meant to be epic, but compared to the songs captured on the "1982 Demos," they come across as cautious and carefully crafted.

My War's Side 2 signals a radical shift: "Nothing Left Inside," "Three Nights," and "Scream" average more than six minutes each and account for almost half of the album's total playing time. Much like Saint Vitus had done, by slowing down the songs on Side 2, Black Flag achieved a heavier sound full of ominous surges and bottomed-out feedback. "If Black Flag had any sort of bad influence," Ginn said, "I think it's that we influenced a lot of bands to play faster and they just rushed into it, whereas we practiced relentlessly every night, to build up our songs faster and faster, but with the full power behind them. And I always thought it was a mistake for bands to just jump right to a fast speed and lose the feel of the music because they want to be fast."[43]

The production doesn't do Rollins any favors, especially on tracks like "Three Nights," where he sounds like he's trapped in a closet, but the slower pace of songs like "Nothing Left Inside" provides a soundscape where it's impossible to ignore the intensity of the performance. "I love 'Nothing Left Inside,'" Stevenson said. "I think it's just a beautiful song. What Henry did to that song is beautiful. It's a ballad."[44]

Black Flag was fond of antagonizing the parochial punk rockers who came to shows demanding to hear "Wasted" or "Six Pack." "Scream" started out as the trudge riff—a slow, plodding jam the band used to enforce the pace of the show and display its dominance over the crowd. "We had a very confrontational stage vibe," Stevenson said. "I'm not saying we brought it upon ourselves, it just wasn't an inviting setting. There was a wall up and we were trying to play through the audience rather than to the audience."[45]

Black Flag's confrontational demeanor made the band unique to promoters like Stuart Swezey. "Messing with your own audience is something I've never seen anyone do. Maybe I'm wrong, maybe Frank Zappa did it in his way. But I really felt like Black Flag through the releases on SST, the tours they put together, the way they presented themselves, were continually challenging their audience."[46]

That tension was a part of the band's live show, but Dukowski's exit eradicated it from the studio, and it shows on *My War*. The ultimate irony—some might say injustice—is that Dukowski doesn't play on the album named after a song he wrote. *My War* was supposed to be the distillation of everything Black Flag had been working toward, but it was hamstrung by forces inside and outside the band. Part of the problem, Carducci explained, was that while

Damaged had two guitarists playing songs written for one, *My War* has just one guitarist playing songs written for two.[47] "*My War* is a really fucked-up record," Carducci said.[48]

The album was mixed and sent off to Rainbo Records to be pressed as quickly as possible so it would be ready in time for Black Flag's tour. But first the band needed to find a new bass player.

8

Kira Roessler came of age in the LA punk scene. Her brother, Paul, had been a member of the Screamers—one of the most exciting and inventive bands to come out of LA. She was also part of the crowd that frequented the Masque and the infamous Canterbury Apartments. She played bass with her brother in Waxx, with Nicky Beat of the Weirdos in the Monsters, and with Pat Smear (and her brother again) in Twisted Roots. Her up-and-down experiences in these bands instilled in her a more pragmatic view toward the music business, and she pursued a degree in economics and system science at UCLA.

Toward the end of 1983, Roessler was jamming with her brother, who had been enlisted to play in D.C. 3, the band Cadena formed after leaving Black Flag. D.C. 3 rehearsed in the same practice space Black Flag was using, and it didn't take long for Ginn to notice Roessler's talent and invite her to join Black Flag. After a quick negotiation—Roessler insisted on finishing up at UCLA—Black Flag had its newest member.

But Roessler was hardly an outsider. She'd partied at the Church during the band's infancy, and after seeing Black Flag perform as a five-piece unit, it became her favorite band. Although she and Rollins had briefly dated and parted on less than amicable terms, they committed to not letting their past differences get in the way of playing together.

Roessler's tenure got off to a rocky start. During her first week in the band, she seriously injured her hand while practicing "Nothing Left Inside." She immediately knew that something was very wrong and went to the hospital. The doctor told her not to play for six weeks; she was back in the practice room in four days, causing permanent damage. "That was my choice,"

Roessler said. "They would have let me not play. They said take whatever time you need. My ego wouldn't let me do it."[49] Roessler knew that because of her gender she would be judged differently, and she refused to give up. She needed to prove to herself and to her new bandmates that she could get the job done no matter what the cost.

Roessler pushed through the pain, which would have lasting consequences. Rollins was impressed with how quickly she learned the songs, but Ginn insisted on extensive rehearsals to prepare for the My War Tour. Roessler went back to work and locked in with Stevenson. "I never really got to know her until she was in the band," Stevenson said. "And then we got to know each other quickly because we were all kind of living like sardines. You become best friends or worst enemies. We became best friends."[50]

During the grueling rehearsal sessions that went on for months, the two got into a groove that bolstered the rhythm section and created a solid platform for Ginn's guitar. But learning *My War* was just the first skirmish. Now she'd have to bring the battle to the people.

Saint Vitus at Club Lingerie, July 6, 1984. Henry Rollins looks on (*bottom right*). (Photo by Wild Don Lewis.)

9

The year 1984 was shaping up to be huge for SST. The turmoil of the Unicorn years was finally behind the label, and SST was ready to unleash one of the most impressive runs by an American independent music label: Saint Vitus's debut in February, Black Flag's *My War* in March, *Meat Puppets II* (SST 019) in April, Hüsker Dü's *Zen Arcade* in July, and a new album from the Minutemen—whenever they finished writing it.

For Ginn, another milestone loomed. In June he would turn thirty, which was ancient by punk and hardcore standards, though these were measuring sticks that Ginn no longer had much use for. With Dukowski's departure, Black Flag was Ginn's to run as he saw fit. In the early days, it was Dukowski who insisted on a strict practice schedule and who indoctrinated new members in the band's way of doing things. Now it was up to Ginn to guide the ship, so to speak.

Ginn had a different way of doing things. Although he could be easygoing and affable, especially when meeting people for the first time, he was extremely serious when it came to rehearsing and recording. There was nothing Ginn enjoyed more than playing guitar, and he would routinely wear his bandmates out during never-ending practice sessions.

Ginn had big plans for both Black Flag and SST. Not only did Black Flag have a new record to promote, but Ginn was sitting on a surplus of songs he'd written and was eager to record. Even after releasing all the material that had been accumulating since 1981, SST had a backlog of records. Ginn knew he couldn't do everything he wanted to do, with both the label and the band, without sacrificing precious rehearsal time. SST was in good hands with Carducci and Mugger, who was now taking business classes at night, but they had more than they could handle. Ginn needed help from someone he could trust. "He could invent things and make things," Mugger said, "but he really had no one to implement what he wanted to do."[51]

Ginn turned to Dukowski, who had recently returned from a trip to his family home in Germany after his grandmother had passed away. He went overseas to help clean her house and clear his mind. Dukowski's mother was German, and he'd been to his maternal homeland several times. The trip had a restorative effect on Dukowski, and he returned to the South Bay with a fresh perspective and some notions about getting his old band back together and possibly starting a new one. But Ginn had other ideas.

Instead of turning his back on the past (as he had with Morris and Reyes), Ginn created a new role for Dukowski (as he had with Cadena). Ginn approached his ex-bandmate and asked him whether he'd be interested in staying with the label and running its touring operations. Dukowski accepted.

SST's first order of business was to find a bigger space for the label. Pettibon had rented a two-story office building on Artesia Boulevard in Redondo Beach for use as a studio, which he agreed to share with SST. Black Flag turned the back end of the studio into a rehearsal space soundproofed with layers of carpet. Dukowski set up his booking operation upstairs: Global and Nixon Management, though everyone referred to it as Global, short for global domination. Dukowski, Ginn, and Rollins had desks upstairs, while Davo, who helped retrofit Pettibon's studio, and the road crew, which now included Tom Troccoli, attended to the gear downstairs.

Carducci and Mugger remained in the Phelan office. Although it was unusual having the business in two separate locations, they were only a block apart, and everyone initially benefitted from the extra breathing room.

While Roessler and Stevenson locked into a groove during daily marathon practice sessions, Dukowski went to work on booking the longest string of dates in Black Flag's history, including a spring tour, a European tour, and a fall tour that stretched into the following year. To promote *My War*, Black Flag was planning an all-out assault. The band's attitude—and its language—became more warlike. "Kill Everyone Now was the agenda," Rollins declared in his journals. "KEN mode all the time."[52] "We've been preparing for a couple years," Ginn said, "and now we're gonna go into 'attack' phase."[53]

10

Hüsker Dü's *Zen Arcade* seemed destined to become one of the most influential albums of its era. Just ask the Minutemen.

After the trio from San Pedro heard the latest record from its labelmates, the Minutemen scrapped its plans for a new album, which the band had recorded with Ethan James at Radio Tokyo the previous November. The Minutemen were so blown away by the ambition of *Zen Arcade*, Boon, Hurley, and Watt wanted *their* next record to be a double album too. SST gave the band the green light, and the Minutemen immediately started writing more material.

The Minutemen went back to the studio in April 1984 to record more songs, but the masterpiece that is *Double Nickels on the Dime* (SST 028) didn't emerge until the album was sequenced. The Minutemen laid out all of the songs like a potluck, and each member took turns selecting his favorite dish until his plate was full. The songs that were left over were put on the album's final side. It was an artful if idiosyncratic way to assemble a record. To Watt, at least, it seemed obvious that the band had borrowed this approach from Pink Floyd's *Ummagumma*.

Although *Double Nickels on the Dime* lacks a concept per se, it does have an organizing principle: cars. Each member's side opens with the sound of the engine of his car turning over, preparing the listener for a musical journey. This motif extends to the elaborate in-joke of the album's title: a reference to the Sammy Hagar song "I Can't Drive 55," a low point in the story of rock and roll as a vehicle for teenage disobedience. "So to wear red leather and say that you can't drive 55," Watt explained, "like that's the big rebellion....[T]o us, the big rebellion thing was writing your own fuckin' songs and trying to come up with your own story, your own picture, your own book, whatever."[54]

Hagar may not have been able to drive fifty-five, but Watt could, and he proved it on the album cover with a photo of him driving down the 10 toward San Pedro at exactly fifty-five miles per hour, double nickels on the dime.

Like Hüsker Dü, the Minutemen had an easier time writing songs than coming up with lyrics, so Watt, Boon, and Hurley reached out for help from their friends: Dukowski, Rollins, Brewer and Baiza of Saccharine Trust, and even Carducci contributed lyrics to the album, with Carducci's "Jesus and Tequila" being a fan favorite.

Double Nickels on the Dime is a mishmash of melodious bass lines, frenetic guitar solos, haunting instrumentals, political spiels, found poetry, ruminations on language, and commentary on the fractious scene. But the effect of these disparate elements is one of convergence rather than collision. While the album is a testament to the Minutemen's exploration in style and sound, Boon's trebly guitar riffs, Watt's prominent bass groove, and Hurley's relentless drumming are instantly recognizable. It's a record no one but the Minutemen could have made.

The Minutemen were never accepted by the Masque crowd in Hollywood or embraced by the hardcore kids in the exurbs. Most people didn't know what to do with the band's short songs and unusual lingo. Members of the Minutemen were often derided as "Martians from planet jazz," Watt said.[55] This gave them the freedom to come into their own as musicians and as a band. The forty-five songs on *Double Nickels on the Dime* constitute a statement that reclaims punk rock as art.

Watt's "Do You Want New Wave or Do You Want the Truth?" repudiates the way commercial forces stunted the punk movement's creativity by applying labels and imposing limits on what it could and couldn't be. For many bands, a song of this nature would call for an anthem with a rousing call-and-response chorus, but that wasn't the Minutemen's style. "I purposely wrote 'New Wave' to be a calmer one," Watt said, "to take us down a little bit. But it really ain't a ballad—in some ways, it's one of the most angry songs."[56]

Like Hüsker Dü, the Minutemen had discovered that sometimes the most effective way to get the message across was to eliminate the noise around it. The autobiographical "History Lesson—Part II," which pays tribute to the band's heroes and is perhaps the best-known tune on the album, has all the ferocity of a campfire song.

Prior to recording *Double Nickels on the Dime*, Watt had read James Joyce's *Ulysses*, and the sprawling modernist novel stayed with him and inspired his own creativity. Watt loved the book.[57] Comparing the trials and tribulations of a common workingman to the heroes of the past in a way that was stylistically innovative and artistically unprecedented was massively appealing to him. *Ulysses* has a reputation for being impenetrable, a book people start but don't finish, but Joyce's masterpiece is full of fucking, fighting, drinking, and singing. It's a work of high art *and* a celebration of the ordinary lives of ordinary people. This notion that art could be both, that it could in fact be many things, is the hallmark of *Double Nickels on the Dime.* "Just finishing the book at that time and getting ready to record," Watt said of reading *Ulysses*, "I was *inspired*. With songwriting, you could talk about anything!"[58]

The lessons for Watt were clear. Elevate your own experience into art and don't shy away from the ugly parts. (This was one area where Pettibon, who turned Watt on to *Ulysses*, didn't need any encouragement.) Why limit yourself to one style, one approach, one viewpoint, when you can make a record that encompasses all of it? "It seemed to me then, and still does now," Watt said of Joyce's *Ulysses*, "that he was trying to write about everything. And in a way the Minutemen were trying to do the same."[59]

Watt pays tribute to *Ulysses* with a song, an instrumental called "June 16th." The song is like a conversation between the bass, the guitar, and the drums, a testament to the sharing of ideas and the constant flow of creativity between the Minutemen. Because June 16 is both the day on which *Ulysses* takes place and Pettibon's birthday, it's also a salute to the visual artist whose work adorns the interior of the cover. Just as the publication of *Ulysses* heralded the arrival of a new kind of novel, *Double Nickels on the Dime* signaled a shift in the rock and roll landscape and immediately created a stir.

11

With all the excitement surrounding the new records from Hüsker Dü and the Minutemen, one can forgive the Meat Puppets for feeling slighted.

The Phoenix trio had recorded the follow-up to its debut a full year before *Meat Puppets II* was finally released, during which time Black Flag's *My War* was fast-tracked and Hüsker Dü and the Minutemen completed their epic albums. "It was hard getting *Meat Puppets II* out in the first place," Bostrom said. "We recorded the damn thing in the spring of '83. And somehow could not arrange to schedule a mix session for like six months. In the meantime, the Hüskers were in there getting their record done. And for some reason, they just weren't following up with us to get the record finished after we had recorded the tracks. We were frustrated by that."[60]

At least the Meat Puppets didn't have to wait as long as Saint Vitus, whose debut album was finally released in February 1984—eighteen months after it was recorded. Perhaps the delay of *Meat Puppets II* was attributable to SST not quite knowing what to make of the new record from the desert rockers. The album ranges from screeching countrified hardcore to melodious acoustic tracks whose lyrics feel like dispatches from the outer limits of an acid trip. The country and western aspects were the hardest to place since the only person at SST who had an appreciation for the genre was Carducci, who would listen to country music when he was alone in the office and had a soft spot for westerns. Was it possible the new record was some kind of elaborate joke? What the hell were the Meat Puppets up to?

All one has to do is listen to the ebullient yowl at the end of "Lost" to know the band was serious and sincere. The Meat Puppets' blend of fast romps and slow ballads was filtered through a love of Neil Young's fusion of rock and Americana, and the Grateful Dead's extended improvisational jams. The result was an album that could serve as a soundtrack for one of Carducci's beloved acid westerns. From the majestic soundscape at the end of "Plateau" to the visionary frenzy of "Lake of Fire," which Curt wrote while tripping on acid, *Meat Puppets II* shimmers with terrifying beauty.

With everything that was going on with the label, SST probably wasn't expecting the Meat Puppets' strange and disarming new album to catch the attention of the national press, but it did. Kurt Loder of *Rolling Stone* called *Meat Puppets II* "one of the funniest and most enjoyable albums of 1984."[61] Joe Sasfy of the *Washington Post* said it was "one of the most impressive and thoroughly American releases of the year."[62]

The Meat Puppets' new record caught listeners off guard. So did *My War*, but many critics found Black Flag's long-awaited follow-up to *Damaged* off-putting and strange. Because Black Flag and the Meat Puppets were touring together, many reviewers tasked with writing about these bands when they rolled into town made no secret of their disappointment in Black Flag's latest. Sasfy's characterization of the songs as "droning pieces that embrace the dirge-like somberness of Birthday Party and other dismal nihilists" was typical of *My War* reviews—when it was reviewed at all.[63]

The members of Black Flag weren't nihilists, but they weren't making music with the "funny" and "enjoyable" qualities that *Rolling Stone* admired in the Meat Puppets' music. Black Flag had done that with songs like "Six Pack" and "TV Party," and they weren't doing it anymore. Meanwhile, the Meat Puppets had recorded its latest record while loaded on MDMA, which a chemistry professor friend had made for them. *Meat Puppets II's* quirky lyrics, upbeat picking, and out-of-tune-but-I-don't-care crooning made for an engaging listening experience. Loder was right: it's a fun record. The same cannot be said of *My War*.

The attention the Meat Puppets received caused an unusual reaction in Black Flag: jealousy. They made their displeasure known to the Meat Puppets with disparaging comments, which heightened tension between the bands. "They seemed to be serious about their music," Rollins said of the Meat Puppets, "but at the same time, not."[64] He was even less charitable in his journals: "The Meat Puppets are a great band but they are children."[65]

Bostrom bristled at this characterization. While it was true the Meat Puppets did not like the way Black Flag toured, finding it "grueling and authoritarian," Bostrom didn't think the members of Black Flag were particularly open minded about how things should be done. "I don't give a fuck what anyone thought about me, my band, my bandmates, or my trip," Bostrom said.[66]

The tour got off to a rough start when the Meat Puppets discovered the band was expected not only to play for basically nothing but to help load in and out every night as well. "They were grievously offended that we didn't care for the terms, especially Chuck," Bostrom recalled. "Chuck found it offensive that we actually wanted to get paid to do shows. And it just goes to show what kind of pressure they were under, how poor the cash flow was."[67]

In addition to the Meat Puppets, Black Flag also brought Nig-Heist with them on the My War Tour, a lineup seemingly designed to provoke the audience. First, Nig-Heist took the stage with its spectacularly offensive blend of cock rock and performance art that walked the line between comedy and misogyny. Somehow Nig-Heist's performances were even more offensive than its name. Mugger regularly performed nude or in women's lingerie. In Denver he and Black Flag roadie Tom Troccoli were arrested for simulating anal sex.

The Meat Puppets fared no better. Curt Kirkwood's hair was longer than anyone's in Black Flag or Nig-Heist, wigs included. He was routinely castigated by the crowd as a "hippie" and a "fag," which only intensified once the Meat Puppets started playing fifteen-minute-long Grateful Dead covers. Fans showed their appreciation by showering the band with spit. *"Hundreds of loogies a night,"* Curt complained. "It was hideous."[68]

Curt seemed to take perverse pleasure in antagonizing the crowd. Though he may not have looked intimidating with his long hair and skinny frame, he was fearless on stage. He didn't back down from the punks in the audience, and he was not above using his guitar as a weapon.

Roessler, who loved the Meat Puppets, felt bad about the abuse they were subjected to night after night by Black Flag's fans. But Black Flag had its own problems, with everyone from critics in the media to kids at the shows reacting poorly to Side 2, which the band sometimes played in its entirety. Fans who were expecting a night of hardcore heaped abuse on the band. Roessler, being the newest member and the only woman, received more than her share.

Despite the negative vibes from the audience, Black Flag was firing on all cylinders again. Roessler and Stevenson were an indomitable rhythm section, and Ginn seized the platform created by Dukowski's vacancy to show the world what he and his Dan Armstrong guitar could do. "I mean, it's got no tone," Troccoli said of Greg's choice of instrument. "It's the deadest guitar ever invented. And yet somehow or another he made that thing roar. He made it work. Dez tried that guitar, I tried that guitar, everybody else I know who tried that guitar only made it go 'plink plink plink.' Greg made it sound like a damn 747."[69]

Although Ginn rewired the guitar and replaced the bridge and the pickups, not even he could say how he was able to achieve his signature sound, but he believed the density of the Lucite was a contributing factor. Ginn maintained it was the passion of the player and not any particular technique that made the difference. "It's not something you can learn—or explain. What makes me different as guitar player is the intensity of feeling that I put into it. I'm not really conscious of my technique. I'll look at my hands and suddenly realize I'm muting this or that string. All of my playing is based on intuition and improvisation."[70]

Not everyone who came out for the My War Tour was disappointed by

Black Flag's new direction. In Seattle, Kim Thayil, Mark Arm, and Kurt Cobain (i.e., future members of Soundgarden, Mudhoney, and Nirvana, respectively) were all in the audience to see Black Flag and the Meat Puppets.[71] Thayil recalled that the crowd really didn't like Nig-Heist, which was nothing new. But if there was an ideal audience for *My War*'s Side 2, it was the Northwest. In punk outposts in Portland, Tacoma, Seattle, and Vancouver where the kids had never been told they had to throw away their Led Zeppelin records, Black Flag's sturdy rhythms and relentless riffage made sense. "We were really into following what Black Flag was doing," Arm said of the band's influence on his band, Green River. "So we were kind of slowing down and getting heavier and trying out some new things."[72]

What stood out to musicians like Thayil was the tempo. "I just remembered this slow heavy change," Thayil said of Black Flag during the My War Tour, "that coincided with the Melvins going from the fastest band of the Northwest to the slowest band in the Northwest. Those two moves: the Melvins slowing down and Black Flag slowing down on *My War* kind of signaled a new direction. Plus, Saint Vitus came out in '84."[73]

Also in attendance that evening was Bruce Pavitt. The future cofounder of Sub Pop Records hosted a radio show in Seattle and had Henry Rollins on as a guest. When he characterized Black Flag's new sound as heavy metal, Rollins corrected him, saying it was "heavy mental."[74]

Rollins was peaking as a performer, flexing his muscles both physically and mentally. In addition to the steady diet of transgressive literature, Rollins began experimenting with LSD. To his associates at SST, it sometimes seemed as though Rollins lacked an off switch. He was always on, always intense. He unnerved strangers and exhausted those who had to deal with him all the time.

Because LSD didn't carry the same stigma as other drugs, it was accepted at SST and—in the case of Rollins—encouraged. Dukowski, who was no stranger to psychedelic excursions under the influence of "laughing Sam's dice," recommended the drug to Rollins as a form of personal growth. Throughout the My War Tour, Rollins took LSD either in the company of

Davo and Troccoli while riding in the van or with Ginn, who would also partake, while performing onstage.

The place where Rollins's LSD experiments had the greatest impact was on the page. Instead of grimly setting down things that happened to him or reflecting on his tormented past, his prose exploded with violent imagery and scenes of unrelenting carnage. The anger and animosity that came to the surface on the stage during a Black Flag performance was just the beginning of a bottomless cauldron of rage that Rollins poured into his journals.

The Meat Puppets were also fond of psychedelics. But some members of the Meat Puppets didn't draw the line at LSD and experimented with harder drugs, which Ginn could not abide, especially when these activities impacted the itinerary. But the frustration ran both ways. Ginn was now smoking marijuana on a regular basis, which the Meat Puppets took credit for. "They were able to explore their nascent interest in weed through us," Bostrom said. "When we first started hanging out with them, they weren't really smoking a lot of pot. But afterwards, slowly but surely, they began to. Not all of them, but some of them."[75]

In addition, Goldenvoice promoter Gary Tovar turned Ginn onto quality strains of weed, and the Grateful Dead–loving guitarist became an acolyte of the green leaf. Some members, including Rollins and Stevenson, never touched it. Pervasive surveillance and routine harassment by the police had made abstaining from recreational drugs a necessity—especially while the band was touring. Black Flag was too busy and too broke to add drug charges to the long list of hassles the band encountered while driving from one club to the next. Although things calmed down as the hardcore movement petered out, the police continued to monitor Black Flag. "They would come and kind of shake down our practice rooms," Stevenson recalled. "They'd even come in when we were gone on tour. They'd basically vacate us out of our practice room. We'd come back and none of our shit would be there."[76]

When drug use became a regular part of the operation, a culture of paranoia and suspicion, which had been in the background from beginning, blossomed. Some members, Rollins in particular, found it more difficult to communicate with Ginn, putting added strain on their relationship.

But the difficulties weren't just about drugs. The Meat Puppets never really knew where the band stood with SST. Record stores couldn't keep *Meat Puppets II* on the shelves, but there were always plenty of Black Flag records in stock. Did SST fail to press enough copies of *Meat Puppets II*? Or was *My War* not selling as well as the new Meat Puppets record? On the road, it was impossible to know.

Bostrom had jokingly told an interviewer for a fanzine that they weren't into Black Flag and were only using the label for promotion. The two bands had been dissing each other in jest on the air and in the press since 1982, but this time Ginn and Dukowski were genuinely upset. "We were in Pittsburgh," Bostrom recalled, "and they got in touch with us via phone saying, 'Well, given the things that Bostrom said in the interview, I don't think you guys are down with the SST program enough for us to want to take a chance with you in Europe.' And we were crushed. Of course, Curt was like, 'Fuck you, Bostrom.' And I was like, 'No, fuck them.'"[77]

Originally, Hüsker Dü was scheduled to go to Europe with Black Flag, but when the band backed out, Black Flag broached the idea with the Meat Puppets, who were all for it. But after the kerfuffle over the interview, Black Flag took Nig-Heist instead. When it came to SST, the Meat Puppets were always on the outside looking in.

Bob and Curt during the Tour. (Photo by Naomi Petersen Photography.)

CHAPTER 7
SST vs. College Radio

1984–1985

1

The Meat Puppets wasn't the Grateful Dead, the Minutemen wasn't Pink Floyd, and Hüsker Dü wasn't the Who, but the albums they released in the spring and summer of 1984 immediately caught the attention of disc jockeys at independent radio stations around the country who subsequently exposed the bands to a new audience: college students.

Long before the terms "indie" and "alternative" were used by music critics to describe bands that typically cruised under their radar, the label "college radio" was used to describe underground music sought by young listeners in their late teens and early twenties. Because this label was applied to bands as diverse as Black Flag, the Violent Femmes, and R.E.M., it wasn't the most useful descriptor, but it was a way for the industry to track the growing interest in independent music, which was challenging to classify but appealed to a growing number of listeners.

The *College Music Journal* began in 1978 as a bi-weekly publication and by 1982 had evolved into the *CMJ New Music Report* that published lists of popular songs played on college radio stations around the country. It was a great way for radio stations, many of which were run by college students, to report on the records that received airplay while getting recognition for their work. SST was one of the first indie labels to capitalize on what it correctly surmised as an essential tool for promoting its artists.

While college radio typically wasn't a driver for record sales, getting songs played on college radio stations made it easier for Global to book shows and get records reviewed in newspapers in those particular cities. Although shipping albums out to radio stations could be expensive, it was another way for SST to generate exposure for its bands.

Hardcore was a tough sell, but Hüsker Dü's pop dissonance, the Meat Puppets' acid twang, and the Minutemen's non sequitur eruptions found listeners at college radio stations. A disc jockey for KXLU at Loyola Marymount University called the Minutemen "the Led Zeppelin of college radio."[1]

Few capitalized on this more than Hüsker Dü, constantly on the move with pop hooks and catchy melodies that energized critics and fans alike. For many college radio stations, Hüsker Dü was the perfect antidote to the afterburn of hardcore: a band that could play loud and fast in a format that was easier on the ear.

Not all college radio stations were alike. Some, such as KAOS 89.3 FM in Olympia, Washington, had a strict policy that 80 percent of all music broadcast had to come from independent artists regardless of genre. Other stations, like WGTB on the campus of Georgetown University in Washington, DC, were subject to intense oversight. Navigating the constant turnover at these student-run radio stations was costly and time consuming. Carducci recognized that staying on top of this emerging platform was a full-time job and started looking for someone he could bring into the fold.

2

Black Flag returned from its European tour in June and immediately went into the studio to record material for its third and fourth studio albums:

Family Man (SST 026) and *Slip It In* (SST 029). The latter was recorded first during a manic forty-eight-hour block. By then all eight songs that would appear on *Slip It In* had been road-tested on the first two legs of the My War Tour, and the band had the material down cold.

The musicianship is solid, impeccable even, and the album offers a variety of styles from the stop-start cacophony of "Wound Up" to the repetitious sludge of "Rat's Eyes"—both of which feature lyrics by Rollins. In "Rat's Eyes" Ginn's guitar deconstructs the song and strips it down to its most rudimentary components while Rollins takes repetition to the extreme. The lyrics rearrange the same three dozen words to the point of redundancy.

Side 2 opens with the instrumental "Obliteration," a muddy jazz-inflected showcase for Ginn's guitar. Where *My War* showed a clear split between Black Flag's punk past and experimental future, *Slip It In* represents a departure from the genre altogether. But *Slip It In* is defined by its title track: a six-minute spew of thinly disguised misogyny. Ostensibly, the song is about women who use their status in monogamous relationships as cover for what they *really* want: to sleep with members of the band. It's not a song about being true to one's self and acting on natural desires. Rather, the narrator of the song takes umbrage with this deception and lambasts these women for their hypocrisy. "Slip It In" isn't a dark fantasy but a sexist complaint that champions coercion and tramples consent. Ginn's exemplary guitar on "Slip It In" is wasted on a song that sinks to disappointing lows.

SST paired the album with Pettibon's illustration of a nun clinging to a man's hairy, naked leg. "Nobody knows more than I that the less girls know the better they are likely to be," the caption reads. Whether he intended it or not, Pettibon's art serves as a commentary on the title track that didn't sit well with Roessler. "There was a moment when I wondered why the first record that a woman played on with them would have that cover," Roessler reflected many years later.[2]

A video for "Slip It In," which starred *We Got Power* cofounder Jordan Schwartz as a horned-up teacher in a classroom full of young women, was shot, edited, and codirected by seventeen-year-old Dave Travis. Travis used gear he inherited from his father, who was a cameraman for the news. "It was all my equipment," Travis said. "We were just figuring it out as we go."[3] The shoot was recorded in the same room where Ginn's father taught at Harbor College.

"Slip It In" had been part of Black Flag's set since 1982, and the version the band recorded with Ginn and Cadena is one of the highlights of the "1982 Demos." Ginn likely thought it was the best of the previously unreleased tracks and would be familiar to fans who had been coming to see them the past few years.

Things were getting more complicated around SST. In early July, *Zen Arcade* and *Double Nickels on the Dime* were released on the same day. A dual release meant double the work for Mugger, Carducci, and whomever they could scare up to help, but because both releases were double albums, it meant quadruple the labor. Schwartz, who was helping Dukowski at Global to book shows, and Black Flag roadies Davo and Troccoli would pitch in at the SST office when needed. Sometimes Boon and Watt, who went by the name "Spaceman" when cold calling record stores, would drive up from San Pedro. But what SST needed most was more space for all the records it was producing. SST finally moved out of the Phelan office and into a garage apartment three-quarters of a mile south on Ralston Lane in Redondo Beach. The apartment sat behind the house of another member of the Ginn clan: Greg's sister Linda Flynn.

Finally, Mugger could hire real employees: people on the fringes of the scene who could be counted on to help manage the label in a professional manner. The first person Mugger called was Linda Kite, who was dating Boon. Kite was a college student and activist with a knack for organizing, but her plate was full, so she recommended her younger sister Jeanine Garfias. Mugger made Garfias SST's first paid employee, and she immediately took over the mail-order operation.

But SST didn't stay in Redondo Beach for long: this time they moved several miles north to 14147 Hawthorne Boulevard, and Carducci moved into the garage apartment left vacant. After all the years of SST's existence, the label was finally headquartered at the edge of a town that fans from all over the world knew by heart: Lawndale, California. The new office was located in a small plaza just north of Rosecrans Avenue—due east of Manhattan Beach.

While the label hustled to find space to accommodate the growing catalog, Black Flag and Global stayed put in Redondo Beach to prepare for the blitz of releases. Whenever SST needed new artwork from Pettibon, Ginn would send Stevenson to the Ginn residence where the artist worked seemingly round the clock. "Ray would just be sitting in that chair in his living room and there would be art just everywhere," Stevenson said. "I mean everywhere on the floor. He'd go, 'Oh, there's those over there' and there'd be like a pile of stuff in the corner on the floor."[4]

Stevenson brought the illustrations back to Global and the crew pored over the drawings, deciding which ones they'd use. Trying to choose the most disturbing Pettibon illustration is like trying to pick the least creepy member of the Manson family, but *Family Man*'s depiction of a man holding a gun to his head after murdering his family is exceptionally disturbing.

Family Man was Black Flag's most experimental album and a harbinger of things to come. Unless you were a fan of Ken Nordine and the Fred Katz Group, an album that was half spoken word, half instrumental would be weird in any year, but it was especially strange in 1984. Rollins's tales of murder and annihilation bore little resemblance to *Word Jazz*, and Black Flag's Ornette-Coleman-by-way-of-Black-Sabbath-influenced instrumentals weren't exactly easy listening.

The first side collects several of Rollins's early spoken word performances—most notably the title track, which first aired on KCRW during Deidre O'Donoghue's show SNAP, which stood for Saturday Night Avant Pop. When Rollins asks at the beginning of the track which bit he should read, it's O'Donoghue who provides the answer.[5] "Salt on a Slug" captures a live performance at a popular reading series at Bebop Records in Reseda, and "Shed Reading (Rattus Norvegicus)" is a home recording Rollins made in the "shed" behind the Ginns' house where he stayed between tours, which was actually Regis Ginn's book-lined study. Rollins rounds out the side with "Armageddon Man," a long, rambling piece written in the style of one of the many alter egos from his journal. Throughout the reading, Ginn, Stevenson, and Roessler pile on top of Rollins and each other with their instruments, and at times it sounds as if each performer is playing their own version of the song.

If Side 1 of *Family Man* left Black Flag fans scratching their heads, the four instrumental tracks on Side 2 really weirded them out. Instrumentals weren't anything new. During the My War Tour, Black Flag frequently opened with an instrumental number and occasionally used the bizarrely titled "I Won't Stick Any of You Unless and Until I Can Stick All of You!" as a kind of interlude, during which Rollins kept himself occupied by joining Stevenson behind the kit and whacking on floor toms and cymbals.

Side 1 of *Family Man* showcases Henry Rollins's enthusiasm for spoken word, and while it's tempting to say that Side 2 serves the same purpose for Ginn and his guitar, it actually makes a statement about Ginn's artistic intentions and represents a critical moment in the history of Black Flag. *My War's* Side 2 was a shot across the bow; *Family Man* is Ginn's declaration of hardcore as a musical dead end.

Bill Stevenson at UCLA in 1984. (Photo by Linda Aronow.)

Family Man stands as a testament to Ginn's willingness to push the boundaries of rock and roll regardless of a record's commercial viability. The album makes a courageous statement, but it suffers from an overall lack of quality. Rollins's spoken word performances are the work of a young writer finding his voice. His presence and command don't come through on the record. *Family Man* fails to capture what it was like to be in the room when Rollins was onstage.

Although "Armageddon Man" attempts to bridge the two sides, *Family Man* tells the story of two artists with very different agendas. Were Ginn and Rollins trying to demonstrate they didn't need the other? Were the two artists competing with each other? If so, it was a one-sided competition. After Dukowski's departure from Black Flag, no one in the band enjoyed equal footing with Ginn. It was his band, his show, his rules.

3

"Carducci wants another album already," the liner notes of *Zen Arcade* declared.[6] He didn't have to wait long for Hüsker Dü to deliver. By the time *Zen Arcade* hit record store shelves in July, Hüsker Dü was ready to record its follow-up, but it wasn't the same band that had cranked out a double album in two weeks. Hüsker Dü was enjoying some success but was confronted by many of the same issues the Meat Puppets had experienced: the new record was receiving favorable press, but fans couldn't find it on the shelves.

Hüsker Dü rolled up to an appearance at a record store that didn't have copies of *Zen Arcade*. The band quickly threw together a flyer and had it printed so the band members would have something to autograph for the fans. The problem was particularly irksome because so much time had passed since the recording session at Total Access the previous October. This delay was partly attributable to SST's desire to release *Zen Arcade* and *Double Nickels on the Dime* on the same day. SST had only printed five thousand copies of *Zen Arcade* and wasn't able to replenish inventory until September. "We had warned them that this was going to be an important record and that they needed to press up more copies than usual," Mould said. "They were not at all prepared for what was happening."[7]

SST's press release touted *Zen Arcade* as "the most important and rele-vant double album to be released since the Beatles' *White Album*." However, outside of the Twin Cities, Hüsker Dü was still operating in the shadow of its best-known record, *Land Speed Record*, which had sold approximately ten thousand copies. At the peak of its speed-enhanced, ultrafast sound, the band boasted it could play the entire album in twelve minutes. Although Hüsker Dü was light years removed from that frenzied pace, critics insisted on sticking the band with the hardcore label long after it had weeded out songs from its set, such as "Bricklayer" and "Tired of Doing Things," that Mould referred to as "hardcore dog-pleasers."[8] "I stopped writing songs for people with mohawks two and a half years ago," Hart said. "I started writing songs for myself."[9]

Those who were taken by surprise by Hüsker Dü's pop sensibilities simply weren't paying attention. Back in March, indie rock sensation R.E.M., whose record *Murmur* was hailed as one of the best albums of 1983, invited Hüsker Dü to play a gig at Harvard University and the following night did a secret set with Hüsker Dü at the Rat in Boston. A few weeks later, SST released a single of Hüsker Dü's cover of the Byrds' "Eight Miles High" (SST 025), a song about a flight to England that was so widely misunderstood it was banned from commercial radio for its presumed drug references. Hüsker Dü's version is faster and more ferocious than the original and fits *Zen Arcade*'s concept of voyaging into the unknown.

It was clear to those who came to see Hüsker Dü play that it was no longer a hardcore band, but shedding the stigma proved more difficult. Hardcore punk was sustained by rigidly enforced aesthetics, a kind of purity test that determined whether you were in or out. To leave hardcore could only mean one thing: you were selling out. Hüsker Dü responded in typical fashion: if you think *Zen Arcade* is a sellout, wait until to you hear our *next* record. "We change our attitude every two weeks about things," Mould admitted. "One week we'll feel real experimental, like 'fuck the world, we're so avant-garde you'll never figure it out.' Then two weeks later we turn around and write like five pop songs."[10]

Despite the constant reinvention, Hüsker Dü's lineup remained intact for the entirety of the band's existence. Yet music journalists were still trying to pin Hüsker Dü to the mat and tag it with labels the band had outgrown. This proved as fruitless as trying to dissect a frog while it's still alive: it makes a mess and upsets the frog.

Hüsker Dü was in a curious position. The band was at least two records ahead of its fans. Mould, Hart, and Norton were almost compulsively creative and continually on the verge on recording or releasing a new album. Every time the band got together to practice, the trio would develop new songs and incorporate them into the set. Hüsker Dü didn't go into the studio with raw material but with songs that had been polished and perfected on the road.

After testing out material for the new record all spring and summer, the trio returned home to make a new album. "Mixing *Zen Arcade* in one forty-hour session makes for a great story," Mould said, "but let's face it, it wasn't ideal. We wanted to spend more time making this next album and have more control over the recording environment. And while sleeping in the van or underneath Rollins's desk was oddly romantic, we also thought it might be nice to make an album while sleeping in our own beds each night."[11]

Hüsker Dü wanted to produce the new record, but SST insisted that Spot be on hand to coproduce. Shortly after *Slip It In* was recorded at Total Access, Spot split Redondo Beach for Nicollet Studios in downtown Minneapolis. Steve Fjelstad, who had worked on all of the Replacements' albums, served as engineer.

Those looking for a radical departure won't find it on *New Day Rising* (SST 031). All the elements of Hüsker Dü are here: Mould's guitar tone, Grant's caveman-in-a-china-shop drumming, Norton's fluid bass lines, held together by the point-counterpoint of Mould's introspective bombast and Hart's neoromanticism. These are the controls to which Hüsker Dü added new musical elements to test the limits of what a pop song could be.

New Day Rising opens with a jaunty declaration that devolves into a guttural howl. The same lyric is repeated over and over again. Nothing changes except the way the phrase is presented and perceived: a message of hopeful optimism that gives way to a snarling, sneering threat.

From acoustic outros ("Celebrated Summer") to the avant-garde ("How to Skin a Cat") and from haunting symbolism ("Girl Who Lives on Heaven Hill") to hardcore stomps that disintegrate into noise ("Plans I Make"), *New Day Rising* is an experiment in song structure. "It's more first-person in a third-person way," Mould said.[12]

New Day Rising achieved several things. First and foremost, it proved that *Zen Arcade* wasn't a fluke and demonstrated Hüsker Dü's potential for widespread appeal. *New Day Rising* also forced rock critics to come up with a new vocabulary for Hüsker Dü's music. The language journalists employed often missed the mark, and "hardcore" wasn't going to cut it anymore. Hüsker Dü, along with SST labelmates the Minutemen and the Meat Puppets, was compelling critics to revisit their tired, dogmatic notions about rock and roll. The only way to describe these bands was to meet them on their own terms.

4

Four years into the Reagan regime, the eyes of the world were on LA as the city prepared for the Summer Olympics. Because the United States had boycotted the Olympics in Moscow in 1980, the USSR returned the favor in 1984, setting the stage for American athletes to dominate the field and provide America with a much-needed feel-good story.

In 1984, Police Chief Daryl Gates's reputation was in tatters. His inflammatory racist rhetoric sparked outrage throughout the city. Gates was given one last chance to salvage his job by making sure that nothing ruined LA's Olympic showcase. Gates broke out the punk playbook, and the LAPD rolled into East LA and South Central with an overwhelming show of force, executing wave after wave of gang sweeps to clear the streets. Gates's officers operated like an occupying army, not a community police force. His tactic of rounding up people of color, charging them with a wide array of bogus crimes, and then releasing them later kept gang violence out of the news.[13]

Black Flag wasn't taking any chances with Gates's goons. As rumors of police raids swirled, Dukowski threw together a short, late-summer tour for Black Flag, Saccharine Trust, and October Faction, an SST house band. Saccharine Trust was celebrating the long-awaited follow-up to *Paganicons*: *Surviving You, Always* (SST 024), a jazz-inspired foray into biblical imagery and punk rock experimentation. Tony Cicero took over on drums when Rob Holzman departed for Slovenly. Earl Liberty left the band to join the Circle Jerks and was replaced by Mark Hodson. But Brewer and Baiza continued to take their nihilist songs in a gleefully cacophonous avant-punk direction. *Surviving You, Always* marks the maturation of Baiza's guitar playing while Brewer's vocals walk the line between a disaffected performance poet and an exuberant rocker in the mold of MC5's Rob Tyner.

October Faction grew out of Dukowski's affinity for jamming with Greg Cameron, a seventeen-year-old drummer from Gardena. Cameron was friends with members of the Descendents and had once tried out for the band. He shared a drum set with Bill Stevenson and would come to Global to practice after Black Flag was done rehearsing. When his booking duties were done for the day, Dukowski would come downstairs and jam with him. Soon others were joining their improv sessions, including Ginn and Baiza, and an idea was born. Ginn believed he played better with Black Flag when he warmed up beforehand, so why not take October Faction out on the road?

At the end of August, Black Flag drove up to San Francisco to record a live album at the Stone nightclub. The Stone was a familiar haunt for Black Flag: the band had performed there as early as 1980 when it opened up for Stiff Little Fingers. The show was typical of Black Flag's set and featured a mix of old, new, and unreleased material. Although *Live '84* (SST 030) was scheduled for release on cassette only, the performance also marked Black Flag's first foray into concert video. SST would eventually make copies of the performance, which featured roadie Troccoli on backing vocals during "Slip It In," available on VHS.

Troccoli got plenty of work that night. SST supergroup October Faction also recorded its performance at the Stone, with Troccoli handling the vocal duties, Dukowski on bass, and Ginn and Baiza playing guitar. Stevenson filled in on drums for Cameron, who couldn't make the trip because he was sick. All the members had logged countless hours jamming together and decided to capture the experience since the recording truck was ready and waiting.

October Faction (SST 036) combines improvisational jazz fusion and acid rock. Although the recording is broken into seven "songs," the session unspools in one continuous jam demarcated by Troccoli's "lyrics," which serve as signposts. The album is at its most daring during "Trail of Tears" when Baiza's and Ginn's guitars seemingly communicate with each other in a newly invented language while Troccoli bellows and howls. The record is very much in keeping with the group's desire to experiment, but compared to Saccharine Trust's new record, *October Faction* feels somewhat retro, like the Mothers of Invention without the spark of Frank Zappa's genius.

Prior to the fall tour, Ginn had given Dave "Rat" Levine a special assignment. Black Flag's mission to play anytime, anywhere meant the band often performed in places with subpar sound systems. Ginn wanted a custom PA system for Black Flag to take out on the road for the fall tour. The cabinets were built using heavy hardwood to help capture the sound that Ginn craved. "That solid, low-end is physical," Ginn said. "To get it you have to use stuff that's twice as heavy. That makes loading in and out backbreaking, but you have to pay a price to get that sound."[14]

The new gear meant more grunt work for the band and the crew. Hauling the massive stacks of cabinets and all of the equipment required a Ryder truck, and the tour van had to be configured to maximize every inch of space for instruments and personnel. The results were unassailable. Now Ginn could unleash hours of sonic fury every day at sound check and during shows at night.

Rollins used the downtime between tours to do more readings and act with Lydia Lunch in Richard Kern's semipornographic *The Right Side of My Brain*. Needless to say, Kern's film never made it to the cineplex, but Rollins's star was rising. He was now headlining shows and preparing to self-publish a zine of his own work that he would call *20*.

In September, Black Flag set out on an extensive fall tour with Saccharine Trust and Tom Troccoli's Dog, another improvisational project, with Troccoli on guitar, Ginn on bass, and Davo on drums. The name was something of an inside joke: if man's best friend was a dog, then Troccoli's most reliable companion was marijuana, which was a constant presence on the tour. Black Flag returned to Southern California only to embark on a winter tour with doom rockers Saint Vitus. The itinerary took them across the United States, deep into the Northeast, and back across Canada during a brutally cold winter.

Two new Black Flag records bookended these tours: *Family Man* came out in September and *Slip It In* squeaked in just before the end of December for an astonishing total of three new releases in 1984, and *Live '84* was scheduled to come out at the top of the new year. But the South Bay crew had no intention of slowing down and had even bigger plans for 1985.

Ginn was considering moving Black Flack to another label. He was convinced that SST was holding the band back. "Greg thought SST wasn't doing anything but issuing the record," Carducci explained, "which in his mind probably meant we were still capitalizing the label on Black Flag's back to the benefit of the other bands."[15]

Ginn, however, needed Carducci's help with setting up a new label for Black Flag, which he and Dukowski would run while Carducci and Mugger handled SST. After everything they'd done to get *My War, Zen Arcade*, and *Double Nickels on the Dime* out the door, Carducci thought Ginn was being shortsighted. "I told him I wasn't interested in that because the other bands weren't working at it like Black Flag," Carducci said. "I wasn't there for the other bands, I was there for Black Flag and to see what could be done with a label."[16]

After Carducci threatened to leave, Ginn scratched the idea. Those "other bands" were keeping SST busy, and Michael Whittaker, a relatively new employee at Global, was moved over to SST to work with Carducci. Whittaker had been in bands, had booked shows, and had worked the sound board at numerous clubs. After moving from Austin to Boston to Los Angeles, he took a job managing Legal Weapon and eventually bumped into Dukowski, who invited him to come work for SST.

One of Whittaker's jobs at Global was to cold-call record stores about stocking SST releases. At Dukowski's request, Whittaker adopted the "Spaceman" moniker that Watt had used while making these calls, and the name stuck. Whittaker promoted new releases, put together press kits, and did publicity for tours. A talented writer, Whittaker had a knack for

Joe Carducci at SST.
(Photo by Naomi Petersen
Photography.)

generating compelling copy that flirted with hyperbole. Whittaker was a
large man with a gregarious personality to match. His humor was a welcome
addition to SST. If there was some mischief involved with a press release or
publicity stunt, Whittaker usually had a hand in it.

5

In late February 1985, SWA, Saccharine Trust, the Meat Puppets, the
Minutemen, and Hüsker Dü embarked on a four-night showcase of SST's
brotherhood of bands that would become known simply as the Tour. This
represented the greatest collection of talent SST had ever assembled: five
bands at or near the peak of their power and popularity. Well, four bands
and SWA.

Although Dukowski was in the process of putting together a new album with his old band Würm, he was enamored with his latest project. SWA was a mixture of old ideas with new players that originally included Ted Falconi of Flipper, who'd jammed with Dukowski and Cameron at Global. When it became clear he wasn't going to work out, Falconi was replaced by Ray Cooper of the Descendents and Richard Ford of Frantic Technoid. Dukowski, who was drawn to extreme personalities in a front man, asked Merrill Ward, formerly of Overkill, to sing.

Saccharine Trust had toured with Black Flag twice the previous year and was in peak form. "We had to learn to kick ass or suffer the consequence," Baiza said of playing with Black Flag every night.[17] After weeks of playing with a band it had little in common with, Saccharine Trust benefitted from playing with SST's more experimental artists.

The Meat Puppets started the year by spending three days recording *Up on the Sun* (SST 039), which was scheduled to drop at the end of March. The Meat Puppets were predictably unpredictable and didn't disappoint with their third album for SST. The title track's elliptical yet surprisingly tender song sets the tone for the rest of the album. If *Meat Puppets II* pays tribute to the band's influences, *Up on the Sun* announces its talent. "The record was better than we were," Bostrom said. "We had crafted a really nice record, but our show was rough. If you put out records that people like, they're going to come to the shows expecting to see something like that. Our shows were all over the map."[18]

The Minutemen had just recorded *Project: Mersh* (SST 034), its follow-up to *Double Nickels on the Dime*. Earlier that year SST had released *My First Bells* (SST 032), a massive sixty-two-song compilation of the Minutemen's discography from *Paranoid Time* to *Buzz or Howl Under the Influence of Heat* that was released only on cassette. *Project: Mersh* was the Minutemen's tongue-in-cheek attempt at selling out with radio-friendly songs with conventional arrangements.

Hüsker Dü's *New Day Rising* had just come out in January. The band was touring heavily and, in typical Hüsker Dü fashion, already playing songs that would appear on the next album.

The SST labelmates kicked off the Tour at the Keystone in Palo Alto where the Meat Puppets confused the audience by playing a thrashy version of the Allman Brothers' "Midnight Rider." The Minutemen brought a hand-made sign on stage, proclaiming "US OUT OF CENTRAL AMERICA." Hüsker Dü also played a number of covers, including the Beatles' "Ticket to Ride," a scorching rendition of "Eight Miles High," and "Love Is All Around," the theme song to *The Mary Tyler Moore Show*. The show ended with various musicians assembling on stage to bash out "Louie Louie" until Curt Kirkwood was all alone on the drum kit.

The SST ensemble played at the Stone in San Francisco the following night, and the performance was recorded by Target Video for SST Records. Saccharine Trust performed a spirited cover of the Doors' "Peace Frog." The Meat Puppets announced, "I guess we're the Meat Puppets and we're supposed to play here" before opening with an off-key cover of the Honeydrippers' "Sea of Love" and playing Little Richard's "Good Golly, Miss Molly" later in the set.

The Tour moved south to Los Angeles and resumed at the Ackerman Grand Ballroom on the UCLA campus. The impact of *Zen Arcade* had finally registered with the music industry, and there was considerable buzz around *New Day Rising*. Having learned from its mistakes with *Zen Arcade*, SST made sure to press up enough copies of *New Day Rising* to satisfy growing demand. Among those in the audience were A&R reps from A&M, Slash, and Warner Bros., and they weren't subtle about their interest in the band. Hüsker Dü, however, didn't finish its set. At the start of the encore, someone threw a beer bottle at Hart. He stopped playing and angrily confronted the crowd, and the headliners pulled the plug.

So many fans from LA drove down to San Diego to see the final leg of the Tour, the gig was moved from Carpenter's Hall to Rock Palace at the last minute. For all the talk of Hüsker Dü slowing down and selling out, it was still the fastest band on the bill. After the show, a fan complimented Mould on the new song "Makes No Sense at All," to which Mould replied, "Yeah, that's the one."[19]

6

Black Flag stayed home during the Tour to rehearse for another balls-to-the-wall, forty-eight-hour recording session at Total Access. The band didn't waste a minute in the studio and recorded material that would appear on at least three new records. The first, *Loose Nut* (SST 035), isn't the heaviest-sounding record Black Flag ever recorded, but it hews closest to the heavy metal that was being produced in the mid-'80s. The album marks the departure of Spot and the return of Dave Tarling, who had worked on W.A.S.P.'s self-titled debut for Capitol Records the previous year.

After *My War*, it often felt as though Ginn was shoehorning his garage prog experiments into a format to which they weren't particularly well suited. If the song was too fast, Ginn's soloing felt spidery and spasmodic, but if the song was too slow, it was easily highjacked by Ginn's angular riffs. With *Loose Nut*, Ginn landed on a formula of mid-tempo songs that were neither too long nor too short. This hybrid of chugging riffs, punishing rhythms, and slick production was designed for mass appeal, but would fans go for it?

Ginn often returned to themes that had worked well for the band in the past, and "Loose Nut" feels like an attempt to recapture the crazed energy of "Depression" and "Nervous Breakdown." Unfortunately, like "Slip It In," the title track suffers from sophomoric lyrics. Ginn's pyrotechnics on the guitar do little to disguise the fact that the player is a thirty-year-old man deploying whimsical euphemisms for "vagina." It's little wonder that Ginn wanted to retreat to instrumentals, where words wouldn't get in the way.

"Loose Nut" is followed by three bangers. "Bastard in Love" features actual singing by Rollins. "Annihilate the Week," an anti–"Fight for Your Right (to Party)" anthem, is a catchy but oddly puritanical dismissal of those who party their lives away, and it may be the closest thing to a commercial song that Black Flag ever released. "Modern Man," one of the strongest tracks, is another song that dates back to the "1982 Demos." "Modern Man" was penned by Chuck Dukowski and Ed Danky, Dukowski's cohort in Würm, but it is completely transformed by Ginn's wailing guitar and Rollins's swaggering vocals. After a slow introduction, "Modern Man" builds with operatic theatricality only to tumble into a bona fide ripper that swerves in and out of multiple time changes. At times, Ginn's mournful guitar sounds like a second vocalist that layers the song and transports the listener.

Loose Nut represents the players at the top of their game. The rhythm section hammers away with machine-like precision, and Rollins's maturation as a vocalist is on full display. While many of the songs are structured around repetitive riffs, it's Rollins's delivery that makes them dynamic, and *Loose Nut* captures the vocalist's full range of charisma and conviction.

The marathon recording session produced an abundance of material that would be parceled out over Black Flag's next three studio albums: *Loose Nut*, *The Process of Weeding Out* (SST 037), and *In My Head* (SST 045). It's impossible to make statements about any of these records without considering the others. For instance, it would be a mistake to say that Black Flag moved away from instrumental experiments just because there aren't any on *Loose Nut*. In fact, the shows Black Flag played the first few months of 1985 were instrumental-only performances that were as baffling to fans as they were to Rollins, who wisely used the time to focus on his spoken word projects, the demand for which was growing. Rollins's literary efforts raised eyebrows at SST and caught the attention of *Spin* magazine—which commissioned Rollins to write an ode to his local 7-Eleven at the intersection of Artesia Boulevard and Felton Lane.[20]

It would be the last time this—or any—lineup would record a Black Flag record at Total Access Recording.

7

Shortly after the Tour, Hüsker Dü returned to Nicollet Studios in Minneapolis to record its next album—this time without Spot. "During the course of producing *New Day Rising*," Grant said, "we got totally fed up with Spot, and henceforth, he isn't and will never work with us again."[21] After spending so much time writing, rehearsing, recording, and touring, the members of Hüsker Dü had a strong sense of what they wanted to achieve.

Hüsker Dü had been playing several of the songs on the road for weeks, including the pop masterpiece "Makes No Sense at All," as well as "Hate

Paper Doll," "Green Eyes," and "Divide and Conquer," a practice that many felt worked against the band. "They were one of the hardest working and most prolific bands, almost to their undoing in a way," said Katzman. "As soon as a record came out, they'd be already playing songs from the next one. When *New Day Rising* came out, they were already doing songs from *Flip Your Wig*. That confused some people, because you're laying so much on them and they haven't even caught up with the other record."[22]

Mould was characteristically unapologetic about the band's habit of working out new material on the road. "If people want to hear us play a bunch of old hits," Mould said, "they picked the wrong band to follow."[23]

Mould, Hart, and Norton took a month off from their exhausting touring schedule and committed to making the next album. Hüsker Dü spent the first week of April recording the basic tracks and overdubs and the second week mixing the album down. The result, *Flip Your Wig* (SST 055), is sonically crisper, cleaner, and—yes—poppier than anything they, or anyone else on SST, had done before.

The melodies are simpler, but brighter and bouncier—a tradeoff the band had strived to achieve on *New Day Rising*. *Flip Your Wig*'s lyrics are simple yet thought provoking, and expansive harmonizing balances the savage with the sublime. "It's more vocal-oriented," Mould admitted, "as opposed to a wall of sound."[24]

"Green Eyes" feels like an "artyfact" from Lenny Kaye's *Nuggets*. Sonically, "Divide and Conquer" could blend in on any of the band's previous SST releases, but the lyrics are a prescient criticism of a world connected so it can be sold off to the highest bidder. *Flip Your Wig* is an unpredictable record. For instance, Mould slows the tempo on the apocalyptically epic "Find Me," and Hart counters the latent optimism of "Keep Hanging On" with guttural bellowing. The album winds down with a pair of instrumentals, "The Wit and the Wisdom" and "Don't Know Yet," which are as evocative as any of the diatribes of disaffection on *Zen Arcade*.

Mould, Hart, and Norton believed they had just recorded their best album, and they were feeling good about their prospects. By early April *New Day Rising* sold thirty thousand copies, notched the top slot of *Rockpool's*

Alternative Chart, and received a rave review in the *New York Times*. With the increase in sales and critical acclaim, critics questioned whether Hüsker Dü had set out to make a commercial album. "If anything ever does make it as a top 40 hit," Norton explained, "that's fine with us, but we're not purposely trying to achieve that goal."[25]

Karin Berg, the A&R representative from Warner Bros., was so intent on signing Hüsker Dü that she flew out to Minneapolis to meet with the band. Hüsker Dü played the new record for her, and she was unequivocal in her enthusiasm. "I wanted *Flip Your Wig* so bad," Berg said. "It might be their best record. For that to come out on Warner Bros., it really would've done well."[26]

But Hüsker Dü was feeling better about its relationship with SST. The success of *New Day Rising* prompted Mould to admit, "There's no more animosity between us and them."[27] The admission is telling. The band's frustration with SST's handling of *Zen Arcade* was widely known. While Mould tended to be circumspect about the band's intentions, Hart was more forthcoming. When the Replacements, Hüsker Dü's friendly rival from the Twin Cities, signed to Sire, it opened a floodgate of questions. Would Hüsker Dü be next?

Ultimately, the band decided to release *Flip Your Wig* with SST. Mould believed they "owed" the label the album. Carducci had a different take. "They gave SST *Flip Your Wig* when Warners wanted it because they were writing so many songs and could impress upon Warners that they didn't need them—and get a better deal." Hart vehemently disputed this claim and asserted that giving *Flip Your Wig* to SST was a miscalculation and that Mould had misled the band.[28] One reason for Hüsker Dü's change of heart was SST's willingness to bring in a new face to improve its publicity apparatus, but the band was already considering a future without the label.

8

"BRACE YOURSELF," commanded the latest dispatch from SST headquarters, only this press release had a new name at the top: Ray Farrell. Carducci lured Farrell away from the Bay Area in April 1985 to help out with SST's publicity and promotion, especially on college radio, which was exploding.

Farrell grew up far from Southern California in Parsippany, New Jersey, where he received his musical education in New York's Lower East Side as a regular guest at CBGB. He attended shows at the infamous club throughout the mid-'70s and witnessed Patti Smith, Television, the Ramones, Talking Heads, and other music for uplifting gormandizers. From an early age, Farrell was fascinated with the music industry. Some fans get into music wishing they could trace the origins of a favorite song back to the first spark of creative inspiration. Farrell wanted to know how radio stations knew what songs to play and how records made it into some stores but not others. Who were these people who pulled the strings behind the scenes, Farrell wondered, and how could he get a job doing that?

On a tip from Patti Smith, Farrell made his way to Rather Ripped Records in Berkeley, California. Rather Ripped was more than just a record store: it served as a hub for writers, artists, and musicians in the Bay Area. When Farrell showed up the owner was too busy to talk to him so Tom Petty, who happened to be in the store, volunteered to conduct the job interview. Farrell impressed the musician with his extensive knowledge of Shelter Records, the label that had released Petty's debut album, and got the job.[29]

From there Farrell bounced around to Maximum Rocknroll Radio, Arhoolie Records, Rough Trade, and CD Presents, making crucial connections along the way. Everywhere he went he soaked up information about scenes, zines, record labels, and radio stations, and used his network to book shows for friends' bands.

Carducci persuaded Farrell to join SST by sending him a trio of SST's new releases: Minutemen's *Double Nickels on a Dime*, Meat Puppets' *Up on the Sun*, and Hüsker Dü's *New Day Rising*. Farrell knew that SST wasn't like other independent record labels that only pressed up records in small batches, but did SST have the muscle to meet the demands of a sustained national campaign?

Farrell fit right in at SST by sleeping under his desk at the office for a few weeks until he found a place to stay. He jumped right into the fray with the "BRACE YOURSELF" press release announcing SST's upcoming releases, which included Meat Puppets' *Up on the Sun*, in March; the Minutemen's *Project:*

Grant Hart and D. Boon at SST. (Photo by Naomi Petersen Photography.)

Mersh, D.C. 3's *This Is the Dream* (SST 033), and October Faction's self-titled debut in April; and a collaboration between Henry Rollins and Lydia Lunch titled *Help Us Hurt You.*

This last project didn't pan out. It was based on a controversial performance they did together at the Lhasa Club in late 1983. Attendees were invited, one at a time, into a back room where they were confronted by Rollins and Lunch. Some participants enjoyed the experience, while others were traumatized by the combination of Lunch's intensity and Rollins's aggression.

Another project that didn't come to fruition was a recording of songs and spoken word pieces that Charles Manson sent from prison in Vacaville. Rollins, who was in direct correspondence with him, advocated for the project and even booked studio time to mix the recordings. The album, which would have been called *Completion,* was mastered and test pressings were created. Word of the album created a stir, and when Dukowski started getting death threats, SST decided to drop it.

After leaving Black Flag, Dez Cadena started a new band with Paul Roessler. Joined by Overkill drummer Kurt Markham, they formed SST's latest trio: the Dez Cadena Three (D.C. 3), a throwback to early '70s rock and roll when there was smoke on the water and fire in the sky. A rugged, rumbling, riff-driven record augmented by Roessler's keyboards, *This Is the Dream* leans on the sounds of Black Sabbath and Hawkwind, but it also takes cues from Frank Zappa's willingness to experiment and explore. "With D.C. 3, we were trying to show these punkers that it wasn't about a Mohawk," Cadena said. "We were punk in our spirit, but we were trying to do our own thing.... Even if we had a two minute song, we'd turn it into an extended jam live; kind of like what Mountain would do."[30]

Two of Cadena's songs, "I Believe It" and "Ain't No Time Here Now," had been worked up by Black Flag under the titles "What Can You Believe" and "Yes I Know" for Black Flag's "1982 Demos." Paul shares writing credit on a couple of tracks and also sings on "Dance of the Imbeciles." Recorded with Spot at Total Access over the course of three sessions spanning June 1984 to January 1985, *This Is the Dream* was Cadena's vision of a band unfettered by the burden of Black Flag's baggage. While the record may have been out of step with punk audiences, it was right at home on SST and bridged the gap between the Meat Puppets and Saint Vitus.

Farrell's approach to publicity and promotion wasn't to send out as many copies of the albums as possible but to target members of the media who might be receptive to them. For newer artists who hadn't cultivated a following, as much as 25 percent of the product went toward promotion. Even if the press didn't like or understand what SST's bands were doing, as when *Creem* compared the Meat Puppets to "the Flying Burrito Bros. on Romilar," the records benefitted from the exposure.[31] Farrell's campaign to get SST's records heard by as many people as possible was particularly effective in the realm of college radio, and he was on a mission to make Hüsker Dü's single "Makes No Sense at All" (SST 051) a hit. "'Makes No Sense at All' was different from everything else," Farrell said. "It has great energy. It isn't a love song."[32]

Before Farrell's arrival, SST had scattershot success with college radio.

There were hundreds of college radio stations across the country. Some stations were high wattage and had listeners throughout the communities they served, while others had such weak signals they could only be heard on campus. For Farrell's purposes, the best college radio stations "were connected to their local scenes. A good college radio station, in tandem with local record stores, clubs, fanzines and local journalists, could help build momentum. More people at shows, more record sales."[33]

Farrell included a one-sheet with every record he sent out and slapped hype stickers on the jacket to call out specific tracks. He knew the most successful college radio stations were getting inundated with releases from major labels, and he wanted to make sure SST's records got a shot at being heard. These materials, along with follow-up phone calls, encouraged student-run stations to report the songs they played, which was a crucial step to landing on the increasingly important college radio charts. "I loved having competition," Farrell said. "Major labels treated college radio as a stepping-stone to commercial rock radio. Having a top ten college radio record seemed to be a good thing in a press kit because it was often repeated by music press."[34]

It was much harder for indies like SST to break into the regular rotation on commercial radio. Most stations stuck to their formats and paid consulting companies that advised them on what songs to play. These companies tracked record sales nationwide and pushed stations to play the most popular songs around the country to drive advertising revenue. SST couldn't compete with that.

9

Two weeks before *Loose Nut* was scheduled to come out, Stevenson got a call from Dukowski to let him know that his time in the band had come to an end. The news upset Stevenson, but with Milo Aukerman back from college, he had been spending more time making music with the Descendents. The freedom and creativity he experienced with his old band contrasted with the rigidity of life in Black Flag, where one person called the shots and everyone else fell in line. Stevenson had trouble toeing that line, and the conflict with Ginn had been making him miserable. "I had gotten into a real negative space because of some personal things in my life that had not gone the way I had hoped they would," Stevenson said. "I think I was craving an environment where I would be one of the main songwriters, but at the same time realizing that my songwriting wasn't really appropriate for Black Flag....So it was very sad to leave, but it was also quite a relief."[35]

Ginn was more interested in where Black Flag was going than where it had been and was always looking for players who could execute that vision. But the timing of Stevenson's dismissal was curious. Black Flag had scheduled a lengthy summer tour that was set to kick off in two weeks. This made replacing Stevenson a top priority. Ginn enlisted Anthony Martinez, a talented drummer with an affable personality. Roessler was tasked with keeping Martinez in check because of his tendency to speed up and play the songs too fast. Roessler did her part, but she was unhappy with the situation and said as much to Ginn. When Roessler joined the band, Black Flag had rehearsed for months to prepare for her first tour. If Ginn wanted a different drummer, why did he wait until two weeks before the band's next tour to get one?

"For the '85 tour, we got this young drummer who was not physically strong," Roessler said, "and we had to break him in in two weeks. Physically, he wasn't up to it."[36] As Martinez's limitations became apparent, Ginn began to have second thoughts. Had he decided too quickly? Was Martinez the right drummer for Black Flag?

Ginn was no longer sure. Wary of repeating the Emil Johnson fiasco, Ginn and Roessler buttonholed SWA's drummer and asked him what he thought. "I like Anthony," Cameron said, "but he's no Bill Stevenson."[37]

Cameron's candid response confirmed their thinking that Martinez might not be the best fit. Ginn and Roessler then shocked Cameron by inviting him to replace Martinez and join Black Flag on tour.

Cameron was a logical choice. He knew the songs and had toured with Black Flag as a member of October Faction. As tempting as it was, Cameron declined the offer, and Martinez remained Black Flag's drummer. Cameron may have been young, but he was loyal to Dukowski. He knew Dukowski had been pushed out of Black Flag, and leaving SWA to play with Ginn felt like a betrayal. "Greg and Chuck already had a strained relationship," Cameron said. "Chuck was one of my best friends at that point and I couldn't do that to him."[38]

But it wasn't a problem for Ginn. His attempt to poach Cameron from Dukowski's band shows how little regard he had for his ex-bandmate. For Ginn, it was nothing new. He'd plucked Roessler from D.C. 3, Stevenson from the Descendents, and Rollins from S.O.A. But this was different. Dukowski and Cameron had started SWA together. After Dukowski's emotionally wrenching exit from Black Flag, it's difficult to imagine he would have taken Cameron's defection well. Would it have spelled the end of Dukowski's partnership with Ginn? Would Dukowski have left SST and set up shop elsewhere?

Ready or not, Black Flag headed up the California coast with the Minutemen and Tom Troccoli's Dog. In June, D.C. 3 and Twisted Roots took over as supporting acts. Then it was SWA's turn, joined once again by Tom Troccoli's Dog, whose self-titled album (SST 047) had just been released, with guest appearances by Dukowski, Cadena, and X's John Doe (appearing under the name Chuy Modello). And on it went into the endless summer with tempers simmering between Ginn, Rollins, and Roessler and a sense that the wheels were starting to come off.

10

Even before the release of *Zen Arcade*, Hüsker Dü had been drawing interest from major labels, but after the recording of *Flip Your Wig*, it was a foregone conclusion the group would leave SST. As early as the Tour, SST suspected Hüsker Dü's departure was imminent, which caused mixed feelings among the other bands on the label. "There was definitely camaraderie among the SST groups," Baiza said. "But just to put it in perspective, there was also a little bit of jealousy."[39]

Baiza's reaction was typical of the South Bay bands that benefitted from being on the SST roster and touring with Black Flag. They saw themselves as integral components of the SST community, but they also longed for the attention the label lavished on bands like Black Flag and Hüsker Dü. This mixture of gratitude and envy became a familiar one-two punch.

The Meat Puppets, however, was a different kettle of fish. The band felt little loyalty to Ginn or to SST and anticipated jumping to a major label at the first opportunity. Although SST was putting more resources behind the trio from the desert—reissuing the *In a Car* EP (SST 044) on vinyl, cassette, and CD—the members of the Meat Puppets were confident their time in the sun would come.

That fall, Farrell, Whittaker, and Schwartz were busy promoting the Meat Puppets, the Minutemen, Henry Rollins, and Hüsker Dü, who were all on tour, plus new releases by Saccharine Trust and Saint Vitus. SST was also spreading the word about Angst, a band that had journeyed from Boulder, Colorado, to London, England, before finally settling in San Francisco. Angst had released an EP on Happy Squid in 1983 before signing with SST and recording *Lite Life* (SST 054).

Farrell's determination to make *Flip Your Wig* a success paid off. The record received favorable reviews and attracted the attention of the rock establishment. It was a hit on college radio and rocketed up to #5 on the *CMJ*. The album also did well abroad, and "Makes No Sense at All" claimed the top spot on the Indie Chart in the UK. As Mould had predicted, it was indeed "the one."

Despite the acclaim with which *Flip Your Wig* was met, Karin Berg made a convincing case that Warner could do more for Hüsker Dü than SST. Mould and Hart countered with the demand that they be given complete creative control. Surprisingly, Warner was amenable. Hüsker Dü notified Ginn of the band's plans. Ginn lobbied for the band to stay, but the Minnesotans had already made up their minds.

On November 1, Hüsker Dü played its last gig with the Meat Puppets, D.C. 3, and Angst at Charley's Obsession, a decrepit club housed in a sleazy hotel in downtown LA. The band officially signed with Warner on November 11—Veterans Day—and celebrated with a party at Nicollet Studios, where Hüsker Dü had recorded its previous two albums. Friends and family flew in from all over the country, and the champagne flowed long into the night.

For Hüsker Dü, the signing further established Minneapolis as an important music scene. First there was Prince, next came the Replacements, and then Hüsker Dü. Just as Suicide Commandos had blazed a trail for Hüsker Dü, its success paved the way for bands like Babes in Toyland, Soul Asylum, and many others that would emerge in the late '80s when indie (an aesthetic) gave way to alternative (a genre of music).

But not all their fans were happy with the move. "A lot of people equate sellout with being on a major label," Norton said. "There were probably people who thought we sold out when we went to SST."[40]

When the checks cleared, Mould, Hart, and Norton each celebrated his success by buying a modest home, but Hüsker Dü did not enjoy a fairy tale ending. Rather, the story proved to be a cautionary tale. From the moment Mould, Hart, and Norton signed on the dotted line, the band was bedeviled by creative differences, personal conflicts, and issues stemming from drug use. Less than two years after signing a deal with a major label, Hüsker Dü was no more.

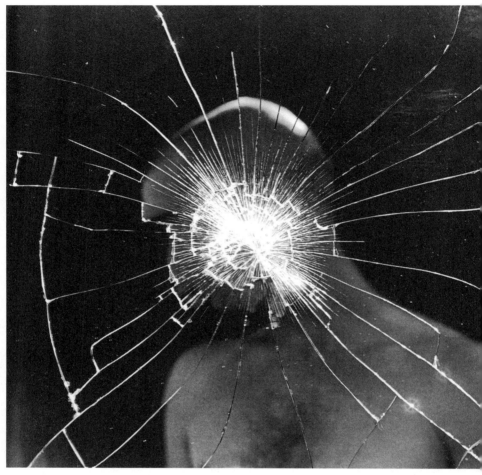

Henry Rollins during the *Damaged* photo shoot. (Photo by Edward Colver.)

CHAPTER 8
SST vs. Death

1985–1986

1

Hüsker Dü's defection from SST Records was a watershed moment in the history of independent music. Hüsker Dü wasn't the first indie band to sign with a major label—it wasn't even the first indie band in Minneapolis to do so—but its departure signaled a shift in the way people perceived the record label. SST was no longer just an arbiter of weirdo cool but a label that could get you a record deal with a major. From the outside looking in, SST had gone from a renegade outpost of outsider music to an indie tastemaker with its proverbial finger on the pulse of the sound of the underground, and it had seemingly happened overnight.

But if Hüsker Dü's signing with Warner made SST more appealing to emerging bands, it also raised the label's reputation with its mail-order customers. For example, when *Loose Nut* shipped in May 1985, the record included a double-sided flyer titled "The SST Factor." The list of products was now so long it took up both sides of the sheet. "The SST Factor" offered offensive artwork packaged in zines that looked like comic books (but weren't); books of writing that looked like poetry (but weren't); and music by punk bands that didn't seem interested in making punk-sounding records (they weren't). The flyer also advertised T-shirts, stickers, skateboards, and a selection of records that was getting deeper by the month. Fans could order Black Flag lyric sheets, Raymond Pettibon posters, and even a videocassette of Black Flag's *Live '84* on Beta or VHS.

These developments displayed Ginn's understanding of the first rule of direct marketing: invest in the customers you already have before you spend money chasing new ones. SST had been at the mail-order game a long time, and its grassroots communications endeared customers to the brand. For those who were unable to see their favorite bands perform or whose small towns lacked a record store where they could purchase (or even find out about) new releases, the catalog was a lifeline to independent music. For some, the records they bought from SST were the first purchases they made with their own money (and often without their parents' permission), which conferred a whiff of the transgressive to the packages that arrived from Lawndale—a place that conjured up images of a mythical suburb in surf-splashed, sunshine-dappled California.[1]

Customers learned they could trust SST—even if they'd never heard of a band before. As long as it had the SST logo on it, that was good enough for them. Imagine sending away for a new record by a band with an odd-sounding jumble of vowels and having *Zen Arcade* show up on your doorstep. How many minds were blown by SST's slow and painstaking process of promoting new releases, soliciting orders, and fulfilling them through the mail? The lessons Ginn learned from his days of running SST Electronics—make products people want, communicate with your customers, and keep up with inventory—were paying off.

Ginn may not have been happy about Hüsker Dü's departure, but the band had been very good for SST. By the end of 1985, SST would ship fifty thousand copies of *Flip Your Wig*, making it the top-selling record on the label by a considerable margin.[2] Not only did Hüsker Dü sell a ton of records, but their records flew off the shelves, giving the label a much-needed infusion of cash. SST's ability to move and ship large volumes of records gave the label credibility and leverage with distributors, who often withheld payment from indies until the label produced another record the distributors wanted. The success meant distributors could no longer afford to gamble with the label by holding back payments. In fact, several distributors were starting record labels of their own and modeling their business plans after SST.

Although *Loose Nut* hadn't performed nearly as well as *Flip Your Wig*, since March 1984 Black Flag had released *five* albums, and it had another two coming in the fall of 1985. While the number of releases depressed the sales of individual records, the total sales were significant, which enabled SST to re-press older material. In a conversation with Michael Goldberg for a long feature that ran in *Rolling Stone*, Ginn estimated that Black Flag had sold 250,000 total units.[3] This windfall prompted Carducci to inform Ginn that SST now had the financial freedom to expand its roster. "I told Greg our cash flow was good and there was no longer a reason not to do something," Carducci said.[4]

SST also benefitted from the increased exposure the press lavished on its bands. That feature in *Rolling Stone* discussed at length the "neo punk" of Black Flag, Hüsker Dü, the Minutemen, and the Meat Puppets. Thankfully, the term never took hold, but the article was a veritable showcase of SST talent that also mentioned Tom Troccoli's Dog, Saccharine Trust, and Saint Vitus, who all had records coming out that summer and fall. The story did not present SST as a punk powerhouse; if anything, it affirmed SST's outsider status with descriptions of Black Flag's strange energy. Ginn confessed that he dreamed of Black Flag opening for the Grateful Dead, and he ranted about the state of the world. "It's time to loosen it up," Ginn said. "A lot of stuff done in the Sixties was important."[5]

This wasn't the first time that Ginn had declared his affinity for the band. In 1983 he wore a Grateful Dead T-shirt during a Fourth of July smoke-in for the California Marijuana Initiative at the Federal Building in Los Angeles. Many assumed Ginn was making an ironic statement. He wasn't. Ginn rarely wore clothing that had any kind of message or logo on it. While his labelmates often wore the latest SST merch on stage, Ginn stuck to his thrift store duds. If anything, Ginn was making his affinity for the Grateful Dead known, and he wasn't the least bit embarrassed about it.

Quite the contrary. When Mark Leviton wrote in *BAM* that "so-called adventuresome people who dig Black Flag probably wouldn't be caught alive at a Grateful Dead concert," Ginn was moved to respond.[6] He wrote a letter to the editor stating that not only was the Grateful Dead his favorite band, but at the Grateful Dead show he'd recently attended in San Diego, fans in the audience were wearing Black Flag shirts. Ginn's admiration for the Grateful Dead's lead guitarist Jerry Garcia was becoming increasingly evident as he threw himself into instrumental and improvisational music. "For Greg it was about Jerry's virtuosity," said Kite, who'd attended many Grateful Dead shows with Ginn and Dukowski.[7]

Ginn wasn't just a fan of the music. He studied the culture the Grateful Dead created by booking its own shows, traveling with its own PA system, and building its own community completely separate from the rock and roll establishment. Kite believed that Ginn was attracted to "the autonomy of not having to be part of that other mainstream world."[8] While stereotypes clung to this community—namely, that it consisted of hippies and acid casualties who hadn't gotten the memo that the '60s were over—the culture had its own identity and thrived on its own terms, according to its own values.

Hadn't SST made something similar? While the notion that only pissed-off punks went to Black Flag shows persisted, the reality Ginn had created—and recreated every time he plugged in his guitar—was much different. The only meaningful outcome of rejecting the status quo was to make something new to take its place. This was precisely what Ginn did with SST Records. He didn't start up a record label to release music that appealed to his personal taste; rather, he created a community that reflected his *values*. As its roster of artists expanded, so did its influence, and now it was bearing fruit for bands not named Black Flag. Even if the long hair and '60s rhetoric struck square journalists who wrote about Ginn's enterprise as oddly retrograde, SST was building something new.

While Ginn was telling reporters about his fondness for the '60s, Rollins was treating interviews like Charles Manson at an open mic, saying things like, "A lot of places to me are like a big open throat waiting to be cut."[9] With his wild eyes, perpetual lack of sleep, and commitment to bringing the intensity 24/7, it was difficult for strangers and intimates alike to tell whether Rollins was being serious.

Rollins's surliness wasn't reserved for the media anymore. As the Loose Nut Tour wore on, he retreated into himself and his journals. There was no questioning his intensity, commitment, or effort on stage, but he seemed miserable and took his anger out on others—both on the page and in person.

2

While the members of Black Flag feuded behind the scenes, it was a busy summer at SST, especially for Dukowski and Ward. That August SST released albums by two of Dukowski's bands: *Feast*, by Würm (SST 041), and the ominous-sounding *Your Future If You Have One*, by SWA (SST 053).

Feast represents more than Dukowski's desire to get his old band back together. In 1983, he expanded the trio into a quartet by enlisting Simon Smallwood. The band's relationship to Smallwood dated all the way back to '77 with an ad in the paper: "Singer Wanted. Into Iggy, Ozzy, and Alice."[10] Smallwood responded and had a productive session with Würm, but he opted to continue with his own project, Dead Hippie, an underground LA punk band that eventually released the album *Living Dead* with Pulse Records in 1983 and gave an electrifying performance on *New Wave Theatre*.

When he returned from Germany, Dukowski reconnected with Smallwood, and they recorded the tracks for *Feast* at Radio Tokyo with Ethan James. Many of the songs on *Feast* were written long before, including "Padded Cell," which Black Flag had recorded for *Damaged*. Yet another Würm song that got the Black Flag treatment, "I've Heard It Before," didn't make it onto *Feast* but was a staple of the band's live performances. *Feast*'s front cover features a striking nude photo of Suzi Gardner, Dukowski's girlfriend at the time, taken by Naomi Petersen at the infamous Spahn Movie Ranch, where Charles Manson and his followers plotted the murders they carried out in August 1969. Unfortunately, Smallwood quit the band in the studio, and the record sat in limbo. Dukowski had better luck with his next project.

While concepts for SWA had been percolating for years, Dukowski teamed up with Ward to write some songs and record an album with guitarists Ray Cooper and Richard Ford and drummer Greg Cameron (a.k.a. Nazi Sex Doctor). Ward worked at a bookstore with an adult section, and he would occasionally bring titles to the office at Global. While waiting for rehearsal, Cameron perused a novel about a German commandant of a labor camp who fell in love with one of his prisoners. When Rollins and Davo returned from getting coffee, they found Cameron engrossed in the book. They were delighted to discover its title was *Nazi Sex Doctor.* "Boom that was it," Cameron said. "I was the Nazi Sex Doctor. . . . Of course, it was so opposite of who I was. In fact, I was still a virgin, but the nickname stuck like glue."[11]

His friends at SST would call him Naz (pronounced "Knots") or Nazi for short, which created some uncomfortable situations for the young drummer. On tour, Dave Rat did SWA's sound, and during soundcheck one day he addressed Cameron by his nickname through the talkback mic, which was also going through the house sound system. Cameron recalled, "He actually said, 'Okay, Nazi, go ahead and hit the kick drum.' Everybody that worked at the venue just stopped what they were doing and all eyes were on the stage."[12]

SST also released a record by Ward's old band Overkill, concluding one of the more bizarre chapters in SST's discography. *Triumph of the Will* (SST 038) was Overkill's first record since the "Hell's Getting Hotter" seven-inch came out in 1982. The band recorded the instrumental tracks for the album in April 1982 and played several dates in California, including opening for Trauma on the night James Hetfield and Lars Ulrich saw the headliner's bassist Cliff Burton play and decided to recruit him for Metallica.

Before Ward could record vocals for the album, he was booted out of the band, which irritated Ginn. Overkill found a new singer, but Ginn was no longer in a hurry to make the record, and the band broke up before it could get in the studio. The recordings languished for many years, but when Ward started playing in SWA, Ginn urged the vocalist to finish the album. Ward met with Spot and recorded one or two songs at a time until it was finally finished. Overkill was essentially a dead band when the record came out in 1985. Naming the album after a Nazi propaganda film and using the insignia of the Waffen-SS on the album cover likely submarined the album's already slim potential. "That was just what the band wanted to do," Carducci explained. "It wasn't considered offensive by any of us....Kurt Markham's girlfriend drew it and we didn't have anything else since the band wasn't together."[13]

Be that as it may, SST was certainly aware that the packaging was provocative, or else Whittaker wouldn't have referred to Overkill as "crypto-fascists" in a press release. (For the record, none of the members of the band were fascists, but SST proved time and again it was comfortable with fascist imagery and language.) *Triumph of the Will* was hamstrung by the lack of participation from the band and didn't reflect the usual care and attention SST put into the design of its albums. For instance, Saint Vitus, who released *Hallow's Victim* (SST 052) in August as the follow-up to its self-titled debut, added a Christian cross to its logo so that listeners wouldn't assume the band's members were devil-worshipping Satanists. SST was no stranger to controversy and took pleasure in agitating the media, but it wasn't 1977 anymore, and with racist skinhead bands like Skrewdriver using Nazi iconography to sell records to like-minded cretins, employing Nazi images and language was blatantly offensive and bad marketing.

With SWA, Dukowski tried to generate an aura of mystique around the band whose unusual name stopped just short of risking offense. (The name is pronounced like the first syllable of the word "swastika.") The back cover of *Your Future If You Have One* features a Naomi Petersen photograph of the band members wearing suits and sunglasses and carrying briefcases like spies from the art department—a marked contrast to the increasingly shaggy look of much of the SST crew. Laid over the photo in capital letters are a series of cryptic messages that repeat like dispatches from an Orwellian ticker tape: "YOU ARE EITHER SWA OR NON SWA....THERE ARE THOSE WHO WILL SHUN SWA WE WILL WATCH THEM DESTROY THEMSELVES."[14] These messages were very much in keeping with the SWA manifesto that Dukowski had been developing as early as 1981 according to the press release from "insanity director" Jordan Schwartz. The album insert also came with a SWA identity card. Fans were encouraged to cut it out, paste their photo, and present it at shows to receive discounts and even free admission.

Some Black Flag fans were averse to SWA, not because of the music or messaging but because of its front man. Ward would put on makeup or wear dresses on stage and vamp in a way that stood in stark contrast to Rollins's performative masculinity. For many closed-minded fans, it was easier to deride Ward for his appearance than to listen to his lyrics. Rollins himself was among Ward's detractors. "Merrill was very flamboyant," Cameron said, "and very much the opposite of what Henry thought SST bands should be like."[15]

Not everyone at the label was put off by Ward's antics. "SWA was fun to watch live because Merrill Ward was charismatic and entertainingly menacing," Farrell said. "SWA was best experienced close to the stage."[16]

Your Future If You Have One opens with the SWA theme song: the up-tempo "Rip It Up," which is about breaking with the past to embrace the future (if you have one) that SWA proposes. Ward is a gifted singer blessed with a wide range and an abundance of charisma that lends his bluesy delivery the weight of authenticity. His gritty vocals pair well with Dukowski's low-end groove.

Dukowski took SWA up to Vancouver to join Black Flag on the final leg of the Loose Nut Tour, where the tension between Ginn, Rollins, and Roessler was reaching a breaking point. Roessler had discovered that Black Flag was planning a tour that conflicted with her schedule at UCLA. In other words, they were moving on without her.

On the last night of the tour, Rollins unleashed a scathing diatribe at Roessler during "Louie Louie." Dukowski, Ginn's axman, gave Roessler the news that her time in the band was over. Even though she knew it was coming, Roessler was devastated. "Being in a band is like a marriage of several people and demands work, just as a marriage does," Roessler said. "It demands acceptance of each other, supporting each other even in disagreement, and all sorts of things I did not get then. I thought it was about playing good and surviving. I guess that is important too, but not nearly enough."[17]

While Ginn sought out a new bass player, Rollins rented the Black Flag van from Global and embarked on a nationwide spoken word tour to promote his books. Rollins went all the way across the country, up the Eastern Seaboard, back across the United States to Vancouver, and down the coast to Los Angeles. The tour gave Rollins some much-needed time away from the band and some degree of financial independence. More than anything, the tour assured Rollins that he could draw a crowd without the rest of Black Flag behind him.

The glut of new releases meant that SST was in the familiar position of looking to expand its brick-and-mortar facilities. Mugger took care of all of the logistics. He handled the lease agreements, hired the movers, negotiated with trucking companies, and got the power switched on. Mugger had learned a great deal about the business and never got on the phone without knowing exactly what he wanted. This caught service providers off guard when, after an intense negotiation over the phone, a young, scruffy-looking kid showed up with the SST checkbook. "The people that I met all wanted to invite me to dinner and set me up with their daughters," Mugger said. "I was like twenty-one and I'm doing all this shit and they're like looking at me going, 'Who gave you that money? Who gave you that power? Who the fuck is this kid?'"[18]

SST moved into its new headquarters in Hawthorne about a mile and a half northwest of the previous location. The building had plenty of office space and a proper warehouse with a roll-up door to facilitate the moving, storing, and shipping of palettes of vinyl. It was considerably larger than any of the previous locations.

SST never wasted an opportunity. As soon as Mugger and Carducci vacated the premises, the Minutemen showed up with John Talley-Jones of the Urinals to make a short music video. The Minutemen had just recorded the Urinals' classic "Ack Ack Ack Ack" at the end of August. The video portrays Boon, Watt, and Hurley as members of a dysfunctional cleaning crew hired to spruce up the office of Sonic Boom Records, a division of Underhanded Industries. As the *Three Stooges*–inspired video unfolds, the crew demolishes the office, the record company executive has a fit, and the boys from San Pedro kick back in the rubble with some brews. In the final scene, Boon flinches as part of the ceiling caves in, and the short video ends with a cloud of dust settling over the band. It's an eerie image that foreshadows the grim fate that was awaiting the Minutemen: the proverbial roof was caving in, but no one could see that far into the future.

3

When SST received the covers for *The Process of Weeding Out*, Ginn and Dukowski realized they'd made a mistake. There was nothing wrong with Pettibon's image—a devil peering into a microscope by the light of a moon, which is also a petri dish—but the word "Instrumental" was nowhere to be found. The word was supposed to be prominently placed on the front cover underneath the band's name, except no one told Cameron, who'd been pressed into serving as a graphic designer. "Apparently that information on *Process* was known but never relayed to me," Cameron said. "So they had to add that sticker later. I just did what I was told."[19]

The word "Instrumental" served as both a description of the record and a modifier of the band, as if to denote an entity separate and distinct from the version of Black Flag fronted by Rollins. This alternate version—Black Flag Instrumental—was fueled by fresh frustrations and old influences.

Ginn was unhappy with the amount of attention Rollins was receiving. By all accounts, it's not any one thing Rollins said or did. The vocalist was compliant to the point of obsequious when it came to the band's business. Ginn dictated when Black Flag rehearsed, what songs would go on the records, and how long it toured, and Rollins went along with all of it.

But the tide had turned. With Hüsker Dü gone, Back Flag was back to being the biggest draw on the label, but it wasn't the same. Sales were down. Attendance was down. Ginn had taken a page out of the Hüsker Dü playbook with an onslaught of new records and relentless touring. But Black Flag was not Hüsker Dü. Hüsker Dü shifted in a direction that made its music more accessible, not less. On the contrary, Black Flag had saturated the market and was losing fans at a greater rate than it was making new ones.

While Ginn was all too happy to put Rollins front and center for the publicity machine when Black Flag's popularity was rising, now that it was on the wane resentment began to fester. The vocalist's rising celebrity as both an author and a spoken word performer added to the acrimony.

Some at SST believed Rollins's success as a spoken word artist had changed him, and that the intellectual superiority he'd always felt over his bandmates and road crew was now out in the open. Others thought Rollins was playing a role. This version of Rollins was unnecessarily antagonistic, especially toward those who had the audacity to point a microphone at him. For Mugger, Rollins "was never a part of the group. I mean he was the singer, but he was sort of aloof and not really a part of this thing."[20]

Perhaps Ginn could handle Rollins becoming popular for what James Parker describes as the vocalist's "educated savagery" on stage, but not as a celebrated creative artist.[21] As for Ginn, he likely believed Black Flag already had a genius, and he was it.

When Rollins wasn't touring with Black Flag, he stayed in the detached study at Ginn's parents' house and enjoyed a close relationship with Regis and Oie, about which their son wasn't thrilled. Unless he was rehearsing with Black Flag or responding to fan mail at SST, Rollins preferred to spend his downtime making tapes and writing in his journal. Rollins had few allies left in Black Flag, and he felt so isolated that he recruited his friend Joe Cole to roadie for the band and keep him company on tour.

SST was also becoming increasingly divisive. Each time SST moved its offices, it took Mugger and Carducci farther from Ginn, Dukowski, and the road crew at Global. Creative decisions were made by all four of the label's partners, and the two camps within SST seldom saw eye to eye with respect to which artists should be brought into the fold. Carducci and Mugger were always looking outside of SST's circle for new bands to bring in, whereas Ginn and Dukowski were focused on their own and their collaborators' projects.

Ginn advocated for SST to put more resources behind Black Flag, whether that meant sending out press materials or purchasing ads. With half of the partners headquartered in Hawthorne and the other half in Redondo Beach, a feeling of suspicion—if not distrust—developed between the two offices, each wondering what the other was up to and getting a deepening feeling that "they" were out of touch.

"We never should have split the band from the label," Carducci said. "It just came to be that once the band was out of the label building, the typical paranoia down there made it impossible to then reconnect."[22] This cloud settling over SST was as thick and murky as the marine layer that shrouded the Beach Cities, and it drove a wedge between the creative partners. Two offices, two realities, one recipe for dysfunction.

4

The Process of Weeding Out picks up where Side 2 of *Family Man* leaves off. Black Flag's instrumental tracks on *Family Man* are experiments in rock and roll. For the new record, Ginn uses a completely different platform: jazz. This shift in emphasis is evident from the album's opening notes. The tracks on *Family Man* were clearly recognizable as songs, some of which had been part of Black Flag's set for years. *The Process of Weeding Out* is more improvisational. "It's something that I've always liked to do," Ginn said.[23]

The album's improvisational elements can be traced back to the legendary jazz performers he saw at the Lighthouse. The urge to experiment was always there—it was part of the foundation of who he was as a musician. "When the Mahavishnu Orchestra came out, I really liked that a lot," Ginn said. "I saw them a lot of times. I was into them when they first came out, and I think that had a big impact on my music."[24]

Stevenson recalled the inspiration for *The Process of Weeding Out* was all over the place. "We were playing stuff that was more like Ornette Coleman," Stevenson said, "or things that were more like Charlie Parker or things that were more like the Mahavishnu Orchestra or King Crimson or Sabbath."[25]

The EP has two long songs and two short ones, though none are "songs" in a conventional sense; rather, they are musical ideas that Ginn explores with his guitar. There are moments in the opening track, "Your Last Affront," when Ginn's guitar sounds like an airplane engine in distress, roaring into a nosedive, as if channeling his father's combat missions in World War II.

Although *The Process of Weeding of Out* is instrumental, Ginn had a lot to say about the record. In the liner notes on the back cover, Ginn declares that "even though this record may communicate certain feelings, emotions, and ideas to some, I have faith that cop-types with their strictly linear minds and stick-to-the-rules mentality don't have the ability to decipher the intuitive contents of this record."[26]

For someone who hated the police as much as Ginn did, "cop-types" was the worst insult he could muster. The double meaning embedded in the EP's title suggests a turning point for Ginn. The reference to Ginn's affinity for weed disguises his intention to thin the herd of Black Flag fans, to weed out those who associated Black Flag with Rollins. Just as *My War* Side 2 had done nearly two years before, *The Process of Weeding Out* announced the band's break with the hardcore hooligans who came to Black Flag shows hoping to thump skulls to the accompaniment of "Six Pack" or "TV Party." Black Flag Instrumental was for thinking people.

Of course, weeding out also referred to smoking large quantities of marijuana. By many accounts, Ginn's marijuana consumption had advanced. He didn't just indulge on the road. Mugger recalled a meeting during which Ginn passed out at the table. "Greg was sitting there and all of a sudden he just passed out in front of me at the restaurant. I thought he was dead. I'm going, 'Greg…Greg…' and he was just fucking so stoned he passed out. A minute later, he wakes up. And he kept talking like nothing happened. I go, 'Greg, you just fucking passed out!'"[27]

Those who were dissatisfied with *The Process of Weeding Out* didn't have to wait long for its follow-up: *In My Head*, Black Flag's fifth studio album, was released the following month in November. The record was cobbled together from two sessions at Total Access in January and March 1985.

In My Head opens with "Paralyzed," a song about being emotionally stuck that is sandwiched between primal screams. From there the album nosedives into "The Crazy Girl" and "Black Love," with lyrics that are too vague to be offensive but embarrassing nonetheless. The album's title track is easily its best song, with chugging riffs and lyrics that feel as though they were ripped out of Rollins's journal. Side 2 kicks off with "Drinking and Driving," yet another tongue-in-cheek take on the perils of partying, which was old hat by now. The album closes with "It's All Up to You," which features harmonizing backing vocals that couldn't be more out of place.

In My Head is a regressive rock and roll record with familiar rhythms and predictable cadences. If Ginn was searching for a format to showcase his guitar solos, this wasn't it. For perhaps the first time, Ginn's guitar feels unmoored from the music, a nonsensical splatter of caterwauling pseudo-blues. The songs are plodding and inevitable. Ginn sets the pace, and the players follow along. Lyrically and musically unimaginative, the songs take the listener to places they've been to many times before, places to which Ginn perhaps found comfort in returning. Even the album art—six Petti-bon images over the silhouette of a head—feels like a rehash of old concepts: mushroom clouds, gun violence, loose women, shady cops. *In My Head* poses the question: Was Black Flag out of ideas?

5

The trio from San Pedro was on a roll. The Minutemen's newest record, *3-Way Tie (for Last)* (SST 058), came out in December 1985, and SST shipped eighteen thousand copies of the band's most political album. Boon and Watt split their material into sides, and three of the four opening tracks on Boon's side—"The Price of Paradise," "The Big Stick," and "Political Nightmare"—address the US government's expansionist policies abroad. These themes are backed by the Minutemen's choice of cover songs with politics at their periphery: Creedence Clearwater Revival's "Have You Ever Seen the Rain?," Blue Öyster Cult's "The Red and the Black," and the Urinals' "Ack Ack Ack Ack." Even Watt's "Spoken Word Piece" deals directly with political ideology.

The record shipped with an insert that had a curious announcement: "Comrades in music! We can make democracy work, if only for ourselves." The reverse side contained a list of 150 songs—every song the Minutemen had ever released. Readers were given instructions to select their favorites by April 1, 1986—D. Boon's birthday—and the top thirty would be recorded for a special live triple album the band was planning. It was an inspired stunt that unfortunately wouldn't pan out as planned.

The Minutemen had just spent three weeks between November 24 and December 13, 1985, opening for R.E.M. on its Fables of the Reconstruction Tour. While R.E.M. hadn't reached superstardom yet, Boon, Watt, and Hurley played in front of much larger crowds than they were accustomed to in cities and college campuses across the Southeast. Sales of *3-Way Tie (for Last)* were bolstered by national attention, college radio, and word of mouth generated by the tour. But what should have been a thrilling experience was tempered by hostile audiences and R.E.M.'s belligerent crew. "No one wanted us on the tour," Watt said. "The only reason we were there is cause the R.E.M. guys really like the Minutemen."[28]

Meanwhile in Hermosa Beach, the SST crew prepared for the Christmas holiday. Black Flag was home but gearing up for a lengthy tour in January, and Ginn was busy with a new side project. For Boon, it was a happy time. He and his girlfriend Linda Kite had traded vows and were planning on getting married the following year. They'd known each other since they were kids. Kite's family moved into the housing project where Boon lived when she was six and he was eight years old. (Watt moved in a few years later.) Both Boon and Kite had attended Dodson Junior High School in San Pedro, and their mothers had been close friends. Even though Boon had been touring with the Minutemen for months, he had plans to travel with Kite and her sister to Tucson, Arizona, to tell Kite's mother the news about the wedding and to celebrate the holidays together. "His mom and my mom had been best friends when we were kids," Kite said, "but his mom died when we were in high school. And so for Dennes it was a big thing to go tell my mom that I had finally agreed to marry him."[29]

Boon and Watt bickered during the tour, which was nothing new. This time the argument between the two headstrong men was about whether the spare tire should be kept inside the van or bolted onto the rear door. Boon believed the tire took up too much space inside the van, but Watt reasoned the tire could be stolen if it was left outside the van. An argument ensued that resulted in Watt kicking Boon out of the band, which happened with such frequency that Hurley refused to get involved, forcing the two songwriters to work out their differences.

"That's just how childhood friends argue," Kite said. "When you've known each other for so long, you're almost family and it's not always a Norman Rockwell existence. Mike is very argumentative and very much into 'I'm right, you're wrong, and I'm going to lecture you and tell you why.' That's how he rolls. Dennes was equally opinionated. He had his own strong opinions and it was the same kind of thing. He was stubborn and he was going to argue until he won his side of the argument. They did that as children and then obviously as young adults."[30]

The two combative performers had yet to mend fences. The Minutemen had just come off a grueling tour, and the holidays were fast approaching, but then Boon got sick. For much of the previous year, he had been following a vegetarian diet, but the night before the trip to Tucson, Boon celebrated with a large nonvegetarian meal, which Kite believed was a contributing factor. He was sick in bed all the next day and unable to make some minor repairs to the van and drop off his amp to Joe Baiza, who needed it for a gig Saccharine Trust was playing with Sonic Youth. Although Boon couldn't complete these tasks, nothing was going to stop him from making the trip to Arizona.

Shortly before Boon's departure, Watt called to discuss plans for their next studio project: a collaboration with Richard Meltzer, who had written lyrics for songs that Boon and Watt planned to write. Although the Minutemen had worked with many songwriters in the past and weren't above hitting up their friends in a pinch, Meltzer was both an icon and an idol. One of the first rock and roll critics in America, Meltzer wrote for *Crawdaddy* in 1966 when it was still a zine and was such a San Francisco institution that he welcomed the Sex Pistols to the stage at Winterland. But it was Meltzer's role as a lyricist for Watt's beloved Blue Öyster Cult that thrilled the Minutemen.

Alarmed by Boon's pitiful-sounding condition, Watt expressed concern for his friend's health. Boon reassured him that he would sleep in the back of the van and arrive in Arizona fully rested.

On the evening of the winter solstice—Saturday, December 21, 1985—Boon, Kite, and Garfias departed San Pedro in the Minutemen's 1979 Dodge van and headed out for the desert. While Boon slept in the back of the van, Kite drove, and Garfias, who was also ill, slept in the passenger seat. Although Kite had put in a full day at her retail job, she was no stranger to life on the road. The plan was to spend the night in Phoenix with the Meat Puppets and then go on to Tucson the following day. Well past midnight, Kite pulled over to a gas station in the town of Quartzsite to gas up the van, check the fluid in the radiator, and grab some coffee. At approximately 4:30 in the morning, about fifty miles east of Quartzsite on Interstate 10, the van violently swerved off the road, rolled over twice, and came to rest in a ditch.

When Kite emerged from the van with a shattered ankle, her sister was seriously injured and her fiancé was simply gone. He'd been ejected through the van's rear doors. Police arrived at the scene of the accident and pressed Kite for details. Various drugs and drug paraphernalia the Minutemen had acquired while on tour were now scattered all over the highway. Disoriented and distraught, Kite told the police that she must have fallen asleep behind the wheel. One minute they were driving along the interstate and the next they were in a ditch. She was at a loss to explain what had happened. Garfias, though seriously injured, was fighting off the EMTs, and they asked Kite to help calm her down. That's when she saw Boon's body on the ground covered in a sheet.

On the longest night of the year, the nimble-fingered giant, the deep-thinking April fool everyone loved was struck down, a cruel casualty of happenstance. Dennes Dale Boon was just twenty-seven years old, cut down in his prime, like so many other rock and roll legends.

Spot and D. Boon in Redondo Beach. (Photo by Naomi Petersen Photography.)

6

In Redondo Beach, Rollins awoke on Sunday morning to the awful news from Ginn's mother, Oie, who told him that Boon had died in a traffic accident in Arizona. Rollins went to Global and for two days fielded calls about the tragedy from freaked-out friends, fans, and journalists around the country. In death Boon was big news, an irony that was not lost on Rollins, who after dozens of calls started answering the phone, "Hello, D. Boon hotline."[31]

One of the callers was Watt, who was struggling with the news. Boon wasn't just his bandmate; Boon was his best friend. Though their fights could be bitter, they loved each other like brothers. For Watt, it was as though half of his personality had died. He couldn't see a path forward. "the minutemen ended when d. boon was killed on december 22, 1985," Watt said. "weird though, I will always be a minutemen—it was not some sort of 'stage' I grew up out of or just went through. I balance everything I do today off what I did then and it gives me perspective."[32]

For Watt, the Minutemen wasn't just a band but a way of making his way through the world. The Minutemen wasn't like Black Flag—a band that existed like a sports franchise with new members frequently replacing those who'd fallen out of favor with management. The trio of Boon, Watt, and Hurley had stayed together through thick and thin. For Watt, being in the Minutemen was as much a part of his identity as being a sailor in the US Navy was for his father.

Carducci was back in Illinois when the accident happened. His sister, Lisa, had died from cancer the previous month, and he went home for the holidays to be with his family. "D. was one of the few at SST who knew," Carducci said about his sister's death. "He'd lost his mother to cancer and so was sensitive to it."[33]

Boon's sensitivity as an artist and as a person set him apart from the others. He cared about people, not because of some moral stricture but because he believed in the inherent goodness of human beings. When Watt was deep in his reading of classic authors like Joyce and Dante, Boon complained that Watt's lyrics had gotten "too spaced out."[34] Boon's proletariat humanism balanced Watt's intellectual curiosity.

Everyone at SST was an outsider, but perhaps none more so than Boon. He was bullied all his life because of his size—he stood five feet ten and weighed more than three hundred pounds at his heaviest and was taunted on the stage and teased behind his back. Doormen, bouncers, and stage security couldn't wrap their heads around the fact that a man built like an offensive lineman was the Minutemen's lead vocalist and guitar player. Boon performed with the energy of an athlete and bounced around the stage as if he were proving to the world that he truly belonged there. Watt wrote, "the man was amazing. he would play his heart out w/total conviction. this was no pose for him, it was a mission."[35]

Although Boon's onstage exuberance thrilled fans, many promoters worried whether the stage would hold up under the strain. At a show in Portland, Boon crashed through the stage and kept on playing. "He was so active on stage," Kite recalled, "with the amount of weight he was jumping up and down with, all of us were worried that he was going to keel over from a heart attack."[36]

But his heart was the one thing that never let him down. Boon's funeral was held on January 4, 1986, at Green Hills Mortuary in Rancho Palos Verdes. Several of his friends couldn't bring themselves to attend. For Rollins, his friend's funeral proved to be too intense, too real. Everyone dealt with the tragedy differently. Some withdrew from it while others tried to move on. Watt's solution was to retreat from SST, music, and the world. For him, December 22, 1985, was the day the music died.

In retrospect, the success of *3-Way Tie (for Last)* seemed cruel, even grotesque. The cover of the album features a painting by Boon that depicts the heads of all three members of the Minutemen mounted on plaques—like trophies killed for sport. In light of Boon's violent death, the cover is eerily macabre.

Disturbed by Watt's reclusive behavior, those closest to him tried to intervene. Kira Roessler was particularly concerned. "When D. Boon was killed, I was dating Mike," she said. "I was out of town when I got the news. I came back to town and Mike was in his room and he didn't want to play bass anymore, and he didn't want to leave his room."[37]

Roessler had been collaborating with Watt, and although she doesn't play on *3-Way Tie (for Last)*, she cowrote four of the tracks with him. She knew how Watt worked as a creative artist and tried to coax him out of seclusion—even though she was working on her master's degree at Yale University. The couple drove back to Connecticut and had many conversations about what the future had in store for them.

Watt's identity as an artist was tied to the Minutemen. "you must understand that I never really saw myself as a musician or a song/lyric writer," Watt said. "music was one way me and d. boon shared our lives together so in a sense, the connection I had w/this art form was much more personal than an aesthetic endeavor. the personal connection is what I found much more important than any other aspiration.... d. boon was my best friend and dearest connection to this world. what we did as minutemen was in a sense a direct reflection of how we saw and shared life together. when I wrote songs, I wrote them for him. when we played gigs and I was on stage w/him, there was a confidence he instilled in me like no other. how could anyone be afraid w/d. boon on stage with them?"[38]

For Watt, Boon's death meant that not only was the Minutemen finished, but so was Watt's musical career. No more mersh, no more spiels, no more gigs.

7

While Boon's friends tried to make peace with his sudden passing, questions about the accident swirled. What happened out there in the desert?

Boon's father, Danny, flew out to Phoenix, where his sister, also named Linda, lived and worked as a nurse at the very same hospital where Kite was being operated on for a severely broken ankle. Boon Sr., who'd worked on cars all his life, went to the site of the accident, studied the scene, and then proceeded to the impound yard to take photos of the van. After careful study, he determined the accident was caused not by Kite falling asleep or by a flat tire but by a broken rear axle.

Danny Boon contacted SST to make sure this information was included in SST's press release about his son's tragic death. Carducci was clear about this in his statement to the press. Despite the fact that the police and the press reached the same conclusion—that the accident was caused by the collapse of the right rear axle—because Kite's confusion at the scene of the accident was recorded in the police report, a different narrative took hold in the public imagination. This falsehood was doubly cruel because it implicated Kite in the death of her fiancé and maiming of her sister, who was left paralyzed from the waist down. Although Kite was never charged by the police or sued by anyone connected to the tragedy, rumors of her culpability persist to this day.

Meanwhile, Mugger needed to find someone to replace Garfias at SST. Out of respect, he asked her who she would recommend for the job, and she suggested her roommate Kara Nicks, who worked as a buyer at the Wherehouse music store in Torrance.

Nicks was no stranger to SST. While living in Tucson, Arizona, she'd gone to see Black Flag in May 1983. After the show, she and a friend got in the van to go see them play in Phoenix the following night. Nicks insisted on helping the band load in and set up the equipment so that no one at the club would mistake her for a hanger-on (a mistake one bouncer made many years later when he called her a groupie and put her in a bear hug; Nicks bit off his ear).

Once she made her way out to LA, Nicks hooked up with SST and roadied for Black Flag, the Minutemen, and the Meat Puppets for one-off shows around Southern California. She didn't have an easy time of it in LA and was homeless on more than one occasion. When Mugger got wind of her situation, he intervened and situated her with Garfias, who was living with D. Boon and Linda Kite at the time. Nicks also had relatives in Arizona and briefly considered joining her roommate on the trip to Tucson. "I was supposed to have been in the van that rolled over," Nicks said, "but I couldn't get off work."[39]

On the day of D. Boon's funeral, Nicks took over Garfias's role at SST Records. "I started out in mail order," Nicks recalled, "and Mugger was really quickly impressed with me, so he handed me the reins to the warehouse and shipping and receiving and, right behind that, distribution and sales."[40]

In addition to new employees, Mugger introduced the first computer to

SST to keep track of the books. A photocopy machine was also added. It was a brave new world for SST.

8

Just as *The Process of Weeding Out* and *In My Head* were hitting the shelves in 1985, Ginn was assembling his new side project, Gone, which was an uncharacteristically involved process. After Ginn kicked Roessler out of Black Flag, he reached out to people in the indie music community to let them know he was looking for a new bass player. One of those people was Randy Ellis (a.k.a. Randy Now), a disc jockey and promoter at Trenton, New Jersey's, notorious punk club City Gardens.

Ellis informed local bassist Andrew Weiss, who had been in Regressive Aid with drummer Sim Cain. Weiss promptly contacted Ginn and offered his services. By then, Ginn had already recruited C'el Revuelta, but he invited Weiss and Cain to join him in a side project. Cain said that Weiss called him up. "If you don't say yes, I'll kill you."[41]

Weiss and Cain were well suited for Ginn's project. They were experimental artists who enjoyed thumbing their noses at the rock establishment. They'd also played together in the noisily scabrous Scornflakes and were part of the early Trenton scene that included Ween.

Weiss and Cain flew out to Los Angeles in December 1985 to begin rehearsing the songs for Gone's first album. That record, *Let's Get Real, Real Gone for a Change* (SST 061), is a great leap forward from *The Process of Weeding Out*. On Ginn's previous instrumental album, the players were creative collaborators in name only, but Ginn's new project benefitted from an infusion of fresh talent.

Let's Get Real, Real Gone for a Change serves up ten songs with a variety of styles in thirty-six minutes. The three opening tracks set the album apart from Ginn's previous instrumental work. "Insidious Detraction" is marked by inventive riffing that constantly corkscrews in on itself yet continues to churn forward. The next track, "Get Gone," makes use of samples from an Elvis Presley performance, which provides the inspiration for the album's title. "Peter Gone" explores the subgenre of surf music used for spy thrillers in film and television, as in Henry Mancini's "Peter Gunn Theme." Three songs, three different styles of play. Ginn's willingness to explore—and have fun with—other genres of instrumental music is what makes the record such a departure. It's hard to imagine Black Flag performing a song dedicated to Ginn's girlfriend ("Rosanne") or a playful nod to porno music ("Ch. 69").

Gone differed from other trios on the SST roster in that it was wholly committed to a variety of instrumental music. Unlike songs on Black Flag records, each attributed to individual collaborators, all the songs on *Let's Get Real, Real Gone for a Change* are simply credited to Gone. Although Weiss and Cain shared Ginn's work ethic and were dedicated players, the SST lifestyle, which included a road trip to Northern California to see the Grateful Dead, took some getting used to. "This was all shocking to me," Cain said. "I realized that whatever preconceived notions I had about Black Flag were wrong."[42]

9

In the shadow of Boon's gruesome death, Black Flag made the final preparations for the epic In My Head Tour, a six-month jaunt to all four corners of the United States. Accompanying Black Flag—though you could say it was the other way around—was Ginn's instrumental project Gone and Painted Willie, which consisted of Phil Newman on bass, Vic Makauskas on guitar, and Dave Markey on drums.

Markey had been kicking around the LA punk scene since he was a teenager and had worn many hats. He played drums in the band Sin 34, wrote the Southern California scene report for *Maximum Rocknroll*, collaborated with Jordan Schwartz on the zine *We Got Power*, and directed the films *The Slog Movie* in 1982 and *Desperate Teenage Lovedolls* in 1984 with friends and members of Redd Kross.[43] He had already shot the film's sequel, *Lovedolls Superstar*, in 1985 for release later in 1986 when he went on tour with Black Flag.[44] All three films were low-budget affairs shot on a Super-8 but had killer soundtracks—thanks in part to Newman. After Sin 34 broke up, Newman started Spinhead Studios in North Hollywood, where he and Markey lived and honed their respective crafts. Out of this intensely creative environment Painted Willie emerged.

After a brief period as a four-piece unit with Nick Delaney of Vancouver's No Exit and Makauskas of Saint Vitus Dance Band (no relation to the boys from Lomita), Delaney exited the band, and Painted Willie settled in as a trio. In the spring of 1985, Painted Willie recorded a demo and submitted it to SST for consideration. Ginn was so impressed that he briefly considered enlisting Painted Willie as his backing band for the songs he would eventually record with Gone.

Later that year, Ginn ventured up to North Hollywood to produce Painted Willie's debut, *Mind Bowling* (SST 057), at Spinhead Studios. "It was just a play on mind blowing," Markey said of the album's title. "It was just mind blowing at the time to be welcomed into that world, to be invited into that by Greg Ginn himself."[45]

The album opens with "405," an instrumental with multiple time changes that builds to a gallop and slows to a crawl—just like driving on LA's most infamous freeway. The dynamic nature of the song must have caught Ginn's ear right off the bat. Like all of Markey's projects, Painted Willie has a sense of humor that comes across in songs like "Chia Pet," in which the eponymous plant grows into a jackbooted Nazi, and "Monkey Mia," a whimsically weird tale of cannibalism. Side 2 includes a spirited cover of "My Little Red Book," a faster, fuzzed-out version of the 1965 hit by Burt Bacharach and Hal David that was made famous the following year by LA's Love. Painted Willie's take on "My Little Red Book" wouldn't be out of place on a Hüsker Dü record.

Mind Bowling announced Painted Willie as the increasingly rare post-punk band that retained the essence of punk rock: fast, driving rhythms with tuneful melodies and a touch of thrash. While many post-punk bands of the mid-1980s were trying to distance themselves from the collapse of hardcore and reinvent themselves into something new, Painted Willie embraced its roots as it explored new territory in a way that was slightly ahead of its time.

Newman's midrange bass lines exude a buttery tone that contrasts with his abrasive snarl. Makauskas's riffs aren't as regimented as some metal-influenced guitarists, but they pull from both ends of the punk-metal spectrum. In addition to contributing vocals, Markey punishes the tubs with old-fashioned smash and bash. Black Flag's Martinez and Gone's Cain may

Phil Newman, Vic Makauskas, and Dave Markey of Painted Willie (and Naomi Petersen's shadow) in Redondo Beach in 1986. (Photo by Naomi Petersen Photography.)

have been more technically proficient, but neither was as fun to watch as Markey when he was behind the kit.

The specter of Boon's death raised its head at the beginning of the In My Head Tour. After a show in Huntington Beach the crew prepared for an all-night drive across the desert to Tucson—the same route that marked Boon's last ride. But C'el Revuelta, Black Flag's new bass player, got drunk, and his performance fell well short of the band's exacting standards. To make matters worse, Revuelta had to return a vehicle he'd borrowed but was no in shape to drive it, delaying the entire caravan.

The fleet comprised a pair of Dodge Ram 350 vans, an International Harvester truck to haul the enormous PA system, nine musicians from three bands, roadie Joe Cole, manager Mitch Bury, and sound engineers Davo and Rat. Thirteen people: one mission. When Saccharine Trust, the Minutemen, or even SWA toured with Black Flag, nearly everyone shared a bond because they'd been gigging together for years. Not this time. Most of the people didn't know one another very well—if at all—including members of their own bands.

Although Markey knew Ginn and Rollins, the new members, Martinez and Revuelta, were strangers to him. Rollins, however, was hostile to Markey because the filmmaker had brought his camera along with an eye toward documenting the tour, which Rollins didn't appreciate. Thanks to the film Markey eventually made—*Reality 86'd*—and Rollins's compulsive journaling, which inspired Cole to do the same, it's a remarkably well-documented tour.

With Ginn at the helm, a tour is never just a tour, but this one felt different. Ginn threw all his energy into Gone and made no secret about his priorities. "I think that Black Flag is his second string project," Rollins wrote in his journal.[46] It was not unusual for Ginn to play several times a day: first at an in-store with Gone, then during the band's opening set at the venue, and once more with Black Flag as headliner. At some venues, the bands played two sets, which meant quadruple duty for Ginn.

"We would play at least three times a day," Cain said. "We would load in this stadium-sized PA, no matter what sized club we were playing. We would load in, then Gone would jump back in the van and go to play a record store or a street corner or whatever, and then go back to the venue and play the opening set. Greg would get a one-set rest while Painted Willie played and then play again with Black Flag. If it was a two show night, he wound up playing six or seven sets a day."[47]

Many—if not most—musicians of Ginn's talent and stature would balk at the prospect of posting up outside a dry cleaner's shop or record store to rock out a short set in sweatpants while passersby went about their business, but not Ginn. He took it all in stride. "Playing that much didn't bother me at all," Ginn said. "I like playing. It's what I do."[48]

The rest of the crew, which had to haul more than thirty pieces of equipment in and out of the club each night, was not as sanguine. The road-weary musicians acrobatically slid down the ramps as they tried to wrangle the heavy road cases out of the truck only to have to load them back in again a few hours later. This process took four hours minimum: two to load in, two to load out. The sameness of the drudgery was slightly offset by the challenge of trying to cram the gear into clubs that often weren't big enough.

Cain recalled that "to be on a Black Flag tour, you were there as a roadie.

Black Flag had a massive amount of equipment because they wanted to be a self-contained unit, so that no outside influences could mess with the show. We were hauling a lot of gear, and the fact that we got to play was a bonus. After I joined that tour, I lost 15 pounds."[49]

Everyone pitched in, some more than others. Rollins saw the load-in process as an obstacle to the only real free time he had during the tour, the brief period between sound check and show time. Afterward, Rollins would try to hide out someplace where he could drink coffee, write in his journal, and attempt to recover from his many ailments exacerbated by the rigors of touring. This wasn't always possible, and on the rare day off he'd retreat to a hotel room or hang out with an admirer, such as Michael Stipe of R.E.M.

But these days were the exception, not the norm. Rollins had lingering issues with his surgically repaired knee. In Houston, he reinjured his wrist during an altercation with a fan, and in Charlotte he collided with Ginn onstage, resulting in an undiagnosed concussion and a swollen eyelid. Dave Rat was attacked by skinheads during a show in Tampa, and when the gang showed up the following night in Orlando, the crew members armed themselves with pipes and hammers. Black Flag generated more trauma and triage than some bands experience in a lifetime, and that was just the first month of the tour.

In his journal, Rollins repeatedly reflects on the animosity he felt from Ginn. "Greg does not like me that much. At least he told me. I can respect that. It makes playing kind of strange sometimes. Makes me feel on the outside of everybody. Makes me wonder if I have any friends at all."[50]

As much as Rollins professed his preference for solitude, it must have been an isolating experience to be five years into the Black Flag experience and find himself surrounded by strangers. Black Flag's touring operation had never been more dialed in, but in other ways the band was falling apart. The elaborate sound system underscored the fact that its audience was shrinking. No matter how strong the logistical apparatus or how talented the players, camaraderie and community are critical to the success of a touring operation. "In all of those six months I never saw the two together other than on stage," Markey said of Ginn and Rollins's relationship, "nor did I ever see the two speak."[51]

But it wasn't all violent skinheads and existential suffering. The crew popped mushrooms like they were corn chips, mugged for Markey's camera, conducted impromptu drum circles, and held sing-alongs in the Rocky Mountains. Ginn, however, never took days off. On March 7, they were back in Southern California to tape a Painted Willie performance, which resulted in the EP *Live from Van Nuys* (SST 085) that Ginn produced. Ginn also found the time to record a new Gone album, *Gone II—but Never Too Gone!* (SST 086), in April at Total Access.

The In My Head Tour continued through the spring and into the summer with an extensive crawl through the Midwest. The tour finally wound down on June 27, 1986, at Graystone Hall in Detroit. It would stand as Black Flag's final show for more than twenty-five years, and the last time Greg Ginn and Henry Rollins performed together. The final song?

"Louie Louie," of course.

10

Back in LA, the dominoes had already started to fall. Spot decided it was time to move on from SST. He gradually severed ties with the label in 1985, and the following year he moved out of LA altogether. He'd been captivated by Austin since he first visited the city in 1977 during its cosmic cowboy days. He'd recorded both the Big Boys and the Dicks in Austin and decided to try his luck there.

Carducci told Ginn that he'd come to SST to work with Black Flag and was determined to see the project through to the end. But it didn't take a mind reader to see that Ginn's priorities were elsewhere. It had been more than fifteen months since Black Flag had been in the studio, and the band hadn't booked any time to record. Ginn had started a new project with Gone and was already planning to go back on the road—without Black Flag.

Carducci had spent almost five years with SST. He was not a musician, nor did he have a desire to pursue a career in music. He was a writer, and he thought it was time to go home and be one. But the decision to leave wasn't just about business. Ever since his sister's death, Carducci felt uneasy about his place at SST. After Boon's funeral, he called up Ginn and Dukowski at

Global and told them his plans. As one of SST's four owners, he wanted to discuss a buyout. Carducci calculated the number of hours he'd put into the label since his arrival in September 1981 at minimum wage.

"They agreed to the figure," Carducci said.[52]

Ginn asked him to stay for another three months, which he did, and to consider going to England to run an SST office in London, which he did not. "They intended to sign some new bands," Carducci explained, "and wanted me to train Rich Ford to walk the new titles through manufacturing."[53]

The next to go was Pettibon. Like everyone who found himself on the outs with Ginn, Pettibon's breakup with SST took place over a long time. Like Carducci, Pettibon had ambitions beyond what he could achieve with SST, yet his work with Black Flag had come to define him. This was a recipe for resentment. Though Pettibon lacked a formal education in the fine arts, he saw himself first, last, and always as an artist and was every bit as dedicated to his art as Greg was to his.

But the relationship between the Ginn siblings had soured. When *Loose Nut* was in production, SST recycled an image Pettibon had provided for a flyer several years earlier without consulting him. Pettibon arrived at Global to discover Stevenson, who was pressed into serving as an art director, cutting up his artwork for use on the lyric sheet. Pettibon was furious.

When *The Blasting Concept Volume II* (SST 043) came out in October 1985, it was released without any artwork on the front cover, and the back cover was plastered with promotional photos, many of which were taken by Naomi Petersen. This, however, was not the original vision for the compilation. Pettibon had provided art and liner notes for the record in August, but Ginn didn't like what his brother had to say. The notes took the form of a direct address to the readers, questioning their taste and speculating on how they came to own the record. Pettibon even takes a shot at SST's growing number of in-house bands: "I wish we could put our SST staff (that's 90% of the band-members and their cousins–Ed.) on the cover."[54]

Carducci, who spent a great deal of time and effort curating the compilation and had enormous respect for Pettibon, considered it better to remove Pettibon's art than to run it without his copy, so the album went forward without either. The result is a fluorescent green cover with Day-Glo orange lettering that's eye-catching for all the wrong reasons: it resembles a brightly colored spacer in a record bin.

Pettibon also had issues with the cover of *In My Head*, which was created once again by Cameron. Only this time he didn't have an image to work with. "When I was doing *In My Head*," Cameron explained, "I came up with the concept of the silhouetted head surrounded by several ideas, and then put a few more images on the back. I got approval and rolled with it. Apparently Ray didn't want more than two pieces of his work used on any cover. So he wasn't happy about it and I believe it may have furthered the rift between him and Greg. Had I known that was an issue, I would have done something different."[55]

In December 1985, when *3-Way Tie (for Last)* came out, Pettibon's posters and zines, which now numbered in the fifties (though many were out of print), were advertised on the SST flyer under the subhead "PETTIBON GHETTO." The same term was used on the flip side of the catalog sheet to denote "NON SST" material—namely, Nig-Heist's records as well as a few releases from New Alliance that SST distributed, but the language seemed designed to provoke a reaction, and it did.

Pettibon went to SST to retrieve the work he'd contributed to Black Flag's live album *Who's Got the 10½?* (SST 060) and the single "Annihilate This Week" (SST 081), ensuring his art wouldn't appear on another SST release. The last new SST record to include Pettibon's art was Black Flag's *In My Head*. When SST issued its first four-page catalog—"GUNS OR RECORDS? SST SURVIVAL CATALOGUE"—in early 1986, all of Pettibon's products were removed. The "Pettibon ghetto" had been torn down.

In Pettibon's absence, SST turned to the creative people in its orbit. Naomi Petersen, whom Carducci writes about at length in his tribute to the photographer, *Enter Naomi*, created the cover for Black Flag's *Who's Got the 10½?*, which was recorded at Starry Night in Portland, Oregon, on August 23, 1985. On the front cover, a twelve-inch ruler sits atop Schwartz's desk calendar, filled with notes, numbers, dates, and doodles. A collage of photos of Ginn, Rollins, Roessler, and Martinez rounds out the back side.

Baiza provided artwork for Saccharine Trust's *We Became Snakes* (SST 048) and Minuteflag's self-titled collaboration between members of Black Flag and the Minutemen (SST 050). Ford painted the cover of SWA's *Your Future If You Have One*. Even Carducci got in on the act. Before parting ways with SST, he contributed artwork for the cover of Saccharine Trust's improvised live album *Worldbroken* (SST 046). None of these artists, however, could fill the immense void left by Pettibon. The artist's exit was comparable to the sudden departure of a founding member of the band. This broaches the question: Was Black Flag really Black Flag without Raymond Pettibon?

Pettibon's iconic logo and images supplied Black Flag's record covers with immediate brand recognition. While the band turned over its lineup, experimented with its sound, and even ventured into unusual formats (doom metal, spoken word, instrumental music), Pettibon's logo and pen-and-ink drawings reassured listeners they were getting a bona fide Black Flag experience. In other words, Black Flag the band benefitted from Black Flag the brand—a brand that Pettibon created and sustained through every step of Black Flag's tumultuous history. One could argue that Black Flag's graphic representation was more stylistically consistent than its music.

Pettibon contributed more than just flyers and album covers. His mordant wit and macabre style made Pettibon's work instantly recognizable to fans who were familiar with it and seized the attention of those who weren't. A Pettibon piece was more than the juxtaposition of image and word; it was a whole mood that somehow managed to capture the residual rot of the late '70s and the creeping menace of the early '80s. It conveyed a terrifying vision of Southern California that was strange yet familiar, whether you encountered it in New York or Newport Beach. Everyone knew the good vibrations the Beach Boys sang about in the '60s were bogus, but Americans went along with it anyway. Pettibon's body of work served as a dark counterpoint to this vision, with scene after scene of intensely bad vibes to which Black Flag provided the soundtrack. Although many have tried, no other independent record label before or since has been so closely aligned with the vision of a single visual artist.

Pettibon's break with SST coincided with the first solo exhibition of his work, at the Semaphore Gallery in New York in 1986. Clearly SST needed Pettibon more than Pettibon needed SST. In interview after interview, Pettibon maintained that his work in punk rock had held him back, which has been borne out by his success as a fine artist. His flyers used to decorate lampposts; now his work hangs in museums and is sought after by collectors from all over the world.

While Pettibon remains loyal to his many friends from the South Bay, he has tried, without much success, to distance himself from the LA punk rock scene that he helped create. He stopped talking to his brother not long after he left SST behind, a silence that persisted through the death of their father, Regis, in 2005 and continues to this day.

11

Henry Rollins was enjoying the summer in Washington, DC, when he got a phone call from Ginn informing him that Ginn was quitting the band and thus ending Black Flag. The news came as a shock, and Rollins wasn't sure how to take it. He hadn't been fired, but it sure felt like it. Ginn made a choice, and he chose Gone over Black Flag. Because Black Flag was essentially Ginn, Rollins, and some hired players, Ginn quitting was no different from firing Rollins.

For those who'd been on the In Your Head Tour, the news of Black Flag's demise didn't come as a surprise. "The negative vibes were apparent from the get go," Markey said. "The tensions between Henry Rollins and Greg Ginn were high.... How the tour went on for six months was a testimony to the thirteen individuals who were on that tour."[56]

In the span of a few short months SST lost not only the talent but the enormous drive of Hüsker Dü, D. Boon, Spot, Joe Carducci, Raymond Pettibon, and Henry Rollins. Where would the label go from here?

Greg Ginn is Gone. Raji's in Hollywood on September 12, 1986. (Photo by Naomi Petersen Photography.)

CHAPTER 9
SST vs. New York

1986

1

Paul Hudson could have been anything he wanted to be. Athletic, intelligent, and creative, he was a seeker whose mind was open to the possibilities of the world around him. Hudson's mother was Jamaican, and his father served as a mechanic in the air force. By the time the Hudsons moved to the Washington, DC, area, they'd lived all over the world, including Liverpool (where Hudson was born), Jamaica, Hawaii, California, Alabama, Texas, and New York. After graduating from high school, Paul strove to make his parents happy by enrolling in a premed program, but his heart wasn't in it, and he dropped out. Discouraged by his apparent lack of drive, Hudson's father urged Paul to pick up a book, which he did, and it changed punk rock forever.

The self-help book Paul plucked off his father's shelf, *Think and Grow Rich*, by Napoleon Hill, advocated a purpose-driven course of mental improvement that focused on positivity and persistence. Hill placed a premium on desire and believed that not only was success impossible without it, but also the greater the desire the greater the reward.

For Hudson and his younger brother Earl, their greatest desire was to play music together, and with the help of their friends Gary Miller and Darryl Jenifer, in '76 they formed a jazz fusion band that was heavily influenced by the Weather Report and Return to Forever. They chose the name Mind Power after Hill's inspirational book, but success didn't come quickly or easily. This, too, was part of Hill's philosophy: he believed failure was the proving ground that weeded out those who were easily discouraged and lacked determination and desire.

On June 16, 1978, the band went to the Capital Centre in Landover, Maryland, to see Chick Corea and Stanley Clarke perform. Although the duo had played together in Return to Forever, it was the opening act—Bob Marley and the Wailers—that made the biggest impression that night. The experience exposed Mind Power to Rastafarian teachings in musical form and put the Hudson brothers in touch with their heritage in a powerful new way. Bob Marley may have planted the seed, but an altogether different style of play provided a conversion experience.

After being exposed to bands like the Sex Pistols, the Dead Boys, and the Ramones by Sid McCray, Mind Power morphed into Bad Brains. It seemed only natural to be intrigued by a genre of music where an abundance of desire was the only prerequisite. "Once I discovered the Ramones and the Damned and all," Jenifer explained, "I said, 'Shit, I can make my own shit like this.'"[1]

Miller adopted the moniker Dr. Know, Jenifer became Darryl Cyanide (although the name didn't stick), and Paul took on the name H. R. Brain. (The initials originally stood for "Hunting Rod" but eventually became "Human Rights.") Though the young musicians may have found the complexities of progressive jazz elusive, they were talented and dedicated players. With Dr. Know on guitar, Jenifer on bass, Earl at the drums, and H.R. front and center, Bad Brains played punk rock with a level of proficiency and intensity no one else could touch.

They threw themselves into DC's quickly evolving punk rock scene, embracing the movement's revolutionary spirit and freedom of expression. While the notion of four Black men playing punk rock was shocking at first, in the predominantly Black city of Washington, DC, which has its own unique musical traditions, it made sense. One thing that punk rock and go-go had in common was a lack of separation between the band and the audience. When Bad Brains took the stage, all were called to get swept up in the frenzy, and audiences responded.

Bad Brains announced itself to the world when it opened for the Damned at the Bayou in Georgetown on June 24, 1979. "It was one of those stupendous shows, an absolute benchmark," said Kim Kane of the Slickee Boys, one of DC's original punk bands. "I loved the Damned but the Bad Brains blew them into outer space."[2] They began playing all-ages shows at Madam's Organ and d.c. space, thrilling one young fan by the name of Henry Garfield. H.R. befriended the future vocalist of Black Flag, sensing there was a place for him on the punk rock stage. "They played like their lives depended on it," Rollins said. "They made you feel that you could do whatever you wanted to do. I couldn't sleep after seeing them. I couldn't even see straight."[3]

While it's true Bad Brains was banned from clubs throughout DC, so were many other fledgling punk rock bands, such as Ian MacKaye's Teen Idles. The music scene was oriented around alcohol sales—the drinking age in DC was eighteen at the time—and venues had little patience for bands that drew kids who weren't old enough to drink and were abstaining from alcohol altogether in increasing numbers.

Frustrated with the small crowds and limited opportunities in DC, Bad Brains took up an offer from the Damned to play in London. In the winter of '79, the band played some shows in New York to raise money for the trip overseas and set off across the Atlantic—without work visas. At Gatwick, authorities detained Bad Brains and confiscated the band's equipment, which was subsequently lost. The band was unceremoniously sent back to New York dead broke and without any gear. In hindsight, the decision to go to London was misguided, but the band—H.R. in particular—often took unconventional steps that favored intuition over reason, and Bad Brains missed out on many opportunities as a result.

Back in DC, the Teen Idles lent a helping hand, sharing its instruments and a place to practice with the beleaguered Bad Brains. The bands rehearsed back to back, and these sessions not only helped Bad Brains get back on its feet but also inspired MacKaye to start a new project called Minor Threat.

H.R. was a charismatic and influential figure in the DC scene, inspiring peers and electrifying fans. Although he was seen as a leader, his pursuits pulled him in different directions. He expanded his mind with marijuana and LSD, but his heroin use nearly brought him to his knees. The knowledge he sought from religious figures in DC's Rastafarian movement led him out of the darkness of addiction, but these teachings also pulled him away from punk rock.

Although Dr. Know and Jenifer also embraced Rasta teachings, neither was ready to give up his dream of making Bad Brains a success. H.R., however, regarded the desire for material things with increasing suspicion, a symptom of the sickness of Babylon. Then again, he could afford to be skeptical as a wealthy new manager named Mo Sussman outfitted the band with new gear and sharp-looking suits to wear on stage.

H.R.'s performances had always been shamanic, but now he began to embrace the shaman's role as truth-teller and bringer of the word of Jah. Bad Brains played reggae songs with greater frequency at a time when hardcore was sweeping across the country. The music was getting faster, but Bad Brains operated at its own speed, on its own schedule. H.R.'s message of peace and love disguised the disharmony within his own band as well as the concern within his inner circle about his frequent mood swings and increasingly erratic behavior.

Bad Brains' fans appreciated the music's revolutionary outlook—punks almost always sided with the oppressed—but religion was religion. As Christianity and conservatism became entangled during the Reagan administration, the band's embrace of Rastafarian reggae left many fans confused and, ultimately, disenchanted.

Around the same time that Rollins left DC to join Black Flag, Bad Brains returned to New York and immediately started playing shows at 171-A, a performance space and recording studio run by Jerry Williams. In May 1981, Williams recorded part of a Bad Brains show and convinced the band to record an album there. The recordings were completed that summer, and the band signed a deal with Reachout International Records, which was something of a misnomer since it was a cassette-only label. The self-titled tape featured an iconic illustration of a lightning bolt striking the Capitol dome; it was created by Dave Parsons, a jack-of-all-trades who ran Rat Cage Records out of the basement of 171-A.

After the record was released to widespread acclaim in early '82, the band embarked on its first national tour. By its end, H.R. and the gang would wish they'd stayed home. Bad Brains played to a packed house in San Francisco but were startled by the openness of the gay community. In an interview the following day, H.R. made homophobic remarks of a violent nature. The situation came to a head in Texas during an ugly confrontation between H.R. and the Big Boys' Randy "Biscuit" Turner and Tim Kerr. Word of Bad Brains' intolerance spread through the punk rock grapevine. Instead of disavowing his hateful comments, H.R. announced his intention to transform Bad Brains into a reggae outfit called Zion Train.

Unfortunately, he didn't inform his bandmates of this decision. While Earl generally went along with his brother, both Dr. Know and Jenifer felt increasingly at odds with the things H.R. said and the problems they caused, which were about to get a lot worse.[4]

At the end of the tour, Bad Brains' equipment was stolen from their van, putting them in the unenviable position of returning to New York without any gear—again. Nor did Bad Brains have a place to stay. Williams had been booted out of 171-A for nonpayment of rent. Apparently, he was under the impression that Bad Brains was taking care of the bills. Understandably upset, Williams took the tapes he'd made for Bad Brains' next record and split.[5]

For someone trying to live his life in peace, H.R. had a knack for stirring up trouble, but just when the situation seemed untenable, someone would appear to bail the band out. This time it was Ric Ocasek of the Cars, a talented producer, who lent Bad Brains a helping hand and produced its next EP, *I and I Survive*, and the full-length album *Rock for Light*.

Anthony Countey was another individual who showed up right when the band needed him. The native New Yorker became a fan of Bad Brains the moment he saw the band perform at Roseland Ballroom as the opening act for Gang of Four and Bush Tetras in late 1981. It was immediately clear to Countey that he was witnessing something special and unique: "When they started playing it was like the floor fell away. I lost track of reality. It was so potent, I couldn't believe it. I was like, 'What's happening?' This is not a blues structure. This is not rock and roll. This is not like anything else. What is this?"[6]

After the show, Countey was convinced he found what he went searching for in the '60s when he left New York to go to San Francisco. Not only was Bad Brains the best live band in existence—a belief shared by many—but it delivered something real. What Countey lacked in qualifications he made up for with insight and intuition, and he committed himself to the cause. Although he'd never managed a band before, he had experience helping musicians get through tough situations, which Bad Brains always seemed to be in. "If you drop me in the middle of almost anything," Countey said, "if it's going well, I'm a good person to have around. And if it's not going well, I'm a better person to have around because I'll do my fucking damnedest to keep it from crashing and burning."[7]

He'd need those skills managing Bad Brains. Keeping the band going, Countey soon learned, proved to be a Herculean task. Countey borrowed money from friends and bought a used Winnebago so the band could go out on another tour. Although Bad Brains was barely making enough to survive, with help from Ocasek, whose band racked up hit after hit for Elektra, Countey set up a meeting in LA with Tom Zutaut, an A&R executive at Elektra who'd just signed Mötley Crüe and would go on to ink Guns N' Roses to Geffen. For once, it seemed as though the stars were aligning.

While the band was excited about signing a deal with a major label, H.R. was at war with himself. His suspicion of corporations and fear of selling out made him apprehensive. Zutaut may have seemed like the answer to the band's prayers, but to H.R. the A&R executive was Babylon incarnate. When Countey introduced him, H.R. asked Zutaut, "Do you know what happens to people who mess with Rasta?"[8] Throughout the meeting, H.R. glowered at

Zutaut. The singer's hostile demeanor so unnerved the executive that afterward he asked Countey whether H.R. had threatened him. Naturally, Elektra declined to sign the band, and a deal rumored to be in the millions was scuttled.

Instead of inking a lucrative record contract and landing *Rock for Light* with a major label, the band released the album in the spring of '83 with an imprint of Passport Records called PVC Records. The album featured seventeen songs, but only seven were new. Six had appeared on the Bad Brains debut album, and the other four were from the *I and I Survive* EP. Nevertheless, the bulk of the record was hardcore, not reggae, though that wasn't always true of Bad Brains' live performances as H.R.'s desire to spread the word of Jah intensified. The record sold well, but within a few years, the label folded without ever sending the band a royalty statement. Bad Brains never saw a penny.

Things continued to unravel during Bad Brains' first European tour. During a show in England, a fan spat on H.R. Though gobbing was standard practice at punk rock shows, especially abroad, it wasn't going to fly with Bad Brains. "H.R. practically killed the kid," Countey said. "He roundhoused him with a 58." The blow left an impression from the mesh covering of the Shure SM58 microphone on the fan's temple. "Luckily the kid had a thick skull," Countey said.[9] Although the fan didn't press charges, H.R. had had enough of punk rock. He wanted to sing about peace, love, and understanding, and he was getting spat on instead. When Bad Brains returned to the United States, H.R. left the band. "He blew the whole thing up," Countey said.[10]

H.R. moved to Washington, DC, but chaos continued to follow him everywhere. He moved into a large three-story rowhouse on Seventeenth Street in Northwest DC with several like-minded musicians and friends. To make ends meet he sold marijuana, which was a risky proposition since the police precinct was located directly across the street from the Dread House, as the quasi-communal setup came to be known.

As H.R. got deeper into Rastafarianism, which involved smoking large quantities of marijuana, his mind took an apocalyptic turn. In New York, he'd joined the Rastafarian sect Twelve Tribes of Israel and was assigned to the tribe of Joseph after his birth month, February, which he shared with Bob Marley. H.R. assumed the name Joseph I, dressed exclusively in camouflage, and was consumed by revolutionary thoughts about the downfall of Babylon and the rise of Black nationalism, as predicted by the prophet Emperor Haile Selassie I based on his reading of the book of Revelation.

The DC punks who welcomed H.R.'s return were baffled by his militant turn. Despite his embrace of Rasta, H.R. finally made good on his promise to get his reggae band Zion Train off the ground, launched an eponymous solo project, and started up a record label. Dr. Know and Jenifer declined to participate in these endeavors, but Earl remained a stalwart supporter of his brother's musical projects.

From the beginning, H.R. was more than just a singer. On stage he was a spiritual force who possessed boundless energy and could express himself in a way that was both transgressive and transcendent. "We're talking about a performer who took the total rage and boundary-breaking of rock and roll and the deep spirituality of Rasta reggae and molded it into one," said DC musician Kenny Dread, who collaborated extensively with H.R. during this period.[11]

Shortly before his band's debut on May 23, 1984, H.R. was arrested on a marijuana charge and had to serve a two-month sentence at Lorton Reformatory in Lorton, Virginia. The fact that he was busted on his son's birthday added to the indignity. Although H.R.'s parole restrictions prevented him from touring, it was an incredibly prolific period for the embattled singer. He recorded the EP *It's About Luv* at Cue Recording Studios in Falls Church, Virginia. He planned to put it out on his own label with support from Julie Bird, who lived at the Dread House and bankrolled the operation.[12] For once, H.R. went into the studio with a plan in place for releasing the record. H.R. recruited guitarists David Jordan of Press Mob and David Byers, who'd played in the Enzymes, one of DC's earliest punk bands, and Outrage. Not only did Byers bring his significant guitar skills, but he produced the EP, beginning a long collaboration with H.R. as a musician and producer.

While H.R. intended Zion Train to be a reggae band, he took a different approach with his own project. *It's About Luv* is musically diverse, which would become a hallmark of his solo records. While few of the tracks match the intensity of Bad Brains, songs like "It'll Be Alright" show H.R. hadn't completely turned his back on hardcore. A press release written by Jimi Riley, who also designed the band's logo, declares, "The velocity and fury of the BAD BRAINS remains intact, but with this record JOSEPH I shows a new MATURITY and DIRECTION in his MESSAGE and SOUND. There is a polished merging of musical influences—from the delicate soulful vocal and Spanish-tinged guitar stylings of 'Who Loves You' to the razor sharp THRASH of 'It'll Be Alright' to the gentle muted reggae of 'Happy Birthday My Son.'"

Unfortunately, Riley and H.R. had a falling out that was directly attributable to Riley's sexuality. When H.R. discovered his friend was gay, he disowned him. Riley was devastated, making H.R.'s decision to do an interview with Riley on the eve of *It's About Luv*'s release bizarre. During the interview, H.R. added to the homophobic statements he'd made years before and made a number of highly unusual remarks, such as calling his new record "a piece of shit."[13] When asked about his relationship to punk, H.R. declared, "Rasta has shown me that I am a dead punk. Rasta has shown me that I love punk and punk rockers. Rasta has taught me that to everything there is a time. If it wasn't for Rasta, I wouldn't play hardcore music. I would probably have sold out by now and started playing disco or funk or something like that."[14]

For many DC punks, H.R. no longer embodied the values of the evolving scene. At a time when many of the old guard were starting new bands, throwing themselves into Revolution Summer, and protesting apartheid in South Africa, H.R.'s homophobia was hostile and regressive. For H.R., it was a good time to get out of town, and Bad Brains came calling with the perfect opportunity.

Earlier that summer, Countey received a call from promoter Chris Williamson at the Rock Hotel in New York. Although the venue had seen better days, he wanted to put on a pair of hardcore shows with Bad Brains. Countey saw no harm in asking. Dr. Know and Jenifer were playing in a band with Ras Michael's son Michael Enkrumah, Mackie Jayson from the Cro-Mags, and Billy Banks, but the project struggled to get off the ground. Countey was surprised to learn that all of the original members were up for a reunion show.

Because so much time had passed since Bad Brains had played together, the band needed time to rehearse. Rather than embark on a nostalgia trip, Bad Brains immediately began experimenting with the material written with Enkrumah, composing new songs, and dusting off "I Against I," which was written long before the band's hiatus.

H.R.'s reputation may have taken a hit in DC and other punk rock communities across the country, but the shows at the Rock Hotel proved Bad Brains' reputation was still bulletproof in New York. After a year-and-a-half hiatus, enthusiasm for the band's return to New York was at an all-time high.

Bad Brains played a pair of sold-out shows with Raw Power and Scab on Friday and with the Cro-Mags and P.M.S. on Saturday. The packed house wasn't limited to punks, rockers, and Rastas. For industry insiders and hardcore fanatics alike, Bad Brains transcended genres. Even Andy Warhol and his entourage made the scene. "Everybody in New York came to that fucking show," Countey said, "and everybody got their minds blown."[15]

Bad Brains unleashed a mind-melting mix of metal and reggae delivered with H.R.'s aggressive athleticism. It was immediately clear to everyone in the audience that Bad Brains hadn't missed a beat. A few minutes into the show, Countey understood why the venue had such a miserable reputation: the building started to shake, and he was afraid the ceiling was going to collapse. "It snowed in that room," he said. "Because that theater space was so fucked up and old and unused that when the band started playing, the asbestos from the ceiling started raining down. I was like, 'We're all gonna die from this!'"[16]

Bad Brains was officially back. Offers to play came in from around the country. With new material to record, Countey made some calls to see whether he could generate interest from the majors. Although enthusiasm from fans was sky high, reception from the music industry was lukewarm—if that. The new songs were bigger than punk, but this unconventional fusion of rock, pop, funk, and metal confused record executives. How do you sell something if you can't put a label on it? Plus, the industry was still wary of Bad Brains. The word was out: H.R. didn't trust corporate rock, and the feeling was mutual.

Countey turned to SST, a label whose enmity of corporate rock exceeded

H.R. and Dr. Know of Bad Brains at La Casa de la Raza in Santa Barbara, November 26, 1986. (Photo by Alison Braun.)

even the band's. SST jumped at the opportunity. For years, Bad Brains sat at the top of a short list of bands with an open invitation to make a record with the label. Furthermore, unlike most bands that signed with SST, Bad Brains was a known quantity that could be counted on to sell records.

To make a record that captured the essence of Bad Brains, Countey needed a producer who understood the power of the band's live show. He reached out to Alan Douglas, who had worked with Jimi Hendrix. In turn, Douglas recommended Ron Saint Germain, a producer, engineer, and remixer who had worked with scores of artists. Intrigued, Saint Germain went to see Bad Brains play at the Ritz with Slayer and Megadeth shortly before the band set off on a West Coast tour, and he was impressed by the performance. Saint

Germain called Countey to tell him he was interested, but could SST afford him? The producer called Ginn to negotiate his fee, and Saint Germain recalled the conversation went something like this:

> **GINN:** We will give you $5,000.
> **SAINT GERMAIN:** Well, which song do you want to do?
> **GINN:** No, no, no, no. That's for the whole album.
> **SAINT GERMAIN:** Really?
> **GINN:** That's what we do, man.[17]

In the past, SST recorded its bands at Media Art, Total Access, or Radio Tokyo as cheaply and efficiently as possible, but as the label began to sign acts from around the country, it became necessary to pay producers outside of LA. However, the amount was always so low that it meant recording had to be done on a shoestring budget over a short time. But the qualities that worried major labels weren't an issue for SST, who seldom encroached on its artists' creativity. For Ginn and company, the rewards of signing Bad Brains far outweighed the risks. This gamble—if it could even be called that—paid off in a big way.

2

Legend has it the first thing Ginn did after Carducci left SST was call up Sonic Youth and offer the band a record deal. Ginn, Dukowski, and Mugger were all enamored with the band, but Carducci wasn't impressed. Because signing new artists to SST required approval from all four partners, only a unanimous vote would do. But like many a good story, this apocryphal anecdote is spoiled by the truth.

Farrell, who was familiar with the band's music and who'd booked some of Sonic Youth's earliest West Coast shows, advocated on the band's behalf almost as soon as he arrived at SST. For Farrell, it was a no-brainer: "Coming from a record label mindset," Farrell said, "any indie label would be lucky to sign them. Everything was in place. The band members are smart, innovative, motivated and very engaging people. I knew that there was no other US indie better suited to them."[18]

Sonic Youth had sent a demo tape to SST, and it landed on Carducci's desk. After Hüsker Dü left for the majors, the number of demos arriving at SST skyrocketed. They were largely ignored as the label was focused on scheduling releases and keeping the back catalog in print. But by 1986 the situation had changed, and SST was actively looking for new acts, particularly touring bands. The label was especially eager to add bands from the East Coast to the roster.

So, when Carducci put Sonic Youth's demo tape in a box to be sent to Global—and not in the trash as has been widely reported—Ginn and Dukowski were excited to see the tape from a group they were familiar with and that checked all the boxes of what they were looking for in a band. Hüsker Dü's departure had created a vacancy. Could Sonic Youth fill the void?

Sonic Youth emerged from the ashes of the No Wave movement of New York's Lower East Side and the burgeoning art explosion south of Houston Street. A native of Bethel, Connecticut, guitarist Thurston Moore moved to New York in '79 after his father's sudden death caused him to reevaluate his priorities. He joined the Coachmen, a fairly conventional guitar rock outfit that wrote its own songs and whose members were remarkable for being rather tall—Moore, the youngest, stood six feet six. Versed in punk rock and hardcore, and a fervent reader of zines, Moore was disappointed to discover the New York punk scene he'd read so much about had all but vanished. The bookish musician began to suspect that he came to New York too late.

Many of the members of New York's early punk bands and No Wave movement were artists. Painters, photographers, and sculptors were taking advantage of the city's cheap rent to create new art forms using video, installation, music, and performance. Being in a band was a way to participate in this outpouring of creative energy.

Moore fell in with Kim Gordon, a Californian who graduated from Otis College of Art and Design and drove to New York in 1980 with her friend and fellow artist Mike Kelley to—well, she wasn't sure why she came, but once she got into New York's avant-garde music scene, she displayed an affinity for the bass guitar and a knack for making things happen.

Gordon encouraged Moore to organize a festival in the summer of '81 for their friends and like-minded musicians. They jokingly called it Noise Fest, and it brought together everyone in their scene who was serious about loud, experimental music. Sonic Youth played its first show at the festival as a trio with Richard Edson on drums. Although the band's name sounded vaguely hardcore, its roots were more esoteric.

From the start, Sonic Youth did its own thing, with a distinctive, albeit unfocused, sound. Moore described the band in its first press release: "Crashing mashing intensified dense rhythms juxtaposed with filmic mood pieces. Evoking an atmosphere that could only be described as expressive fucked-up modernism. And so forth."[19]

Shortly after Noise Fest, Edson quit the band to pursue a successful career in acting that included roles in *Desperately Seeking Susan, Ferris Bueller's Day Off*, and *Platoon*. At Gordon's suggestion, Lee Ranaldo, a guitarist who was part of Glenn Branca's experimental guitar group, started playing with Sonic Youth, and the band began to develop the songs that would appear on its first, self-titled EP. The band played several gigs as a trio before asking Edson to play another festival in September. Branca saw Sonic Youth's show and invited the band to put out an album on the label he was starting: Neutral Records.

The first flares of the punk movement may have been fired in New York, but a network of independent labels didn't generate there like it did in LA, because all of the popular New York punk rock bands were snapped up by major labels. For bands in New York, a recording contract was a realistic possibility—until it wasn't. In LA, the punk and hardcore movements operated in opposition to that reality and created their own outlets out of necessity. Branca somewhat naively followed the path of those who had gone before him. This led to Sonic Youth recording its debut five-song EP for Neutral at Plaza Studios, where Blondie, the Ramones, and Richard Hell and the Voidoids had recorded their debuts.

A lot of what Moore knew about the punk rock scenes outside of New

York he'd gleaned from zines. He corresponded with Eddie Flowers of the West Coast zine *Search and Destroy* and Gerard Cosloy of Boston's *Conflict*. He would eventually start his own zine, *Killer*, in 1983 for the same reason that all punk fanatics get involved with zines—better access to the music they love.

Gordon's knowledge of West Coast punk rock was firsthand. She'd actually seen Black Flag play with Keith Morris and was so enamored with Raymond Pettibon's illustrations that she would eventually write a critical appreciation of his work for *Artforum*. She had a broad appreciation for many genres of music; Moore's musical scope of interest was more limited. Gordon recalled that early in her relationship with Moore, "all he would listen to was hardcore."[20]

Naturally, the next step for Sonic Youth was to play some shows outside of New York. Joined by new drummer Bob Bert, Sonic Youth embarked on a pair of short tours with the Swans, whose lead singer, Michael Gira, Gordon had known back in LA. Sonic Youth seemed mild mannered, even lethargic off stage, but on stage the musicians attacked their instruments with drumsticks, power drills, and screwdrivers.

Back in New York, the band prepared to release another record—a single—with Neutral Records, but the label was suffering from financial setbacks. Sonic Youth moved from Plaza Studios to a basement in Chelsea where the band's friend Wharton Tiers was experimenting with a new 8-track he'd bought. Tiers had played in Branca's band Theoretical Girls and used the empty basement where he was a building supervisor as a rehearsal space. The son of a tape recorder salesman, Tiers grew up experimenting with tape machines and was predisposed to recording the bands that he and his friends played in.[21]

Sonic Youth had let Bert go after the grueling tour with Swans and invited Jim Sclavunos of Red Transistor to record with them, but he was discouraged by the dungeon-like setup in Tiers's basement and stuck around just long enough to record his tracks.

What started as a single became a full-length album titled *Confusion Is Sex* that featured a collaboration with Michael Gira and a cover of the Stooges' "I

Wanna Be Your Dog." *Confusion Is Sex* also marked the beginning of Sonic Youth's experimentation with alternate tunings. Moore and Ranaldo played a variety of cheap guitars—they would bring a dozen or more with them onstage—for different sounds, tones, and effects. Some were missing strings; others had their frets removed. For Ranaldo and Moore, a guitar's deficiencies and limitations were crucial to the experience they were trying to create. Sonic Youth was deconstructing the myth of the guitar player as a super-gifted maestro with top-line gear and rewriting the rules of rock and roll.

In '83, Moore joined Ranaldo as a member of Branca's experimental guitar ensemble for a European tour. Branca fused art, noise, and rock to create droning repetitive soundscapes at punishing volumes. There wasn't much opportunity for creative expression under Branca's strict direction, so Moore and Ranaldo made the most of the trip by booking shows for Sonic Youth at the gigs where Branca performed.

With this jaunt across Europe, Sonic Youth established its method for touring. Instead of putting together a repertoire of polished songs, Sonic Youth stuck to its new material, figuring out the songs as the tour progressed. Songs took on new forms that differed from the way they were played in rehearsal or on the record. "Each night is a roll of the dice," Ranaldo wrote in his journal.[22]

With its high-stakes approach and aggressive performances, Sonic Youth won over crowds. In Europe, audiences brought different expectations to art and didn't come to experimental musical events expecting to be entertained. Sonic Youth was different; the New York rockers were both arresting to listen to *and* thrilling to watch.

Although the band occasionally played shows to empty halls, at the end of the tour, Sonic Youth received glowing reviews in the notoriously difficult British music press. The band returned to New York feeling that perhaps the tide had turned. The members of the band were perpetually broke and had to work odd, and in some cases demeaning, jobs to pay the rent. Gordon waited tables while Moore worked as a street vendor selling ice cream sandwiches. Ranaldo and Bert worked in the visual arts, helping other artists get famous while they struggled to make ends meet. It was all so hard, but wasn't it supposed to be?

Despite not having any money, in June 1984 Moore and Gordon got married just as they were assembling material for the next album. Sonic Youth was probing California, looking for an entry point. During one of Gordon and Moore's visits to LA to visit her family, the couple explored the former site of the Spahn Movie Ranch. The Manson family was a source of fascination for the band, who devoured Ed Sanders's *The Family* and Vincent Bugliosi's *Helter Skelter*. Gordon's brother, Keller, had dated a woman who disappeared under mysterious circumstances, and Gordon claimed in interviews that she had been murdered by the Manson family. "America is a country built on people seeking utopias," Gordon said of her fascination with Manson, "and being from California, that was all very interesting to me. The whole Charles Manson thing was the most obvious symbol of what was wrong."[23]

Gordon and Moore were also familiar with how Manson's bad vibrations ran like an electric current through Raymond Pettibon's work and how Black Flag had co-opted Manson's concept of "creepy crawl." Eventually this fascination with the Mansons made its way into the band's music. Moore shared some ideas on the subject for a song he was writing with Lydia Lunch, who was back in New York after her sojourn in California, and the two came up with lyrics on the spot.

Sonic Youth recorded "Death Valley '69" with Tiers in July 1984, and it was released as a single, backed with "Brave Men Run (in My Family)," by Michael Sheppard's Iridescence Records. Sheppard was an LA promoter who "embraced the outré, the outsider, the offbeat."[24] He had shaken up the city's cultural landscape by being the first to bring Throbbing Gristle to Culver City's Veterans Auditorium. The label on the front side of "Death Valley '69" featured an image of Manson member Susan "Sadie" Atkins, and the flip side had a close-up of Henry Rollins's creepy crawl spider tattoo. Sonic Youth wanted to record another album but didn't have the money or the support of a label. Was the band attempting to send a signal to SST on its own wavelength?

With a loan from some wealthy friends, the band turned to Martin Bisi, who, with support from Bill Laswell and Brian Eno, had been running BC Studio in Gowanus, Brooklyn, since he was seventeen years old. Bisi had

238 CORPORATE ROCK SUCKS

recorded a mix of post-punk and rap artists, including Grand Mixer DXT's turntablism on "Rockit," the hit from Herbie Hancock's *Future Shock* that won a Grammy. The son of a classical pianist, Bisi had a profound love of the avant-garde, and he turned the dankly oppressive yet acoustically pleasing L-shaped room in the bowels of the building into a home for artists with eclectic tastes.

The eight tracks recorded that fall for *Bad Moon Rising* marked a turning point for Sonic Youth. While far from conventional, the songs on *Bad Moon Rising* are more structured. It's as if the players realized they could craft songs in a variety of modes without being defined by them. *Bad Moon Rising* is steeped in Americana and filtered through a pagan lens. For Sonic Youth, songs began with musical ideas: textures, tones, chords, riffs (and so forth) that the band expanded upon during rehearsals—a process that could take months. Lyrics came last and were written to match the feeling of the song, not the other way around.

Gordon and Moore share the vocal duties on the record, but between the long instrumental sections and spoken word pieces, there's not a lot of singing in the traditional sense. The title of the song "Society Is a Hole" hinges on Moore's mishearing of a lyric in Black Flag's "Rise Above." The track ends with a sample from Iggy and the Stooges' "Not Right" that Sonic Youth cut right into the song as an inside joke.

"Death Valley '69" marks the high point of the album and shows the way forward. Vocals by Moore and Lunch echo one another as a creepy commentary on the notion of killers following orders from a murderous mastermind. Despite the laconic maybe-I'll-kill-you, maybe-I-won't lyrics, "Death Valley '69" is Sonic Youth at its most propulsive—eddies of swirling guitars rocketing forward independent of the relentless rhythm section. Sonic Youth had found a way to incorporate both the horror at the end of the '60s and the nihilism of the mid-1980s in one terrifying soundscape of psychedelic hardcore. With its opening howl, Sonic Youth announced itself as more than a noisy New York band. However, the gory video, directed by Judith Barry and Richard Kern and filmed in New York on the day Ranaldo's first son was born, made it hard to forget the band's arty origins. The video aired on MTV but was eventually deemed too provocative for the video channel's sensibilities. "We're a rock band and we're proud of it. We're not an art, noise or an extreme band. We just do what we do,"[25] Ranaldo declared, but the music industry wasn't so sure.

Bad Moon Rising was released on Long Island's Homestead Records, which was run by the band's old friend Gerard Cosloy. In the UK, the record came out on Blast First, a new offshoot of the London independent label Rough Trade. Both labels were run by people who were just getting their feet wet in the record business and whose good intentions were often hamstrung by a lack of experience.

Sonic Youth couldn't resist the lure of California. In late '84, Gordon called up LA promoter Stuart Swezey, whom she'd met at a club called the Loft inside the Metropol in Berlin. Swezey invited the band to participate in a desert show, and Sonic Youth decided to take him up on his offer. Gordon informed Swezey that she would be on the West Coast for the holidays and the band was available for a gig. Could he put a show together?

Though the date was only two weeks away, Swezey accepted the challenge. Desolation Center had put on two previous generator shows in the desert plus a raucous concert on a boat in San Pedro Harbor with the Minutemen and the Meat Puppets called Joy at Sea. Swezey's previous shows had generated enough buzz to ensure his next event would be his biggest gig yet. The Gila Monster Jamboree featured Sonic Youth, the Meat Puppets, Redd Kross, and Psi Com, which was fronted by one of Swezey's roommates Perry Farrell.

Sonic Youth had flirted with the dark underbelly of the California dream in its songs; now the band was going to get its West Coast debut in the wilderness. Sonic Youth's forty-minute set ranged from the thundering cacophony of "Brother James" to the moodily disconsolate "Brave Men Run (in My Family)" before roaring into a full-on freak-out on the desert floor with "Death Valley '69." Sonic Youth closed out the set with an extended version of one of the band's earliest tracks, "Burning Spear," that ended with the players crouched in the sand making primitive sounds as people have been doing for thousands of years.

For the three hundred or so revelers in the audience, most of whom were tripping on acid, Sonic Youth was a revelation. During the course of the performance, it unleashed a series of pummeling escalations that overwhelmed the senses as it reached its climax, a phenomenon that Lydia Lunch referred to as the band's signature "sonic holocaust."[26]

With a single performance, and the help of some hallucinogens, Sonic Youth put the band on the map in all-important California. "I think that Sonic Youth was perceived differently on the West Coast after the Gila Monster Jamboree show," Swezey said. "First of all, because that was their first West Coast show. Second, because the outlaw nature of the gig gave them a lot of credibility."[27]

Initially, some of the resistance to the band came from SST. Swezey recalled, "I remember somebody at SST saying, 'Why are you booking this Loft Rock? Why are the Meat Puppets opening for this Loft Rock band? After that gig, they were signed to SST."[28]

But it didn't happen right away. While in California, Sonic Youth played a series of West Coast shows, including a gig at LA's Anti-Club with Lawndale, a South Bay band that played instrumental surf rock. Sonic Youth's performance at the Anti-Club made a big impression on Boon, Watt, and Markey, who'd all come to see the band again in a more conventional setting.

Despite making inroads with its favorite label, Sonic Youth returned to New York without a contract. *Bad Moon Rising* was ignored by the national press, and the band still didn't have much of a following outside of New York. Nor was the punk rock community eager to embrace Sonic Youth. For all of Moore's desire to connect with underground hardcore scenes, those scenes weren't reciprocating. "I wanted Sonic Youth to be a part of a community," Moore said. "I wanted to make a real impression on people and I had a real anxiety that we weren't really able to do it. I felt we needed to work on the same level as Black Flag or the Dead Kennedys, and I felt we were a little too outside that system."[29]

Bad Moon Rising did substantially better in the UK, shipping five thousand copies, and the band embarked on a lengthy European tour. During a planning meeting at the end of the tour with Paul Smith of Blast First, Bert unexpectedly quit the band. As luck would have it, Sonic Youth didn't have to

Gordon, Moore, Ranaldo, and Shelley of Sonic Youth in downtown Los Angeles, 1985. (Photo by Naomi Petersen Photography.)

look far for his replacement—he was already staying in Gordon and Moore's apartment on Eldridge Street.

3

Back in the summer of '83, Moore and Ranaldo had attended the Rock Against Reagan Tour at CBGB, where an unusual hardcore band from Lansing, Michigan, called the Crucifucks caught their attention.

The band was fronted by Doc Corbin Dart, an agitator who succeeded in making a first-class nuisance of himself in Lansing and its surrounding townships owing to his profound contempt of the police. After the show, Gordon and Moore introduced themselves and stayed in touch with the drummer, Steve Shelley, who sensed the Crucifucks would run its course sooner rather than later. When Shelley wrote to Sonic Youth to tell them he was thinking of moving to New York, they reassured him that there were always plenty of bands in the city looking for a drummer. At the time, they didn't realize they'd be one of them.

Gordon and Moore invited Shelley to stay in their apartment while they were on tour in Europe, and when they returned, they promptly invited him to join the band. The kid who'd recorded "Hinkley Had a Vision" with the Crucifucks, the terror of Lansing, was now a member of Sonic Youth.

Shortly after Shelley signed on, Sonic Youth started working on new material and returned to Tiers's basement studio to record a cover of Alice Cooper's "Hallowed Be Thy Name" for the soundtrack to Dave Markey's film *Lovedolls Superstar* (SST 062), which included a song by Black Flag and featured tracks by SST bands Gone, Painted Willie, and Lawndale, whose SST debut *Beyond Barbecue* (SST 087) would come out the following year. Sonic Youth didn't know it yet, but it was on a collision course with SST Records.

In the aftermath of Boon's passing, Roessler coaxed Watt to drive back to the East Coast with her. While she caught up on her studies at Yale, the grief-stricken Watt found himself at loose ends in New York City. Gordon and Moore invited the bassist, who was clearly still devastated by Boon's death, to come stay with them.

Sonic Youth had already begun recording songs at BC Studio for the album that would become *EVOL*. At the time, Sonic Youth was fascinated with pop culture and as likely to name-drop Bruce Springsteen and Madonna during interviews as they were Black Flag and Saccharine Trust. Madonna was especially compelling for the New York band because she had played at the same clubs where Sonic Youth and its peers performed, and then suddenly she was a huge star.

The band invited Watt down to the studio, thinking it would be good for him to be in a creative environment. Watt accepted and even played bass on a track the band was working on—the first time he'd picked up the instrument since Boon's death. From this session a collaborative project emerged called Ciccone Youth. The musicians goofed around with a cover of Madonna's "Burnin' Up," with Watt playing bass and providing vocals. They also worked on an interpretation of Madonna's dance hit "Into the Groove" from the *Desperately Seeking Susan* soundtrack, which Ciccone Youth dubbed "Into the Groove(y)." In addition, the group performed a tongue-in-cheek rap song with Moore on the mic called "Tuff Titty Rap," which name-checks Watt and New Alliance.[30]

Ciccone Youth demonstrated a humorous side of the band that wasn't always apparent. Sonic Youth's reputation for taking experimentation further than most guitar rock bands were willing to go lent an aura of seriousness to Sonic Youth that, from the outside looking in, resembled art-rock pretentiousness.[31] Although the individual members pursued their interests to an obsessive degree, the results were as likely to be silly as dark.

Despite Sonic Youth's wild and at times ferocious stage show, its members were fairly conservative off stage. No up-all-night drug orgies or wild displays of hedonism for this crew. Band members went to shows out of a genuine love of music, but they attended parties to network with people who could help spread the word about the band. Sonic Youth was an ambitious group that approached the business of being in a band with rigor, and while its members were aware of what critics wrote and peers said about Sonic Youth in the press, it didn't stop them from pursuing "unserious" projects like Ciccone Youth.

For all the fun and games Sonic Youth had with Watt in the studio, the recording sessions went to some very dark places. Watt plays bass on "In the Kingdom #19," a spoken word piece written by Ranaldo about a car crash.[32] Sonic Youth had its own connection to Boon's death. On the night of the accident, Sonic Youth played a winter solstice warehouse show in Los Angeles with the Swans and Saccharine Trust that was organized by Swezey. For that performance, Ranaldo played through Boon's amp.

EVOL, which is both a homonym of EVIL and LOVE spelled backward, was also the name of a short film created by Tony Oursler that featured Mike Kelley. These were artists that Sonic Youth would continue to collaborate with for years to come. While Madonna's rise to global stardom struck the members of Sonic Youth as absurd, they were interested in the intersection of art and fame, and this played out in different ways on EVOL. One of the earliest songs on the album, "Expressway to Yr Skull" had the alternate title "Madonna, Sean, and Me" and would eventually be listed that way on the album's back cover. The song "Starpower," which also deals with the lure of celebrity, has a fairly standard structure whose middle collapses on itself. Like a wolf in sheep's clothing, this allowed the musicians to conduct their radical guitar experiments within a pop format.[33]

After finishing *EVOL*, the band was reluctant to hand the album off to Homestead Records. While it had a good relationship with Cosloy, Homestead wasn't a true indie, nor was it the former zinester's label. Homestead was a subsidiary of Dutch East India Trading, a music distributor unironically named after a company that was synonymous with exploitation. Dutch East India Trading was operated by Barry Tenenbaum, a graduate of the University of Pennsylvania's Wharton School, who could fire Cosloy at any time. The members of Sonic Youth worried that if Cosloy left Homestead, the band would be stuck with someone who didn't understand what it was trying to do. Sonic Youth had a reputation as a noise band, which, despite being largely inaccurate, followed them everywhere. "Next to our friends the Swans," Gordon said, "who were very loud and had a percussionist who pounded metal, we were total wimps."[34]

Sonic Youth didn't have a lot of options, but the band's fortunes changed with a single long-distance phone call from California when Ginn inquired if Sonic Youth wanted to release *EVOL* on SST. The band was overjoyed. "It was like a lottery ticket," Moore said.[35]

4

Another New York band that signed with SST was a hard-rocking group from Queens that called itself Das Damen.

After the hardcore band the Misguided broke up, guitarist Alex Totino and drummer Lyle Hysen joined guitarist Jim Walters and bassist Phil Leopold von Trapp to form Das Damen. The quartet established a reputation as a hardworking rock band that loved to play loud. This attracted the attention of Sonic Youth, and Moore released the band's self-titled EP on his label, Ecstatic Peace!

The EP also intrigued Ginn, but he wanted to hear the band with his own ears. An opportunity arose for Das Damen to play with Black Flag during a Sunday matinee at Rick's Cafe in East Lansing, but there was a problem: Das Damen already had a gig opening for Big Black the night before in New York. Immediately after the show, Das Damen drove all night to Michigan to get to the Black Flag gig on time. Ginn was impressed and agreed to sign the band, starting with a reissue of Das Damen's debut EP (SST 040).[36]

The band quickly established itself as a workhorse that played with SST acts all over the country, following the trail that Black Flag had blazed. But a not-so-subtle shift was taking place, and the action was moving from the stages of clubs to television screens as kids across the country clamored for three letters...

Paul Hudson (a.k.a. H.R., a.k.a. Joseph I). (Photo by Naomi Petersen Photography.)

CHAPTER 10
SST vs. MTV

1986–1987

1

Bad Brains assembled at Long View Farm, a studio in North Brookfield, Massachusetts, where the J. Geils Band had recorded and the Rolling Stones had rehearsed. The remote location ensured that everyone could focus on music and nothing else. It was the perfect situation for H.R., who had multiple projects going and a lot on his mind.

This isolation nearly worked against the production team when Saint Germain announced he was unhappy with the drum sound and had to send someone to Boston to get another kit. The gear was procured, and after some difficulty finding the best place for Jenifer's bass cabinets, which proved to be at the bottom of a flight of stairs facing a pasture full of cows, everything was ready to go.[1] On the second day, Saint Germain recorded the drums, bass, and guitar, leaving the third and final day for H.R.'s vocals and Dr. Know's overdubs. There was no margin for error because, unbeknownst to Saint Germain, H.R. was due at Lorton for another drug charge the following day.

Back in February, H.R.'s brother Earl had been pulled over by the DC police, and marijuana was found under the passenger seat where H.R. was sitting. Because it was Earl's car, he was also charged, and the brothers were both sentenced to serve their time at the correctional facility where their father was a captain. H.R. had a contentious relationship with his father, which added shame and strain to an already difficult situation.

Saint Germain was incredulous, not because he had less time to record the vocalist—they'd booked all the time they could afford—but because of the incredible pressure H.R. was under. It was bad enough that time was limited, but his imminent return to prison was a heavy load to bear. For singers and songwriters, the studio is a crucible, and many a band has cracked up during the recording process from the pressure. But when it came time to deliver, H.R. sang with the urgency of a man whose freedom was about to be taken away.

Bad Brains finished recording all of the songs save one, "Sacred Love," which was surreptitiously recorded over the telephone while H.R. was incarcerated. This unorthodox recording session was carried out like an espionage operation with coordination from all parties so that Saint Germain would be ready to record when the time was right. H.R.'s familiarity with Lorton—and its with him—created an opportunity where he could sing his song in relative peace.

I Against I (SST 065) was a major step forward delivering on the promise of Bad Brains' reunion shows at the Rock Hotel. In *Dance of Days*, DC punk historians Mark Andersen and Mark Jenkins write, "This material charted a course between hardcore and reggae, forging a sound that was slower than the band's blistering rastacore and much heavier than its reggae. The songs were sinuous, assured, and more accessible than much of the quartet's earlier work. They were as powerful as early Bad Brains hardcore but less frenetic, a progression rather than a repudiation."[2]

The accessibility was key. This tantalizing middle ground was precisely what record executives had been dreaming of since Bad Brains first appeared on the scene. Still, *I Against I* is virtually impossible to classify. While H.R.'s dynamic performances often overshadowed the other players on stage, Saint Germain's clean recording made it impossible to ignore Dr. Know's groundbreaking guitar playing, a mind-blowing blend of rock and metal that left the one-chord wonders of rap-rock in the dust. Soaring over Jenifer's funk-driven bass lines and Hudson's steady beat, Dr. Know's unapologetically technical guitar playing was no less ferocious for its precision. Although the songs "She's Calling You" and "Sacred Love" sound nothing alike, they show off an unmistakable groove. The band may have started in dingy clubs with subpar sound systems, but the new record declared that no stage was too big for Bad Brains.

Perhaps more importantly, the time was right for *I Against I*. Heavy rock music was getting more airplay on MTV, bringing the hair metal bands of the Sunset Strip into living rooms across America. Run-D.M.C.'s cover of Aerosmith's "Walk This Way" went platinum and put rap-rock crossover on the map in the summer of 1986. Bad Brains wasn't a rap act, but its members were Black artists in a genre dominated by white musicians. The ubiquitous video in which Run-D.M.C. literally broke down the wall separating it from Aerosmith signaled a change in the way rock was perceived and who was allowed to make it.

SST was poised to take advantage of this new platform. Typically, the decision to make a music video came from the bands and hinged on knowing people who had the right equipment. In 1985, Black Flag recorded a video for "Drinking and Driving" but it didn't receive extensive airtime. Although regional cable shows would sometimes air videos and interview touring bands that were passing through town, SST had limited success with music videos and struggled to get them broadcast. MTV commanded the largest audience, and what had once been a wide-open field had become intensely competitive. Even though MTV started a new program in March 1986 called *120 Minutes* that featured "alternative" music, most of the songs on the show came from recording artists on major labels. There were a few exceptions; SST was able to get the Descendents' video for "Kids" on the program.

Despite the show's focus on music outside the mainstream, *120 Minutes* didn't become a showcase for indie artists until Dave Kendall became more involved with curating the show's playlist. With Bad Brains' name recognition, SST hoped to crack MTV's rotation with a video for the song "Hired

Gun." It was a strange choice for a single and an even stranger video: a moody black-and-white piece directed by Kurt Feldhun with a subdued live performance and a gangster subplot. "Every video submitted to MTV went through the standards and practices department," Farrell explained. "They responded quickly, but they required the lyrics as part of the process. I recall the show's host telling me that he was not sure what the Bad Brains video was about. I told them to think of the video as a Scorsese tribute."[3]

Farrell had better luck getting Bad Brains on the radio. The ascendance of hair metal made *I Against I* appealing to program managers at heavy rock stations. New York's WBAB was especially excited about the record, and Farrell was able to secure an on-air interview. There was just one problem, Farrell recalled: the radio station was located in Babylon, Long Island. "I said 'H.R., this will be easy. All you have to do is to take the train to Babylon!'"[4]

Naturally, H.R. refused.

2

Twenty-two-year-old Ed Crawford was living in Columbus, Ohio, when he attended a Camper Van Beethoven show at a local punk rock club called Slashes. After the show, the young guitarist spoke with a member of the band, and the two had a fateful exchange. "I happened to ask him after a gig what was happening with the remaining Minutemen," Crawford said, "and he said he heard they were auditioning guitar players. I don't know if he was making that up just to get rid of me, but that's what he told me."[5]

That exchange set in motion a quixotic quest. Crawford looked up Watt's number in the phone book and inquired about auditioning for the new band. Watt brushed him off; there was no new band. Undeterred, Crawford kept calling and eventually drove to San Pedro, California, to make his case in person. Crawford didn't know that neither Watt nor Hurley had discussed playing music together. Watt, however, was at least playing his bass again.

Roessler and Watt continued writing songs together after she returned to New England, sending tapes back and forth between San Pedro and New Haven. "[He] had to get past the idea that he couldn't play bass with anyone else," Roessler said.[6]

Gradually, Watt began to shake off his grief. While the collaboration would eventually bear fruit as a project called dos, a unique exploration of what two musicians could do with the same instrument, the idea of playing in a band without Boon still seemed impossible to Watt.

Then Crawford showed up for his nonexistent audition. Watt and Hurley reluctantly jammed with the persistent, yet inexperienced, guitarist from Ohio. While Crawford's vocal style differed from Boon's, his trebly and frenetic guitar playing was remarkably similar. Moved by Crawford's raw passion and determination, they agreed to start a new project together, and fIREHOSE was born. For Crawford, Watt's words in "History Lesson—Part II," which had served as an inspiration for the young musician, had literally come true.

Watt wrote about his trepidation in the liner notes to *The Whitey Album*, a Ciccone Youth project that expanded on the Madonna-influenced songs of the *Burnin' Up* EP: "I had once again gotten caught up in the sound of my own engine and dove right in where the rubber meets the road."[7]

3

When *EVOL* (SST 059) came out in May 1986, Sonic Youth had already embarked on its fifth European tour. The album cover featured an image of the actress Lung Leg from a still of a Richard Kern film titled *Submit to Me*.[8] The band returned to New York in time to play CBGB with Gone and a band from Massachusetts called Dinosaur—though it wouldn't play under that name for long.

Less than a week after returning from Europe, Sonic Youth set out on the EVOL Tour, booked by Global. The flyers for the tour announced the band as "SST Recording Artists The Sonic Youth." For the first time, Sonic Youth could afford to travel with a crew that included a sound engineer and lighting technician, though in typical SST fashion everyone did a little bit of everything. In Tucson, Sonic Youth hooked up with Saccharine Trust, with whom the band was enamored, and they played several dates together, including a gig at the Roxy with Watt's new band fIREHOSE. Watt took the stage with Sonic Youth to play "Starpower."

Not everything went smoothly. When fans failed to come out for Sonic Youth, club owners would withhold the guarantees that Global had so painstakingly secured. Early in the tour, the proprietor of the Uptown Lounge in Athens, Georgia, told the band that the Meat Puppets had sold out the venue not too long ago. A show at the I-Beam in San Francisco had to be cut short when fIREHOSE cancelled because of car trouble, and Moore snapped the neck of his favorite guitar before an unsympathetic crowd.

In the Midwest, Dinosaur joined the tour. Guitarist J Mascis and bassist Lou Barlow had played in a hardcore band together called Deep Wound. With Emmett Jefferson Murphy III (a.k.a. Murph) on drums, the noisy trio had put out its self-titled debut on Homestead Records the previous year. Mascis's performance betrayed a baffling range of influences that was made almost unrecognizable by intense volume and distortion. Moore loved Mascis's guitar playing, and the two became fast friends.

Sonic Youth had a second American tour booked with fIREHOSE in the fall, but first the band returned to Los Angeles to score a soundtrack for the film *Made in the U.S.A.* Sonic Youth set up shop at Spinhead Studios and played along to videocassettes of the film. The band got its first taste of Hollywood when the soundtrack was released—without any of the band's music on it, and the film didn't come out until '95.[9]

In August, the Meat Puppets released a new EP called *Out My Way* (SST 049), an homage of sorts to Phoenix, Arizona. Recorded in Scottsdale, the EP includes a blistering cover of "Good Golly Miss Molly," which the band had been playing during its live show for years. Support for *Out My Way* was put on hold after a roadie slammed a van door on Curt's finger, which forced the Meat Puppets to cancel the remainder of the tour.

October Faction recorded its second and final album, *The Second Factionalization* (SST 056), but it would be a mistake to call it a reunion. Each member of the band laid down his tracks individually, which was fairly conventional practice, except that the band hadn't prepared any songs in advance and the work was entirely improvised, including the drums. The musicians spontaneously jammed on top of the previous tracks without the benefit of having heard them or even being in the same room when they were recorded. The dubious experiment was recorded in Mystic Studios but augmented with equipment from Rat Sound Systems.

Watt, Hurley, and Ed from Ohio went to Radio Tokyo in Venice Beach to record fIREHOSE's first album, *Ragin', Full-On* (SST 079), over the course of twenty-nine hours between October 14 and 27. Like the early Minutemen albums, *Ragin', Full-On* includes songs with music and lyrics composed by all the players. Roessler also contributed to a third of the songs and wrote more lyrics than anyone in the band, even though she doesn't play on the record.

fIREHOSE was not a continuation of the Minutemen, but it belonged in the same conversation. As a band, the Minutemen never reached a point where the members looked back to recapture the spark of the early days—always a sign that a band has lost its way or is attempting to appease a dwindling fanbase. The Minutemen had a distinct style that was immediately recognizable, yet the band didn't adhere to a template. After *Double Nickels on the Dime*, the band had a plan for what it was trying to achieve. From attempting to get songs on the radio, to making a political record, to compiling live performances of the band's greatest hits selected by the fans, which was the organizing principle for *Ballot Result* (SST 068), there was intention behind these records.

The only objective driving *Ragin', Full-On* was to play music together. Crawford's dynamic vocal range marks fIREHOSE as a distinct musical project. The record benefits from a wealth of ideas and a heady dose of youthful enthusiasm to compensate for Crawford's inexperience. The opening track, "Brave Captain," explores Watt's uncertainty about moving forward without Boon. Watt had always been partial to nautical metaphors, but the song also alludes to Walt Whitman's elegy for Abraham Lincoln, "O Captain! My Captain!," written after the president's assassination by John Wilkes Booth. Just as Lincoln had steered the ship of state, Boon had helmed the Minutemen in his own incomparable fashion. "It was very difficult without D. Boon," Watt confessed. "But I had guitarist Ed helping me. He was very enthusiastic. First tour with Sonic Youth...they helped me. But it was rough. I didn't think that people wanted to see me play without D. Boon. My pop once told me, 'Don't think. Do.' And that's what I did. I got back in the saddle."[10]

The fall tour with fIREHOSE was dubbed Flaming Telepaths Tour after a song by Blue Öyster Cult, which continued to influence Watt. He would occasionally ride with Sonic Youth and take over the stereo, blasting T. Rex, the Beastie Boys, Janet Jackson, and, of course, his beloved Blue Öyster Cult. He even coaxed Sonic Youth into playing a cover of "The Red and the Black" that turned into a jam featuring Hurley, Crawford, and Roessler, who accompanied Watt on the tour.

One thing hadn't changed since the Minutemen days: Watt continued to bicker with his bandmates. He would get into arguments with Hurley that would become so heated they would throw each other out of the band, much to the befuddlement of the even-tempered members of Sonic Youth and the amusement of Davo, who was back behind the wheel.

In terms of attendance the shows were hit or miss, and on one occasion Sonic Youth felt so bad for the promoter they gave back some of the band's guarantee. Highlights included raucous shows in Texas where Sonic Youth met Daniel Johnston and played with the Butthole Surfers. In Florida, Sonic Youth shared the stage with Saccharine Trust for one night. Ranaldo wrote, "jack brewer is a god...i can't understand how they can be this great band that's been around for so long and still be so under-appreciated."[11]

Sonic Youth refused to pander to its audience, playing mostly new material off the album. "Death Valley '69" seldom made its way onto the set list, and the band occasionally worked on new songs, such as "White Cross." Many bands tested out tracks on the road, making minor tweaks and subtle changes along the way. Sonic Youth's approach was much more radical. The band continued to experiment with songs long after they were recorded, and the musicians felt little fidelity to the album version. A performance might be altered by the contours of the room, the energy from the audience, or the mood of the players. By the end of a tour, a song might be transformed. In his journals, Ranaldo declared, "we do not try to pinpoint what we do. we leave it open and rely on collective intuition to make it happen. we lean outwards towards infinity by leaving the things open-ended."[12]

Greg Ginn and Zoogz
Rift at SST in 1986.
(Photo by Naomi
Petersen Photography.)

4

As bad as things seemed after the demise of the Minutemen and Black Flag,
SST actually increased the number of records it released in '86. It accomplished this feat by signing new bands and by releasing multiple albums by
the same artist. For instance, Gone dropped the follow-up to its debut earlier
in the year with *Gone II—but Never Too Gone!* Angst also had two records:
a reissue of the self-titled EP originally released on Happy Squid (SST 064)
and the LP *Mending Wall* (SST 074). Not to be outdone, D.C. 3 laid down
two more retro rock records: *The Good Hex* (SST 063) and *You're Only as
Blind as Your Mind Can Be* (SST 083). Zoogz Rift, the titan of rock that

was rude, crude, and unspeakably lewd—sometimes all at the same time—started his improbable rampage through the SST catalog with a pair of records: *Island of Living Puke* (SST 077) and *Looser Than Clams...a Historical Retrospective (Greatest Hits, Vol. 1)* (SST 088).

Zoogz Rift was in a band in New Jersey with Scott Colby and Richie Hass called Zobus. The band went through a number of iterations before moving to LA. Alan Carl Eugster, who played the violin on SWA's *Your Future If You Have One*, introduced Zoogz to Dukowski. Although the larger-than-life musician and wrestling fanatic frequently clashed with his collaborators, he had a remarkably good relationship with Ginn and Dukowski, which led to a career that was as unique as it was unlikely.

Other artists new to the label included a trio of LA bands that would each release many records with SST. After the Flesh Eaters broke up, Chris D. started up a new Americana-infused band with his wife, Julie Christensen, called Divine Horsemen, which was also the name of the final track on the Flesh Eater's epic *A Minute to Pray a Second to Die*. SST wasted no time in issuing *Devil's River* (SST 091), which was produced by Chris D. and engineered by Brett Gurewitz at Westbeach Recorders. The records *Middle of the Night* (SST 090) and *Snake Handler* (SST 140) and the EP *Handful of Sand* (SST 176) followed soon after, as well as the Flesh Eaters' compilation *Destroyed by Fire—Greatest Hits* (SST 094).

Like Divine Horsemen, the Leaving Trains started out on Enigma Records before jumping ship to SST. Founded by Falling James Moreland in the early '80s, the original lineup featured future SST artist Sylvia Juncosa on keyboards. Starting with *Kill Tunes* (SST 071), the Leaving Trains issued a slew of grungy pop records for SST, including *Fuck* (SST 114) and *Transportational D. Vices* (SST 221). A productive run, considering Moreland was married to Courtney Love long enough to produce Hole's first single for Sympathy for the Record Industry before the relationship crashed and burned.

While Slovenly's *Thinking of Empire* (SST 067) marked the band's SST debut, it had already released a full-length and a pair of EPs on New Alliance, but its South Bay roots went deeper than that. Slovenly emerged from the ashes of Toxic Shock, a band that made its debut on Happy Squid's *Keats*

Rides a Harley compilation. Originally named Slovenly Peter after a German fairy tale, the band dropped Peter and recruited Holzman to play drums. After leaving Saccharine Trust, Holzman hung out at SST HQ on Phelan Lane but couldn't get the label interested in his new band. It took moving to San Francisco for SST to appreciate Slovenly's sound. Of all the SST bands that featured members who graduated from Mira Costa High School, none were as hard to pin down as Slovenly. Equal parts angular and groovy, Slovenly were seemingly influenced by artists from everywhere but the South Bay.

Two bands from Richmond, Virginia, with alliterative names and similar aesthetics also put out new records: *Hold Your Tongue* (SST 075) by Alter Natives and *Black Pyramid* (SST 078) by Always August. Both bands emerged from the same scene that produced GWAR—Alter Natives' Jim Thomson even played drums in GWAR under the name Hans Sphincter—but they sounded more psychedelic than psychopathic.

Not to be outdone, doom rockers Saint Vitus cranked out another album, *Born Too Late* (SST 082), with new vocalist Scott "Wino" Weinrich, formerly of the Obsessed, a metal band from the DC suburb of Potomac, Maryland. Though listed as an album, *Born Too Late* has just six songs and clocks in at under thirty-five minutes. What it lacks in length it makes up for in low-end, rib-rattling sludge. It's also one of the last records Carducci worked on before leaving the label.

SST also released a pair of compilations: *Program: Annihilator* (SST 066), a double album of SST's heaviest material issued between 1983 and 1986, and *The Sacramental Element* (SST 084), a cassette that brings together Saccharine Trust's *Paganicons* and *Surviving You, Always*, as well as tracks that appeared on singles and compilations. In addition, *The 7 Inch Wonders of the World* (SST 070) collects all of the singles SST had released up to that point on cassette. The pun in the title overlooks the fact that nine singles are sampled and not all of them were issued as seven-inch records, but SST never let accuracy get in the way of a joke.

Last but not least, SWA put out its sophomore effort: *Sex Doctor* (SST 073), a record that would mark Ford's final contribution to the band. Things were getting so busy at SST that Carducci's replacement had to quit SWA to keep up with his workload, which was about to get even heavier as the label prepared to ramp up its production in '87. Ford's replacement was none other than Sylvia Juncosa, who made her first appearances on the LP *XCIII* (SST 093) and the single "Arroyo" (SST 153). SST subsequently released *Evolution 85–87* (SST 157), a CD compilation of cuts from SWA's first three albums.

During an interview with *Flipside*'s Al Kowalewski after a show at the Music Machine, Dukowski was pressed once again on the meaning of SWA. Dukowski responded in typical fashion: "I'm not into this verbal linear approach. I think the real truths in people are in their hearts. Words are only an expression of those things and capable of being inaccurate. Thoughts that come by you verbally tend to lead you astray from what you are truly doing and wanting. Therefore I'm not into that whole thing."

"Unfortunately we are a printed publication," Kowalewski said.[13]

Not all of SST's plans came to fruition. At the premier of *Lovedolls Superstar*, Ginn told David O. Jones that he wanted to sign his band to SST.

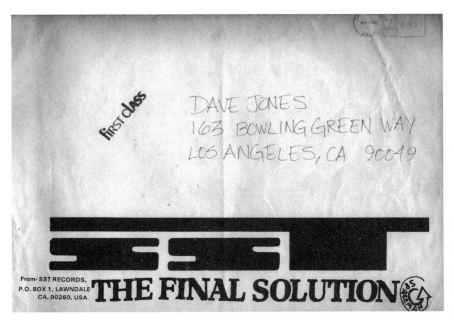

SST envelope that contained the contract for Magnolia Thunderpussy. Note the Spaceman doodle. (Image provided by David O. Jones.)

Magnolia Thunderpussy had played with Black Flag the previous year at a generator show thrown by Dave Travis, who served as the band's manager. Jones was thrilled—"It was the greatest thing I'd ever heard in my life"—but also alarmed. His bandmates had graduated from high school and were spread out across the country at different colleges and universities. Jones convinced them to come back to LA, and SST sent Magnolia Thunderpussy a contract. However, because of creative differences within the band, the album was never made. "Chuck called me every week to ask, 'When are you coming down to record?'" Jones said, "and I'd have to tell him, 'I don't know.'"

5

SST suffered another setback when Greenworld, one of the label's key distributors, went bankrupt. Greenworld, like many indie distributors, started out as an import operation. It intuited there was a market in the United States for new music from overseas. To put it in oversimplified terms, Greenworld gambled that consumers who liked bands such as the Sex Pistols and the Clash would also like the Dead Kennedys and Black Flag, and it was right. Greenworld, and other companies like it, began to distribute records from small independent labels around the country and became a vital part of the indie ecosystem. These companies filled a growing need. As artists realized that virtually anyone could make a record, it was considerably harder to get it on record store shelves.[14]

Based in Torrance, Greenworld collaborated with a number of indie labels and occasionally worked with bands as a third partner. For instance, when New Alliance wanted to release a Minutemen or Hüsker Dü record but was short on cash, Greenworld would advance funds to press the record in exchange for being its sole distributor. "It was more like, 'Hey, it's us against the rest of the music business' rather than competing against each other," said Bill Hein, who—along with his brother Wes—were two of Greenworld's owners.[15]

Distributors knew how to make records and how to sell them. Naturally, most came to believe they knew what types of records would sell as well. Greenworld started up a label under its own name and a second label called Enigma Records. Enigma's first release was a little record by Mötley Crüe called *Too Fast for Love*.

When Greenworld showed signs of struggling, the Hein brothers made Enigma its own company in 1985. Greenworld's remaining owner, Stephen Boudreau, filed for bankruptcy the following year. Because of the lag between shipping and billing, Greenworld owed SST an undisclosed sum that it was unable to pay back. Greenworld also had a great deal of inventory tied up in its network of retailers, causing a massive headache for SST. There was a trickle-down effect as well. Greenworld owed money to other labels and distributors that SST worked with, such as Rough Trade and Mordam, who were counting on funds from Greenworld to stay afloat.

One silver lining of Greenworld's downfall was the signing of the Santa Cruz hardcore band Bl'ast. Black Flag had played with the band in the summer of '84, and Rollins mocked the band in his journals for copying Black Flag's sound. This criticism wasn't entirely without merit. Bl'ast featured two guitarists who both played Dan Armstrong guitars, and at times the band was able to replicate Ginn's signature tone with uncanny accuracy. The band continued to develop and grow, and after Black Flag disbanded, Bl'ast's brand of hardcore felt necessary, even essential. "We got signed to SST," vocalist Clifford Dinsmore said, "by playing a ghetto blaster recording of 'It's in My Blood' for Greg Ginn in our van."[16]

Ginn liked what he heard. Not only did SST release the LP *It's in My Blood!* (SST 106) and the single "School's Out" (SST 124) the following year, but it also picked up *The Power of Expression* (SST 148), the last record Greenworld released on its own label before it folded.

6

Paul Rachman woke in his apartment in Hell's Kitchen early one morning to the ringing of the telephone. The native New Yorker had returned to the city from Boston, where he made his mark on the hardcore scene recording shows and making videos. He moved back to Manhattan in hope of finding work as a video director and took a job as a junior offline editor at Windsor Total Video.

"Hey, this is Mark Pellington from MTV," said the voice on the other end of the line, "and I hear you have some videos."

"Yeah?" Paul said. The videos he made were for punk, post-punk, and hardcore bands, and only a handful of people had ever seen them.

"Well, we'd love to play them on *120 Minutes*."

That got Rachman's attention. As he sprang out of bed, Pellington explained the show was shifting its focus to alternative music produced by independent labels that didn't fit into MTV's regular rotation. This was music to Rachman's ears. In college, he fell into filmmaking the same way he stumbled into punk rock. His roommate at Boston University, Alec Peters, was a local promoter who became the manager of the hard-partying band Gang Green. With access to touring punk acts and local hardcore bands, Rachman felt compelled to document the scene that was unfolding in front of him. As his reputation as a filmmaker grew, he was invited to film one of Mission of Burma's final shows and made some videos for Gang Green.[17]

While Rachman's introduction to the punk scene may have been accidental, it was Bad Brains that made him a fan for life. "The first time I saw this band, they blew my mind," Rachman said of a show he attended in 1982. "It hit my guts, it hit my nerves, the energy was overwhelming. I couldn't believe there was this hardcore punk band that was so tight, so perfect-sounding, and so fast. You could hear these arrangements going at a thousand miles per hour. The adrenaline was unforgettable. From that moment on, if I was within fifty miles of a Bad Brains show, I did not miss it."[18]

After hearing that Bad Brains had an album in the works with SST, Rachman approached Countey about shooting a video and got the green light from the band. Although Rachman hadn't seen the video for "Hired Gun," he took a very different approach to "I Against I": "The Bad Brains was about being in the pit, hearing this music that turns you into somebody else for ninety minutes, almost like a trance. For me, being at their shows was overwhelming, taking over all of your senses. When I made the 'I Against I' video, that was my vision: you are there."[19]

Rachman filmed the video at the Living Room in Providence, Rhode Island, an intimate space where he knew the energy would be intense. Although video technology was becoming more affordable, he shot the video with actual film to capture the chaos of the show, using three different types of cameras: a Super 8, a 16-millimeter movie camera, and a small plastic camera that he gave to someone who could handle himself in the pit.

Shooting the video was the easy part. Because the record was already out, Rachman was under intense pressure to develop the film, transfer it video, and edit it into shape. He worked after hours and over the holidays so he could sneak into the film lab at his job and use the expensive film transfer and editing equipment.

When Rachman finished the video, he turned it over to the band and called up SST to see if the label was interested. "Yeah, cool, send it," Rachman recalled Dukowski saying.[20] The video played on a few cable channels around the country, but not very many people saw it. As hard as it was for indie bands to break into radio, it was even harder to get on TV. Making a video was no different from making a record: the real challenge was getting it to people who would appreciate it. Rachman took the video to the Ritz, which had the largest video screen in the city, and the club added it to its rotation. At least his friends would be able to see it.

Then the biggest broadcaster of music videos on the planet came calling. The next day, Rachman met Pellington and Kendall at MTV in Manhattan and handed over the masters for Gang Green, Mission of Burma, and Bad Brains. Within a matter of weeks, all three videos were on the air.

Although the video for "Hired Gun" aired on *120 Minutes*, the song didn't stick as a single or as a video. It also didn't help that Bad Brains rarely played "Hired Gun" during the I Against I Tour. Rachman's videos, however, were an instant success. "Those videos were on *120 Minutes* for the next eighteen months," Rachman said.[21] This push from MTV helped make Bad Brains' *I Against I* one of the most successful releases in SST's history. The video for the title track gets close to the band and captures the feeling of being in the audience at a Bad Brains show. Shot in black and white, it feels timeless. Unfortunately, the video was on the air longer than the band stayed together.

7

Although *I Against I* didn't enjoy the kind of mainstream success to which Saint Germain was accustomed, it was a major windfall for SST and funded the release of countless other projects. Flush with cash, SST had more freedom to allocate its resources. Thus began a voluminous run of new releases unmatched by an independent record label before or since.

To accommodate this increase in production, SST moved into a larger building in Carson, just north of Long Beach at a cost of $5,000 a month. The facility was large enough to accommodate SST Records, Global, and a warehouse for the label's extensive mail-order operation. Ginn, Dukowski, and Mugger all had offices. For the first time, SST had a conference room where Ginn and Dukowski could hold staff meetings and conduct job interviews for new employees as the label ramped up its operations.

More space meant more people, and a new cast of colorful characters came into the fold. Brian Long had seen Gone and Black Flag play less than a year earlier when he was a student in Columbia, Missouri. After graduating, he moved to LA and parlayed his experience working at his college radio station into a gig at Spin Radio. One day he got a call from Farrell at SST suggesting that Spin record an upcoming Meat Puppets performance at the Roxy. Long pitched the idea to his boss, Ed Rasen, who'd worked with Rollins on his pieces for *Spin* magazine. Rasen signed on, and a recording of the Meat Puppets' performance on August 16, 1986, was pressed up by Special Forces Radio Concert in association with SST.

Six months later, Long was out of a job. After a brief stint at Bomp!, Long received a call from Farrell to see whether he was interested in working at SST. With the success of Bad Brains, Farrell was trying to crack the code of commercial radio and needed someone to focus on college radio while Whittaker continued to work on press. Long came in for what he described as one of the strangest job interviews he'd ever had. "Here's Ginn next to me, and Dukowski to my left, awkwardly asking me questions. There was one tiny light on in the room. So it was really kind of dark and shadowy. It was just a bizarre experience."[22]

Also hired that day was a New Yorker named Steve Kaul, who had some experience as a booker. Kaul went to work with Dukowski at Global to help book shows for the label's growing stable of touring bands. Another relatively new employee, Ed O'Bryan (a.k.a. Keltic Runes), had just come off the disastrous Shitheads Across America tour with Zoogz Rift. Originally from Ashland, Kentucky, O'Bryan was hired as a production artist and was tasked with making print ads for SST releases. The warehouse had its own expanding crew of contract employees managed by Nicks, including Linda Trudnich, who worked in the reception area, and Petersen's role as house photographer was made official when she finally became a paid employee.

In some ways, working at SST was not unlike working other nine-to-five jobs. Employees carpooled to Carson. The company had a travel agent. Thanks to Mugger, full-time staff had health insurance with Permanente. But in other respects, SST remained a very unusual place to work. "I remember 4:00 pm daily 'weed breaks,'" Farrell said. "Joints were passed around. We had a small basketball court on the side of the building. I went to one weed break. I have a bad reaction to pot, but I felt pressure to fit in. I was too busy to shoot hoops, pot or no pot."[23] With shows to attend almost every night of the week, there were plenty of opportunities to socialize, and employees bonded both with each other and the bands with whom they worked.

With so many of the new employees coming from places well beyond the South Bay, it was inevitable that the culture at SST began to change in subtle and not-so-subtle ways. Those with previous experience brought some music industry practices with them, such as hiring college interns. Some musicians who'd been with the label for years no longer bothered to get to know the new faces at SST—there were just too many.

What all the employees at SST shared, regardless of age, background, or experience, was a sense that they were joined in a war against the major labels. They imagined each record they shipped, show they booked, or song they got on the radio as a victory for SST and a blow against the enemy of corporate rock. "There was definitely an us-against-them mentality that ran through the ethos of the company," Long said, "and it was awesome. I loved it, ate it up, because we were the underdog, and we were winning."[24]

8

Just a few months after the completion of the EVOL Tour, Sonic Youth returned to the studio in March 1987 to record a second album for SST. The band chose Sear Sound, which was located on the mezzanine of the Paramount Hotel just west of Times Square. The studio had fallen on hard times, and its equipment was as old school as the location. Sonic Youth was interested in exploring the tones created by tube amplifiers, especially at high volume.

Sonic Youth's experimentation with antiquated equipment was seemingly at odds with the album's subject matter, much of which was inspired by the prolific California science fiction writer Philip K. Dick, whose novels the band devoured during long hours on the road.[25] Dick enjoyed something of a resurgence after the success of the film *Blade Runner* in '82, which was based on his 1968 novel *Do Androids Dream of Electric Sheep?*[26]

Dick didn't traffic in hard science fiction or space operas set in galaxies far, far away; he was interested in the psychological impact of ideas that radically transform the world in some meaningful way. For example, *The Man in the High Castle* investigates what America would look like under totalitarian rule several years after losing World War II. Sonic Youth was especially interested in the novels Dick wrote toward the end of his life, such as *Valis,* in which the author makes use of his own religious experiences, mental breakdowns, and drug addiction. Throughout his life, Dick was obsessed with the death of his fraternal twin sister, Charlotte Jane, who died shortly after birth, and this fixation with his ghost sister fueled many of his projects.

Much like Dick's work, Sonic Youth's *Sister* explores alternate futures, dual consciousness, and unreliable memories. "Schizophrenia," the opening track, announces themes of madness and religion that play out throughout the record. These ideas are so prevalent the band considered naming the album after this track. Gordon's older brother was diagnosed with schizophrenia, but the song isn't *about* him per se, nor is it about the vision that informed Dick's later work alluded to in the song. A Sonic Youth song is never about one thing. "Schizophrenia" is soothing *and* unsettling, elusive *and* hypnotic.

"(I Got a) Catholic Block" picks up where "Schizophrenia" leaves off before kicking up the pace with jangly guitars over which Moore's lyrics bemoan the hang-ups in his head. The song builds to a hyperkinetic climax before tumbling into a prolonged comedown, a progression that would become one of the band's signature moves. "(I Got a) Catholic Block," like "Schizophrenia," marries fast and slow, punk and pop, madness and religion in ways that are both bewildering and beguiling. This fusion of disparate ideas continues in "Stereo Sanctity" with tinfoil-hat lyrics, howling guitars, relentless drumming, and a bass line so subdued it's barely there at all. *Sister* reaches its apotheosis with "Kotton Krown." The song begins with guitars that echo the trumpets heralding the arrival of heavenly beings and slowly unfurls with a seductive refrain that cuts through the clamor with the precision of a vision. More important than the meaning behind the music—"That's for the writers," Gordon said—with *Sister* the band finally captured the essence of its live shows on an album.[27]

"We just didn't get a sound that in any way approximated what we do live, and we feel this record is a lot closer to that," Ranaldo said.[28] *Sister* reflects the band's live sound while serving as a statement of where Sonic Youth intended to go. Using edgy science fiction and outdated tubes, Sonic Youth was looking both forward and back to dream a new kind of music into existence.

9

"This is the next Bad Brains record," Mugger said as he plucked a cassette off his desk and held it up for Long's inspection.[29] The two were discussing SST's plans to release a Bad Brains live album and to record a second studio album. The songs on the tape were recorded during the I Against I Tour. Countey had hired Phil Burnett, an engineer who worked with Saint Germain on *I Against I*, to serve as the band's soundman on tour. His stellar work on the soundboard gave the album a seamless quality despite the tracks being recorded at various stops on the tour.

The album, which would be released the following year as *Live* (SST 160), captures the band's electrifying live performance and what Bad Brains was capable of with hardcore stompers like "At the Movies" and "Right Brigade" alongside reggae scorchers such as "I and I Survive." It's a portrait of the band at the peak of its power.

Unfortunately for SST, after a year of nonstop touring, a new record, and a popular video, Bad Brains was back on the major labels' radar. This time it was Island Records. Bad Brains headlined a show with the Circle Jerks, Living Colour, and Leeway for the New Music Seminar, the music industry's annual showcase in New York City. Bad Brains was electric on stage, but it short-circuited off it. Countey arranged for Island's Chris Blackwell to meet with H.R. after the show, but the mercurial singer blew off the meeting, sabotaging another opportunity for a huge payday and driving a wedge between the Hudson brothers and the rest of the band.

H.R. wanted to focus on his true love: reggae music, but Dr. Know and Jenifer were determined to carry on as Bad Brains—with or without its singer. Countey briefly considered helping H.R. but stayed with the band. "Doc and Darryl wouldn't have put up with my going to make H.R.'s career while I'm trying to find one for them," Countey said. "I had to go one way or the other. So I went all in with Bad Brains. It was either Bad Brains or nothing."[30]

Although Bad Brains' coveted second studio album with SST never materialized, H.R. remained on good terms with the label. In fact, he moved to California and set up shop in LA, where he was a frequent visitor to Carson. SST rewarded H.R. for his loyalty with a slew of solo records that included a new album called *Human Rights* (SST 117) as well as reissues of the single "Keep Out of Reach" (SST 177) and *It's About Luv* (SST 179) from Olive Tree Records.[31]

Human Rights is even more musically diverse than *I Against I*. Rather than make a record that was 100 percent reggae, H.R. experimented with synth-driven dance and pop music. H.R.'s gift to the universe can't be summarized in a list of artistic achievements or a catalog of records. That he felt the call to use these gifts to spread a message of peace and love through Rastafarianism was both a blessing and a curse.

10

Sister (SST 134) was released in June 1987, a quick turnaround for a label that was cranking out an incredible number of records. However, Sonic Youth's sophomore effort for SST immediately ran into problems. The album cover features a collage of images that included Mickey and Minnie Mouse, a portrait of a young girl by the photographer Richard Avedon, and a photo of a half-naked model named Audrey Rose taken by Richard Kern. The band had permission to use Kern's photo but not the others, and both Disney and Avedon sent cease-and-desist letters to SST.

Whittaker handled the press campaign for *Sister*, which included a provocative ad that read, "Have you ever seen your sister naked?" that many magazines declined to run. Under legal pressure, new covers for the album had to be printed with the images blacked out, much as the label had done on *Everything Went Black*.

Unfortunately, the problems that plagued Hüsker Dü became an issue for Sonic Youth as well. Although the Sister Tour was planned long in advance, the production of the album lagged behind, and in many stops it wasn't available. The number of records that SST was churning out exacerbated the band's feeling that perhaps the label was moving too fast and neglecting one of the bands on the roster whose success made signing all those others feasible.

While it was working up the material for *Sister*, Sonic Youth played a show at 9:30 Club in Washington, DC, with Das Damen and Always August. Both bands had a new record out on SST: *Jupiter Eye* (SST 095) and *Largeness with (W)holes* (SST 135), respectively. It was around this time that Jim Thomson of the Alter Natives got the impression Sonic Youth wasn't too psyched about his band being on the label. "I remember talking to them and getting a sense that they were already starting to think, 'What the fuck is Ginn doing? The big groups were selling records and making money. Then all of a sudden all these no-name groups were showing up on the label!'"[32]

Mugger felt much the same way. He believed that after Black Flag broke up, Ginn sought more creative control of the label. "My suspicion is Greg only wanted the bands that he brought in. If somebody else brought in a band it wasn't going to work because it needed to be his idea. It was his record label, right? And so he started bringing all this other crap like Zoogz Rift that really made Joe and I go, 'This is not what we envisioned.'"[33]

SST was committed to releasing records regardless of their commercial viability. If Ginn thought a band was doing something interesting and cool, he supported it. Vitus Mataré, who helped produce his own projects and worked with a number of SST bands, considered Ginn's support essential to the indie ecosystem. "There was always money to pay for tape and studio time. He came to listen to everything. He cared about everything. It isn't like you brought him an album and he said, 'Okay, we'll put it out.' He was really listening to it. He didn't want to meddle; he just wanted to see it get out there. It was the ideal situation for so many bands."[34]

One of those bands was Treacherous Jaywalkers, a trio of talented but raw musicians from LA whose debut EP *Sunrise* (SST 126) was produced by Watt and led to a full-length record, *Good Medicine* (SST 207), and a second EP, *La Isla Bonita* (SST 217), that Mataré helped produce: "They should have rehearsed a bit more maybe and matured a little bit and done that record six months later, but Greg didn't care. If they're gonna get better we'll put out another record, but let's put this out now."[35]

Some bands seemingly took advantage of this largesse. Zoogz Rift, for example, pushed through seven records in 1987, most of them reissues: *Water* (SST 099), *Ipecac* (SST 120), *Interim Resurgence* (SST 121), *Amputees in Limbo* (SST 122), *Idiots on the Miniature Golf Course* (SST 123), *Water II: At Safe Distance* (SST 137), and *Son of Puke* (SST 174)—a cassette-only extravaganza of tape manipulation. *Son of Puke* comprises elements of all its previous releases and a bootleg of Beatles covers purportedly by a band known as the Transients.

Sonic Youth believed SST was damaging its reputation by signing bands that weren't worthy of the label. Furthermore, the avalanche of new releases at the end of '87 clogged up the promotion pipeline and drew attention away from Sonic Youth. While sales were steady, the quarterly payments stipulated in the band's contract often fell short of what Sonic Youth believed it was due. Even worse, sometimes the statements would arrive without the checks. As the band members started thinking about recording a new album, the prospect of giving another record to a label that owed them money gave them pause.

Still, there were unmistakable perks to being on SST. Although Sonic Youth was on a record-to-record contract, the band went all in with the label and vice versa. SST rereleased the band's self-titled debut (SST 097) and *Confusion Is Sex* (SST 096) in October and Lee Ranaldo's *From Here* → *Infinity* (SST 113) in November. Suddenly Sonic Youth's hard-to-find records were available again on vinyl, cassette, and CD.

After the *Sister* sessions at Sear Sound, Sonic Youth continued to experiment in the studio. The song it recorded there, "Master-Dik," a rap-rock anthem of the sort that the Beastie Boys were making ubiquitous on MTV, fused Moore's rapping over heavy guitar riffs. But it's also much more than that, with sampling, tape loops, drum machines, and a title that serves as a tribute to the mastering studio in New York City where Moore had briefly worked. The flip side features a medley of covers including "Beat on the Brat" with Mascis on guitar, snippets of interviews, found audio, and other assemblages from a host of sources—much of which had been recorded at Wharton Tiers's basement studio in Chelsea over the previous five years.

Farrell was amused, but Smith at Blast First was convinced the record was a ruinous mistake. Smith may have felt the stakes were higher in the UK where Sonic Youth's singles and side projects performed well. Sonic Youth urged Smith to release it, which he did against his better judgment. That decision would prove to be a prudent one. The EP wasn't worth souring his relationship with the band, which was about to take a big step forward.

When *Master-Dik* (SST 155) was released, the inner sleeve reprinted a screed penned by Ben Weasel published in *Maximum Rocknroll* earlier that year. Weasel takes shots at SST, and several of its bands, for the crime of turning its back on punk rock. "Yep, it's the big thing now for halfway decent bands to regress back to the shittiest music ever created by man and call it 'progression.'"[36]

Weasel wasn't talking about SST's jam bands like October Faction or Tom Troccoli's Dog but rather Hüsker Dü, Das Damen, and Sonic Youth, bands that played loud and aggressive music and earned whatever recognition came their way by performing all over the country. In general, SST had a good relationship with the zines, particularly *Maximum Rocknroll*. "We sent them most of our records and we advertised in many of them," Farrell said. "There was occasional snark, but it was all in good fun. I doubt that the owners sat around reading these things."[37]

If Ginn was aware of Weasel's screed, one imagines he would have been pleased by the provocation. After all, he had been openly antagonizing the hardcore contingent since before the release of *My War*, so it's only natural that its more outspoken members would lash out. "SST, what the fuck," Weasel whined, "when was the last time this grandpa-assed label put out a good record?"[38]

Sonic Youth was poised to answer this question with one of its finest albums, a record that would stand alongside *Zen Arcade* and *Double Nickels on the Dime* as one of the best independent releases of the '80s, but it wouldn't be for SST.

Kim Thayil of Soundgarden at the Santa Monica Civic. (Photo by Alison Braun.)

CHAPTER 11
SST vs. the Northwest

1987–1988

1

When Ray Farrell heard that Greg Ginn was planning a compilation of instrumental music, he saw it as an opportunity to expand SST's repertoire of artists. He immediately reached out to Pell Mell, an instrumental band he'd briefly managed in the Bay Area. Because the members had spread out to different cities, Farrell asked Ginn whether they needed to tour—typically a critical component in SST's decision to sign a band. Ginn said it didn't matter. Farrell recommended one of his favorite bands: Pell Mell. "I was determined to bring the band to any label I worked for," Farrell said.[1]

Pell Mell first came to Farrell's attention while he was working at Rough Trade Distribution in the United States. Pell Mell sent him a copy of its debut, *Rhyming Guitars*, and Farrell took an immediate liking to the band. Although originally from Portland, the musicians relocated to the Bay Area, where Farrell managed the band for a while. Farrell said his duties "consisted mainly of booking shows, hustling the music press in that city, and making sure we got paid."[2]

By the time Farrell left for SST in the spring of 1985, the band was no longer playing shows, but it had a great deal of recorded material. Ginn liked it all. He not only gave Pell Mell a spot on the compilation he was planning but also offered to put out an album of its unreleased material: *The Bumper Crop* (SST 158).

Ginn's interest in instrumental music was no secret, and the compilation featured songs from each of the instrumental albums he'd played on in Black Flag and Gone. Ginn also selected cuts from Lee Ranaldo's *From Here→ Infinity* and the first self-titled record from Joe Baiza's new jazz rock project Universal Congress Of (SST 109). While Lawndale's second album, *Sasquatch Rock* (SST 125), was in the works and the incorrigibly improvisational Paper Bag had two albums in the pipeline—*Ticket to Trauma* (SST 076) and *A Land Without Fences* (SST 170)—Ginn needed more musicians to flesh out the compilation. "I brought a few other instrumentalists to Greg's attention," Farrell said, "including Blind Idiot God at Tim Yohannan's suggestion."[3]

Experimental, talented, and absolutely ferocious, Blind Idiot God was exactly what Ginn was looking for. Taking its name from a deity created by horror novelist H. P. Lovecraft, the St. Louis trio drew from a long list of influences—ranging from hardcore and noise to classical and jazz—to create something unmistakably unique. In addition to including the track "Dark and Bright," on the compilation, SST released the band's self-titled debut (SST 104), which was recorded on the banks of the Gowanus Canal at BC Studio.

But Farrell wasn't done yet. "Henry Kaiser was another old friend that I thought Greg would like," Farrell said, "especially with their mutual love of the Grateful Dead."[4] Kaiser was an avant-garde guitarist in the San Francisco scene who seemingly knew everyone, including Herbie Hancock and Captain Beefheart drummer John French. Just as Farrell predicted, Kaiser and Ginn clicked, which led to three records in 1987: *Crazy Backwards Alphabet* (SST 110), a project that included French and featured album artwork by cartoonist Matt Groening; the solo record *Devil in the Drain* (SST 118); and *With Enemies like These, Who Needs Friends?* (SST 147), which combines two previous collaborations with Fred Frith and adds some unreleased live cuts.[5]

Kaiser subsequently brought multi-instrumentalist and composer Elliott Sharp into the fold, and SST released records from several of his musical projects, including the solo album *In the Land of the Yahoos* (SST 128), *Tessalation Row* (SST 129) and *Hammer, Anvil, Stirrup* (SST 232) with the Soldier String Quartet, and *Bone of Contention* (SST 167) as the bass player for Semantics.

Kaiser also introduced Ginn to two more musicians who would make significant contributions to SST's explosion of experimental instrumental music: Glenn Phillips and slide guitarist Scott Colby. Phillips recorded *Elevator* (SST 136) with the Glenn Phillips Band, and Colby, a frequent collaborator with Zoogz Rift, recorded *Slide of Hand* (SST 151).

Ginn called his instrumental project *No Age: A Compilation of SST Instrumental Music* (SST 102), a verbal play on No Wave and new age music. For the cover, SST returned to Lewis, who had snapped photos for D.C. 3's *You're Only as Blind as Your Mind Can Be* and the Leaving Trains' *Fuck*. Lewis went down to the Wilmington Refinery, not far from SST headquarters, searching for images that fit the idea of "no age." "I spent the whole day from dawn until about midnight," Lewis explained, "walking around this no man's land of smoke and dead dogs. A real wasteland. At sunset, I came across a storage tank that was broken down and took some shots. They were in the process of demolishing it, so it was half torn down. It reminded me of the Roman Colosseum with the walls eaten away."[6]

That photo ended up on the cover of *No Age*. Originally, the compilation was going to be presented in a double gatefold package decorated with Lewis's photos of industrial ruin, but because of budget constraints those plans were scrapped.

No Age announced another shift in the label's direction. Not only did the process of assembling *No Age* establish a new frontier of instrumental music; SST's association with Pell Mell opened up a new region that was on the verge of changing literally everything.

2

All towns are small in their own way, but when counting down the days until you get away, they can shrink to the size of a prison cell. Through a strange web of connections, Screaming Trees broke out after becoming the first band from Washington State to sign with SST.

Screaming Trees emerged from the small, rural town of Ellensburg, a place so out of the way that Black Flag had never played there. Farmland surrounded the town of eight thousand souls sitting in the center of the state. Seattle was only one hundred miles away to the northwest, but Ellensburg sat on the opposite side of the Cascade Range, so it felt more remote, especially when winter snowstorms and freezing rain made passage across the Cascades treacherous.

Mark Lanegan knew Lee (who now goes by Gary Lee) and Van Conner from around town. Both of the Conner brothers were over six feet tall and three hundred pounds, making them hard to miss. Lanegan and Van bonded over a shared love of punk rock, which would have made them pariahs if they hadn't already been outcasts in the conservative-minded town. As a teenager, Lanegan earned a reputation as a hard-drinking troublemaker who didn't take shit from anyone. When he put his muscle to use working for Van's father as the repo man for the video store's electronics equipment rent-to-own operation, he discovered the Conner boys had formed a band and they wanted him to join. Intrigued by the band's garage rock sound and Gary Lee's songwriting skills, Lanegan signed on as the singer. Gary Lee played guitar, Van manned the bass, and their friend Mark Pickerel pounded the drums.

Before the band had played a single gig, Screaming Trees recorded a demo at Ellensburg's only recording studio, Creative Fire. The studio's new in-house producer, Steve Fisk, would have a huge impact on the band's fate. Fisk had moved to Ellensburg, from Lakewood, California. "I hated Los Angeles," Fisk said, "always hated Los Angeles, always hated Lakewood. Washington just seemed like a cooler place to be."[7]

After a few years at Central Washington University, Fisk moved to Olympia to enroll at Evergreen State College. A talented musician with a knack for audio engineering, Fisk hosted a show every other week at the school's radio station. The station's music director, John Foster, also launched *OP* magazine, which quickly became an essential guide for indie musicians, zines, and record labels. The culture at Evergreen was something of a DIY training ground—Fisk received college credit for helping run a record label—that inspired indie enthusiasts like Calvin Johnson and Bruce Pavitt, who also briefly managed Pell Mell and accompanied the band on a national tour that Fisk helped organize in 1982. Pell Mell released a tape of a live performance with the whimsical title *Live Cassette*, produced and mixed by Fisk, who joined the band shortly afterward.

Pell Mell parted ways with Pavitt when it relocated to Berkeley, California, but despite a period of intense creativity and Farrell's best efforts, the group struggled to get anything going in the Bay Area. When a record deal with Sixth International, an imprint of Rough Trade, fell through, the band dissipated. Pell Mell put together what it thought would be its last recording, *For Years We Stood Clearly as One Thing*, which was both the slogan of a financial institution and the band's epitaph. The cassette was released on Johnson's label, K Records, to wide acclaim, but the band members had all moved away.

When Fisk returned in Ellensburg to run Creative Fire, he already had a fan in Pickerel, who worked at Ace Records. The drummer had sent him a fan letter, and Fisk reached out to Pickerel when he returned to town. "We became pretty good friends," Fisk said. "We had a lot of musical tastes and ideas in common, and I met the rest of the Screaming Trees shortly thereafter."[8] This relationship led to Fisk producing the Screaming Trees' six-song EP *Other Worlds* in just his second session at the studio. Fisk also played electric organ on a pair of songs that fit right in with the band's psychedelic, garage-rock vibe.

Recorded in 1985, the EP was released by the studio's in-house label Velvetone Records in 1986. *Other Worlds* is a remarkably self-assured record even though the band was very green. Lanegan, in particular, was new to being a vocalist and still learning what his instrument could do. Fisk and Lanegan were both acquainted with Johnson, who'd lived in Ellensburg before moving to Olympia. Oddly enough, Lanegan's mother had been Johnson's fifth-grade teacher.

Johnson distributed the Screaming Trees' demo tape through K Records and helped the band get shows in Olympia, including a gig with Portland legends the Wipers. Pickerel did his part by passing the demo on to Greg Ginn at a Black Flag show at Serbian Hall in Seattle on May 31, 1986. "I was still a senior in high school," Pickerel said, "and we had just finished our recordings with Steve Fisk. We went to see Black Flag and I somehow elbowed myself through the slam pit to the front of the stage and put the *Other Worlds* cassette right next to Greg's monitor. He picked it up in between songs and put it on top of his amp, and apparently that was his first introduction to the Screaming Trees."[9]

Pleased with the demo, the Conners' parents footed the bill for another recording session and a full-length release on Velvetone called *Clairvoyance*, which drew interest from Greg Sage of the Wipers, who was recruiting bands for Pink Dust, an imprint of Enigma. Pink Dust had signed several garage rock revival acts and was in the process of reissuing records by Roky Erickson of the 13th Floor Elevators, godfather of psychedelic rock. Pink Dust seemed like a perfect fit for Screaming Trees, but the label was looking for an extensive commitment from the band, which caused some trepidation.

Because of the band's relationship with Fisk, Screaming Trees was able to record new material whenever the studio was available. While in the process of recording a third album, the band headed to California to play some shows. Fisk had sent copies of *Other Worlds* and *Clairvoyance* to Farrell, who was now at SST, and asked for help booking shows for the band. Farrell obliged and talked to Schwartz at Global about pairing Screaming Trees with an SST band in town, but he ultimately secured a gig a bit off the beaten path. "Texas Records in Santa Monica was a very cool indie-leaning store that had a small stage," Farrell said. "It was owned by two great people, Michael Meister and Susan Farrell. They later started the Texas Hotel label. They wanted the band to play at the store. Should the Trees play the opening slot at a local club with no audience or at a free record store gig with a full house? No brainer."[10]

Farrell put the band up in his apartment as a favor to Fisk, but his opinion of Screaming Trees changed after he saw the band play. Like D. Boon, the Conner brothers were big men who played with a lot of energy, stomping around the stage and whipping their long hair around like headbangers. Gary Lee was especially fond of windmilling his arm like Pete Townshend. The music drew on the Northwest's rough-edged garage rock tradition of the Wailers, the Ventures, and the Sonics, and the band had a powerful physical presence that was impossible to ignore. "That's really what sparked it all," Lanegan said. "Ray got really excited when he saw us play live."[11]

After the band returned to Ellensburg, Lanegan answered the phone at work one day and was shocked to discover Ginn on the line. Lanegan considered that someone might be playing a prank on him, but it quickly became apparent it really was Ginn. He told Lanegan how much he enjoyed *Other Worlds* and that he wanted to put it out on SST.

The call couldn't have come at a better time. The band was seriously considering joining Sage at Pink Dust, in spite of the deal's unfavorable terms. "We were on the verge of signing some ridiculous seven-record deal with Pink Dust," Lanegan said, "when Greg called, and he said, 'It's one record at a time, but nobody's ever been dropped by SST.' Of course that was very attractive."[12]

Although the band was thrilled that SST wanted to put out *Other Worlds* (SST 105), Screaming Trees had grown since that EP and wanted to show SST what it could do. Gary Lee, who was constantly writing new songs, recording them on his four-track and sharing them with the band, was eager to get back in the studio with Fisk to finish making the album that would be called *Even If and Especially When* (SST 132). Since the last session, Gary Lee had taken LSD for the first time, and it had a profound impact on his songwriting. His already trippy material became even more so, which is evident on tracks like "Transfiguration," a fuzzed-out homage to the life-changing power of altered states.

After the album's release in March 1987, Screaming Trees played several shows with fIREHOSE, including the FeaSST to ExiSST festival on the campus of UCSD, where Screaming Trees opened for Lawndale, fIRE-HOSE, and Opal, featuring Dave Roback of Rain Parade and Kendra Smith of the Dream Syndicate.[13] "That was a great day," said Long, who drove down with the rest of the SST crew to see the show. "It was really well attended and great bands. It was Opal. We were all so into Opal. I mean absurdly into that record."[14] Opal was gearing up to release *Happy Nightmare Baby* (SST 103) at the end of the year, but Smith would leave the band in the middle of the tour.[15]

Fisk also released a record of his own—*448 Deathless Days* (SST 159). The title comes from a sign posted on the old highway boasting of Ellensburg's traffic safety record. The numbers hadn't changed for as long as anyone could remember, and it took an outsider to notice how strange that was. "Steve definitely helped us view Ellensburg through a set of ironic spectacles," Pickerel said. "We could only see what we didn't like about Ellensburg, and Steve helped us see Ellensburg almost the way David Lynch might."[16] It was an indie sci-fi film called *FertiliChrome* directed by P. S. O'Neil and shot in the deserts of Eastern Washington that provided Fisk with the get-up he wore on the album cover. In the film, Fisk plays the villainous Dr. Stimson, who terrorizes the locals with a crew of thugs, played by Lanegan, Pickerel, and Van.

Screaming Trees went on its first nationwide tour in the fall of '87 with fIREHOSE to support the release of its new record, *If'n* (SST 115). Although the notoriously frugal Watt often made fun of Sonic Youth for

Steve Kaul of SST sandwiched between Mark Lanegan and Van Conner of Screaming Trees, at Bogart's in Long Beach, October 1987. (Photo by Naomi Petersen Photography.)

splurging on motel rooms during the Flaming Telepaths Tour, he wasn't shy about crashing with Screaming Trees whenever the band had booked a room.

In Connecticut, Screaming Trees played with Dinosaur. Lanegan recalled a woman at the show was upset because she drove a long way thinking she was going to see the Dinosaurs, a '60s psychedelic supergroup. This Dinosaur was a completely different entity. Not only did the band not play music that would appeal to nostalgic hippies, but it was much louder than the band with whom it shared a name—or anyone else for that matter. "I remember it was so incredibly loud," Lanegan said, "when Mascis started playing his guitar that I had to leave the room."[17]

3

Like Screaming Trees, the members of Dinosaur hailed from a small town. Amherst, Massachusetts, is located approximately one hundred miles west of Boston, and like Ellensburg, Amherst is home to an institution of higher learning—three, in fact. Although Mascis played drums in his high school hardcore band, after graduation he switched to guitar and began an advanced study in noise at the University of Massachusetts Amherst. In the ultimate slacker move, Mascis moved into a dorm room even though his parents lived just minutes away at 27 Jeffrey Lane.

With Barlow on bass and Murph on drums, the stripped-down trio started playing shows as Dinosaur. Mascis sang—seemingly with great reluctance—with occasional help from Barlow, who was more of a screamer. Mascis's laconic vocal style was so laid back it bordered on indifference. This was part of Dinosaur's charm but also a necessity because Mascis's guitar was always going to be the loudest instrument in the room. Dinosaur's seesaw between Mission of Burma–style aggression and pensive pop songs earned them fans all over New England.

At the invitation of former UMass Amherst student Gerard Cosloy, the trio recorded its first self-titled album for Homestead Records. Released in 1985, the songs are a lo-fi patchwork of incongruous parts. Stylistically all over the map, the record works backward through '80s hardcore, '70s guitar rock, and '60s garage pop and ends up someplace entirely new.

Despite Mascis's low-key demeanor on and off the stage, he was demanding of his bandmates and had a strong sense of what he wanted to do. Dinosaur became notorious around Western Massachusetts for insisting on playing at ear-splitting volumes. While Dinosaur struggled to get noticed on its home turf, in New York the band caught the attention of Sonic Youth. "They were nice to us," Mascis said, "which we didn't get a lot of back then."[18]

In September 1986, Dinosaur went on the road with Sonic Youth and played several dates in the Northeast and Midwest. In his journals, Moore raved about Mascis's guitar playing and encouraged Mascis to consider a switch to SST. Dinosaur scratched together a three-song demo with the songs "Raisans," "In a Jar," and "Tarpit," and Sonic Youth dispatched the tape to Ginn, who had already seen the band play and wasted no time in offering Dinosaur a contract.

The new record was pieced together from three different recording sessions. The first took place in Holyoke in the basement of David Pine's parents' house, one of the few places to record in Western Massachusetts. The second session was held at Wharton Tiers's Fun City in New York. Mascis didn't have quite enough material for a full-length, so Barlow's song "Poledo," which he recorded himself, was added to the end. Three sessions, one dynamic record.

The album was called *You're Living All Over Me* (SST 130), which Mascis explained was about "living in a small town, about not being able to express yourself."[19] Despite Sonic Youth's assistance in luring Dinosaur to the roster, sonically the band owed a debt to the Meat Puppets, who released two new albums that year: *Mirage* (SST 100) in the spring and *Huevos* (SST 150) in the fall, but no one on the label played as loud as Dinosaur. Long recalled paying a visit to Ford's cubicle at SST. "'You gotta check this out,' Ford said. He was playing the master of *You're Living All Over Me* and both meters were totally in the red. 'I've never seen a record recorded this hot before!'"[20]

Between the time Dinosaur's SST debut hit record store shelves in July 1987 and a single for "Little Fury Things" (SST 152) was released in November, SST was contacted by a lawyer representing the Dinosaurs, whose members had been in the Grateful Dead, Big Brother and the Holding Company, and Country Joe and the Fish. These Dinosaurs hadn't gone extinct, and their lawyers were upset.

O'Bryan said that even though the Dinosaurs could have made trouble for both the band and the label, it chose not to. Instead, Barry "the Fish" Melton negotiated with SST to find a solution. "He was a real gentleman about it," O'Bryan said. "He basically ran interference for the record label to keep the lawyers out of it. You could tell it wasn't about the money."[21]

As a result, Dinosaur changed its name to Dinosaur Jr, and a legal matter was settled amicably—a rarity for SST.

4

Fall was shaping up to be huge, and SST needed more help, especially in the art department. Nicks's boyfriend, a local skater named Craig Ibarra, had been doing some freelance assignments designing flyers and stickers for bands like fIREHOSE, Bad Brains, and Screaming Trees. Ibarra, who had just turned nineteen, was brought in for an interview and arrived at SST headquarters in Carson fresh from a skate session. "I showed up to the interview with my skateboard in hand," Ibarra recalled, "grasping the strap of my helmet, my Rector knee pads down at my ankles and a bit sweaty. I had no knowledge of job interview etiquette."[22]

Ibarra got the job and was immediately put to work designing an album cover for a Black Flag compilation called Wasted...Again (SST 166). To add to the pressure, Ibarra took creative direction directly from the man in charge. "Greg Ginn described his cover idea to me like this: 'I want it to be colorful, but wasted looking.' I recall him coyly smirking and saying, 'Wastey!' in a surfer-stoner tone."[23] Ginn got what he asked for: a psychedelic swirl of shapes that were as colorful as they were cartoonish and stood out from the rest of Black Flag's album art.

Reissues were a big part of the workload. Included in the wave of new releases at the end of 1987 were some familiar names. Preoccupied with his new band, Watt sold New Alliance Records to Ginn, who promptly began to reissue the label's most popular records on SST, making many available on compact disc and cassette for the first time. SST reissued Hüsker Dü's hardcore classic *Land Speed Record* (SST 195) and the Descendents' *Milo Goes to College* (SST 142) and *I Don't Want to Grow Up* (SST 143). In addition, SST reissued *Bonus Fat* (SST 144), which is the *Fat* EP plus some early tracks, and *Two Things at Once* (SST 145), which (as the title suggests) combines two records: *Milo Goes to College* and *Fat*. The Descendents also put out a new studio album called *All* (SST 112) and the live record *Liveage!* (SST 163). Blood on the Saddle, who'd put out an album on New Alliance in 1984, brought its cow-punk twang to SST with *Fresh Blood* (SST 116). With help from Kubernik, Ginn primarily used New Alliance Records for new jazz, poetry, and spoken word releases.

SST also reissued a pair of Minutemen compilations that combined records that hadn't been released on CD: *Post-Mersh, Vol. 1* (SST 138) included *Paranoid Time* and *What Makes a Man Start Fires?*, and *Post-Mersh, Vol. 2* (SST 139) brought together *Buzz or Howl Under the Influence of Heat* and *Project: Mersh*. A third and final edition, *Post-Mersh, Vol. 3* (SST 165), came out the following year.

As if running two labels wasn't enough, Ginn started another one: Cruz Records. The label started small by showcasing ALL—the band that emerged from the ashes of the Descendents with Bill Stevenson, Karl Alvarez, and Stephen Egerton—and cranked out a deep run of records. Cruz would also serve as a clearing house for Ginn's solo records released under his own name.

By any measure imaginable, '87 was an impressive year for SST. The crew in Carson released close to seventy singles, studio albums, compilations, and reissues in a single calendar year, more than doubling the number of records it released in 1986 and easily exceeding the total number produced between 1978 and 1985. "SST released more records in 1987 than in any other year," Farrell said. "A friend at Warner's told me that we surpassed their number."[24]

SST was not a multinational corporation with decades of industry experience and massive budgets for production and promotion. Yet somehow SST put out a greater number of records than one of the largest labels in the country—a feat that did not escape the attention of the music media. Writing for the *Village Voice*, Chuck Eddy considered the outpouring of releases: "I think SST's just determined to make certain unheard music gets heard no matter what, and from their fecundity alone it's obvious they're succeeding. Coming from an organization that not too long ago did its business from phone booths, I'd say that's an accomplishment worth commending."[25]

SST represented what a group of outsiders could achieve when it believed in what it was doing and committed to the cause. But how do you sustain that mentality when you are no longer the underdog, when you are, in fact, kicking corporate rock's ass?

Not everyone at the label was drinking the Kool-Aid. Some artists believed that SST was simply beating corporate rock at its own game.

5

Michael Whittaker was working in the office at SST when one of the members of Negativland called to ask whether he knew anyone in the Minneapolis press. A sixteen-year-old boy named David Brom had murdered his father, mother, brother, and sister with an axe. One detail in the shocking tragedy seemed like it had been planted to provoke a media firestorm: Brom's murderous rampage was instigated by an argument between Brom and his conservative Catholic father about music. Negativland wanted to know if Whittaker would tell the media that the music in question was none other than "Christianity Is Stupid" from the band's SST debut *Escape from Noise* (SST 133).

Whittaker was game. "Christianity Is Stupid" features samples from a sermon delivered by a scare-mongering Mississippi preacher named Reverend Estus Washington Pirkle who gave inflammatory speeches, wrote several books, and even made films in which his interpretations of what the Bible said about heaven and hell are every bit as strange as Negativland's sonic experiments.

Whittaker called up a journalist he knew in Minneapolis and fed him the fabrication. The story, in twenty-first-century parlance, went viral. When SST and Negativland saw how easy it was to stir up the media, it concocted a press release with additional details. The press release announced that the band was canceling its North American tour after being cautioned by federal officials against leaving town until the Brom murder investigation was complete.

This, of course, wasn't true—Negativland canceled its tour when it realized it would lose money—but when reporters called, the lie provided cover.

The press release was widely circulated, and the sensational story grabbed headlines across the country, having grown from a small item in the music press to extensive television coverage. For Negativland the hoax illustrated the fallibility of the news media and called into question the legitimacy of its practices. As the story gained traction, it became "abundantly clear that the major source for news is other news."[26] If an experimental rock band could generate national attention over a fake story that could have been debunked with a few phone calls, what else were these news organizations getting wrong?

Negativland's bogus claims gained credence through the media's eagerness to run stories that demonized rock and roll as a negative influence on youth culture. For every story about a deranged teenager committing heinous crimes, there were hundreds more warning about the corrupting influence of rock and roll. In other words, Negativland got the press to fall for its own lies.

For SST it wasn't so much a hoax as a case of giving the media a taste of its own medicine. Black Flag had a target on its back for most of its existence, with journalists, music critics, and media personalities lining up to paint the band and its fans as thugs who reveled in violence. In the early '80s, Ginn earnestly explained the reasons for the band's actions to anyone who would listen. He, along with many others, soon realized that the mainstream media interviewed punk rockers to use their own words against them and make the movement look foolish.

At many record labels, Whittaker would have lost his job. Not at SST. No one sat Whittaker down to remind him of the rules because there weren't any. Although the label had developed a set of practices for getting SST's records into stores and on the radio and for soliciting coverage for its bands in magazines, newspapers, and zines, they couldn't compete with the marketing departments at major labels. Any time an SST record broke through the noise and received recognition, it was a win for the label. Stunts like the Negativland press release not only fed the David versus Goliath narrative at SST, but the occasional victory suggested the label was holding its own.

While SST was open to innovative approaches, Whittaker's stunt wasn't new. Dukowski seemed to thrive on misleading the media and wasn't above spreading disinformation about his projects. Those who saw Negativland's manipulations as spurious and opportunistic simply weren't paying attention. Manipulating media was Negativland's reason for being. From widespread sampling to free-form radio shows, the bandmembers were masters at reconfiguring media and recontextualizing it into new forms.

Named after a song by the Kraftwerk splinter group Neu!, Negativland began in 1979 in Concord, California, when Mark Hosler started hanging out at Rather Ripped Records in Berkeley. There he met Ray Farrell, who was just as enthusiastic about Krautrock as he was. Hosler began collaborating on sound-collage experiments with his classmate Richard Lyons after school. David Wills (a.k.a. the Weatherman) joined not long after, and the band formed the record label Seeland and recorded its first, self-titled, self-produced album with help from Peter Dayton in 1980.

Negativland attracted the attention of Chris Grigg and Don Joyce, who hosted *Over the Edge*, a late-night radio show broadcast out of Berkeley on KPFA 94.1. Joyce had the band on the show, which enlarged the scope of Negativland's operations. *Over the Edge* evolved into "the longest running big block of weekly free form radio in radio history."[27] Negativland released heavily edited cuts from the show, the first of which was *JamCon'84*.[28] Radio jamming was the practice of pirating public frequencies. Negativland took this idea a step forward with culture jamming, a term coined by Joyce to describe the hijacking of consumer culture for noncommercial purposes. With its affiliation with *Over the Edge*, Negativland wasn't just critiquing culture from suburban bedrooms and basements anymore; it became part of the apparatus it sought to dismantle.

Negativland signed with SST after several more albums. *Escape from Noise* was a surprise hit, selling thirty-five thousand units—a shocking amount for an arty, experimental outfit that didn't tour and wasn't even a band in the conventional sense.

To Ginn, Dukowski, and Mugger, it must have felt as though they were at the top of the world. It wasn't that long ago that thirty-five thousand units was a number only SST's most experienced and hardest-working bands could achieve. That a band like Negativland was moving so many records was a testament to the strength of the brand. No other indie could match SST in production or sales. Bad Brains and Sonic Youth were the label's top performers, which wasn't surprising considering they were established bands. But the success of newer and more experimental bands like Dinosaur Jr and Negativland revealed how powerful SST had become. The question on everyone's mind was, *How big can this get?*

Success, however, doesn't run in a straight line. In SST's case, the metaphor of a wave is more apt, and its momentum was on the verge of crashing.

6

In 1988, Long added a new task to his list of duties at SST: driver. H.R. had decided he was going to teach himself to play the trumpet, but he needed a place to practice. That's where SST—and Long in particular—came in. "Three days a week, Mondays, Wednesdays and Fridays," Long explained, "I would pick him up from a Safeway parking lot in Hollywood and drive him down to the office. Every morning, he'd get in the car and he'd light up a spliff, and it was a huge spliff, which would last way longer than the forty-five minutes it took to drive to the office."[29]

Long, who didn't partake in the four o'clock weed break, kept his windows open. When they reached SST HQ, H.R. would lock himself in the conference room and play his trumpet. Sometimes he'd take breaks and loudly recite passages from the Bible. Then, at the end of the day, H.R. would repeat the ritual and light another spliff for the ride home. This went on for four or five months, and in the process Long got to know the enigmatic singer. "He was full of great stories, wisdom, and just H.R.-isms," Long recalled.[30]

Everyone at the label soon had a story or two about H.R. O'Bryan recalled that he liked to smoke weed behind the bushes in front of the building. "He's really out there," O'Bryan said. "Nice as hell, but he's out there. A true believer. I got along with him just fine."

O'Bryan drove H.R. around as well, picking him up at the airport and taking him to see friends. It wasn't always clear where H.R. lived. He even stayed with Nicks and Ibarra at their apartment in San Pedro for a week or two. Then H.R. hopscotched over to another SST employee's apartment: Roger Ahlsforth, who replaced Trudnich as SST's receptionist. He moved on, and when Ahlsforth's phone bill arrived, he discovered that H.R. had made long distance calls all over the United States and Jamaica. As H.R.'s vagabond ways continued, rumors—as well as warnings—about his eccentric exploits traveled throughout the punk community.

Ibarra remained on good terms with H.R. and worked on many of his solo projects, including the art and design for *HR Tapes '84–'86*, "Now You Say" (SST 173), the dub-heavy *Singin' in the Heart* (SST 224), *Charge* (SST 256), and *Rock of Enoch* (SST 274). As a result, Ibarra wasn't shy about asking H.R. to perform at the occasional house party he threw for his friends in San Pedro. On one occasion, dozens of people packed into an unventilated garage to hear H.R. sing, but after a confrontation with locals who tried to crash the party, the night ended in chaos.

H.R. liked to have a good time, but he wasn't the only one. Whittaker was fond of the four o'clock weed breaks and sometimes he boosted his creativity at work with a hit of LSD. If he had a long day of writing ahead of him, Whittaker would occasionally drop acid while carpooling with Long so that by the time they got to Carson the drugs had kicked in. "Mike was a wonderfully quirky guy to work with," Long said. "He'd sit at the only computer in the office with a big smile on his face."[31]

SST artists frequently visited the office in Carson. Whether they were stocking up on merch or visiting to discuss recording a new album, there were always people coming and going. Mugger might be on the phone with Mascis in Amherst while Ginn negotiated licensing agreements with record labels overseas. Dukowski gave tours of the warehouse, which was always a popular spot with musicians, who marveled at the stacks and stacks of records, tapes, and CDs and were encouraged to help themselves. Some bands would show up after a tour utterly destitute, without enough money to pay for gas to get home. After tours for *Group Therapy* (SST 185) and *Buzz* (SST 245), Thomson recalled Ginn helped the Alter Natives get back to Richmond by giving them marijuana instead of money.[32]

Always August with Jordan Schwartz at SST. (Photo by Naomi Petersen Photography.)

For bands like the Leaving Trains or Divine Horsemen, a trip to working-class Carson was a break from the Hollywood dream factory. For artists beyond LA, SST was another facet of the weird, sprawling megacity.

Screaming Trees enjoyed coming to sunny Southern California and hanging out at SST headquarters, where the staff was augmented by interns from Loyola Marymount University, including one named Alexandra whose mother, Nancy, was involved in politics. How involved? She would eventually become Speaker of the House of Representatives. "The vibe around SST at the time was pretty exciting and really positive," Pickerel recalled. "Ironically, the only person that we rarely had any personal contact with was Greg because he was often behind closed doors."[33]

7

The first time Lanegan saw Nirvana play, he didn't want to be there. The band had somehow scored a gig at the Hal Holmes Community Center in Ellensburg on June 17, 1988. Lanegan only went as a favor to a friend, but those feelings changed after he saw Nirvana perform a set that was cut short after a fight broke out. Nirvana was something of an enigma: a noisy thrash band with huge hooks. "I immediately thought they were greatness," Lanegan said.[34]

Lanegan and Cobain became fast friends and close confidants who shared a number of interests. Nirvana was on the verge of releasing its first single, a ripping cover of Shocking Blue's "Love Buzz" from 1969 backed with "Big Cheese," on the label Bruce Pavitt created with Jonathan Poneman. Nirvana's version of the song had an extensive intro culled from children's records that Sub Pop insisted be trimmed down. "Kurt was unhappy because of the micromanaging that was happening at Sub Pop," Lanegan recalled. "Of course, I didn't really rate Sub Pop at that time. I was already on the coolest indie in the world."[35]

SST had reissued Screaming Trees' first EP *Other Worlds* (SST 105) and had just released the band's new album, *Invisible Lantern* (SST 188). The art for the album was literally plucked off the studio wall at Velvetone: a pop surrealist painting that Lanegan had always admired called *Belem Is Here* by an art student at Central Washington University. The record opens with "Ivy," a track steeped in snarling guitars and collapsing riffs that steers a course between MC5 and the Stooges. On "Grey Diamond Desert" Lanegan experiments with the gravelly, been-through-some-shit sound of his solo albums to come. *Invisible Lantern* checks all the boxes for the noise that would emerge from the Northwest in the '90s.

Lanegan told Cobain that SST was very hands off and never interfered with Screaming Trees' recordings or artwork, which was rare for a label, no matter its size or stature. This appealed to the young songwriter from Aberdeen. "He asked me if I would send a tape to Greg," Lanegan said, "which I did. Then I sent another one. And he listened to them both. I had three different conversations with him at Kurt's request."[36]

Lanegan's efforts to secure a record deal for his friend's band fell on deaf ears. "He just didn't get it," Lanegan said. "Didn't like it. Didn't see it as something he'd want to put out, which of course is his right, but I couldn't believe it because I thought Nirvana was great. I really tried to talk him into it, but he didn't want to go for it."[37]

Ginn's refusal to sign Nirvana puts to rest the idea that SST was just handing out record contracts to its circle of friends. Of the sixty or so releases SST put out in 1988, approximately ten were by artists who were new to the label. While former SWA guitarist Sylvia Juncosa's *Nature* (SST 146), Paul Roessler's *Abominable* (SST 196), and Grant Hart's single "2541" (SST 219) were new creative projects, each artist had made records for the label with their previous bands.

While Juncosa introduced her scorching guitar riffs with the song "Eat My Pussy, Eddie Van Halen," Hart's "2541" had a compelling backstory. The song was written when Hart was in Hüsker Dü, but Mould rejected it. Mould came to regret that decision and speculated that it may have driven a wedge between the two songwriters: "I often wondered if it might have been the beginning of the end."[38] The song would appear as "Twenty-Five Forty-One" on Hart's LP *Intolerance* (SST 215) the following year.

As in 1987, the number of new releases was boosted by bands putting out multiple records in 1988. Guitar maestro Henry Kaiser had his hand in three: Everett Shock's *Ghost Boys* (SST 182), the solo album *Those Who Know History Are Doomed to Repeat It* (SST 198), and *Re-marrying for Money* (SST 222), which was a reissue of an earlier LP on CD and cassette. Elliott Sharp also got in the act with a pair of experimental electronic records with the band Carbon—*Larynx* (SST 194) and *Monster Curve* (SST 208).

Zoogz Rift continued its unlikely run with *Nonentity (Water III: Fan Black Dada)* (SST 184) and *Murdering Hell's Happy Cretins* (SST 211), which was the difficult-to-please songwriter's favorite record. *Torment* (SST 251), the band's twelfth record with the label, marked the end of Zoogz Rift's stint as SST's resident Dadaist.

Brian Ritchie, the extraordinary bass player for the Violent Femmes, followed up *The Blend* (SST 141) in 1987 with three new records that included a pair of EPs—*Nuclear War* (SST 186) and in German, *Atomkrieg* (SST 187)—as well as the LP *Sonic Temple & Court of Babylon* (SST 202).

Ritchie wasn't the only celebrated new addition to the label. After recording with Lydia Lunch in Berlin, Australian Rowland S. Howard of the Birthday Party started These Immortal Souls in London with his brother Harry and his girlfriend Genevieve McGuckin. The band recorded an album and a single for Mute Records in the UK, which were reissued by SST in the US: *Get Lost (Don't Lie)* (SST 164) and "Marry Me (Lie! Lie!)" (SST 183).

The onslaught of records released in 1988 included more reissues from New Alliance; namely, the compilations *Chunks* (SST 069) and *Cracks in the Sidewalk* (SST 092), plus a new live album from the Descendents called *Hallraker* (SST 205) that features tracks from a pair of shows in 1987. The glut was so great that some bands broke up before SST could get their records out the door and into stores. After releasing Painted Willie's *Upsidedowntown* (SST 098), SST planned to reissue two early records—the EP *My Fellow Americans* (SST 107) and a self-titled single (SST 108). But after the band broke up, SST issued a compilation of these cuts titled *Relics* (SST 178) instead.

SST also made an unusual foray into emerging technology by issuing a series of three-inch miniature compact discs. These mini-discs could hold only about twenty minutes of music, compared to regular-sized CDs, which could store up to approximately seventy-five minutes of music—more than a record or cassette.

The first SST mini-CDs, the Descendents' *Fat* (SST 212) and the Minutemen's *Joy* (SST 214), came out in 1987. These were followed up in 1988 by Brian Ritchie's *Sun Ra—Man from Outer Space* (SST 227); Bad Brains' *Spirit Electricity (Live)* (SST 228); Henry Kaiser's *Alternate Versions* (SST 237); and *Mini Plot* (SST 234), a mini-disc companion to the full-length compilation *The Melting Plot* (SST 249). *The Melting Plot* was made in collaboration with Markey's We Got Power Films and featured a mishmash of amusing and unusual covers, such as Chemical People performing "It's Not Unusual," L7's take on the bubblegum pop of "Yummy Yummy," and Sonic Youth covering Saccharine Trust's "I Am Right."

As SST released more mini-discs, it stopped using a separate catalog number for the format. However, it was a short-lived experiment as these discs were neither practical nor cost-effective and were a drain on the label's resources. But SST also experimented in mini-albums and cassettes. Always August's *Geography* (SST 193) was released as a four-song mini-album, concluding the Richmond jazz rockers run with SST.

The Last finally put out a record for SST with *Confession* (SST 189) followed by *Awakening* (SST 230) in 1989, this time without Vitus Mataré, who was busy with Trotsky Icepick, the band he formed with Kjehl Johansen after 100 Flowers broke up. Trotsky Icepick began a long run of experimental pop records it would release with SST with *Baby* (SST 197).

In addition to all these familiar faces, SST welcomed recordings from a raft of new artists not named Nirvana to the label. Some of these included *The Birth of the Cruel* (SST 127), by the Southern California free jazz band Cruel Frederick; *Zion Train* (SST 168), by H.R.'s mentor in Rastafarianism Ras Michael; *Bugged* (SST 191), by New York City alt-rockers Mofungo with Elliott Sharp; *Hardly, Not Even* (SST 192) and a self-titled record (SST 199) by Minneapolis post-punkers Run Westy Run; a self-titled album (SST 203) by anti-folk rocker Roger Manning; *Farced* (SST 210), by Mission of Burma drummer Peter Prescott's band Volcano Suns, who'd made the jump to SST from Homestead; and *Go Man Go* (SST 223), by bluesman Kirk Kelly. Kelly's record bears the distinction of being the least like any other album on the label because of its utterly conventional sound. Why was there room at SST for a blues shouter like Kirk Kelly but not Kurt Cobain?

Of course, SST wasn't the only label that missed out on signing Nirvana, and Ginn clearly wasn't buying what Lanegan was selling, but perhaps that's because another band from the Northwest had already caught his ear.

8

By 1988, not only were bands angling to get on SST, and major labels trying to lure its artists away, but one group schemed to get on SST after being offered a contract by the majors—like a baseball prodigy going to the minors for some seasoning before stepping up to the big leagues. What made the plan all the more audacious was that it worked.

Susan Silver had already managed the legendary Seattle band the U-Men and booked shows at the notorious all-ages club Metropolis when she took on Soundgarden as a client in 1986. She knew the band intimately because she was dating its singer, Chris Cornell. A pair of transplants from Park Forest,

Illinois—Kim Thayil and Hiro Yamamoto—played guitar and bass, and local Matt Cameron manned the drums.

In March 1986, Soundgarden appeared on a compilation of underground Northwest bands called *Deep Six* that included songs by Green River, the Melvins, Malfunkshun, Skin Yard, and the U-Men. In her review of the record in the *Rocket*, Dawn Anderson observed that the bands were neither punk nor metal "but a third sound distinct from either."[39] In a few years that third sound would become synonymous with Seattle.

The following year, Sup Pop put out a pair of Soundgarden releases: the single "Hunted Down" backed with "Nothing to Say" and the EP *Screaming Life*. Both records were limited to five hundred copies. In 1987, Soundgarden cut a second EP for Sub Pop, *Fopp*, which was produced by Fisk, whose influence can be felt on this dub version of a song by the Ohio Players. The band's Sub Pop connection was hardly accidental: Pavitt was also from Park Forest. In fact, back in Illinois Thayil had played in the punk band Identity Crisis with John Pavitt, Bruce's younger brother.

Despite the fledgling label's limited ability to promote the band, Soundgarden began to draw serious interest from major labels. A&M Records was so enamored with Cornell's talent that it helped pay for the band to record demos. Soundgarden was admired by musicians and industry insiders alike, but it didn't have much of a following outside of Seattle. Silver shrewdly understood that jumping to a major label without a national audience was a recipe for disaster. It would give all the leverage to the label and put the band in a position where it might feel compelled to take direction from outside influences.

Silver tried to reach out to SST but wasn't able to make headway. As a rule, the label didn't take solicitations from music managers. However, Pickerel of Screaming Trees saw Soundgarden play in Ellensburg and was so impressed with the band that he sent a tape of the performance to Ginn. That caught Ginn's attention, and he invited the band to join the label.

For Thayil, signing with SST made sense. He had been buying records from the label since the early days of Black Flag and was especially impressed with Saint Vitus. He was so enamored with the doom metal band that he gave a copy of the debut album to his girlfriend on Valentine's Day. "A lot of punk rock guys had a secret place in their heart for Sabbath," Thayil said. "There are a lot of guys in Seattle who are into Alice Cooper. I was not one of them. I filed Alice Cooper away with my '70s classic rock stuff and put it behind me. But Sabbath was still important. The Stooges were important. The first two Stooges albums are heavy three-chord grinders. They're not fast like *Raw Power*. When Saint Vitus came out, Mark Arm told me about it. 'Oh you gotta check out Saint Vitus, they're kind of Sabbath-y!' I had to deal with the whole cognitive thing: a Sabbath-y band on a punk rock label? But what it said to me was that there was an open-mindedness and a progressive embrace of the indie ethos that was separate from a particular style or punk rock taxonomy. SST was independent of all that."[40]

Soundgarden tapped into the ultra-rock groove that had always appealed to Ginn, Dukowski, and Carducci. Saint Vitus had it. D.C. 3 had it. Even Würm had it. After Saint Vitus released *Mournful Cries* (SST 161), its fourth and final studio album for SST, it passed the proverbial torch to Soundgarden.

News of Ginn's interest in the Seattle rockers was met with confusion at SST, especially by those who were under the impression that Soundgarden had already made a deal with a major. "We were surprised," Long said, "because the rumor was they had signed to A&M. Whether that had happened already, I don't know, but it was definitely a strategic move on the band's part to build credibility."[41]

Soundgarden courted attention from indie and major labels alike. While this was anathema in punk rock circles, the band made no secret of it, which bothered some of the labels that Soundgarden met with. Thayil recalled meeting with an executive at Capitol who asked why they were wasting her time. Ginn, however, wasn't bothered in the least, especially since the band was up front about its plans.

SST was always at the top of Soundgarden's list. "I think our view at that point was the major labels probably aren't going to go away," Thayil said. "If they're interested now, they'll be interested next year. But right now we have this opportunity at SST. The more work we do ourselves, building our brand

and our audience, the less that a major label is going to tell us what to do. SST isn't going to tell us what to do, or how to be, or what kind of audience we should try to reach. And we don't want people to do that. We're not gonna let them do that. The more we do ourselves, the less that'll happen."[42]

Soundgarden's DIY ethos extended to carefully reading its contract, where Thayil found a word he didn't like: "perpetuity." At an LA show with Slovenly and SWA at Club Lingerie, Thayil approached Ginn about it. "We're on SST because we like you guys, we trust you guys, and we like the catalog but what if you and Chuck fly out to New York to see Sonic Youth or something and the plane crashes? Who would inherit SST?"[43] Ginn saw Thayil's point and was convinced to change perpetuity to six or seven years, after which the two parties would reevaluate the contract. By changing one word, Thayil helped Soundgarden retain the rights to its debut album.

Ginn suggested that Drew Canulette produce the record. Drew had recorded Black Flag's live album *Who's Got the 10½?*, and Ginn wanted to hear what the band could do with Canulette's sixteen-track mobile recording unit. Soundgarden had used Jack Endino's bare-bones studio, Reciprocal Recording, to record its demos and was happy with the sound, but since SST was paying, Soundgarden agreed. "It was an experiment," Thayil said, "and an opportunity to take advantage of that offer from Greg."[44]

Canulette hauled Dogfish Sound up to Seattle from Portland to record the drum and guitar tracks and then went home. Over a period of several weekends, Cornell and Thayil went down to Portland to record vocals, solos, and overdubs. Canulette had the studio parked in his driveway with cords running through his window to power the generators. "We'd track during the day, have dinner, and hang out and drink at night," Thayil recalled.[45]

Soundgarden released its SST debut, *Ultramega OK* (SST 201), in October, but the band wasn't happy with the way it sounded. "There are some weird phasing issues with guitars and some cymbals," Thayil explained.[46] The band approached Ginn about remixing the record and he was open to it, but before anyone could do anything about it, the band had moved on. By the time the single "Flower" (SST 231) was released the following year, Soundgarden was long gone.

Mugger, Ginn, and Dukowski at SST in 1988. (Photo by Naomi Petersen Photography.)

CHAPTER 12
SST vs. Negativland

1988–1992

1

When Greenworld went bankrupt in 1986, it didn't hurt SST as much as other labels because of SST's practice of working with numerous distributors rather than the exclusive licensing arrangements distributors preferred and urged their clients to sign. But it was a different story when Jem folded in 1988.

SST was doing more business with Jem because there were fewer distributors to do business with, so the economic impact was higher. How much did Jem owe SST when it went under? Whittaker suggested the number was around $80,000.[1] This latest financial setback must have struck Ginn as yet another example of so-called professionals acting in an unprofessional manner to the detriment of his business. The financial fallout was felt throughout SST. "The first thing to go was the Coke machine," O'Bryan said. "The coffee service and the Coke machine were gone."[2]

There were several reasons distributors were failing, but they played a role in their own undoing. Many had started labels that failed to generate hits. For every Mötley Crüe there were dozens, if not hundreds, of hair metal bands scooped up by overeager labels who never had their moment in the sun. This was especially frustrating for indie labels who believed their distributors were funding these labels with money withheld from them.

Another contributing factor was major labels were poaching bands in increasing numbers. "When things started to get popular," said Derrick Bostrom of the Meat Puppets, "the majors were able to co-opt it."[3] Once major labels started creating "alternative music" departments, Bostrom and other artists observed, it was only a matter of time before they started siphoning off talent from independent labels—similar to what SST had been doing to Homestead, but on a larger scale. "Slowly but surely as bands started moving from SST and the other indies to the majors," Bostrom said, "the smaller labels weren't able to hang on to artists or attract artists that could make the pipeline pay. The next thing you know distributors are starting to run into trouble, and then the labels are starting to run into trouble, and then it becomes a bigger squeeze."[4]

Major labels scoured the scene and found plenty of bands willing to make the jump—provided the circumstances were right. Bizarrely, SST played a role in making the circumstances not only right but perfect.

It started with the firing of Ray Farrell. Although he declined to go into details as to why he was let go, he noted, "It was an incredibly busy time. My wife recalls that my stress level was high."[5] "Busy" was an understatement. In terms of the volume of records released, 1987 and 1988 were SST's two most productive years by a large margin. The intense amount of effort that went into the production and promotion of these albums put an enormous strain on the people working at the label. Still, those who worked closest with Farrell were stunned by his sudden departure, none more so than Long. "It was a complete shock when it happened," Long said, "and it gutted me. He was my mentor really and just an incredible resource with so many layers of knowledge. . . . So it was weird. It was weird when he was let go."[6]

SST didn't offer an explanation and Long never asked, but he suspected that either Ginn or Dukowski felt threatened by how close Farrell was to some of the bands, Sonic Youth in particular. It was no secret that Sonic

Youth was unhappy with the label and was grousing about not being paid. "We didn't have a happy parting," Ranaldo said, "let's just put it that way."[7]

"I left SST before Sonic Youth did," Farrell said, "but I think they were already assessing their future with the label."[8] While that's certainly true, Farrell's firing was likely the last straw for the band. In much the same way that Hüsker Dü stayed with SST because of Farrell, his absence was a contributing factor in Sonic Youth's decision to leave the label and release its next album elsewhere. The band hired a law firm that promptly sent SST a letter, decrying the label's "consistent failure to pay Sonic Youth."[9] The band's departure didn't stop SST from reissuing *Sonic Death* (SST 181), a compilation of raw live recordings that took place between 1981 and 1983.

The next defection from SST was even stranger: Mugger put in his notice and requested a buyout. He'd completed his college courses, earned his degree, and was serving as the label's accountant—all in addition to his other duties at SST. "He was the glue," Long said. "He oversaw the office, but he wasn't overbearing in any sense. He was the guy you'd go to and talk about office bullshit."[10]

That, too, was part of the problem. Mugger's day-to-day activities at SST were not commensurate with the role of a part owner. In the past, Mugger had worked closely with Carducci on production. He'd always been the guy who fixed what was broken and did whatever needed to be done, but now he was basically an office manager whose day-to-day duties had little to do with the making and selling of records. But in his role as accountant he also had one of the most important jobs at the label. It was his responsibility to make sure there was enough money to book studios, make records, and pay artists. No one else at SST could do that as well as Mugger, which quickly became apparent after he left. "It was a very good business," Mugger said, "a very lucrative business, but then when I left they stopped paying bands and that's when the problems started."[11]

Whittaker was the next SST employee who was invited to explore opportunities elsewhere. He wrote his last spiel just before the Volcano Suns record came out at the end of the year. O'Bryan lasted another six months or so before he was "let go with cause." As far as O'Bryan was concerned, there was a direct link between the distributors going belly-up and the reductions in staff. "When Jem and Greenworld went under, they didn't need me anymore," O'Bryan said. "There wasn't anything to advertise."[12]

These departures were sudden, strange, and secretive. For some of the younger staffers, it felt like a series of ugly divorces rather than people leaving a professional work environment. And they kept happening. Ibarra recalled coming to work one day and Ford wasn't there. "I don't know what happened to Richard," Ibarra said. "I remember all of a sudden he was gone. There was no farewell party or anything, no goodbyes that I remember."[13]

Ginn and Dukowski hired people to replace those who left, but the pattern they'd established with Black Flag reemerged at SST. The new staffers tended to be young; some were right out of college. One new employee, twenty-four-year-old Daniel Spector, showed up for his interview at SST wearing a pinstripe suit. Spector recalled Ginn and Dukowski grilling him about the way he was dressed. "'Did you tie your own tie?' they asked. 'Yes, I tied my own tie.' 'That's cool, because forty people work here and we don't have anybody with that skill.'"[14]

Even though Spector had never worked at a record label and didn't have any management experience, he was hired to be SST's new general manager. (The fact that he was a Deadhead may or may not have been a factor in his hiring.) As in the past, job descriptions meant very little at SST. For instance, one task Spector was given involved disposing of the contents of a storage locker filled with Pettibon's old lithographs, pasteups, and zines. "The role of general manager," Spector learned, "was do things that were unappealing to Greg."[15]

Despite the many changes at the label, SST remained Ginn's company, and he did things his way. "We would have these Monday morning meetings in the conference room," Long recalled, "and by this point it was all kids my age.... Chuck was always silent. He would sit at one end of the table and doodle, and Greg would be the one on the other end of the table, running the meeting."[16]

When Long realized that many of the new employees weren't fans of the music, he knew it was time to go. For instance, Patrick Manning, who had been hired as a pasteup artist, eventually became the head of the art department despite not liking any of the music. "He didn't get the SST thing at all," Ibarra said.[17]

These hirings and firings had a huge impact on the label. Mugger, Whittaker, and O'Bryan had been a part of every facet of the alternative music experience. They played in bands and worked soundboards in grimy clubs. They chewed up the road and slept on floors. They did more than get their hands dirty. Whittaker saw the Sex Pistols in Texas. O'Bryan threw a show for the Adolescents at a scout house. Mugger was a living embodiment of the punk rock lifestyle. Music was their life—not their livelihood—and they left SST with something more valuable than a paycheck: their integrity.

2

It wasn't just employees that parted company with SST; bands left the label too. Joe Baiza released two more Universal Congress Of projects with SST—*Prosperous and Qualified* (SST 180) and *This Is Mecolodics* (SST 204)—but subsequent albums were released on other labels. Das Damen also wrapped up its SST experience with a final LP called *Triskaidekaphobe* (SST 190) and the EP *Marshmellow Conspiracy* (SST 218) before moving to Twin/Tone. The EP contained "Song for Michael Jackson to $ell," which incorporated lyrics and melodies from the Beatles' "Magical Mystery Tour" and had to be withdrawn. Though it marked the end of Das Damen's run with the label, it was just the beginning of SST's problems with unauthorized recordings.

That fall, Soundgarden went on tour with Sylvia Juncosa. Soundgarden bought a red 1986 Chevrolet Beauville van with black racing stripes, which Yamamoto customized to make room for the band's gear and provide a space to sleep. Soundgarden went all over the United States and even played the CMJ showcase at CBGB that summer. Cornell electrified crowds belting out songs while climbing rafters, trellises, ductwork, even a basketball hoop. A European tour followed, and when the band returned to the States, it promptly jumped ship to A&M. The label signed a distribution deal to get *Ultramega OK* into more stores, and Soundgarden was nominated for a Grammy in the heavy metal category. The following year it was playing stadiums opening for Guns N' Roses, superstardom all but assured.

Soundgarden's tenure with SST was one of the shortest—less than a year. In the beginning some bands waited that long for SST to put out their records, but those days now seemed very far away.

In December 1988, Screaming Trees left Ellensburg to record its final album for SST at Reciprocal Records with Endino—the same producer who'd made Soundgarden's *Ultramega OK* demos.[18] "We made so many records together," Fisk said, "the idea that they would work with somebody else made sense."[19] Also, the band was spending more time in Seattle after Lanegan moved there, leaving Ellensburg for good.

Buzz Factory (SST 248) is more of a throwback to the psychedelic '60s than any of the three previous albums. The record opens with a wail of distorted guitars on "Where the Twain Shall Meet," and it's not until the third track, "Black Sun Morning," that Screaming Trees hits the sweet spot between the '60s and '70s that contains the DNA of the Seattle sound. The album closes with "End of the Universe," a rambling ultra-rocker with extensive guitar solos—a fitting end to the band's run with SST.

3

The deluge of records SST unleashed in 1989 wasn't as mighty as the previous year, but it was impressive nonetheless. SST showcased these acts with *Program: Annihilator II* (SST 213), a second soundtrack for destruction, featuring Soundgarden, Saint Vitus, Sylvia Juncosa, the Descendents, Bad Brains, SWA, D.C. 3, and Bl'ast!, whose latest album, *Take the Manic Ride* (SST 225) affirmed it was the only hardcore band left on the label.

Many SST acts recorded new albums after months of touring. For Slovenly's follow-up to *Riposte* (SST 089), the Bukowski-inspired title *We Shoot for the Moon and Jack Off in the Closet* was shortened to *We Shoot for the Moon* (SST 209).[20] The album was produced and engineered by Vitus Mataré and recorded in his studio Lyceum Sound where the Last, the Leaving Trains, and Savage Republic had all recorded.

Many bands who came to SST during the peak years didn't stick around for much longer. Wisconsin's Tar Babies released three punk-funk albums between 1987 and 1989—*Fried Milk* (SST 101), *No Contest* (SST 169), and

Honey Bubble (SST 236)—but broke up in 1991. Angst issued *Mystery Spot* (SST 111) in 1987 and *Cry for Happy* (SST 206) in 1988 before calling it quits. After D.C. 3 disbanded, SST released *Vida* (SST 156), a compilation of live tracks from late 1987 and early 1988. Vida concludes with a spirited cover of Black Flag's "Thirsty and Miserable," which Cadena had helped write.

Experimental music remained in vogue at SST. Paper Bag followed up *Music to Trash* (SST 200) with a third, and final, completely improvised record called *Improvised...My Ass* (SST 229). E. Sharp returned with another album from Mofungo titled *Work* (SST 240). Roger Miller's art rock project No Man came back with *Win! Instantly!* (243). SST issued its share of clunkers in 1989, but none clunkier than the Black Flag single "I Can See You" (SST 226), four unreleased tracks from recording sessions that took place during the Roessler era.

4

The history of rock and roll is filled with stories of how a single song changed a band's fortunes. "Freak Scene," the opening track on Dinosaur Jr's *Bug* (SST 216), didn't make the band rich or famous, but it altered the musical landscape and paved the way for many guitar-driven indie rock artists of the '90s. The song's appeal was so obviously massive that SST released "Freak Scene" (SST 220) as a single a month before *Bug*. Its earworm hook, unconventional structure, and emotional sledgehammer finish cemented Dinosaur Jr's reputation as a band on the rise.

But within the band it was a different story. The members couldn't get along, and there was little distance between the personal and the professional. All one had to do was listen to the final track "Don't," in which Barlow screams "Why don't you like me?!" over and over to know that things were at a breaking point. After months of tense touring when the band's performances sometimes broke into shoving matches, Mascis kicked Barlow out of the band.

Due to his close association with Sonic Youth, Mascis had a better sense than most musicians on SST's roster that there was trouble brewing at PO

Box 1 Lawndale—not that he could do anything about it. But when several bands reported missing royalty checks, alarms sounded throughout the indie community. For years, Keith Morris told a story about Bad Brains loading up its van with weapons and heading to SST to demand the money they were owed—or else. While that story is largely apocryphal, the tide had turned and not in SST's favor.

Long realized he needed an exit plan, and when Ginn returned from a trip to the East Coast expressing interest in opening an SST office in New York, Long lobbied hard for the job. Ginn went back to New York and found a tiny office a block down from Madison Square Park on East 23rd Street near Baruch College. Long left LA to open SST East. Long's duties were threefold: continue with college radio, which he could do from anywhere; interface with distributors on the East Coast; and serve as point person for SST artists who lived in the area or passed through New York. But that's not how it worked out. "When I got out there, [Ginn] started reeling in the responsibilities, and it was kind of a bummer because all the SST bands and artists on the East Coast would come by my office and they were excited to have someone from the label there, but I was not given the freedom to be the guy for them. Any questions they had had to go to the West Coast."[21]

This put Long in a difficult position. Not only did he lack the authority to solve problems bands brought to him, but when SST failed to send royalty payments, he was often the first to hear about it. "These artists would come to me with their complaints, asking why they're not getting statements, why they're not getting paid. That was hard because here I was this enthusiastic young gun, in love with the music and the culture, but suddenly I'm being held to the fire by these artists because the label wasn't treating them right. I couldn't justify supporting the label when the label was doing them wrong. I was very conflicted. That's when I decided to leave in June of '89. I was just tired of knocks on the door, and in comes Murph from Dinosaur Jr, 'Hey, how come we're not getting paid?'"[22]

Unfortunately, that was a question Long couldn't answer. When Dinosaur Jr left SST, fIREHOSE followed its labelmate out the door. After releasing the single "Sometimes, Almost Always" (SST 131) and the LP *fROMOHIO*

(SST 235), Watt and company parted ways with SST. Although fIREHOSE wouldn't sign with a major label for a few more years, it had had enough of nonstop touring with nothing to show for it. Thanks to Natas Kaupas's skateboarding video *Streets of Fire*, which featured the Santa Cruz street-skating star turning gravity-defying tricks to "Brave Captain," fIREHOSE had never been more popular.

5

The Meat Puppets also wanted out. After the release of *Huevos* and *Mirage* in 1987, the band was worn down from so many years on the road and more than a little discouraged to see bands like Soundgarden blowing up on MTV. The Meat Puppets recorded its next record, *Monsters* (SST 253), with the intention of getting off of SST and onto a major label. "So we went with the big, ugly-sounding reverb and electronic drums, and the big anthemic chorus crap," Bostrom said.[23] *Monsters* is a Frankenstein-esque fusion of over-the-top riffs, tinny drums, and prog-country crooning—like ZZ Topp on acid.

The band didn't have much luck wooing the majors and sent the record off to SST. Suddenly, Peter Koepke, who started the alternative department at Atlantic, reached out to the band. He was interested in the album and wanted to sign the Meat Puppets for what Curt characterized as "a *huge* amount of money."[24]

Curt called up SST to explain the situation, but Ginn was remarkably unsympathetic. "No. You're a traitor. You gave it to us," Ginn told Curt.[25] Ginn refused to budge and insisted that the record come out on SST. The Meat Puppets tried to negotiate a deal that would allocate a sizable portion of the advance from Atlantic to SST, but Ginn wasn't interested.

Curt started talking to other artists on the roster. Some had contracts with SST; others, like the Meat Puppets, did not. What nearly all of the records on SST had in common was that most of the songs were published by Cesstone Music, which was Ginn's publishing company. That meant Ginn held the copyright to virtually every song SST had ever released. Conversely, most SST artists didn't own the rights to the music they had created.

This was standard practice in the music industry dating back to when sheet music and songbooks were big business. Artists ceded the rights to their songs to companies that published the music in exchange for a share of each item sold. As times changed, the copyright holder's role changed from publishing the music to ensuring the artist was compensated every time a song was reproduced or performed. When the label failed to pay royalties, artists discovered they had no recourse other than to take legal action, which could be time consuming, cost prohibitive, and emotionally draining.

SST benefitted from the fact that many of its artists were young, inexperienced, and didn't have lawyers or managers looking after their interests. The vast majority of bands were simply happy to have the opportunity to put out a record. When Ginn offered a contract to a new artist, in many cases he also offered the services of Global and Cesstone. Many artists, like Screaming Trees, didn't understand what this meant. They figured if it was good enough for the Meat Puppets, the Minutemen, and Sonic Youth, it was good enough for them. "We basically just signed away all our publishing for those first three records to Ginn," Lanegan said.[26]

Although the Meat Puppets acquiesced and *Monsters* came out on SST as originally planned, the songs were registered to Meat Puppets Music—not Cesstone. *Monsters* marked the end of the Meat Puppets' creative partnership with SST, but a dramatic new relationship was only beginning.

However, SST's new general manager discovered there were problems with the label's copyrights. Although virtually every record SST released up to that point bore the copyright for Cesstone Music, very few of those copyrights had actually been filed with the US Copyright Office—a crucial step in protecting the work from infringement. Even more concerning, Spector learned that the contracts SST had been issuing to its artists all these years probably weren't enforceable. "Because of all the fuckery that happened with music publishing in the 1950s," Spector explained, "you could not legally have one document that was both a publishing contract and a recording contract, and all SST contracts were both. So, to the best of my knowledge, no SST contract made before 1990 would hold up in court."[27]

Spector went to work remedying the situation, but Ginn didn't make it easy. Spector was frequently assigned other tasks, like helping to produce a live show or assisting in the studio, but there were perils here too. Ginn told Spector that his name was not to appear on any albums he worked on and that if he was credited on a record, Ginn would fire him.

"Greg hired me to introduce structure," Spector said, "but Greg hated structure. So if I actually started to introduce structure, he would come in and kick it all down."[28]

6

Negativland elevated irreverence into postmodern art. *Helter Stupid* (SST 252), the band's follow-up to *Escape from Noise*, explores the fallout from the Brom murders and the controversy that ensued. It employs excerpts from sensational news coverage and mixes them with samples from a wide array of media, including news broadcasts, carnival music, and snippets of "Christianity Is Stupid." Negativland even included excerpts from a taped phone call with a journalist from *Rolling Stone* who, by calling the band to get the inside scoop, unwittingly became part of the prank.

Everything is fair game on *Helter Stupid*: from the outrage the band generated when the media realized it was all a not-so-elaborate hoax to the moral gray area into which the band had insinuated itself. "Our act of creating a false association with such a tragedy," the liner notes declare, "will remain open to ethical interpretation."[29] Even the title is an appropriation of the Beatles song that inspired Manson, who is also sampled on the record.

The flip side of *Helter Stupid* contains seven tracks from "The Perfect Cut" by the fictional radio announcer Dick Vaughn. Performed by Richard Lyons, Vaughn was part of Negativland's cast of characters that also included Pastor Dick Seeland, who is a central figure in *Negativland Presents Over the Edge Vol. 2: Pastor Dick: Muriel's Purse Fund* (SSTC 901). Vaughn returns in *Vol. 4: Dick Vaughn's Moribund Music of the '70s* (SSTC 904). These recordings, along with *Vol. 3: The Weatherman's Dumb Stupid Come-Out Line* (SSTC 902), were issued on cassette only and consisted of excepts from the band's *Over the Edge* radio program.

But the hysteria surrounding the "Helter Stupid" track on Side 1 lends an ominous and unsettling feeling to the listening experience. Even with an insert covered with copy detailing every step of the fiasco, there's a whiff of danger that hangs over the song. *Helter Stupid* is a masterpiece of Dadaism, an art movement that leaned on satire and the surreal, and that Negativland kicked into high gear at the twilight of the twentieth century.

7

SST's output in 1990 didn't just drop off, it fell off a cliff. The number of records SST released in 1990 was equal to its production in 1984 and a fraction of what it cranked out in 1987.

The timing wasn't a coincidence. At the end of 1989, Dukowski sold his partnership in SST, leaving Ginn the last man standing. Dukowski continued to work for the label, but he no longer had a stake in the company or a say in how it ran its business. By then he'd been relegated to running the label's sales, which were thriving. The problem was getting record chains and distributors to pay. Spector recalled the amount owed to the company was approximately $1.5 million.

Chuck Dukowski makes a flyer in Minneapolis, Minnesota, December 1980. (Photo by SPOT.)

In the summer of 1990, Ginn fired Kara Nicks after the two got in a heated argument. "He had a couple of guys watch me box up my desk and get my stuff together," Nicks said. "I was tripping. 'Do you think I'm going to fucking steal from you?' I think that was what we had a fight about, about him stealing from people."[30] Nicks's firing marked the end of the old way of doing things. Even the way Nicks was escorted off the premises—there were police cars waiting outside—indicated that SST's transformation from a maverick indie into a soulless corporation was complete.[31]

Instead of looking to the future, SST plundered its past, releasing records that were essentially "greatest hits" compilations by some of the label's more popular artists: the Descendents' *Somery* (SST 259), Screaming Trees' *Anthology* (SST 260), the Flesh Eaters' *Prehistoric Fits Vol. 2* (SST 264), the Meat Puppets' *No Strings Attached* (SST 265), Saint Vitus's *Heavier Than Thou* (SST 266), and Dinosaur Jr's *Fossils* (SST 275).[32] (The previous year, SST issued *Past Lives* (SST 149), a double-album compilation of Saccharine Trust recordings that included seven unreleased tracks.) SST even packaged two of Hüsker Dü's biggest early hits as a single product: *Eight Miles High / Makes No Sense at All* (SST 270).

The label also released a pair of high-concept compilation albums: *Duck and Cover* (SST 263), a spirited collection of cover songs recorded by SST artists with original cover art by Ibarra. The anthology featured songs from recent releases, including Dinosaur Jr's cover of the Cure's "Just like Heaven" (SST 244), Chris D.'s project Stone by Stone's version of Eric Martin's "Ghost" on *I Pass for Human* (SST 247), and Volcano Suns' rendition of MC5's "Kick Out the Jams" from the double album *Thing of Beauty* (SST 258). SST also produced an anthology of acoustic material called *SST Acoustic* (SST 276). These compilations comprised nearly a third of the albums the label released between 1990 and 1992.

Solo artists continued to crank out material: H.R. dropped *Charge* and the CD EP *Rock of Enoch*, and Grant Hart released *All of My Senses* (SST 262), his final record for the label. Pell Mell also issued its last two albums with SST: a reissue of the band's extraordinary first EP *Rhyming Guitars* (SST 241) and *Flow* (SST 278), a sampling of alternative rock anthems recorded in early 1991.

SWA followed up *Winter* (SST 238) with *Volume* (SST 282), the band's fifth and final studio album. More than any other record in SWA's catalog, *Volume* is Dukowski's baby; he wrote most of the songs and sings on it as well. It's his swan song as an SST performer before he finally pulled the plug on the band, but not before approaching Lanegan. "Chuck and one of the other dudes in SWA took me out to lunch in LA and asked me to be the singer," Lanegan said. "That was very flattering because Chuck was part of Black Flag. We used to go see SWA in LA. I actually liked them. I was kind of weighing that offer....Just to be in the same ballpark with those guys was kind of a big deal for a small-town boy."[33]

Not everyone was jumping ship. Many artists considered SST home and continued to put out new records with the label. The Leaving Trains released four new records with a variety of musicians: the LP *Sleeping Underwater Survivors* (SST 271), the seven-inch EP *Rock 'n' Roll Murder* (SST 283), the twelve-inch EP *Loser Illusion Pt. 0* (SST 284), and *The Lump in My Forehead* (SST 288).

Trotsky Icepick followed up its SST debut in 1988 with a trio of clean-sounding pop records in 1989: a reissue of its first album *Poison Summer* (SST 239), *El Kabong* (SST 246), and *Trotsky Icepick Presents: Danny and the Doorknobs in "Poison Summer"* (SST 254), which represented a plan to change the name of the band with every album that thankfully didn't stick.

SST even released the debut album of Boston's Buffalo Tom (SST 250), produced by none other than J Mascis, before the band found its groove with Beggars Banquet. For many of the artists, the work was already complete. The musicians were doing what Ginn himself had done in the mid-1980s: pressing up old recordings and putting them into the world. It would be several years before the label signed any new bands. But at least one of its artists continued to push the envelope in a way that would generate an incredible amount of media attention, just not the kind SST was looking for.

8

It was only a matter of time before a recording of Casey Kasem losing his temper found its way into Negativland's hands. Kasem was the beloved voice of the nationally syndicated radio program *American Top 40*, and a record-ing of the announcer angrily berating the Irish band U2 was captured by an engineer. The outtake never made it onto the airwaves, but for Negativland the material was too good not to use. The sound of Kasem cursing was jarring for those who grew up listening to the good-natured host count down the hits each week.

Negativland worked its satirical magic, cutting up the recording and laying it on top of other samples and song fragments to create a compelling collage. Because U2 prompted Kasem's diatribe, Negativland incorporated fragments of the song "I Still Haven't Found What I'm Looking For" into its send-up.

In the fall of 1990, Negativland sent two versions of "I Still Haven't Found What I'm Looking For" to SST for release as a twelve-inch single (SST 272). The artwork featured an image of a U-2 spy plane superimposed over the let-ter U and the numeral 2 with the band's name in much smaller letters along the bottom. The first person at the label to listen to the record was Spector, who expressed his concerns to Ginn. "I said to Greg, 'Listen to this Neg-ativland. It's amazing,' and he listened to it and it's amazing. I said, 'We're gonna get sued by Casey Kasem, we're gonna get sued by Island Records, we're gonna get sued by U2.' I went through all the lawsuits that I could see in that one piece of material that we would not probably break even on. Greg said, 'We're putting it out.'"[34]

Spector understood that cleaning up Ginn's messes was part of the job, but the new Negativland record represented a minefield of legal jeopardy that he was not willing to navigate. "I was not gonna stick around for the bullshit that generated," Spector said, "and he did not want me to stick around because I was a coward who didn't want to take on the man."[35]

Spector left SST, and Negativland's new EP was released in August 1991. Ten days later, SST was served with a temporary restraining order by U2's label, Island Records—just as Spector had predicted. Thus began what Neg-ativland described as a "modern saga of criminal music."[36]

Island's complaint was twofold: that the packaging of Negativland's *U2* EP was "deceptive and misleading," and the music itself constituted an "unau-thorized use of a sound recording and musical composition."[37] The main issue was the cover, which Island deemed "nothing less than a consumer fraud."[38] Island was afraid music lovers would pick up Negativland's EP, mistaking it for the long-awaited release from U2. This was absurd, of course, because SST's operations were miniscule compared to Island's—U2's album *The Joshua Tree* had sold more than twenty-five million copies worldwide. Indeed, Island's restraining order pointed out *The Joshua Tree* was the first album in history to sell one million copies in CD format.

Island outlined several demands and called for an immediate end to the manufacture, distribution, promotion, and sales of Negativland's *U2*. The label also insisted that SST account for all copies sold, recall outstanding copies of the record, and turn over all inventory, masters, promotional packaging, and sales media for destruction. Furthermore, the document outlined that Island was seeking damages from SST for violations of the Lanham Act and the Copyright Act of 1976. Lastly, as a final indignity, SST would be required to account for its sins, so to speak, in trade publications like *Billboard* magazine.

Neither Negativland nor SST saw the restraining order coming, though perhaps they should have. The two parties discussed the matter on the phone and worked together to come up with a solution, which appears to have been to put more Negativland material into the marketplace to account for the losses incurred by the U2 EP. One thing was obvious to both SST and Negativland: someone was going to have to pay.

Negativland had two projects in the works: a cassette-only LP and a live album. SST promptly cut a check to Negativland for $4,500 as an advance against royalties so these projects could be completed. On November 10, 1991, Negativland issued a lengthy press release titled "The Case from Our Side" that constituted "a more humane attempt at reasonable discourse about artistic integrity and the artless, humorless legalism that controls music today."[39] The band outlined its motives for making the record, asserting its right "to create with mirrors" and to "plunder the ocean of media we all swim in."[40] As far as Negativland was concerned, as the biggest rock band in the world, U2 was part of culture, which can't be owned.

Negativland received another batch of humorless legalism—this time from its own record label. SST had sent the band a one-page agreement stating that SST bore no responsibility in the matter and had the right to recoup damages from the band. This raised several red flags, and the Negativland camp was alarmed by SST's attempt to absolve itself of all culpability in the affair. Negativland interpreted the document as a license to sue and refused to sign it. The band responded with a counterproposal that the two parties split the cost, which SST could deduct from Negativland's royalties once the precise amount was mutually agreed upon.

While it waited for SST's response, Negativland appealed to U2's producer Brian Eno and the band itself with mixed results that set the tone for the next several years. Chris Blackwell, the president of Island Records, responded to Negativland that although he had "been getting a huge amount of hassle from the members of U2," he was "not prepared to eat these legal fees," which he estimated were at least $55,000.[41]

In his reply, Eno expressed sympathy for Negativland's predicament but washed his hands of the affair, suggesting that artists had little power over the corporations that owned the rights to their music. This position baffled Negativland: If the biggest rock band in the world doesn't have the power to influence the company that profits from it, who does? Is this ocean we all swim in really just a corporate-controlled pool polluted with noise that artists cannot criticize or comment upon without being attacked by lawyers?

Surprisingly, in spite of the way Negativland had misled the media in the past, music journalists were sympathetic to the band's plight, and music magazines and daily newspapers across the country covered the story. SST realized it was once again in the familiar position of being in a fight it couldn't win and agreed to settle with Island before the costs ballooned to the point they would sink the label.

Negativland, however, wasn't done. The band appealed to Island and requested that Blackwell return the copyright of the U2 EP to SST so that Negativland could get on with the business of making music and Island and U2 could repair their image as humorless goons.

Negativland also severed ties with SST, but not before releasing another EP titled *Guns* (SST 291). *Guns* critiques the role of firearms in American

316 CORPORATE ROCK SUCKS

history and culture, while taking a shot at those who'd obstructed its previous record. "This recording is dedicated to the members of our favorite Irish rock band, their record label, and their attorneys. The music is two U."[42]

In a letter dated December 11, 1991, the band stated, "As business partners, we have the right to expect that we are working together in each other's interest. This situation makes it clear that, when the chips are down, SST will sacrifice its artists for its own gain."[43] In essence, Negativland was disappointed by SST's attempt to place the blame for the U2 imbroglio onto the band in a way that "distinguishes you little from the rest of the corporate music industry you claim to stand in opposition to."[44]

These were fighting words, but SST responded in curiously contradictory fashion. First, SST unveiled a new T-shirt for sale with "KILL BONO" superimposed over the image of a handgun.[45] Then, in a December 20, 1991, press release, SST announced the settlement and proposed a collaboration with U2 to throw a benefit concert to pay the legal fees. But U2 was not Black Flag, and the days of staging a fundraiser at Mi Casita seemed like a distant memory. The request was ignored.

Upset that Negativland was manipulating the media by feeding it what SST deemed to be false information, on February 3, 1992, Ginn distributed a four-page press release that made his feelings on the matter known in no uncertain terms: "I contend that Mark Hosler is a lying motherfucker."[46] Ginn made all kinds of unusual suggestions, including that he and Hosler take a lie detector test and "that publications who have printed underresearched misinformation in this case volunteer to pay the cost of this test."[47] Although it had been more than a decade since Ginn's feud with *Flipside*, he was still railing at journalists who didn't follow up with him to get the truth—in other words, his side of the story.

The ill-advised press release exposed SST to further legal jeopardy by acknowledging that other Negativland releases included unlicensed samples by Phil Collins and Simple Minds—a band Ginn professed to hate. Ginn also asserted that Island had spent more money "recording the latest U2 record than we have recording our entire catalog of over 400 records in our 14 year history."[48] The most unusual aspects of the press release were the personal attacks Ginn made on Negativland's members, decrying the band as a "hobby" of people with "cushy day jobs." He characterized Negativland as "paranoid upper-middle class malcontents" who were "isolated from the 'real world'" and "victims of the media cocoon they frequently lampoon."[49]

Later that month, Negativland received a letter from Evan S. Cohen of Cohen and Luckenbacher declaring SST's intention to sue the band unless it repaid the label's losses to Island. This was a serious miscalculation on Ginn's part but consistent with the way he responded to perceived slights in the past. Up until this point, the media had painted the story as Negativland versus U2 and unanimously sided with Negativland. This was a narrative that music fans could get behind; they were far less interested in legal disputes between record labels, which was the real story.

Ginn, perhaps resenting the favorable attention that Negativland received while SST footed the bill, decided to set the story straight. Ginn's truth, however, painted him and his label in an unflattering light, and the threat to sue Negativland exposed the hypocrisy at the heart of SST's stance against corporate rock. Moreover, Negativland had focused its energy on U2 and Island Records, but now that Ginn had provided the band with fodder for its irreverent impulses, that was about to change.

9

Negativland was not the only band SST had a beef with: the Meat Puppets were also proving to be a nuisance. After *Monsters*, the Meat Puppets went to work on a new album for Koepke at Atlantic. There was just one problem. Koepke wasn't there anymore; he'd taken a new position at London Records. Once he got settled in, he invited the Meat Puppets to release its new record there. Signing with London Records made perfect sense. In addition to the connection with Koepke, one of the band's idols, ZZ Top, was also on the label.

The Meat Puppets had plenty of complaints about SST, but signing with a major label didn't make those complaints go away. "Turns out if you get on a major label," Bostrom quipped, "the level of horseshit that you deal with is upped quite a bit."[50] Be that as it may, a major label can offer support in areas that have nothing to do with the making of records: namely, protecting its clients' publishing rights. Jamie Kitman, the Meat Puppets' manager, dug into the band's royalty statements and found "serious irregularities."[51] When Kitman couldn't get through to Ginn by telephone, he sent him a letter designed to get his attention.

It worked a little too well. In fact, Ginn was so incensed that he sued the Meat Puppets for libel. The band countersued, affirming it owned the rights to the five studio albums and three EPs it had released with SST. The Meat Puppets hired an attorney, who promptly urged the band to settle out of court, which it did, and Ginn was able to license the Meat Puppets' body of work for another seven years, after which the rights would revert to the band.

Typically, the terms of an out-of-court settlement stipulate that neither party discuss the case with the public. The Meat Puppets ignored this pesky detail by circulating an open letter to the music business, drafted by Kitman. The letter was a shot across the bow: "Friends don't let friends sue bands," it declared.[52] The message was clear: by using the tools of corporate rock, SST was violating an unwritten rule of the indie aesthetic. What kind of label sues its own band?

Unfortunately, SST was just getting started.

10

"The New Faces of Rock 1992," declared the cover of the April 18, 1992, issue of *Rolling Stone*. The headline was positioned next to Kurt Cobain wearing a green cardigan that partially covered a handmade T-shirt that screamed, "CORPORATE MAGAZINES STILL SUCK."

The shirt was an homage to the "CORPORATE ROCK STILL SUCKS" bumper sticker and T-shirt that SST sold through its mail-order operation (and continues to sell today). Apparently, Cobain had no hard feelings toward the label he'd idolized in his youth that—despite Lanegan's best efforts—declined to sign his band.

Nirvana's signing to Geffen Records, the epitome of corporate rock, muddled Cobain's message. When he scrawled the message on his T-shirt, was Cobain thinking about his friend Kathleen Hanna of Bikini Kill—who helped name the song that made Nirvana famous? Or was he just irritated that Geffen was making him do dumb shit he didn't want to do?

Either way, the seemingly carefree musician who cavorted on the railroad tracks with Kim Gordon during the opening scenes of Dave Markey's documentary *1991: The Year Punk Broke* does not look pleased to be on the cover of *Rolling Stone*. The project was inspired by Thurston Moore's viewing of *Reality 86'd*, Markey's documentary of the final Black Flag tour with Gone and Painted Willie, which Ginn prevented from being distributed by refusing to release the music that SST owned the rights to, meaning all of it. So, when Sonic Youth embarked on a European tour with Nirvana and Dinosaur Jr, Markey and his camera were invited along for the ride.

1991: The Year Punk Broke was a triumph not only for the filmmakers (Markey hired Dave Travis to edit the project) but for its subjects as well: Dinosaur Jr, Sonic Youth, and even Ray Farrell, who had taken a job at Geffen Records. Farrell brought Sonic Youth to Geffen, who brought Nirvana.[53] Just as the title of Markey's previous documentary had had a double meaning—*Reality 86'd* referred to both the year it was filmed and the fact that when on tour with Black Flag anything like reality was canceled—there were layers of meaning in *1991: The Year Punk Broke*. It was the year bands from the punk underground broke into the mainstream, but it was also the year SST's machinery broke down.

By 1991 it was clear that SST had missed out on not one but two of the most important records of the '80s and '90s: Sonic Youth's *Daydream Nation*, released by Enigma, and Nirvana's *Nevermind*, released by Geffen. Revenue from the former would have seen the label through the squeeze; the latter would have completely transformed SST. Consider Sub Pop: the label was on the verge of going under when "Smells like Teen Spirit" hit the airwaves. The single generated enormous attention for Nirvana's Sub Pop debut, *Bleach*, which subsequently went platinum. That could have been, perhaps should have been, SST.

Nevertheless, new records continued to sputter out of SST. Chris D. dropped a double album of new material from the Flesh Eaters called *Dragstrip Riot* (SST 273), which was followed by *Sex Diary of Mr. Vampire* (SST

292). The label finally got around to reissuing the Minutemen's *The Politics of Time*, which New Alliance originally released in 1984. Slovenly's final album, *Highway to Hanno's* (SST 287), was issued after the band had more or less fizzled out. Cruel Frederick put out another record of experimental jazz with the *We. Are. The. Music. We. Play* (SST 290)—a bold claim since half the record was covers of songs by Thelonious Monk and Ornette Coleman.

Although SST had throttled back its release schedule, it wasn't exactly hurting for cash, thanks to its back catalog. "Our biggest sellers are somewhere around one hundred thousand copies," Ginn said. "The ones that have hit that level have taken years to do it. We've done over four hundred albums now, and only a few have hit that level. Black Flag, Bad Brains, and Soundgarden are the best-selling artists. We've had a lot of records in the thirty-to-fifty thousand range including fIREHOSE, Meat Puppets, Sonic Youth, Dinosaur Jr and a number of other groups."[54]

SST's treatment of its bands varied. According to Thayil, royalties were never an issue for Soundgarden. "I remember Mark from Negativland calling me, and they wanted to know if we were being screwed by SST. We said, 'No, we consistently got paid by them.' We heard from the guys in Negativland and the Meat Puppets that they weren't getting paid. We believe we were getting paid because we had management and a lot of the other bands did not."[55]

SST's preferential treatment toward Soundgarden made its behavior toward other artists on the roster all the more galling.[56] Negativland didn't have management, but the band members were persistent, and their tenacity wore down some of the biggest names in the music industry.

11

The members of Negativland proved they were master media manipulators, tireless campaigners for their cause, and relentlessly provocative, but first and foremost they were artists. Negativland was different from other musical groups in that its chief ambition was not to entertain but to provoke. What the band did with its letters, faxes, and press releases went hand in glove with its larger ambition to get people to think about who owns culture and who gets to exploit it.

Negativland embarked on a second campaign under the banner Universal Media Netweb, which described the band members as residents of an undersea dome called Howland Island that broke the surface of the Pacific each morning at sunrise. This alternate reality was cleverly spun from the "truths" Ginn asserted in his press releases about cushy jobs and being out of touch.

The band continued its campaign to get the rights to its *U2* EP back from Island, which now held the copyright as part of SST's settlement, while sparring with SST and its lawyer in letters and magazines. In a letter to Ginn's lawyer, Negativland acknowledged that its complaint with the label wasn't limited to the U2 affair; it included "cross-collateralization of royalties and chargebacks across all projects without authorization; cross-collateralization of mechanicals with royalties without authorization; habitually late royalty statements; habitually even later royalty checks; and not paying the agreed-upon royalty rate on CD releases."[57] In other words, Negativland had plenty of issues with the way SST conducted business and was not shy about articulating them.

Negativland also kept the pressure on U2, with assistance from the media, which kept pestering the band. In June 1992, Negativland collaborated with R. U. Sirius of *Mondo 2000* to ambush U2. When the Edge agreed to an interview with the magazine to discuss the group's Zoo TV Tour, Hosler and Joyce sat in on the call. After getting the Edge to admit that U2 sampled copyrighted material as part of its live performance, they revealed their identities to the Irish musician, who took the surprise in stride and participated in a substantial conversation. The Edge repeatedly asserted he was in favor of Negativland getting its music back, but it was Island's call to make. Island's vice president of business affairs Eric Levine promptly informed U2's manager Paul McGuinness this was impossible because Casey Kasem's attorneys had informed the label that re-releasing the record would result in a lawsuit. Thus, the affair came full circle back to Casey Kasem.

In September 1992, Negativland published the first edition of *The Letter U and the Numeral 2*, a zine that included the band's correspondence with SST, Island, and various parties; numerous press releases; excerpts of legal documents; reprints of magazine articles; as well as photos of Bono,

Blackwell, Kasem, and Ginn, with a caption that featured Black Flag lyrics from "Gimme Gimme Gimme." The zine also included a CD with Crosley Bendix, an alter ego Joyce employed on his radio show, discussing the US Copyright Act.

Perhaps the most provocative document in the dossier is the first page of a credit report on SST Records, listing the label's net worth as of September 1991 at $1.2 million. The report was prepared for Gary Powers, the name of the pilot whose U-2 spy plane was shot down over the Soviet Union in 1960.

The Letter U and the Numeral 2 was an unusual document, especially for Negativland. The band that had made a name for itself by manipulating the media had scrupulously documented the U2 affair in a way that allowed the facts to speak for themselves. Anyone curious about the case could read what the parties had said in their own words and draw their own conclusions, which was typically not how Negativland operated. Although the zine is shot through with images of spy planes and updates from fictional Howland Island, Negativland comes across as sincere in its efforts to resolve the issue in a way that would satisfy all parties. The same could not be said of Island or SST.

To the surprise of absolutely no one, SST served Negativland with a lawsuit the day after Thanksgiving. Upset by the publication of *The Letter U and the Numeral 2*, Ginn launched his attack on a number of fronts, including copyright infringement, noncompliance with the Fair Credit Reporting Act, and breach of contract. The suit was neatly summarized by the *Village Voice*: Ginn was "suing the band for printing his threat to sue the band."[58]

This time, however, Negativland had the advantage. The band had secured pro bono legal counsel from a San Francisco law firm and had no assets. SST already owned the rights to the band's most popular records. As for SST's complaint that Negativland refused to deliver the master tapes for the two albums for which the label had paid, the band argued that it could not provide what didn't exist. The records weren't finished so there weren't any masters to turn over. Because Negativland wasn't paying for its defense, it could afford to let the case drag out in court while SST's legal bills accumulated. If that was the game SST wanted to play, Negativland was more than happy to play it.

Meanwhile, newspapers and magazines were digging into the dispute between SST and Negativland, investigating the case and interviewing both parties. *Creem* magazine acquired copies of Negativland's contract with SST and sent them to legal experts, who found the contract poorly worded and surmised it would be challenging to enforce.

Ginn had been railing against "underresearched" newspaper and magazine articles for years, but the more research journalists did, the more dirt they found. Bands had been complaining to journalists about SST's business practices for years, and now the label's ongoing fight with Negativland gave the media a reason to write about it. Each time a new article was published, Ginn came out looking like the bad guy. Though the lawsuit dragged on and on, in the court of public opinion, Negativland was the clear-cut winner. "We've done a rather unusual thing," Hosler said, "which is to document everything that happened and release it to the people, and it ends up making [Ginn] and his record company look like the hypocritical and unethical people that I think they are."[59]

Much to Hosler's chagrin, the public didn't care all that much about the Copyright Act of 1976, but it understood a vindictive bully when it saw one. Somehow, the independent label that had taken on corporate rock transformed from David the underdog into a humorless Goliath hell-bent on making its opponents pay, even when it was in everyone's best interest to put down the sword and walk away.

Eugene Robinson of OXBOW. (Emma Porter Photography)

CHAPTER 13
SST vs. Techno

The '90s

1

Andy Batwinas answered an advertisement in the *Recycler* for an opportunity to work as an engineer in a new studio in North Long Beach called Casa Destroy. Batwinas had cut his teeth in the business recording wannabe Black Flag bands in the '80s at his own demo studio in San Pedro, so he was well aware of Greg Ginn and SST Records, but while working at Larrabee Sound in North Hollywood, he helped with a variety of projects, from recording R&B acts to remixing dance tracks. During the job interview, Ginn was less interested in Batwinas's qualifications than his taste in music.

"What's your favorite band?" Ginn asked.

"I really love Oingo Boingo records," Batwinas replied. "I think they're some of the best produced records."[1]

That was good enough for Ginn. The last person he wanted at the consoles of his new studio was someone with strong opinions about Black Flag's sound. "The way I've heard him express it over the years," Batwinas explained, "was other people had a perception of what his music should sound like, and he didn't want to keep dealing with that. He wanted to do his own experiments, figure out the things he liked, and do what he wanted to do—without other people's preconceived notions."[2] Many years later, after they'd worked on dozens of records together, Ginn admitted to Batwinas he absolutely hated Oingo Boingo.

Batwinas immediately began working on a pair of albums that Ginn would release under his own name on Cruz Records the following year. Most of the tracks were already recorded, with Ginn providing all the guitar, bass, and vocal parts. Steve Fisk engineered the bass tracks, and David Raven, an experienced studio drummer, programmed the drums. Batwinas believed these solo records provided the impetus for Casa Destroy.

After an eight-year hiatus, Ginn also resurrected Gone. With the help of drummer Gregory Moore and bassist Steve Sharp, Ginn recorded and released *The Criminal Mind* (SST 300).[3] Batwinas characterized Sharp and Moore as in-house studio musicians who, like him, were full-time contract employees at Casa Destroy.

Casa Destroy was not part of SST Records, nor did it occupy the same building. The studio was equipped with a 24-track machine, an Akai S950 sampler, and an Atari 1040ST for MIDI sequencing. Casa Destroy wasn't a studio for hire, although Ginn would occasionally make it available to associates who needed a studio. Chuck Dukowski mixed his United Gang Members project there with Paul Cutler and Bill Stinson for New Alliance, and Scott Reynolds's band Goodbye Harry and Craig Ibarra's Rig recorded albums for Cruz Records.

Casa Destroy was Ginn's playground. A project might begin with recordings of Ginn on guitar, edited down into a dozen or so "songs." Then Sharp and Moore would do their parts. Depending on the scope of the project, other musicians might get involved to provide keyboards, saxophone, and occasionally vocals—though most of the work was instrumental. Around this time Ginn was sharing an apartment with his former October Faction bandmate Greg Cameron, who did not share Ginn's fascination with sequencers and drum machines. "If I could," Ginn confided to Cameron, "I would get rid of everybody in the band."[4] At the time, Cameron thought Ginn was joking, but he was serious.

Sometimes Ginn would provide both the bass and the guitar parts as well as the vocals, as he appears to do on Poindexter Stewart's *College Rock* (SST 299), which feels like a swipe at SST alums Dinosaur Jr. "I can neither confirm nor deny that Poindexter Stewart was a real person," Batwinas said.[5] Ginn's pseudonymous persona was thrust into the limelight when SST launched *Screw Radio*, an irreverent show broadcast twice a week on 97.1 FM.

"Screw Radio started out on a local, mid-power FM station," Batwinas said. "We used to produce it and send them tapes, and they would just play the tapes. Eventually we had a telephone line put in, and they would flip over to our feed out of our studio, and we would do it live. That phone line went to the transmitter up on Mount Wilson and broadcast out to pretty much all of LA and Orange County."[6]

The show ran for six months in 1992 and 1993. The liner notes from *Best of Screw Radio* (SST 342), which highlight this period, describe the show as a mix of "comedy with social/political commentary and other unusual entertainment."[7] In its attempts to be edgy, the show blends offensive humor with casual misogyny. *Screw Radio* was cohosted by Poindexter Stewart (a.k.a. Greg Ginn, whose voice was manipulated to make it both irritating and unrecognizable) along with various members of the "Screw Crew," including Jimbo, Buford, and Andy Dunkley, who did promotion for SST. "There's a certain amount of snobbishness in college radio land about SST," Dunkley said in a *Los Angeles Times* article that didn't exactly paint a flattering picture of the label.[8]

SST was no longer at the top of the heap, and Ginn's boast that "One day every radio will be a SCREW RADIO" did not come to fruition.[9]

SST released only six records in 1993, including *Carpetbomb the Riff* (SST 295), a live album by Trotsky Icepick; *Perfectly Square* (SST 296), by the Orange County jazz powerhouse Bazooka, with Tony Atherton on saxophone, Bill Crawford on bass, and Vince Meghrouni behind the drum kit; and *Crucified Lovers in Woman Hell* (SST 297), a CD EP by the Flesh Eaters. A jazz rock project from Richmond, Virginia, that went by the name Hotel X began its run of six records for SST with *A Random History of Avant-Groove* (SST 298). Alter Natives drummer Jim Thomson played on the first four records. All of these albums were released on CD or cassette only. With a few exceptions, SST rarely released new albums on vinyl.

2

In November 1993, Nirvana invited the Meat Puppets to join the band at Sony Music Studios in New York for a taping of *MTV Unplugged*. The Meat Puppets had played with Nirvana for several dates in the Midwest and Canada, and it was during one of these shows that Cobain invited the Kirkwood brothers to play a few songs with him at the acoustic showcase. MTV wasn't thrilled with the selection, but Cobain was determined. Toward the end of the program, the Kirkwoods were invited onstage to perform three songs from *Meat Puppets II*, "Plateau," "Oh Me," and "Lake of Fire." Cobain had been in the audience when the Meat Puppets played these songs live nearly a decade before. "It was like a real show with a real vibe," Curt said of *MTV Unplugged*. "There were no retakes or anything. What you see is what happened."[10]

The Meat Puppets weren't the only SST recording artists on stage. Nirvana brought in Pat Smear as second guitarist to bolster the lineup because of concerns about Cobain's heroin addiction. Smear had recorded two solo albums with SST: *RuthenSmear* (SST 154) in 1987 and *So You Fell in Love with a Musician…* (SST 294) in 1992. When Smear was asked to join, he was working at the SST Superstore, a four-hundred-square-foot retail space at 8847 Sunset Boulevard. The name was a riff on the Virgin Megastore that had opened down the street. "Everyone has their own idea of what super is," said Ron Coleman, who was managing the label at the time.[11]

Although he wasn't physically present at Sony Studios, Mark Lanegan was there in spirit when Cobain performed Lead Belly's "Where Did You Sleep Last Night?" The two musicians worked on the arrangements together for a record that wasn't meant to be. *MTV Unplugged* was broadcast in December to immediate acclaim, and the Meat Puppets benefitted from the attention. The band's new record, *Too High to Die*, its eighth studio album and second for London Records, produced by Paul Leary of the Butthole Surfers, came out in January 1994. The sludgy single "Backwater" charted, and *Too High to Die* sold over five hundred thousand copies, more than the Meat Puppets' entire catalog combined.

While being picked to perform on MTV was a bolt out of the blue, a once-in-a-lifetime event, the steps the Meat Puppets had taken to secure its independence from SST guaranteed the band would make the most of it. Sadly, just five months after the performance aired on MTV, Cobain died by suicide on April 5, 1994. The subsequent release of *MTV Unplugged in New York* in November drew enormous attention from grieving fans and brought even more admirers into the fold. Because the Meat Puppets had three songs on the record, this represented a significant windfall for the band. "If it hadn't been for Nirvana," Bostrom said, "we never would have made any money at all."[12]

3

In May 1994, Negativland reached a settlement with SST—sixteen months after it filed its countersuit. The settlement was as strange as it was expansive. The two parties agreed to split the losses incurred in the Island lawsuit, but instead of the 50/50 split that Negativland had originally proposed, they agreed to a disposition of 75/25, with SST paying the smaller portion. SST claimed the lawsuit cost the label $90,000, but in court it could account for only a little over $41,000. As a result, Negativland was on the hook for approximately $30,000, which was what it estimated SST had withheld from its royalty payments since the release of the *U2* EP.

Even though the court threw out several aspects of Ginn's claim that the publication of *The Letter U and the Numeral 2* infringed upon SST's copyright, Ginn demanded that he be allowed to print pages taken from the publication in a forthcoming magazine of his own. In other words, he insisted on doing the very thing for which he'd taken Negativland to court. He also insisted on complete editorial control of eight pages in Negativland's next publication so he could tell his side of the story, but he settled for four. Lastly, Ginn demanded royalties for each copy sold of *The Letter U and the Numeral 2.*

The settlement also called attention to a business practice that raised eyebrows among SST's community of artists. The label had been paying royalties on CDs sold based on the much lower royalty rates for vinyl, which in the early '90s had a lower price point. SST requested a gag agreement, meaning neither party would discuss the terms of the settlement, but Negativland refused and SST's irregularities became common knowledge.

For the noisemakers from Negativland, the U2 affair was far from over. Once the band identified Casey Kasem as the main obstacle to getting the U2 EP rereleased, Negativland focused its attention on persuading the radio personality to agree not to sue.

Kasem was an intriguing character. The Lebanese American had served in Korea, where he began his broadcasting career in the US Army. In addition to distinguishing himself as a DJ, he was the voice of Shaggy on the popular cartoon *Scooby Doo*. On air, Kasem was the voice of the American dream, but off he was active in politics and an outspoken supporter of a number of progressive causes, from pro–animal rights to anti–nuclear power. Unfortunately for Negativland, doing away with the Copyright Act of 1976 wasn't one of his causes.

The announcer and the band engaged in a spirited conversation, trading letters and even exchanging books. Kasem counseled Negativland not to be so, well, negative and sent the band a copy of Norman Vincent Peale's *The Power of Positive Thinking*. Negativland returned the favor with a copy of Fredric Dannen's *Hit Men*, the book that exposed corrupt business practices at major record labels. Negativland encouraged its fans to contact Kasem through his show and request he release the band's single. Kasem responded to every message with a form letter explaining his reasons, but after receiving a death threat from an irate fan, he was far less congenial.

Another case caught Negativland's attention. The Florida hip-hop group 2 Live Crew had been sued for including the Roy Orbison song "Oh, Pretty Woman" on its record *As Clean as They Wanna Be*. The lawyers for 2 Live Crew argued that parodies were entitled to the exceptions outlined in the fair use doctrine of the Copyright Act. The case went all the way to the Supreme Court.

Naturally, Negativland was interested in the outcome and offered its opinion on the criminalization of copying. In a letter to the band's attorneys, Negativland argued, "There is a big difference between the simple reselling of whole works (either 'cover' versions or 'bootlegging') and the creative use of fragments from existing works."[13] Negativland made similar arguments in a piece that ran in *Billboard*, linking sampling to other forms of artistic appropriation.

Negativland changed tactics by putting pressure on U2 and Island Records. By correctly accusing the band and its label of courting public opinion without taking action, Negativland coerced agreements out of U2, Island, and PolyGram, which owned U2's publishing. "Negativland refuse to go away," U2's manager wrote on the band's behalf urging Island and PolyGram to release the recordings back to Negativland, which, incredibly, they did.[14]

When the Supreme Court weighed in favor of 2 Live Crew, it struck a bittersweet chord for Negativland. Fair use was finally being interpreted in a way that favored artists over corporations, but if the ruling had come down before Island's lawsuit, Negativland had every reason to believe it would have won.

4

In 1995, Negativland published the book *Fair Use: The Story of the Letter U and the Numeral 2*. The book expanded on both the printed matter and the contents of the CD that came along with the previous edition. In addition to updating the articles, letters, and press releases, the new edition included four pages from Ginn, who backpedaled on telling his side of the story and used the space as an advertisement for a booklet of his own titled *O.J.* with a CD called *Positivland*, which could be preordered from SST for twelve dollars. The remaining three pages were dedicated to a bizarre contest in the form of a multiple-choice quiz with questions about the jobs Negativland's members held, the vehicles they drove, and how much money they made. The last question was the strangest: "Who is the whiniest/whimpiest [sic] singer in rock and roll? A. Liz Phair B. Poindexter Stewart C. Evan Dando D. Mark Hosler."[15] Readers were invited to take the quiz and send in their answers for a prize.

Negativland's new CD included "Crosley Bendix Discusses the U.S. Copyright Act" from *The Letter U and the Numeral 2* as well as nine new tracks listed under Dead Dog Records that sampled over a hundred sources, including U2, Casey Kasem, and, incredibly, Black Flag. The track "Gimme the Mermaid," makes extensive use of Black Flag's "Gimme Gimme Gimme" in drastically altered form. The song opens with a series of ominous sounds and gets stranger from there: a barking dog gives way to a recording of a lawyer ranting into an answering machine, which yields to an abbreviated rendition of "The Little Mermaid." Three minutes into the song the familiar drumbeat to "Gimme Gimme Gimme" kicks in, but instead of Morris, Reyes, Cadena, or Rollins, it's the Weatherman, who sings the chorus on a loop.

The book concludes with a lengthy appendix titled "A Fair Use Reader" that serves as a guide to how the Copyright Act has been interpreted at various stages in the late twentieth century. With the publication of *Fair Use*, Negativland hoped to bring its costly and time-consuming project to disrupt the music industry to a close, but there were still more chapters to be written.

5

New releases from SST in the early to mid-1990s were limited to a handful of prolific artists. Roger Miller put out a second No Man album titled *How the West Was Won* (SST 281), the art rock album *Unfold* (SST 307) by a project called Roger Miller's Exquisite Corpse, and a pair of albums under his own name—*Elemental Guitar* (SST 318) and *The Benevolent Disruptive Ray* (SST 331).

There was no slowing down the Leaving Trains, who unleased four more records: *The Big Jinx* (SST 293), the CD EP *Drowned and Dragged* (SST 311), the album *Smoke Follows Beauty* (SST 338), and the CD compilation *Favorite Mood Swings* (SST 334) for a total of eleven releases with SST before leaving the station for good. Bazooka was also extremely prolific during this period and released a total of seven records on SST and New Alliance between 1993 and 1997, occasionally along with Brewer and Joe Baiza, who were frequent collaborators.

Another SST favorite was Mario Lalli, whose 1985 demo for his band

Across the River was at one time seriously considered for release by the powers that be at SST. Across the River came out of the high desert scene nurtured by Dave Travis's generator parties that ranged from the desert to the sea. Across the River bassist Scott Reeder went on to play in Fu Manchu, who along with Kyuss helped shape the scene's stoner rock sound.

Mario Lalli formed Fatso Jetson with his brother Larry and put out a pair of records for SST: *Stinky Little Gods* (SST 321) and *Power of Three* (SST 341). The Lalli brothers simultaneously played in the Sort of Quartet, which cranked out *Planet Mamon* (SST 315), *Kiss Me Twice, I'm Schitzo* (SST 329), and *Bombas De Amor* (SST 332) during the same period.

Trotsky Icepick put out *The Ultraviolet Catastrophe* (SST 279) and *Hot Pop Hello* (SST 286), a collection of fourteen studio outtakes the band had never put to use. Last but not least, the Last completed *Gin & Innuendoes* (SST 323). Although the Last's final record for the label was completed in '94, it wouldn't be released for another two years.

SST Records lumbered on at a slower pace than in years past, but at Casa Destroy Ginn was busier than ever, playing and making music in multiple new projects. With the help of a four-track Pro Tools system, Ginn and Batwinas were able to speed up the recording process and expand into new genres, including techno, jazz rock, and audio collage. The foundation for these "bands" was Ginn on bass and electric guitar and Batwinas programming the percussion, with other musicians adding their parts as needed.

In Mojack, for example, saxophonist Tony Atherton added a free jazz element. Sometimes Greg would record his parts for guitar and leave space for Atherton to fill, and sometimes it was the other way around. "It was always this sort of reactionary musical thing," Batwinas said, "but Tony and Greg really clicked in the way they played their parts. When people talk about Greg's guitar style, Tony could do that on saxophone. You'd listen to it and go, that's really fucking weird. It's really cool, but it's really fucking weird."[16] That weirdness was captured on Mojack's debut, *Merchandising Murder* (SST 320), and continued over the course of six CDs spread out over nearly twenty years.

Hor, Ginn's techno project, featured faster beats and Ginn's signature

Greg Ginn at the Vampire Lounge in Simi Valley, 1993. (Photo by Fred Hammer.)

guitar solos. "Greg loved techno music," Batwinas said.[17] Given Ginn's interest in the intersection of music and community, it's perhaps not that surprising that he enjoyed attending raves in Orange County and LA. As much as Ginn loved the music, he liked experimenting with it even more. "He liked taking the beats and speeding them up to get really outrageous tempos going," Batwinas said. "He was really trying to blend these different interests that he had just to see what would come out of it."[18] Ginn's experiments with techno introduced a droning, machine-like menace to his guitar playing. Hor wasn't a short-lived project, and Ginn created material for a half-dozen Hor

CDs over the years. Like most things Ginn was passionate about, he went all the way.

A pair of side projects, Confront James and El Bad, undermine claims of Ginn's complete immersion in instrumental music. The five CDs Confront James put out between 1994 and 1997—four albums and a CD EP of remixes—featured vocals by Richard Ray, who also contributed lyrics. El Bad put out only two albums, and both feature lyrics and vocals by Reece.

It's helpful to think of these various musical projects not as bands per se but rather as expressions of Ginn's interests. "I'm not very calculating about music," Ginn said. "I just kinda do it and see where it goes. So I don't have a 'this is this kind of band' sort of thing. I don't even know what to call most of the music I do."[19] Despite the many changes at SST, Ginn's passion for experimentation remained as strong as ever.

"Greg's taste in music is far more diverse than people who appreciate Black Flag understand," Batwinas explained. "People that were his contemporaries may have known, but that second generation or third generation of Black Flag fans don't seem to understand. Greg was far more than just a punk rocker."[20]

Not only did Gone put out several new records; it even toured every so often. Gone's new releases included the EPs *Smoking Gun* (SST 303) and *Damage Control* (SST 319) and the LPs *All the Dirt That's Fit to Print* (SST 306) and *Best Left Unsaid* (SST 313). Now that Ginn had a place to play and record, he spent more and more time there. "We would just record hours of raw material that would get edited together into different projects," Batwinas said. Sometimes the tracks were shaped into songs, edited, mixed, and sent off to the record pressing plant right away. Other times the material sat for long stretches. Batwinas recalled how some of the tracks he'd mixed didn't get used until long after he'd stopped working for Ginn.

In 1996, Ginn purchased a massive piece of commercial real estate in downtown Long Beach that was large enough to encompass SST, Casa Destroy, and a multipurpose space called the Idea Room. Ginn outfitted this part of the building with a sound system, a large stage, and even a coffee shop. The Idea Room hosted live shows, movie nights, and even dance parties for the community. Because the building was so big, half of it would sit empty, and Ginn would set up huge speakers for his techno parties, which generated complaints from the neighbors. "Sometimes it'd be a DJ, sometimes it would be Greg's music," Batwinas said. "We really tried to build a little eclectic, localized dance music, techno punk scene."[21]

Screw Radio resumed as an internet show, and Batwinas recalled editing commercials, producing bumper drops, and recording station identification clips with whomever was in the studio. When the internet radio project faded away, Ginn continued to use the name for his audio collages. While Ginn was out on tour with Gone, he'd scan through radio stations and make tapes with a recorder that had an FM tuner. He'd capture bits of talk radio, religious sermons, or people calling into stations across the country. When Ginn returned to Casa Destroy, he'd cut them up and put the sequences into a sampler. Of course, this is very similar to what Negativland had built its reputation doing, but Ginn seemed oblivious of the hypocrisy.

Ginn released two additional records under the Screw Radio moniker: *Talk Radio Violence* (SST 324) and *I'm a Generation X* (SST 333), but these were guitar jams played over manipulated audio samples culled from political talk radio with titles like "President Hillary," "Feminist Banter (I Need to Be Degraded)," and "Pissed White Man." The songs tended to run together, and while Screw Radio came across as a knockoff Negativland, the messages were predictable, the background music forgettable.

Ginn continued making more records under different monikers like the Killer Tweeker Bees and Bias, incorporating faster beats and keyboards. Batwinas said Ginn seldom gave much in the way of instructions to his collaborators: "'Here's thirteen songs. Do stuff to it.' That's the way Greg liked to work."[22]

6

Despite the preponderance of compilations, reissues, and Ginn's various projects, SST occasionally brought exciting new artists into the fold. Ginn plucked a Bay Area band called Transition. out of the pile of demo tapes. "We got signed via a self-produced demo cassette that we mailed," recalled singer David Benson. "No press pack, just a hand-written letter."[23] Ginn liked the band's Helmet-meets–Jane's Addiction style so much he took them out on the road with him to promote the band's nine-song LP *Spine* (SST 302).

Another surprise signing was the Muddle, a young, inexperienced guitar-driven post-punk band that sent its demo to SST. Ginn became enamored with the band and had Batwinas work with the Muddle on its self-titled debut (SST 310).

Perhaps the most exceptional of these new signings was OXBOW's *Serenade in Red* (SST 340). The San Francisco experimental art rock band had recorded its fourth studio album with Steve Albini and Gibbs Chapman. After the album was released in Germany on the label Crippled Dick Hot Wax!, SST expressed interest in releasing the CD.

Vocalist Eugene Robinson was no stranger to the label. A veteran of the scene, Robinson had seen Black Flag play in New York in 1980 and had interviewed the band for his zine *The Birth of Tragedy* during Rollins's first trip to San Francisco. Robinson sent Dukowski a copy of the album when it came out, and Ginn was impressed by what he heard.

Robinson wasn't sure what ultimately convinced SST to release OXBOW's new record. "I remember Greg and Chuck descending on a show we played at Spaceland…and the deal was made very soon after that."[24]

It all started with Robinson. A large, tattooed Black man whose passions included writing and fighting, Robinson spent his entire life making himself at home in places he wasn't welcome. In the whitest of punk spaces imaginable, the native New Yorker barged right in. (You can see Robinson front and center on the back cover of SSD's compilation *Power.*) In 1980, the graduate of Bedford-Stuyvesant High School left New York to attend college at Stanford University. There he formed the hardcore band Whipping Boy with three other Stanford students, and the band got its first show thanks to none other than Keith Morris.

After Whipping Boy ran its course, Robinson found himself at the end of his rope. Depressed and alone in a room full of guns, Robinson started writing what he thought might very well be a suicide note. "I remember feeling poorly served by the music that we had been making at that time," Robinson recalled, "as well as having some really horrible, terrible relationships that were putting my head through changes."[25] This led to what Robinson characterized as his Peggy Lee moment: "This can't be all there is."[26]

Robinson, along with two other members of Whipping Boy's final lineup—guitarist Niko Wenner and bassist Dan Adams—and drummer Greg Davis, started a new creative project called OXBOW, the impetus of which Robinson attributed to Jello Biafra. While discussing his frustration with the limitations of hardcore with the Dead Kennedys' singer, Robinson said, "I'd like to somehow capture the music that's in my head."

"You know," Biafra replied, "that's what we're all trying to do?"[27]

OXBOW is not a band that can be evaluated in conventional terms. "It's not rock not metal nor punk," said Joe Chiccarelli, a producer who would work with the band many years later. "It's just big, cinematic and daring."[28] With its blend of unconventional arrangements and Robinson's howling performances, OXBOW creates an intimate—albeit uncomfortable—space where powerful emotions are exchanged between the audience and the band. "This is the sound of somebody expressing themselves in a very clear and honest way," Wenner said of Robinson's vocals.[29]

Robinson channeled his anguish into OXBOW's debut album *Fuckfest* and its follow-up *King of the Jews*; both albums were released on the band's own label. OXBOW's relationship with Steve Albini began in 1993 when he produced the band's third studio album, *Let Me Be a Woman*, which was essentially a live album recorded in forty-eight hours over four days. The record sat for two years until a label released it in Europe. This caught the attention of the German label Crippled Dick Hot Wax! that wanted to put out the next OXBOW record. The band enlisted Albini's services again for *Serenade in Red*.

By then OXBOW had taken several unconventional turns in its creative process, such as incorporating piano and adding a fifth string to Adams's fretless bass for a thunderous bottom. The most striking change was Robinson writing the lyrics and Wenner composing the music independently so that no one in the band had any idea how the songs would sound until they were in the studio recording them. "I never wanted to sing a song until the microphone was on," Robinson explained. "I wanted to think about the song.

I never liked the idea of scratch vocals. I couldn't do it because I would write something and then I could never unwrite it."[30]

While Robinson had access to the demos, the musicians were kept in the dark with regards to the content of the lyrics and the way the vocals were arranged, but in the studio it all came together. "There's an element of improvisation," Adams explained. "We kind of sit on this fence between doing things in very structured ways, but in some cases doing things in very unstructured ways. All those things are kind of jazz-like in my concept of what jazz is all about."[31]

Recorded over the course of eight days in San Francisco in a vast, high-ceilinged room, *Serenade in Red* tells the story of a doomed relationship that ends badly, shot through with film noir imagery. One of the many standout songs is "3 O'clock," an epic eleven-minute-long blues track turned inside out with a seductive bass motif that captures the album's doomful air of creeping paranoia and suspense. "We recorded it on tape," Wenner recalled, "and when we mixed it we slowed the tape down a little bit. That makes that song stand apart from the other songs."[32] The band recorded three versions of the song that came in at seven, nine, and eleven minutes. OXBOW went with the longest.

Perhaps the strangest things about *Serenade in Red* are the contributions from the legendary Marianne Faithfull. A huge fan of her work, Robinson thought she'd be perfect for "Insylum": OXBOW's reinterpretation of Willie Dixon's "Insane Asylum." "We were like, 'Screw it. Let's ask,'" Robinson recalled. "It's not gonna hurt our feelings if she says no. So we wrote her an actual letter."[33]

Incredibly, Faithfull agreed to fly to New York to record the track, but the authorities wouldn't let her into the country due to past legal issues related to her much-publicized drug problems. "If you can't come to us," Robinson said, "we're going to come to you."

Undaunted, OXBOW flew to Dublin, Ireland, with Chapman to record Marianne Faithfull at Windmill Studios, the same studio where U2 recorded much of *The Joshua Tree*. It took some trial and error to get the track down. Robinson suggested they sing the song together, but Faithfull flinched when

Robinson started screaming and left the room. "When she came back in to sing it after I'd finished my stuff," Robinson said, "she absolutely killed it."[34]

"Insylum," a duet between estranged lovers whose failed romance has all but destroyed them, is the final track on the album. It appears on "Side Z" of the double album released by Crippled Dick Hot Wax! and as a secret track on the CD that SST put out.[35]

Serenade in Red is not only a masterpiece of mood and a challenging work of art in its own right, it just might be the last great album SST released. Even the artwork, a photograph taken by Richard Kern, whom Robinson met through Lydia Lunch, was something of a throwback to SST's more prosperous days.

Although the band's signing raised some eyebrows from friends in the industry who considered it a mismatch or didn't realize that SST was still signing bands, OXBOW wasn't concerned. "We had heard complaints from our friends in Bad Brains and so on about problems with the label," Robinson said, "but I'd been friends with Chuck for a long time and I didn't anticipate that we would have any of those problems. There was nobody else in the US who was hearing what we were saying, and these guys invited us down and came to our shows and were really aggressive about their interest, so it seemed to be something that made a lot of sense."[36]

When OXBOW visited SST headquarters in Long Beach, they found the inventory stocked with CDs from Ginn's many side projects. It also didn't hurt that SST paid the band up front. "He was always nice to us," Robinson said, "paid us prior to the record being released, and outside of a weird dislike for Steve Albini, whose name he consistently and purposefully mispronounced as AL-BYN-E, I saw nothing amiss...before it all got weird."[37]

7

SST's release schedule for 1997 was dominated by Ginn's side projects. These included the fifth and final Confront James record, *Black Bomb Mountain* (SST 343); more Hor, with the suggestive title *A Faster, More Aggressive Hor* (SST 347); another effort from El Bad, called *Trick or Treat* (SST 348); and a second Mojack record, called *Homebrew* (SST 359). Ginn also introduced releases by three new "bands": the Killer Tweeker Bees' *The Tweeker Blues* (SST 345), Bias's *Model Citizen* (SST 352), and Get Me High's *Taming the Underground* (SST 353)—all of which reflected Ginn's growing passion for the possibilities of combining live musicians with computer sequencing. Ginn even gave this amalgamation a name: "guitartechno."

That year also saw the release of several experimental jazz records, including the final Bazooka record, *Sonic Business Environment* (SST 356), as well as the self-titled album for Jeremy Keller's side project, *Guns, Books, and Tools* (SST 357). SST also released Brother Weasel's second record, *Swingin' n Groovin'* (SST 365)—its follow-up to its self-titled album (SST 335) from the year before—and *The Binary System Live at the Idea Room* (SST 349), featuring Roger Miller on piano and Larry Dersch on drums in Ginn's giant café.

By far the strangest SST release that year was Negativland's *Negativ(e)land: Live on Tour* (SST 355), which was recorded at the Knitting Factory in New York all the way back in 1989. The album was ceded to SST as part of the Negativland's settlement with the label, but everything about the finished product shows how much disdain Ginn still had for the group. Released against Negativland's wishes, the CD contained several digs at the band, including the insertion of the *e* in the band's name and the use of the word *tour*, which the band didn't do in the conventional sense. The record coincided with the release of Negativland's *Dispepsi* on the band's own label, its first new release in four years. The timing suggests SST sought to capitalize on Negativland's promotion for its new record—just as Island Records had accused SST of doing with the release of the U2 EP. The biggest indignity, however, was the sloppy and careless manner in which a recording originally conceived as a double album was condensed into a single CD and rushed out the door.

SST put out only a handful of new records in 1998, including a new release from Gone titled *Country Dumb* (SST 344), which the label described as "a fusion of metal-punk-funk-techno-noise" or "hyphen-rock."[38] Although Gone was an instrumental project, it didn't prevent Ginn from taking shots at politicians and former business associates through the song titles. The song

"'PUNK' and the Cash Narcotic" is clearly a swipe at the title of Carducci's book of rock criticism, *Rock and the Pop Narcotic*, which was originally published by Rollins's publishing company, 2.13.61.

In 1998, SST also put out two new compilations of old music: *Anthology* (SST 361), a collection of songs from H.R.'s solo albums released between 1985 and 1990, and an unusual compilation of Minutemen material from 1980 to 1985 that contained at least one song from every release. The comp was given the title *Introducing the Minutemen* (SST 363), although they certainly didn't need one.

With the help of Batwinas, SST also reissued Black Flag's *Live '84*, and it was one of the last projects the engineer worked on before leaving the employ of Casa Destroy. The original recording only came out on cassette. Ginn wanted to put it out on DVD, but he couldn't get the rights back to the video, and the audio tapes were badly damaged. "They were falling apart," Batwinas said, "because they were done on half-inch eight-track tape and they weren't stored very well."[39] Batwinas painstakingly copied the tape song by song onto two-inch tape and then synched it up in Pro Tools.

Batwinas set up the Idea Room as if for a live performance. Then he isolated the tracks from the recording at the Stone in San Francisco so Ginn's guitar played through his guitar amps and Roessler's bass came through the bass cabinets on stage. The drums and vocals were played through the house speakers. Then Batwinas miked up the room and hit play. "That was the closest I ever got to being at a Black Flag concert," Batwinas said.[40] While Batwinas listened to the guitars "tear his head off," Ginn sat at the console and twisted the knobs to get the exact sound he wanted.[41] Batwinas blended the recording with the original tracks. Subsequently, the CD reissue of *Live '84* was actually a completely different mix of the performance.

That was it for 1998. The label didn't sign any new bands or release any new records for the next five years. Aside from the SST Superstore (which moved online the same year), live shows in the Idea Room, and the revival of Screw Radio, for all intents and purposes, the label went dark.

Ginn and Cadena at the Black Flag Benefit for Cats at the Hollywood Palladium, September 12, 2003. (Photo by Paul Rachman.)

CHAPTER 14
SST vs. History

Twenty-first century

1

What do Everlast's "Jump Around," Cypress Hill's "Hits from the Bong," Snoop Dogg's "Murder Was the Case," and Black Flag's "Nervous Breakdown" have in common?

They were all performed at the Smoke Out Festival in the parking lot at the LA Memorial Coliseum in 2003. Ironically, this is where Keith Morris, who'd performed the Black Flag cover with the Circle Jerks, found out his old band was playing a pair of reunion shows at the Hollywood Palladium. Paul Tollett and Rick Van Santen of Goldenvoice insisted Morris be a part of it.

Morris was intrigued by the prospect of playing with his former bandmates again. Visions of doing some damage with Dukowski, Robo, and Ginn ran through his imagination. Morris reached out to Ginn, and Ginn invited him to Long Beach to rehearse. When the day arrived, Morris drove down to Ginn's all-in-one performance space, recording studio, record label office, coffee shop, and cat shelter. Ginn had become interested in rescuing feral cats and threw himself into the cause. "I got into it gradually," Ginn said at the time, "and just got more and more involved to the point where I now have probably eighty cats."[1]

Ginn played a CD of some of the Black Flag songs he wanted to rehearse, but the tempos seemed off to Morris. The drums, bass, and guitars struck him as much too slow. That wasn't the only thing that seemed fishy. The only other musician present was Ginn's drummer Gregory Moore. The reunion was being billed as Black Flag: The First Four Years. Where was Robo? What about Dukowski?

Ginn said he hadn't talked to them yet. Morris went ahead and rehearsed with Ginn, Moore, and the CD player but struggled to get anything going. Like many singers, Morris was accustomed to being counted in by the drummer. Moore was no help, which struck Morris as a bad sign.

Morris went back for another session a few days later. This time Ginn was in Dale Nixon mode, noodling away on the bass guitar, and the results were even worse than before. Feeling that things would be better once the rest of the band was on board, Morris decided to take matters into his own hands. He called Cadena and explained the situation. A week later Ginn called and took Morris to task for reaching out to people on his own and accused him of spreading rumors.

Morris changed the subject and asked Ginn about compensation for participating in the reunion. Ginn said they'd talk about it after the show. Morris started to get a sinking feeling that was all too familiar. He checked in with Goldenvoice and found out the reunion show was actually going to be a benefit for cats. Morris could appreciate that, but he thought Ginn should use his own money if he felt so strongly.

Shortly afterward, Morris was informed by Goldenvoice that his services were no longer needed. While it upset Morris to be cast aside, he was relieved that he wouldn't be part of what he sensed was quickly becoming a clusterfuck. Morris released a statement that he wouldn't be participating in the reunion and that he believed the lineup fell well short of what was advertised. Caveat emptor.

Black Flag played three shows September 11–13: two at the Hollywood Palladium on Friday and Saturday and a surprise warm-up show Thursday at

Alex's Bar in Long Beach. The Friday show quickly sold out, but there were still plenty of tickets available when the doors opened on Saturday night. Tickets were $27.50, but some fans paid as much as $40 with fees.

Mike V and the Rats and 1208 were the opening acts Friday night. Shortly after Black Flag took the stage, Ginn announced they would be playing *My War* in its entirely. Unfortunately, the band was incomplete. Ginn played guitar, Moore filled in on drums, Dez Cadena sang, and "Dale Nixon" returned on bass. Because Ginn couldn't play the guitar and the bass at the same time, he used a sampler loaded with prerecorded bass tracks. Ginn dressed up what one attendee referred to as "his synthetic bandmate" with a sombrero, and off they went.[2]

While Ginn and Moore were old hands at playing along to prerecorded tracks at Casa Destroy, it was a new experience for Cadena, and the performance was marred with several gaffes. "The audience quickly realized Black Flag's bassist was just one step above a Mr. Coffee," one critic observed, and some fans threw a garbage can on stage.[3]

When *My War* concluded, a new lineup took the stage, with Robo replacing Moore, skateboarder Mike Vallely stepping in for Cadena, and Revuelta—an actual Black Flag bassist—replacing "Dale Nixon." This lineup wasn't received much better. Although Vallely had recently performed with Ginn in Good for You, he wasn't part of Black Flag's first four years. The so-called reunion felt like a bait and switch.

Paul Rachman was in town to interview Ginn for his documentary *American Hardcore*. He attended the show and was befuddled by the experience. "The Benefit for Cats was weird," he said. "It was good to see the guys on stage, but it wasn't the Black Flag I remembered."[4]

The following night's performance wasn't nearly as full and just as poorly received. After Fu Manchu and Good Riddance played, a new combination of Black Flag players appeared. This time Cadena started out on guitar and Vallely sang. Surprisingly, the ghost of Dale Nixon also returned. Don Seki, who was photographing the show from between the barrier and the stage, reported being drenched with beer thrown at the performers.[5]

The strange, sad affair raised more questions than answers: Where were

Morris, Dukowski, and Reyes? Hell, where was Bryan Migdol? How was the show a reunion if it featured performers who'd never played together before? Why didn't Ginn use the former members of Black Flag he'd recruited—namely Robo, Cadena, and Revuelta for the entire show? Also, cats?

The whole thing was a bit of a head-scratcher. If one is only good by virtue of comparison, then the "reunited" Black Flag was very, very bad compared to shows put on by the Rollins Band as it barnstormed across the United States that summer playing Black Flag covers. The Rollins Band was also raising funds for a noble cause: the West Memphis Three. Rollins roped Morris into singing a few songs at the top of the set. By all accounts, these shows were far superior to Ginn's attempt at getting the band together.

In interviews leading up to the reunion, Ginn hinted at new SST releases in the works and attributed the lack of output since 1998 to distribution woes. This time the culprit was DNA (Distribution North America), which went belly-up when its parent company, Valley Media, declared bankruptcy in November 2001, taking down several indie labels with it. "When distributors go bankrupt," Ginn explained, "they generally have large reserves, and it's a lot harder to change distributors than it might seem, because they get their hooks into you and pool large reserves, which is understandable for insurance, but when they go bankrupt, we can have very substantial losses. We lost a lot of money. But the records sold. We had small interruptions in the distribution, but large interruptions in getting paid."[6]

These comments got the attention of many of SST's artists. Ginn's relationship to distributors echoed many of his artists' relationships to him: the records sold but the money didn't make it to where it was supposed to go.

Although Ginn boasted in interviews that he'd never stopped jamming or recording, SST hadn't released any new material since 1998. Prior to the Black Flag reunion, Ginn touted new releases. SST signed a new distribution deal with Koch; however, these records never saw the light of day even though they were given titles and catalog numbers: Hor's *Bash* (SST 366), Mojack's *Rub a Dub* (SST 367), Fastgato's *Feral* (SST 368), Confront James's *We Are Humored* (SST 370), and Limey LBC's *Life of Lime* (SST 371). *Bash*, which was originally titled *How Much?*, and *Feral* made it into the production pipeline with promo copy and cover art. Naturally, *Feral* features a photograph of a cat.

2

In 2006, SST Records struck a digital distribution deal with the Orchard to make a portion of its catalog available on digital music platforms around the world. For the first two weeks of the partnership, eMusic was given exclusive rights to the electronic catalog, then the music spread to other platforms, most notably iTunes, before becoming available on other streaming platforms.

The announcement stated that for the first time SST was making "tracks from 94 of its top-selling albums" available for digital distribution.[7] This wasn't really the case. While listeners could stream Black Flag, the Minutemen, the Descendents, and Bad Brains, the services were also stuck with Bias, El Bad, Hor, Mojack, and many other Greg Ginn side projects.[8]

Today, when an artist samples a song from SST's catalog without clearing it with the label and plays it on YouTube or Spotify, as was the case in 2021 when Philadelphia's Old City sampled Dukowski's bass line from Black Flag's "Six Pack," it can expect to hear from the Orchard, which polices copyright infractions across digital media. If that seems like a lot of trouble for one of Dukowski's bass lines, it's helpful to remember the bass line doesn't belong to Dukowski; it belongs to SST, and good luck getting clearance from the label.

That same year Ginn sold the massive commercial property in Long Beach and relocated to Talbot Street in Taylor, Texas, a small town approximately thirty miles northeast of Austin and fourteen hundred miles from Lawndale. This was an odd move for someone so preoccupied with the cutting edge of culture and technology. One suspects there weren't too many places in Taylor, Texas, that played punk or techno.

In 2007 SST released three new records, including one called *Bent Edge* (SST 373), by Ginn's new band, Greg Ginn and the Taylor Texas Corrugators. This was a real band with a rotating cast of players with whom Ginn performed and occasionally toured. *Bent Edge* features bluesy melodies laid over jazzy bass lines. It might be the mellowest record Ginn has ever played on.

The other two records released that year were Mojack's *Under the Willow Tree* (SST 372) and Gone's *The Epic Trilogy* (SST 374), a double CD that is one of the strangest releases of Ginn's post–Black Flag career, which is saying something. The trilogy consists of three instrumental songs on the first disc, each approximately fifteen minutes long, and the exact same songs on the second disc with vocals from H.R. that had been tracked many years before when Batwinas was running Casa Destroy.

The following year saw another handful of releases from various vanity projects: Jambang's cosmic *Connecting* (SST 375), Mojack's hilariously titled album *The Metal Years* (SST 376), and Greg Ginn and the Taylor Texas Corrugators' sophomore effort, *Goof Off Experts* (SST 377). Ginn's honky-skronk was a long way from Black Flag, which wasn't such a bad thing because before too long there would be more Black Flag in the world than anyone knew what to do with.

In 2010, SST released a CD compilation that combined Saint Vitus's *The Walking Dead* EP and *Hallow's Victim* LP—twenty-five years after they were originally issued. *The Walking Dead / Hallow's Victim* (SST 378) represented the first release that wasn't affiliated with one of Ginn's bands in more than a decade.

Perhaps the most unusual development that year was the release of a Jambang DVD with a film that features extremely low-budget sci-fi scenes over which Ginn plays spacey, repetitive riffs. With songs like "El Musica de la Robot" and "Extracting the Ergo Tryptachloride," it's not meant to be taken seriously, but *200 Days in Space* (SST 379) showed that Ginn was still capable of surprises.

3

How much Black Flag is too much Black Flag? After more than twenty-five years of very little Black Flag, the punk community was about to find out.

Goldenvoice, which had a knack for stirring up discord among the band members, approached Dukowski about giving a speech at a party celebrating the company's thirtieth anniversary. Dukowski thought he could do better than that. He rounded up Morris, Stevenson, and Stephen Egerton to play the *Nervous Breakdown* EP. Why those players? Because the Descendents were headlining the party.

The show was a huge success, and afterward it was almost a foregone conclusion the players would do it again. "So we're backstage," Morris said, "me, Chuck, Billy, Stephen, and Dez Cadena, and we're looking at each other. We've had a great time, and among the four of us, we decided that maybe we should play out as a band."[9]

Over a year later, in January 2013, the group announced it would be playing festivals in Europe and at Punk Rock Bowling in Las Vegas under the name FLAG. Almost immediately, Ginn announced that Black Flag had re-formed with Reyes, Moore, and "Dale Nixon" and would also be playing shows soon.

This was somewhat surprising as Ginn was on the verge of releasing a slew of records from his latest project, Good for You, with Mike Vallely as vocalist. This included the vinyl LP *Life Is Too Short to Not Hold a Grudge* (SST 385), the single "Fucked Up" (SST 388), the double LP *Too!* (SST 389), and the triple CD *Full Serving* (SST 390), which contains all of the material from the previous two albums as well as six unreleased tracks.

At first blush, Good for You seemed like a return to form of sorts, with an actual band fronted by an aggressive vocalist and dynamic guitar playing. But Good for You also showcased another one of Ginn's new passions: the theremin, an instrument he'd experimented with on the records he released as Greg Ginn and the Royal We. Was Ginn's desire to re-form Black Flag driven by the public's lack of interest in Good for You?

The punk community was split into two camps: those who supported FLAG, and those who didn't know any better. Although it had been ten years since Ginn's universally panned reunion-cum-benefit-for-cats, no one had forgotten. "Since Greg Ginn's Black Flag has become a bloated, monotonous carcass of everything we hate about rock 'n' roll," wrote Legs McNeil, "FLAG got together to pass the torch to a new generation of headbangers and shame Greg Ginn's band by showing the world how the noise should be played."[10]

But Ginn had another surprise up his sleeve. Not only was Black Flag re-forming, but it was releasing an album of new material in March: its first since 1985's *In My Head*. Ginn released a digital single in May, but the record's release kept getting pushed back. In August, the other shoe finally dropped when Ginn filed lawsuits against the band members for trademark infringement. The court denied the injunction. As much as Ginn wished FLAG would stop playing, there was nothing he could do about it.

Oddly enough, the camp that cared the most about the band's legacy was not the one that had a commercial stake in it. "It's not meant to be 'easy' music," Dukowski said about Black Flag's enduring appeal. "It is music that speaks to a kind of pain. It is intense and that is its power. It is music that speaks to people and tells them that they are not alone. It is music that tells the truth. That's why people care about it so much."[11]

Even though the album was delayed, the tour went on as scheduled. Not surprisingly, there was plenty of drama within the Black Flag camp. During a show in Australia, Ginn had Mike Vallely kick Reyes off stage, essentially firing him on the spot. Many saw this as Ginn's revenge for Reyes quitting on Black Flag all those years ago at the Fleetwood. But Reyes had the last laugh when, once again, a new Black Flag album came out with his vocals on it after he'd left the band.

What The...(SST 391) has twenty-two songs, and the majority of Black Flag fans couldn't name one of them. The influence of electronic music can be heard in the repetitive riffage, and it bears some similarity to Fastgato, a project featuring Scott Reynolds's vocals, or Gone's "collaboration" with H.R. Unfortunately, Reyes sounds like he's singing in a storm that keeps raining down riffs. *What The...*was recorded in both Texas and Long Beach, which was telling—that meant some of the tracks had been parked on Ginn's hard drive since 2006, if not earlier.

Vallely was named the new singer for Black Flag in 2014, and this incarnation of the band has performed on a semi-regular basis. In 2019, Black Flag played some shows with a completely new rhythm section, and the band embarked on an extensive winter tour in 2020. And so it goes. The man who once said, "I never go to those punk reunion shows," has apparently changed his thinking.[12] It's difficult to imagine any of the former members of Black Flag ever playing with Ginn again.

4

The story of SST Records isn't over. Its history, for better or worse, is still being written. SST operates as a twenty-first-century version of the mail-order outfit the label spearheaded in the late '70s. The label maintains the SST Superstore, an online retail outlet where fans can purchase records, CDs, DVDs, T-shirts, and other merch. Although SST creates new merchandise, like the face masks printed with Pettibon's Black Flag logo during the pandemic in 2020, there aren't any new records in the pipeline, new tours being promoted, or new artists clamoring for attention.

SST doesn't act like a typical record label. It hasn't put out a new record since 2014, which saw the release of *Gumbo and Holy Water* (SST 392), by Greg Ginn and the Taylor Texas Corrugators, and *Can't Make It Up* (SST 393), by Hor. For now, Ginn's ongoing experiment with high-voltage guitar-techno and anxiety-inducing BPM stands as SST's last statement.

As of 2021, the website's "About Us" section was curiously blank (and had been for some time) and in 2022 was taken down, a strange omission for a label with such a rich and provocative history. For a while, SST Records was the most important independent record label on the planet, but the empty space registers as a taunt: you know who we are or else you wouldn't be here.

Only a fraction of the catalog is available on vinyl: ALL, Bad Brains, Black Flag, the Descendents, fIREHOSE, H.R., Hüsker Dü, the Minutemen, Negativland, Saccharine Trust, Screaming Trees, and Saint Vitus, along with a few others. These are some of SST's best-known and best-selling bands. Many of Ginn's side projects, from Mojack to Greg Ginn and the Royal We, are also available. Missing from the list are Dinosaur Jr, the Meat Puppets, Sonic Youth, and Soundgarden—bands that have taken back the rights to their music through legal channels.

The quality of the records isn't as good as it once was. The cardboard covers have gotten thinner, and the graphics have gotten shoddier. Edward Colver watched with dismay as his image that graces the cover of *Damaged* degraded over the years. "I am furious about the reissues of *Damaged*," Colver said. "That washed-out color edition and the horrible black and white ones. I've got good photos. I've got beautiful black and white photos. It's embarrassing to me and to them that they'd release a milestone record and then treat it with such disregard."[13]

Other than the anthologies released in the late '80s and early '90s, SST has not sought to capitalize on its legacy by remastering records with today's technology and reissuing them with bonus material in slick anniversary editions. Though similar campaigns have been cash cows for other labels, SST has opted out. "It's time for an anniversary boxed set with a bunch of outtakes and stuff like that," Colver said, speaking for fans around the world.[14]

Much of SST's back catalog is out of print, with many of the early records going for extraordinary sums on the resale market. While it's a frustrating situation for bands that never sold many records in the first place, one of the most glaring omissions is from one of the label's best-known bands. Many of the Minutemen's records and T-shirts are available in a variety of formats, but not its opus *Double Nickels on the Dime*.

As interest in punk, post-punk, and independent music from the '70s, '80s, and '90s has increased over the years, many artists would like to share these early recordings with their fans. For some bands, SST has a strong financial incentive to keep the records in print, but the motive for making the rest of the catalog unavailable is much murkier. Why hold onto a title if you're not going to do anything with it?

"I feel like if you're not going to release it," said Lisa Fancher of Frontier Records, "then give it back to the band. If it hasn't been in print for decades, just let them have it back. That's the cool thing to do. I would do that. It's been over forty years. Let it go."[15]

There's a large gap between what most labels would do and SST's current business practices. One possible explanation for SST's curious disregard for its own history is that it no longer has access to those original recordings. Consider the story of how Black Flag's *Live '84* had to be painstakingly remixed. Those tapes fell into disrepair in less than fifteen years. What do the original masters look like now? What about recordings made even earlier?

SST's location in LA's South Bay may have played a role in this mystery. When the sun goes down in the Beach Cities, the marine layer creeps in and hangs around until morning. This mass of air is created when cool offshore temperatures collide with warmer inland temperatures. These damp conditions can have a catastrophic effect on analog tapes, which are sensitive to both heat and humidity and should be kept in a cool, dry, temperature-controlled atmosphere. To put it another way, the South Bay may have been the worst possible place for SST's tapes.[16]

SST didn't really have a stable environment in which to store them until 1987. Over the years stories have emerged about the reckless handling of masters, such as when Emil Johnson retaliated against Black Flag by stealing them. SST was able to get them back, but the temporary solution was to hide them in Mugger's girlfriend's closet. When Spector was general manager at SST, he didn't have access to the masters, which meant responsibility for their safety and storage fell to Ginn. According to the Meat Puppets, when the band requested that SST turn over the masters, the band was told they were lost. That sounds like an evasion, but what if it were true? How many other recordings are missing?

"That's the million-dollar question," Spector said. "Probably a ten-million-dollar question."

SST can't reproduce what it doesn't have. Given the lack of safe storage, perhaps this is one reason SST hasn't issued lavish editions of milestone albums like *Damaged*, *Double Nickels on the Dime*, and *Zen Arcade*. For whatever reason, whether they were lost in all the moves, misplaced out of carelessness, stolen due to insecure storage, or unintentionally damaged, SST's inability to produce quality tapes would explain a lot.

Then there's the production. Many audiophiles take issue with the quality of the recording on SST's milestone albums. Critics frequently blame subpar production on Spot. This conveniently ignores the fact that the vast majority of these records were produced for very little money during a short period of time in studios rented by the hour. These recording and mixing sessions were typically collaborative affairs that often took place late at night on little or no sleep.

A campaign to remaster the albums that made SST great is long overdue. However, there is a great gulf between what SST's fans want and what the label will allow. The most honest, least corporate rock thing to do would be to release the records back to the musicians and let them decide how to make it available to the public.

Artists consulted for this book reported reaching out to Ginn directly about reacquiring the rights to their music only to receive the "Hollywood no": not a yes, not a no, just silence. "For many years the label was paying us," said Mark Pickerel of Screaming Trees. "Not necessarily annually, but often. We were receiving royalty checks, and we were really happy with our professional relationship with them. But I would say by the late '90s, things had started to sour and now there just isn't a relationship at all."[17]

Some of these artists and musicians not only collaborated with Ginn on their records but toured with him, shared the stage with him, and socialized with him. Ginn's silence is not only inexplicable but in many cases painful to those who'd shared a friendship with someone who was once so supportive. "Everything about Greg is unfathomable," said Mark Lanegan of Screaming Trees. "He is a huge enigma."[18]

That said, Lanegan does not discount the fact that without SST his career would be very different. "Still to this day the most thrilling thing that's ever happened to me in music or any entertainment business bullshit was when he called me on the phone at work and said he wanted to put out our records. Because we loved Black Flag. We loved everything on SST. We listened to all those records—even *Tom Troccoli's Dog*. I owe him because that's where it started for us."[19]

Of course, Screaming Trees' time with SST was a springboard to signing with a major label, which brought more attention and opportunities to the band. Most SST artists did not benefit from this kind of exposure, and some bands are at risk of being forgotten. But even those who didn't make the jump are grateful for being a part of SST. "It was a huge deal for us to get on SST," Rob Holzman said of SST's signing of Slovenly. "It was a very influential label for a lot of bands and a lot of people."[20]

For many in the music industry, SST served first as an inspiration, then as a cautionary tale. Brett Gurewitz, an original member of Bad Religion and founder of Epitaph Records, became a fan of Black Flag the first time he heard the *Nervous Breakdown* EP. When he started Bad Religion, he used the same font—Friz Quadrata Bold—from a pack of Letraset press-on letters when he made flyers for the band. "I wanted people to know we were punk," Gurewitz explained, "and I thought that it was a punk font."[21]

Gurewitz imitated more than just the font. He saw similarities between himself and Black Flag's guitarist and strove to emulate the band's success. "I really looked up to Black Flag, in the early days especially, as something to aspire to," Gurewitz said. "Greg Ginn was a songwriter-guitarist in his band but not the singer, and I was the guitarist-songwriter in my band but not the singer. He put out the records for his band and built a label around that idea. So did I. In many ways, I was following in his footsteps."[22]

Bruce Pavitt, cofounder of Sub Pop Records, also paid close attention to SST: "I was impressed with the consistency of the label through the art of Raymond Pettibon and the production of Spot. To a certain extent, we emulated that with photography of Charles Peterson and production by Jack Endino. An aesthetic emerged from that."[23]

However, as rumors circulated about SST's business practices and bands initiated legal action, other indie labels took heed. "They were a big influence on me," Gurewitz explained, "but they were also an influence on what not to do. At first I wanted to be like them. I wanted to be a DIY musician who put out other people's records and had a cool label. But then when I started hearing stories about SST not treating bands fairly, it also influenced me not to ever put myself in that position, and to always treat my artists fairly and keep my nose clean in business."[24]

Although SST's reputation as a creative force may be tarnished, for Gurewitz one thing will always be true: "I hope that SST is remembered as the incubator of American hardcore. Because that's really what it was. Black Flag is ground zero for hardcore as an art form."[25]

For many musicians, the way SST cultivated that art was just as important. "They created a network for bands that benefited other bands," said Derrick Bostrom of the Meat Puppets. "They went into towns and fought with local promoters and with local audiences when no other bands had ever been there before. They were trailblazers."[26]

Pavitt echoed this sentiment: "They were pioneers who made alternative music possible through the touring network they established, particularly with Black Flag, and the records they put out. SST put out some brilliant records."[27]

Even those who criticize the label for its business practices (and its owner's proclivity for suing its artists) grudgingly acknowledge SST's rich history. "As an artistic project and as a business idea, I got nothing but respect for those guys," said Bostrom. "In spite of the fact that they have had lawsuits with many of their artists, including myself—and if there's ever any conflict between me and SST I wish to win—in terms of their historical legacy, you've got to give it to them."[28]

The story of SST's clashes with its many antagonists often overshadows the thing that made SST great: its music. "I think there's an amazing musical legacy that Ginn has been involved in as a guitar player, as a composer, as a bandmate," said Niko Wenner of OXBOW. "It's really important stuff that they did with the aggression, the timing, the feel, the level of complexity. If you were to try to put it on paper, it would look like twenty-first-century music. I think that because nobody bothered to put it on paper, it doesn't get some of the respect that it deserves."[29]

SST's multifaceted legacy is perhaps most bittersweet for those who poured their blood, sweat, and tears into the label not as artists but as coconspirators. "I can't think of another record label in indie rock," said former employee Brian Long, "that put out so many important underground rock records in that period of time as SST did."[30]

Carducci put it more succinctly: "We seemed to win battles but then lose the war."[31] Not only does this echo some of Ginn's most extreme lyrics but it exemplifies the mindset that dominated SST during its peak years: going toe-to-toe with the enemy, whether that was corporate rock, the local media, or the band's own fans. SST never backed down, even when it knew it couldn't win.

But if SST did indeed lose the war, is it destined to be a footnote in the history of rock and roll? Steve Fisk believes "SST will be the cool thing that the cool kid brings up at the party when people are talking about Sub Pop."[32]

What do the experts think? Ryan Rodier and Brant Palko host the *You*

Don't Know Mojack podcast, in which they examine every single SST release. They've been at it since 2017 and have interviewed scores of musicians, producers, and former employees. For Rodier, there are multiple threads to consider, including the legacy of the touring circuit that Black Flag helped establish and the legacy of the label's irregular business dealings. What stands out for Rodier is the impact on indie culture of the label's willingness to make art for art's sake. "People took a chance on a record," Rodier said, "because it had an SST logo on it. They picked up Zoogz Rift or Blind Idiot God, and they didn't hate it. They loved it and it influenced them."[33]

There's a tendency to think of SST in monolithic terms: the legendary label that released *Damaged* or *Zen Arcade* or *Double Nickels on the Dime*. But SST wasn't a static entity. The label that released *Nervous Breakdown* wasn't the same label that put out the Meat Puppets' first record, and by the time Dinosaur Jr joined the roster, the makeup of the label had changed and would continue to change throughout the '80s and '90s and into the twenty-first century. Each phase of its history represents a different entry point for fans. "I think everybody gets to decide what the legacy of the label is to them," Palko said. "I mean, to me it's the timeless music and the fact that they didn't let a lack of funds stop them."[34]

What, if anything, can be done about SST? If it were up to Palko, he'd release everything that's out of print back to the artists. "This is a popular opinion," Palko said, "but the way that we fix SST is by allowing the Slovenlys and the Trotsky Icepicks and the Angsts to have their back catalog and do what they wish with it. If that's pressing a couple thousand vinyl copies of something, and then having it available digitally, so be it. I don't think it makes economic sense for Laura Rift to press physical copies of a Zoogz Rift record when she can sell it on iTunes and have it available for streaming on Spotify. That is how people are going to be able to access those records, hopefully, for the next fifty years."[35]

With magic wands in short supply, Rodier is in favor of a more direct approach. "I would love to have a chat with Greg and find some common ground to say, 'Bygones, man! Put it all behind you. The music is what matters. Everyone benefits if these artists can get the music back.'"[36]

Throughout the history of SST, artists remember Ginn as open and generous. In a musical environment, he was someone you wanted in your corner, and he was that person for countless artists. One didn't have to know Ginn very well to be the recipient of his generosity. "He would give you anything," Mugger said.[37] But we're also talking about someone who has been nursing a decades-long grudge with his brother. Reconciliation doesn't seem likely, but it may not be necessary.

Artists who created work after 1977 can petition to have their copyrights terminated after thirty-five years. That means the vast majority of work released by SST is eligible to be reclaimed. Although it can be a long, time-consuming process, there are legal entities adept at copyright termination and reversion, including one run by none other than Evan S. Cohen.

While a collaborative spirit may be lacking within SST, perhaps that spirit can be harnessed by its fans to work in favor of the artists that the label has exploited. Bands that have succeeded in the courtroom, like the Meat Puppets and Sonic Youth, demonstrate there's a path for returning music to its creators.

Anyone who has ever been in a band knows how hard it can be to reach consensus, especially after the band has called it quits. But in this age of collaborative fundraising, would it be so difficult to use a tool like GoFundMe or Kickstarter to help SST artists reclaim the rights to their music? Would fans contribute funds today for a chance to purchase a reissue of their favorite SST record tomorrow?

Fans have a tendency to forgive and forget, which often works in favor of transgressors who go underground for a while and reemerge with a new story to sell. To its credit, SST has never tried to rebrand itself, but there's still plenty of time for the label to begin a new chapter in its history. It would be simple for SST to restore the rights to the music it has no intention of releasing, but it would require considerably more effort to make things right with the bands that continue to generate income for the label. It could be done, perhaps with the assistance of third-party mediators. While there are many musicians who are angry, bewildered, and upset by the label's lack of cooperation and transparency over the years, there are many more who are genuinely grateful to have had the opportunity to work with SST and to be a part of its story. Virtually all of them would love to sit down with the head of the label to talk about the past, present, and future.

It doesn't have to end like this. One suspects that for most people it would take only a handful of successful reissue campaigns for SST to redeem the sins of its past, restore its reputation, and ensure its legacy. Or the label could continue on its present course as a third-rate record mill and T-shirt manufacturer, a cut-rate imitation of corporations SST used to ridicule.

When it comes to the end of SST, which Ginn will emerge: the bitter entrepreneur who uses the courts like a weapon or the visionary musician who nurtured the dreams of so many artists and changed the course of rock and roll?

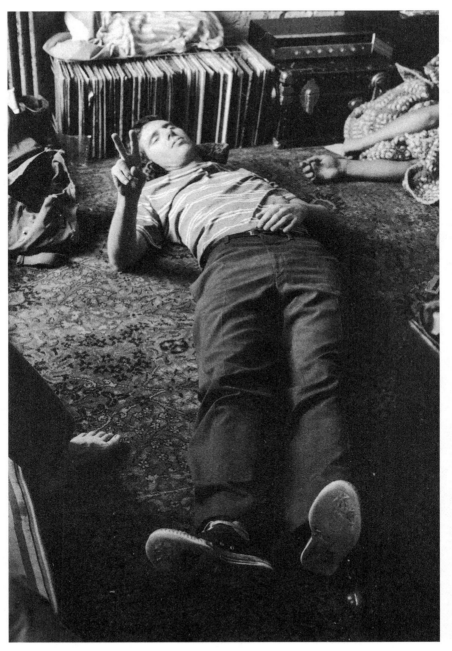

Greg Ginn in 1981. Photo by SPOT.

ACKNOWLEDGMENTS

Corporate Rock Sucks: The Rise & Fall of SST Records is a story about a record label. By using books, newspaper and magazine articles, interviews in fanzines, and interviews that I conducted, I have attempted to tell a story that acknowledges the work done by others and opens the door to future obsessives.

Corporate Rock Sucks represents the final installment of an unlikely trilogy that began with a collaboration with Keith Morris on his memoir *My Damage* and continued with Bad Religion's narrative history *Do What You Want.* Without Keith Morris, Greg Graffin, Brett Gurewitz, Jay Bentley, and Brian Baker, I never would have had the opportunity to write this book. Thank-you to Joshua Bodwell for putting me on the path and to Scott Crawford, Paul Rachman, and Bobby Schayer, who convinced me it was a journey worth taking. Again, without the blessing of Keith Morris, this project never would have gotten off the ground.

Extra special thanks go to my agent, Peter McGuigan, who somehow sold this project at a time when some were privately wondering whether the global economy was on the verge of collapse. (OK, it was me.) People will tell you that corporate publishing sucks just as hard as its counterpart in the music industry, but working with Ben Schafer on three successive books—all about LA punk—has been extremely rad. I'm also indebted in no particular order to Quinn Fariel, Kristin Flinn, Fred Francis, Michael Giarratano, Carrie Napolitano, John Pelosi, Amy Quinn, Carrie Watterson, Timothy O'Donnell, Thomas Mis, Melissa Mathlin, and everyone at Hachette Book Group.

There is plenty of room for further study of SST Records, which is demonstrated with each new episode of the *You Don't Know Mojack* podcast, whose archives are a treasure trove of SST-related arcana. If this book is at all compelling, it's because of generous contributions from the following: Dan Adams, Chris Ashford, Andy Batwinas, Robert Becerra, David Benson, Derrick Bostrom, Greg Cameron, Joe Carducci, Jenny Cohl, Edward Colver, Anthony Countey, Lisa Fancher, Ray Farrell, Steve Fisk, Brett Gurewitz, Bill Hein, Wes Hein, Rob Holzman, Craig Ibarra, David O. Jones, Linda Kite, Mark Lanegan, Wild Don Lewis, Brian Long, Vitus Mataré, Dave Markey, Cindy Mora, Keith Morris, Mugger, David Nolte, Joe Nolte, Ed O'Bryan, Brant Palko, Archie Patterson, Bruce Pavitt, Raymond Pettibon, Mark Pickerel, Paul Rachman, Jack Rivera, Eugene Robinson, Ryan Rodier, Jordan Schwartz, Daniel Spector, Spot, Bill Stevenson, Stuart Swezey, Kim Thayil, Jim Thomson, Dave Travis, and Niko Wenner.

When I imagined *Corporate Rock Sucks*, it was my hope that it not look, well, corporate. Thanks to the talent and skill of the following photographers who brought these pages to life: Linda Aronow, Alison Braun, Edward Colver, Fred Hammer, Wild Don Lewis, Naomi Petersen Photography by Chris Petersen Images / Punk Life LLC All Rights Reserved, Emma Porter Photography, Paul Rachman, and the incomparable Spot.

For editorial oversight, I turned to a pair of veritable punk rock encyclopedias: Mike Fournier and Todd Taylor (*Razorcake* por vida!). Joe O'Brien played the role of cranky Gen Xer with considerable restraint. The indispensable Amanda Johnston, as always, saved me from embarrassment in a thousand different ways. *Corporate Rock Sucks* also benefitted from hundreds of recommendations from friends, associates, and strangers on the internet who pointed me to where I needed to go. Whether they know it or not, I am also grateful to Evan Fay Earle of the Division of Rare and Manuscript Collections at Cornell University, Paul Hilcoff, Brad Knetl, Ian MacKaye, Ben Merlis, Ryan Richardson, James Sinks, Hank Shteamer, and Zack Wentz. It goes without saying all errors are my own. If you have any comments about the content of *Corporate Rock Sucks*, send a message to corproxsux@gmail.com.

Although I started working on *Corporate Rock Sucks* in the spring of 2019, it was written during the COVID-19 pandemic in 2020 and 2021. While the isolation made it an ideal time to lose myself in old records and zines, it was a challenging time for my family. I'm immensely grateful for my wife, Nuvia, and my daughter, Annie, for granting me the space to work on this book. They were a daily reminder that while the story of SST has many twists and turns, at the heart of it there is some real magic.

SST DISCOGRAPHY

01	Black Flag	*Nervous Breakdown*	EP
02	Minutemen	*Paranoid Time*	EP
03	Black Flag	*Jealous Again*	EP
04	Minutemen	*The Punch Line*	LP
05	Black Flag	"Six Pack"	single
06	Saccharine Trust	*Paganicons*	LP
07	Black Flag	*Damaged*	LP
08	Overkill	"Hell's Getting Hotter"	single
09	Meat Puppets	*Meat Puppets*	LP
10	Stains	*Stains*	LP
11	Würm	"I'm Dead"	single
12	Black Flag	"TV Party"	single
13	Various Artists	*The Blasting Concept*	comp
14	Minutemen	*What Makes a Man Start Fires?*	LP
15	Black Flag	*Everything Went Black*	comp
16	Minutemen	*Buzz or Howl Under the Influence of Heat*	LP
17	Dicks	*Kill from the Heart*	LP
18	Subhumans	*No Wishes, No Prayers*	LP
19	Meat Puppets	*Meat Puppets II*	LP
20	Hüsker Dü	*Metal Circus*	EP
21	Black Flag	*The First Four Years*	comp
22	Saint Vitus	*Saint Vitus*	EP
23	Black Flag	*My War*	LP

024	Saccharine Trust	*Surviving You, Always*	LP
025	Hüsker Dü	"Eight Miles High"	single
026	Black Flag	*Family Man*	LP
027	Hüsker Dü	*Zen Arcade*	2LP
028	Minutemen	*Double Nickels on the Dime*	2LP
029	Black Flag	*Slip It In*	LP
030	Black Flag	*Live '84*	LP
031	Hüsker Dü	*New Day Rising*	LP
032	Minutemen	*My First Bells*	CS
033	D.C. 3	*This Is the Dream*	LP
034	Minutemen	*Project: Mersh*	LP
035	Black Flag	*Loose Nut*	LP
036	October Faction	*October Faction*	LP
037	Black Flag	*The Process of Weeding Out*	LP
038	Overkill	*Triumph of the Will*	LP
039	Meat Puppets	*Up on the Sun*	LP
040	Das Damen	*Das Damen*	EP
041	Würm	*Feast*	LP
042	Saint Vitus	*The Walking Dead*	EP
043	VA	*The Blasting Concept Volume II*	comp
044	Meat Puppets	*In a Car*	EP
045	Black Flag	*In My Head*	LP
046	Saccharine Trust	*Worldbroken*	LP
047	Tom Troccoli's Dog	*Tom Troccoli's Dog*	LP
048	Saccharine Trust	*We Became Snakes*	LP
049	Meat Puppets	*Out My Way*	LP
050	Minuteflag	*Minuteflag*	EP
051	Hüsker Dü	"Makes No Sense at All"	single
052	Saint Vitus	*Hallow's Victim*	LP
053	SWA	*Your Future If You Have One*	LP
054	Angst	*Lite Life*	LP
055	Hüsker Dü	*Flip Your Wig*	LP
056	October Faction	*The Second Factionalization*	LP
057	Painted Willie	*Mind Bowling*	LP
058	The Minutemen	*3-Way Tie (for Last)*	LP
059	Sonic Youth	*EVOL*	LP
060	Black Flag	*Who's Got the 10½?*	LP

061	Gone	Let's Get Real, Real Gone for a Change	LP
062	VA	Lovedolls Superstar	comp
063	D.C. 3	The Good Hex	LP
064	Angst	Angst	EP
065	Bad Brains	I Against I	LP
066	VA	Program: Annihilator	2LP comp
067	Slovenly	Thinking of Empire	LP
068	Minutemen	Ballot Result	LP
069	VA	Chunks	comp
070	VA	The 7 Inch Wonders of the World	comp
071	Leaving Trains	Kill Tunes	LP
072	VA	Desperate Teenage Lovedolls	comp
073	SWA	Sex Doctor	LP
074	Angst	Mending Wall	LP
075	Alter Natives	Hold Your Tongue	LP
076	Paper Bag	Ticket to Trauma	LP
077	Zoogz Rift	Island of Living Puke	LP
078	Always August	Black Pyramid	LP
079	fIREHOSE	Ragin', Full-On	LP
080	Sonic Youth	"Starpower"	single
081	Black Flag	"Annihilate This Week"	single
082	Saint Vitus	Born Too Late	LP
083	D.C. 3	You're Only as Blind as Your Mind Can Be	LP
084	Saccharine Trust	The Sacramental Element	CS comp
085	Painted Willie	Live from Van Nuys	LP
086	Gone	Gone II—but Never Too Gone!	LP
087	Lawndale	Beyond Barbecue	LP
088	Zoogz Rift	Looser Than Clams...a Historical Retrospective (Greatest Hits, Vol. 1)	LP
089	Slovenly	Riposte	LP
090	Divine Horsemen	Middle of the Night	LP
091	Divine Horsemen	Devil's River	LP
092	VA	Cracks in the Sidewalk	comp
093	SWA	XCIII	LP
094	Flesh Eaters	Destroyed by Fire—Greatest Hits	comp
095	Das Damen	Jupiter Eye	LP
096	Sonic Youth	Confusion Is Sex	LP

097	Sonic Youth	*Sonic Youth*	LP
098	Painted Willie	*Upsidedowntown*	LP
099	Zoogz Rift	*Water*	LP
100	Meat Puppets	*Mirage*	LP
101	Tar Babies	*Fried Milk*	LP
102	VA	*No Age: A Compilation of SST Instrumental Music*	2LP comp
103	Opal	*Happy Nightmare Baby*	LP
104	Blind Idiot God	*Blind Idiot God*	LP
105	Screaming Trees	*Other Worlds*	EP
106	Bl'ast	*It's in My Blood!*	LP
107	Painted Willie	*My Fellow Americans*	unreleased
108	Painted Willie	*Painted Willie*	unreleased
109	Universal Congress Of	*Universal Congress Of*	LP
110	Crazy Backwards Alphabet	*Crazy Backwards Alphabet*	LP
111	Angst	*Mystery Spot*	LP
112	Descendents	*ALL*	LP
113	Lee Ranaldo	*From Here⟶Infinity*	LP
114	Leaving Trains	*Fuck*	LP
115	fIREHOSE	*If'n*	LP
116	Blood on the Saddle	*Fresh Blood*	LP
117	H.R.	*Human Rights*	LP
118	Henry Kaiser	*Devil in the Drain*	LP
119	Saint Vitus	*Thirsty and Miserable*	LP
120	Zoogz Rift	*Ipecac*	LP
121	Zoogz Rift	*Interim Resurgence*	LP
122	Zoogz Rift	*Amputees in Limbo*	LP
123	Zoogz Rift	*Idiots on the Miniature Golf Course*	LP
124	Bl'ast	"School's Out"	single
125	Lawndale	*Sasquatch Rock*	LP
126	Treacherous Jaywalkers	*Sunrise*	EP
127	Cruel Frederick	*The Birth of the Cruel*	LP
128	Elliott Sharp	*In the Land of the Yahoos*	LP
129	Elliott Sharp / Soldier String Quartet	*Tessalation Row*	LP
130	Dinosaur Jr	*You're Living All Over Me*	LP
131	fIREHOSE	"Sometimes, Almost Always"	Single

132	Screaming Trees	*Even If and Especially When*	LP
133	Negativland	*Escape from Noise*	LP
134	Sonic Youth	*Sister*	LP
135	Always August	*Largeness with (W)holes*	LP
136	Glenn Phillips Band	*Elevator*	LP
137	Zoogz Rift	*Water II: At Safe Distance*	LP
138	Minutemen	*Post-Mersh, Vol. 1*	comp
139	Minutemen	*Post-Mersh, Vol. 2*	comp
140	The Divine Horsemen	*Snake Handler*	LP
141	Brian Ritchie	*The Blend*	LP
142	Descendents	*Milo Goes to College*	LP
143	Descendents	*I Don't Want to Grow Up*	LP
144	Descendents	*Bonus Fat*	comp
145	Descendents	*Two Things at Once*	comp
146	Sylvia Juncosa	*Nature*	LP
147	Fred Frith & Henry Kaiser	*With Enemies like These, Who Needs Friends?*	comp
148	Bl'ast	*The Power of Expression*	LP
149	Saccharine Trust	*Past Lives*	2LP
150	Meat Puppets	*Huevos*	LP
151	Scott Colby	*Slide of Hand*	LP
152	Dinosaur Jr	*"Little Fury Things"*	single
153	SWA	*"Arroyo"*	single
154	Pat Smear	*RuthenSmear*	LP
155	Sonic Youth	*Master-Dik*	EP
156	D.C. 3	*Vida*	live comp
157	SWA	*Evolution 85–87*	CD comp
158	Pell Mell	*The Bumper Crop*	LP
159	Steve Fisk	*448 Deathless Days*	LP
160	Bad Brains	*Live*	LP
161	Saint Vitus	*Mournful Cries*	LP
162	Sister Double Happiness	*Sister Double Happiness*	LP
163	Descendents	*Liveage!*	LP
164	These Immortal Souls	*Get Lost (Don't Lie)*	LP
165	Minutemen	*Post-Mersh, Vol. 3*	LP
166	Black Flag	*Wasted…Again*	LP

167	Semantics	*Bone of Contention*	LP
168	Ras Michael	*Zion Train*	LP
169	Tar Babies	*No Contest*	LP
170	Paper Bag	*A Land Without Fences*	LP
171	H.R.	*HR Tapes '84–'86*	comp
172	Fred Frith	*The Technology of Tears*	2LP
173	H.R.	"Now You Say"	single
174	Zoogz Rift	*Son of Puke*	CS comp
175	Black Flag	"Louie Louie"	single
176	Divine Horsemen	*Handful of Sand*	EP
177	H.R.	"Keep Out of Reach"	single
178	Painted Willie	*Relics*	comp
179	H.R.	*It's About Luv*	LP
180	Universal Congress Of	*Prosperous and Qualified*	LP
181	Sonic Youth	*Sonic Death*	CD comp
182	Everett Shock	*Ghost Boys*	LP
183	These Immortal Souls	"Marry Me (Lie! Lie!)"	single
184	Zoogz Rift	*Nonentity (Water III: Fan Black Dada)*	LP
185	Alter Natives	*Group Therapy*	LP
186	Brian Ritchie	*Nuclear War*	EP
187	Brian Ritchie	*Atomkrieg*	EP
188	Screaming Trees	*Invisible Lantern*	LP
189	Last	*Confession*	LP
190	Das Damen	*Triskaidekaphobe*	LP
191	Mofungo	*Bugged*	LP
192	Run Westy Run	*Hardly, Not Even*	LP
193	Always August	*Geography*	Mini LP
194	Elliott Sharp / Carbon	*Larynx*	LP
195	Hüsker Dü	*Land Speed Record*	LP
196	Paul Roessler	*Abominable*	LP
197	Trotsky Icepick	*Baby*	LP
198	Henry Kaiser	*Those Who Know History Are Doomed to Repeat It*	LP
199	Run Westy Run	*Run Westy Run*	LP
200	Paper Bag	*Music to Trash*	LP
201	Soundgarden	*Ultramega OK*	LP
202	Brian Ritchie	*Sonic Temple & Court of Babylon*	LP
203	Roger Manning	*Roger Manning*	LP

204	Universal Congress Of	*This Is Mecolodics*	LP
205	Descendents	*Hallraker: Live!*	LP
206	Angst	*Cry for Happy*	LP
207	Treacherous Jaywalkers	*Good Medicine*	LP
208	Elliott Sharp / Carbon	*Monster Curve*	LP
209	Slovenly	*We Shoot for the Moon*	LP
210	Volcano Suns	*Farced*	LP
211	Zoogz Rift	*Murdering Hell's Happy Cretins*	LP
212	Descendents	*Fat*	mini-CD
213	VA	*Program: Annihilator II*	comp
214	Minutemen	*Joy*	mini-CD
215	Grant Hart	*Intolerance*	LP
216	Dinosaur Jr	*Bug*	LP
217	Treacherous Jaywalkers	*La Isla Bonita*	EP
218	Das Damen	*Marshmellow Conspiracy*	EP
219	Grant Hart	*2541*	EP
220	Dinosaur Jr	"Freak Scene"	single
221	Leaving Trains	*Transportational D. Vices*	LP
222	Henry Kaiser	*Re-marrying for Money*	LP
223	Kirk Kelly	*Go Man Go*	LP
224	H.R.	*Singin' in the Heart*	LP
225	Bl'ast	*Take the Manic Ride*	LP
226	Black Flag	"I Can See You"	single
227	Brian Ritchie	*Sun Ra—Man from Outer Space*	LP
228	Bad Brains	*Spirit Electricity (Live)*	mini-CD
229	Paper Bag	*Improvised…My Ass*	LP
230	Last	*Awakening*	LP
231	Soundgarden	"Flower"	single
232	Elliott Sharp / Soldier String Quartet	*Hammer, Anvil, Stirrup*	LP
233	Negativland	*Jam Con '84*	CS comp
234	VA	*Mini Plot*	mini-CD comp
235	fIREHOSE	*fROMOHIO*	LP
236	Tar Babies	*Honey Bubble*	LP

237	Henry Kaiser	*Alternate Versions*	mini-CD
238	SWA	*Winter*	LP
239	Trotsky Icepick	*Poison Summer*	LP
240	Mofungo	*Work*	LP
241	Pell Mell	*Rhyming Guitars*	EP
242	Descendents	*Enjoy!*	LP
243	No Man Is Roger Miller	*Win! Instantly!*	LP
244	Dinosaur Jr	"Just like Heaven"	single
245	Alter Natives	*Buzz*	LP
246	Trotsky Icepick	*El Kabong*	LP
247	Stone by Stone with Chris D.	*I Pass for Human*	LP
248	Screaming Trees	*Buzz Factory*	LP
249	VA	*The Melting Plot*	comp
250	Buffalo Tom	*Buffalo Tom*	LP
251	Zoogz Rift	*Torment*	LP
252	Negativland	*Helter Stupid*	LP
253	Meat Puppets	*Monsters*	LP
254	Trotsky Icepick	*Trotsky Icepick Presents: Danny and the Doorknobs in 'Poison Summer'*	LP
255	Opal	"Rocket Machine"	unreleased CD single
256	H.R.	*Charge*	LP
257	Volcano Suns	*Thing of Beauty*	2LP
259	Descendents	*Somery*	comp
260	Screaming Trees	*Anthology*	comp
262	Grant Hart	*All of My Senses*	LP
263	VA	*Duck and Cover*	comp
264	Flesh Eaters	*Prehistoric Fits Vol. 2*	comp
265	Meat Puppets	*No Strings Attached*	comp
266	Saint Vitus	*Heavier Than Thou*	comp
267	No Man	*Whamon Express*	LP
270	Hüsker Dü	*Eight Miles High / Makes No Sense at All*	EP
271	Leaving Trains	*Sleeping Underwater Survivors*	LP
272	Negativland	*U2*	EP
273	Flesh Eaters	*Dragstrip Riot*	2LP
274	H.R.	*Rock of Enoch*	CD EP

275	Dinosaur Jr	*Fossils*	singles comp (925)
276	VA	*SST Acoustic*	comp
277	Minutemen	*The Politics of Time*	LP
278	Pell Mell	*Flow*	LP
279	Trotsky Icepick	*The Ultraviolet Catastrophe*	LP
281	No Man	*How the West Was Won*	LP
282	SWA	*Volume*	LP
283	Leaving Trains	*Rock 'n' Roll Murder*	LP
284	Leaving Trains	*Loser Illusion Pt. 0*	EP
286	Trotsky Icepick	*Hot Pop Hello*	comp
287	Slovenly	*Highway to Hanno's*	LP
288	Leaving Trains	*The Lump in My Forehead*	LP
290	Cruel Frederick	*We Are the Music We Play*	LP
291	Negativland	*Guns*	EP
292	Flesh Eaters	*Sex Diary of Mr. Vampire*	LP
293	Leaving Trains	*The Big Jinx*	LP
294	Pat Smear	*So You Fell in Love with a Musician...*	LP
295	Trotsky Icepick	*Carpetbomb the Riff*	LP
296	Bazooka	*Perfectly Square*	CD
297	Flesh Eaters	*Crucified Lovers in Woman Hell*	CD EP
298	Hotel X	*A Random History of Avant-Groove*	LP
299	Poindexter Stewart	*College Rock*	EP
300	Gone	*The Criminal Mind*	LP
301	Hotel X	*Residential Suite*	CD
302	Transition.	*Spine*	LP
303	Gone	*Smoking Gun*	EP
304	Hotel X	*Engendered Species*	CD
305	Confront James	*Test One Reality*	CD
306	Gone	*All the Dirt That's Fit to Print*	LP
307	Roger Miller's Exquisite Corpse	*Unfold*	CD
308	Bazooka	*Blowhole*	CD
309	Confront James	*Just Do It*	CD
310	The Muddle	*The Muddle*	CD
311	Leaving Trains	*Drowned and Dragged*	CD EP
313	Gone	*Best Left Unsaid*	LP

314	Confront James	*III Gotten Hatred*	CD
315	Sort of Quartet	*Planet Mamon*	CD
316	Hor	*House*	CD
317	Hotel X	*Ladders*	CD
318	Roger Miller	*Elemental Guitar*	CD
319	Gone	*Damage Control*	EP
320	Mojack	*Merchandising Murder*	CD
321	Fatso Jetson	*Stinky Little Gods*	CD
322	Confront James	*Chemical Exposure*	CD EP
323	Last	*Gin & Innuendoes*	CD
324	Screw Radio	*Talk Radio Violence*	CD
325	Bazooka	*Cigars, Oysters & Booze*	CD
326	Hor	*Slo n' Sleazy*	CD
328	Hotel X	*Uncommon Grounds*	CD
329	Sort of Quartet	*Kiss Me Twice, I'm Schitzo*	CD
330	El Bad	*Bad Motherfucker*	CD
331	Roger Miller	*The Benevolent Disruptive Ray*	CD
332	Sort of Quartet	*Bombas de Amor*	CD
333	Screw Radio	*I'm a Generation X*	CD
334	Leaving Trains	*Favorite Mood Swings*	CD comp
335	Brother Weasel	*Brother Weasel*	CD
336	Bazooka	*Poor Mr. Rock Star*	CD
337	Hotel X	*Routes Music*	CD
338	Leaving Trains	*Smoke Follows Beauty*	CD
340	OXBOW	*Serenade in Red*	CD
341	Fatso Jetson	*Power of Three*	CD
342	Screw Radio	*Best of Screw Radio*	2CD comp
343	Confront James	*Black Bomb Mountain*	CD
344	Gone	*Country Dumb*	CD
345	Killer Tweeker Bees	*The Tweeker Blues*	CD
347	Hor	*A Faster, More Aggressive Hor*	CD
348	El Bad	*Trick or Treat*	CD
349	Binary System	*Live at the Idea Room*	CD
352	Bias	*Model Citizen*	CD
353	Get Me High	*Taming the Underground*	CD
355	Negativland	*Negativ(e)land: Live on Tour*	CD

356	Bazooka	*Sonic Business Environment*	CD
357	Guns, Books, and Tools	*Guns, Books, and Tools*	CD
359	Mojack	*Homebrew*	CD
361	H.R.	*Anthology*	CD
363	Minutemen	*Introducing the Minutemen*	CD
365	Brother Weasel	*Swingin' n Groovin'*	CD
366	Hor	*Bash*	unreleased
367	Mojack	*Rub a Dub*	unreleased
368	Fastgato	*Feral*	unreleased
370	Confront James	*We Are Humored*	unreleased
371	Limey LBC	*Life of Lime*	unreleased
372	Mojack	*Under the Willow Tree*	CD
373	Greg Ginn and the Taylor Texas Corrugators	*Bent Edge*	CD
374	Gone	*The Epic Trilogy*	2CD
375	Jambang	*Connecting*	CD
376	Mojack	*The Metal Years*	CD
377	Greg Ginn and the Taylor Texas Corrugators	*Goof Off Experts*	CD
378	Saint Vitus	*The Walking Dead / Hallow's Victim*	CD comp
379	Jambang	*200 Days in Space*	DVD
380	Greg Ginn and the Taylor Texas Corrugators	*Legends of Williamson County*	CD
381	Hor	*Culture Wars*	CD
382	Mojack	*Hijinks*	CD
383	Greg Ginn and the Royal We	*We Are Amused*	CD
384	Greg Ginn and the Royal We	*"We Are One"*	single
385	Good for You	*Life Is Too Short to Not Hold a Grudge*	LP
386	Greg Ginn and the Royal We	*Fearless Leaders*	LP
387	Mojack	*Car*	CD
388	Good for You	*"Fucked Up"*	single

389	Good for You	*Too!*	2CD
390	Good for You	*Full Serving*	3CD
391	Black Flag	*What The...*	CD
392	Greg Ginn and the Taylor Texas Corrugators	*Gumbo and Holy Water*	CD
393	Hor	*Can't Make It Up*	CD

NOTES

Chapter 1: SST vs. Bomp!

1. De Visé, Daniel. "SST Defies Industry, Defines New Music." *San Diego Union-Tribune,* October 1, 1995.

2. Ginn, Greg. Interview with Hank Shteamer. *Heavy Metal Bebop,* July 2012.

3. Morris, Keith. Interview by Jim Ruland. January 10, 2014.

4. Dukowski, Chuck. Interview with Dave Lang. *Perfect Sound Forever,* May 2007.

5. Spot. Interview by Jim Ruland. January 18, 2021.

6. This letter was reprinted in Ryan Richardson's book *Panic!* in 2018.

7. Grad, David. "Fade to Black: The Rough and Unruly History of Hardcore Legends Black Flag." *Guitar World,* July 1997.

8. Pettibon, Raymond. Interview by Jim Ruland. July 28, 2015.

9. The Germs were cut from the film for instigating a food fight with the audience and were subsequently banned from the Roxy Theatre, but Bobby Pyn (a.k.a. Darby Crash) and Pat Smear can be seen as extras. Ashford left the label on Side 2 blank to avoid possible complications with the film's producers. Unfortunately, the labels were printed on the wrong side and the records had to be re-pressed. This track, food fight and all, can be heard on the Germs album *MIA: The Complete Anthology.*

10. Ashford, Chris. Interview by Jim Ruland. May 16, 2020.

11. Face, Kickboy. Review of "Forming" by the Germs. *Slash,* vol. 1, no. 4, September 1977.

12. Ashford, interview.

13. In Alex Cox's 1984 film *Repo Man,* when Otto goes to visit his parents, the sign on the bus marks the destination as "Edge City."

14. Dewar MacLeod's *Kids of the Black Hole: Punk Rock in Postsuburban California* provides rich historical context for the forces that shaped the landscape Southern California punk rockers would inhabit.

15. Mike Nolte joined the Last first. David was writing songs with Frank Navetta in a very early version of the Descendents before joining the Last in 1978.

16. Nolte, Joe. Interview by Jim Ruland. May 22, 2020.

17. Danielle Faye, the bassist and vocalist with the Zippers, had previously performed in Venus and the Razorblades, the band the infamously sleazy Kim Fowley managed after the Runaways. Nolte wrote the lead sheets for these songs so they could be submitted for copyright purposes.

18. Mataré, Vitus. Interview by Jim Ruland. May 23, 2020.

19. Mataré, interview.

20. Fancher, Lisa. Interview by Jim Ruland. February 12, 2021.

21. Nolte, Joe, interview.

22. Nolte, David. Interview by Jim Ruland. May 27, 2020.

23. Nolte, David, interview.

24. Nolte, David, interview.

25. Nolte, David, interview.

26. Nolte, Joe, interview.

27. Stevenson, Bill. Interview by Jim Ruland. October 24, 2020.

28. Nolte, Joe, interview.

Chapter 2: SST vs. Hollywood

1. *Popular Electronics*, April 1969.

2. *Radio Amateur*, August 1971.

3. Gnerre, Sam. "SST Records Blazes Musical Contrails across the South Bay." *Daily Breeze*, October 27, 2017.

4. Carducci, Joe. *Enter Naomi: SST, L.A. and All That* (Centennial, WY: Redoubt Press, 2007), 85.

5. Carducci, *Enter Naomi*, 86.

6. Pettibon, interview.

7. Ginn, Regis C. (1960). "The Imaginary World Created by Graham Greene" (Unpublished master's thesis, University of Arizona, Tucson, Arizona).

8. Another literary-minded military veteran who moved to the South Bay during the aerospace boom was the author Thomas Pynchon. Pynchon lived for a time in Manhattan Beach and has written about a fictionalized version of the place in his books *Vineland* and *Inherent Vice*. While Ginn was writing his novel in Hermosa Beach, a few blocks away Pynchon was working on his book set after the war, the postmodern classic *Gravity's Rainbow*. Did the two novelists ever bump into each other and chat about their works in progress?

9. Spot, interview.

10. Pettibon, interview.

11. Pettibon, Raymond. *Captive Chains*. 1979.

12. Pettibon, *Captive Chains*.

13. Pettibon, Raymond. Interview with Eric Nelson. *American Suburb X*, January 25, 2015.

14. Nolte, Joe, interview.

15. Dukowski, Chuck. "A History of L.A. Punk Rock." *NO MAG*, 1982.

16. After opening its doors in July 1977, the Masque closed for the first time the day after the Sex Pistols' show at Winterland in January 1978. It reopened at a new location in January 1979 only to shut down again for good in May of that year.

17. Morris, Keith. *My Damage* (New York: DaCapo, 2016), 29.

18. Spot, interview.

19. Grad, "Fade to Black."

20. Dexter, Dave, Jr. "New Talent Behind Success of L.A.'s 'Rebel' Hong Kong Café." *Billboard*, December 8, 1979.

21. Nolte, Joe, interview.

22. Nolte, Joe, interview.

23. Ginn, Greg. Interview with Tim Tonooka. *Ripper* #3, 1980.

24. Nolte, Joe, interview. David Nolte taped Black Flag's performance, and it can be found without too much effort on the internet. "The way I can identify my tape," Nolte said, "is I can hear Bill Stevenson talk to me at one point, and I can hear Jeff Pierce." He believes it's the only recording of the event.

25. Welsh, Kerry. "Manhattan Meets Punks." *Easy Reader*, July 1979.

26. Spot, interview.

27. Welsh, "Manhattan Meets Punks."

28. Nolte, Joe, interview.

29. Ginn, Greg. Interview with Al Kowalewski. *Flipside* #22, December 1980.

30. Morris, Keith. Interview with Jay Babcock. "A 12-Step Program in Self-Reliance: How L.A.'s Hardcore Pioneers Black Flag Made It Through the Early Years." *L.A. Weekly*, June 28, 2001.

31. Spot, interview.

Chapter 3: SST vs. the Media

1. Reyes, Ron. Interview with Jim Lindberg. *Punk Guru*, September 12, 2016.

2. Rettman, Tony. "The Complete Oral History of Legendary Rock-Doc Series 'The Decline of Western Civilization.'" *Vice*, June 10, 2015.

3. Reyes, Ron. *The Decline of Western Civilization*, directed by Penelope Spheeris. 1981.

4. Marcus, Greil. *In the Fascist Bathroom: Punk in Pop Music 1977–1992* (Cambridge, MA: Harvard University Press, 1993), 183.

5. Fancher, interview.

6. Reyes, Ron. Interview with Jim Lindberg.

7. Morris, Keith. Interview with Chris Marlowe. *Damage* #11, December 1980.

8. Bartell, Bill. Quoted in *Lexicon Devil: The Fast Times and Short Life of Darby Crash and the Germs*, by Brendan Mullen with Don Bolles and Adam Parfrey (Los Angeles: Feral House, 2002), 214.

9. Reyes, Ron. Interview with Jim Lindberg.

10. Much of the background information about the Minutemen and Saccharine Trust comes from Craig Ibarra's excellent *A Wailing of a Town: An Oral History of Early San Pedro Punk and More* (San Pedro: END FWY Press, 2015).

11. Watt, Mike. Quoted in Ibarra, *A Wailing of a Town: An Oral History of Early San Pedro Punk and More* (San Pedro: END FWY Press, 2015), 92.

12. The gig was part of Western Front, nine nights of independent music, film, and art with bands from all over the world, including Vancouver's D.O.A. and Belfast's Stiff Little Fingers. Ginn recognized it was an important gig.

13. Mullen, Brendan. *Damage* #7, July 1980.

14. Ginn, Greg. Interview with Tim Tonooka. *Ripper* #3, 1980.

15. Goldstein, Patrick. "Violence Sneaks into Punk Scene." *Los Angeles Times*, June 29, 1980.

16. Ginn, Greg. Interview with Tim Tonooka. *Ripper* #3, 1980.

17. Goldstein, "Violence Sneaks into Punk Scene."

18. Ginn, Greg. Interview with Al Kowalewski.

19. Belsito, Peter, and Bob Davis. *Hardcore California: A History of Punk and New Wave* (San Francisco: Last Gasp, 1983), 46.

20. Dukowski, Chuck. Interview with Eric Davidson. *Please Kill Me*, December 17, 2018.

21. Morris, interview.

22. Jones went by at least two aliases, Rosa Medea and Medea Rosalinda Lack, but on songs cowritten with Ginn, she is credited simply as Medea.

23. Babcock, "A 12-Step Program in Self-Reliance."

24. Prato, Greg. *Too High to Die: Meet the Meat Puppets* (CreateSpace, 2012), 41.

25. Dukowski, Chuck. Interview with Tim Tonooka. *Ripper* #3, 1980.

26. Grad, David. "Everything Went Black: A Complete Oral History." *Punk Planet* #20, September/October 1997.

27. Fancher, interview.

28. Incidentally, when I reached out to Ginn for this book, he responded, "I retired from interviews a long time ago."

29. Ginn, Greg, and Chuck Dukowski. Interview with Steve Stiph, *Outcry* #1, 1980.

30. Ginn, Greg. Interview with Al Kowalewski.

31. Full disclosure, I wrote for *Flipside* beginning in 1995, long past its heyday, until the zine's demise in 2000. I wonder what Al's up to these days. I hope he's doing OK.

32. Dukowski, Chuck. Interview with Steve Stiph. *Outcry* #1, 1980.

33. Ginn, Greg. Interview with Tim Tonooka. *Ripper* #6, 1980.

34. Stevenson, interview.

35. Rivera, Jack. Interview by Jim Ruland, September 30, 2021. When Rivera played drums in the Stains, he went by the name Gilbert Berumen.

36. Becerra, Robert. Interview by Jim Ruland. October 1, 2021.

37. Morris interview.

38. Colver, Edward. Interview by Jim Ruland. September 15, 2020.

39. Ginn, Greg. Interview with Al Kowalewski.

40. Campbell is the subject of one of Colver's best-known photographs: the trio of boots shot at Oki-Dog. The photo was widely published and was later used for the Bad Religion record *80–85*. Campbell's boots are on the left.

41. Cadena, Dez. Interview with Tony Rettman. "Dez Cadena of Black Flag, Misfits, and More on the Fight for His Life." *Vice*, September 3, 2015.

42. Grad, "Everything Went Black."

43. Barrett, Rona. *The Tomorrow Show with Tom Snyder*. NBC Studios, November 10, 1980.

44. Goldstein, Patrick. "Rona, Pin in Cheek, Meets the Punks." *Los Angeles Times*, November 16, 1980.

45. Tucker, Ken. *Los Angeles Herald-Examiner*, July 24, 1981.

46. Spheeris, Penelope. "Mission Possible: Serena Dank." *NO MAG*, 1982.

47. Even though these beach cities sit in different counties and are separated by nearly thirty-five miles of freeway—an hour's drive if you're lucky—the media constantly lumped the two together. This was particularly true of writers from London, New York, and even San Francisco, who tended to view Southern California as one endless beach.

48. Schneider, Mitchell. "The Black Flag Violence Must Stop!" *BAM*, January 30, 1981.

49. After Black Flag, for a hardcore band to be taken seriously, it needed a name, a type treatment, and a logo.

50. Black Flag. *Everything Went Black*. SST Records. 1982.

51. Gates also had a tendency to make inflammatory and racist remarks. In May 1982, Gates made awful statements about Blacks being more genetically disposed to dying from a chokehold because of weak vascular systems. Sadly, this issue hasn't gone away, and the LAPD remains one of the most lethal police departments in the nation.

52. Ginn, Greg. Interview with Tim Tonooka. *Ripper* #6, 1980.

53. Bale, Jeff. Review of *Nervous Breakdown*. *Damage*, July 1980. Incidentally, this issue of *Damage* features reviews of Polish cinema and Japanese Samurai films by a writer named Joe Carducci, who would play a large role in the SST story.

54. Dukowski, Chuck. Interview with Dave Lang. *Perfect Sound Forever*, May 2007.

Chapter 4: SST vs. MCA

1. Ginn, Greg. *The Coolest Retard*. December 13, 1980.

2. Randy, Black. Quoted in Mullen, *Lexicon Devil*, 211.

3. Spot, interview.

4. Watt, Mike. Quoted in Ibarra, *A Wailing of a Town*, 97.

5. Watt, Mike. Quoted in Ibarra, *A Wailing of a Town*, 97.

6. The image would be used in a flyer for a Black Flag show at the Ukrainian Hall on December 10, 1982, with D.O.A., the Descendents, and—fittingly—the Minutemen.

7. Henley was Darby Crash's on-again, off-again lover. Tatu was a Hollywood native and one of the punks interviewed in Penelope Spheeris's *The Decline of Western Civilization*.

8. Mugger. Interview by Jim Ruland. September 26, 2020.

9. Mugger, interview.

10. Mugger, interview.

11. Dukowski, Chuck. Interview with Tony Lombardi. *Capitol Crisis* #5, May 1981.

12. This notion of purity in punk, hardcore in particular, led to the creation of unwritten rules that governed acceptable wardrobe, length of hair, and style of play. This rubbed many punks the wrong way, particularly those who could no longer find places to play.

13. Amezquita, Jesse. Interview with Jimmy Alvarado. "An Oral History of East Los Angeles's First Punk Band." *Razorcake* #67, April 1, 2011.

14. Becerra, interview.

15. Rivera, interview.

16. Becerra, interview.

17. Viscarra, Ceasar. Interview with Jimmy Alvarado. "An Oral History of East Los Angeles's First Punk Band."

18. Rivera, Jack (as Gilbert Berumen). Interview with Jimmy Alvarado. "An Oral History of East Los Angeles's First Punk Band."

19. Rivera, Jack. Interview with Jimmy Alvarado.

20. Amezquita, Jesse. Interview with Jimmy Alvarado.

21. Spot, interview.

22. Baiza, Joe. Quoted in Ibarra, *A Wailing of a Town*, 120.

23. Holzman, Rob. Interview by Jim Ruland. September 29, 2021.

24. Other members of the Jetsons included Tom Watson, who would go on to play in Toxic Shock and Slovenly; and Dennis Jarvis, who is the founder of Spyder Surfboards in Hermosa Beach.

25. Holzman, interview. "A Christmas Cry" was released on the New Alliance comp *Chunks* and as a promotional single for SST.

26. SST would reissue "Louie Louie" (SST 175) in 1987.

27. Marsh, Dave. *Louie Louie* (New York: Hyperion, 1993).

28. Morris, interview.

29. Spot, interview.

30. This, too, was an echo from the past: the day before the Kingsmen recorded "Louie Louie," the band played the song for ninety minutes straight during a dance marathon.

31. Spot, interview.

32. Carducci, *Enter Naomi*, 44.

33. Mugger. Interview with Richie Charles. "Scoring a Three with Mugger." *Vice*, November 1, 2011.

34. Turgeon, Dave. Interview with Michael Patrick Welch. "Dee Slut Is Not Mad at Henry Rollins." *Vice*, August 27, 2014.

35. Turgeon, Dave. Interview with Michael Patrick Welch.

36. Rollins, Henry. Interview with Ally Schweitzer. "Henry Rollins at the Smithsonian: 'Rock Is Dead—to Gene Simmons.'" WAMU, October 16, 2014.

37. Carducci, *Enter Naomi*, 18.

38. Carducci, interview by Jim Ruland. December 2020.

39. Carducci, Joe. Quoted in Prato, *Too High to Die*, 38.

40. Cooper, Aimee. *Coloring Outside the Lines: A Punk Rock Memoir* (Texas: Rowdy's Press, 2003), 96.

41. Spot, interview.

42. Babcock, "A 12-Step Program in Self-Reliance."

43. Rollins, Henry. Interview with Jacob McMurray. *Taking Punk to the Masses: From Nowhere to Nevermind* (Seattle, WA: Fantagraphics Books, 2011), 37.

44. Rollins, Henry. Interview with Will Welch. "Fifty Years of L.A. Rock: A Punk Rock Reunion." GQ, March 16, 2009.

45. Parker, James. *Turned On* (New York: Cooper Square Press, 2000), 77.

46. Spot, interview.

47. Colver, interview.

48. Mugger, interview.

49. Cadena, Dez. Quoted in Parker, *Turned On*, 79–80.

50. Rollins, Henry. *Get in the Van: On the Road with Black Flag* (Los Angeles: 2.13.61 Publications, 2004), 28.
51. Grad, "Fade to Black."
52. Pettibon, interview.
53. Colver, interview.
54. Bergamo, Al. *Los Angeles Times.* September 27, 1981.
55. Ginn, Greg. *Action Now.* February 1982.

Chapter 5: SST vs. Unicorn

1. Prato, *Too High to Die,* 28.
2. Bostrom, Derrick. Quoted in Prato, *Too High to Die,* 20.
3. Bostrom, Derrick. Interview by Jim Ruland. March 16, 2021.
4. Bostrom, interview.
5. Kirkwood, Cris. Quoted in Prato, *Too High to Die,* 28–29.
6. Spot, interview.
7. Details about the recording session supplied by Joe Carducci. Interview by Jim Ruland. December 2020.
8. Bostrom, Derrick. Interview with Chris, Scott, Kelly, and Helen. *Flipside* #29, December 1981.
9. Carducci, interview.
10. Carducci, interview.
11. Carducci, Joe. Quoted in Ibarra, *A Wailing of a Town,* 120.
12. Holzman, interview.
13. Mugger, interview. Mugger maintains that Rob Henley wrote the lyrics to "Walking Down the Street."
14. Holzman, interview.
15. Holzman, interview.
16. Stevenson, interview.
17. Stevenson, interview.
18. Stevenson, interview.
19. Ginn, Greg. Interview with Dave Markey, Alan Gilbert, and Jordan Schwartz. *We Got Power* #4, September 1982.
20. Holzman, interview. Johnson wasn't the first choice. Black Flag asked Jack Rivera to join the band for the spring tour. However, Rivera turned them down because his girlfriend was pregnant.
21. Ginn, Greg. Interview with Boz and David Camp. *Suburban Relapse* #6, May 20, 1982.
22. Holzman, interview.
23. Mugger, interview.
24. Watt, Mike. Quoted in Ibarra, *A Wailing of a Town,* 106.
25. Watt, Mike. Quoted in Ibarra, *A Wailing of a Town,* 109.
26. Carducci, Joe. Quoted in Prato, *Too High to Die,* 40.
27. Davis, Wyn. Quoted in "Total Access Recording: Evolving with the Business," by Barbara Schultz. MixOnline.com, April 27, 2010.

28. Mugger, interview.
29. Ginn, Greg. Interview with *Smash! Smash!* #4, 1983.
30. Johnny "Bob" Goldstein was Keith Morris's nickname.
31. Watt, Mike. *Spiels of a Minuteman* (Montreal: L'Oie de Cravan, 2003), 106. Please note Watt's inconsistent and unorthodox usage of capital letters in this book.
32. Rollins, *Get in the Van*, 192.
33. Parales, Jay. "Hardcore Rock: 2 Bands." *New York Times*, March 11, 1983.
34. Ginn, Greg. Quoted in McMurray, *Taking Punk to the Masses*, 13.
35. Parker, *Turned On*, 106.
36. Court of Appeal of the State of California Second Appellate District. Petition for a Writ of Habeas Corpus and Stay in re. Gregory Regis Ginn. November 29, 1983.
37. Grad, "Everything Went Black."
38. Cohan, Brad. "FLAG's Chuck Dukowski Pretty Much Confirms Greg Ginn Is a Total Douchebag." *Village Voice*, September 18, 2013.
39. Heylin, Clinton. *Babylon's Burning: From Punk to Grunge* (New York: Viking, 2007), 550.
40. Carducci, *Enter Naomi*, 51.
41. Parker, *Turned On*, 124.
42. Carducci, interview.
43. Carducci, *Enter Naomi*, 175.

Chapter 6: SST vs. Hardcore

1. Earles, Andrew. *Hüsker Dü: The Story of the Noise-Pop Pioneers Who Launched Modern Rock* (Minneapolis: Voyageur Press, 2010), 48.
2. Hart, Grant. Quoted in "SST Defies Industry, Defines New Music," by Daniel de Visé. *San Diego Union-Tribune*, October 1, 1995.
3. Carducci, Joe. Quoted in "A Tale of Twin Cities: Hüsker Dü, The Replacements and the Rise and Fall of the '80s Minneapolis Scene." *Magnet Magazine*, July 12, 2005.
4. Katzman, Terry. Quoted in "A Tale of Twin Cities."
5. Katzman, Terry. *Sweet Potato*, November 26, 1980.
6. Mould, Bob. Interview with Jed Hresko and Marc. *Smash!* #5, July 1983.
7. Norton, Greg. Quoted in "Inside Hüsker Dü's Early-Years Box Set Treasure Trove," by Kory Grow. *Rolling Stone*, September 5, 2017.
8. Hazelmyer, Tom. Quoted in "A Tale of Twin Cities."
9. Hart, Grant. Quoted in McMurray, *Taking Punk to the Masses*, 75.
10. Carducci, Joe. *New Vulgate* #75, December 8, 2010.
11. Pettibon, interview.
12. Stevenson, interview.
13. Stevenson, interview.
14. The band's name came from the Black Sabbath song "St. Vitus Dance." The title is derived from an inexplicable mania for dancing that spread across Europe during the Middle Ages.
15. Carducci, *New Vulgate* #75.
16. Spot, interview.

17. Stevenson, interview.

18. Rauzi, Robin. "In So Many Words." *Los Angeles Times*, April 4, 1996.

19. Kubernik, Harvey. *The Blasting Concept*. SST Records, 1983.

20. Kubernik, *The Blasting Concept*.

21. For his written work, Dukowski generally preferred Charles to Chuck, much to the annoyance of the poet Charles Bukowski.

22. Rollins, Henry. Interview with *Last Rites* #7, 1984.

23. Rollins, *Get in the Van*, 120.

24. Rollins, Henry. Interview with Lee Randall. Bookslut.com, October 31, 2011.

25. Lewis, Wild Don. Interview by Jim Ruland. November 21, 2020.

26. Becerra, interview.

27. Floyd, Gary, with David Ensminger. *Please Bee Nice: My Life Up 'til Now* (CreateSpace, 2014), 4.

28. Blashill, Pat. *Texas Is the Reason: The Mavericks of Lone Star Punk* (Callicoon, NY: Bazillion Points, 2020), 141.

29. According to Carducci, during Spot's absence the members of Bad Brains arrived at SST headquarters and announced their intention to record an album with him. Because Spot wasn't there and studio time hadn't been booked, nothing was recorded. Carducci told the story on the air on WMFU on October 5, 2012. Imagine an alternate universe where Spot is present, Total Access is available, and Bad Brains records *Rock for Light* for SST. What if this record comes out on SST in the spring of 1984 and Bad Brains joins Black Flag on the My War Tour? In this alternate future, Kurt Cobain doesn't see the Meat Puppets play and draws inspiration from Bad Brains instead. 😎

30. Spot, interview.

31. This studio was also connected with Unicorn and was located *in* Santa Monica several miles west of Unicorn's studio *on* Santa Monica Boulevard.

32. Albini, Steve. "Hüsker Dü? Only Their Hairdresser Knows for Sure." *Matter*, September 1983.

33. Mould, Bob. Interview with *Smash! Smash!* #6, 1983.

34. Hart, Grant. Interview with *Smash! Smash!* #6, 1983.

35. Mould, Bob. Interview with *Smash! Smash!* #5, 1983.

36. Mould, Bob. Interview with Gerard Cosloy, *Conflict* #34. 1984.

37. Lee, Craig. "Hüsker Dü a Product of Minneapolis' Rock Scene." *Los Angeles Times*, December 15, 1984.

38. Mould, Bob. "Eight Miles Over Minneapolis." *New Musical Express*, September 15, 1984.

39. Spot, interview.

40. Jones, David O. Interview by Jim Ruland. October 28, 2020. Magnolia Thunderpussy had an unusual relationship with SST. After playing with Black Flag at a generator show organized by Dave Travis, Jones dropped off a copy of its demo at SST. The band was rejected by Carducci, only to be offered a contract a year later by Ginn, but Magnolia Thunderpussy broke up before recording an album for SST.

41. Hüsker Dü. *Zen Arcade*. SST Records, 1984.

42. Spot, interview.

43. Ginn, Greg. Quoted in McMurray, *Taking Punk to the Masses*, 37.

44. Stevenson, interview.

45. Grad, "Everything Went Black."

46. Swezey, Stuart. Interview by Jim Ruland. January 4, 2021.

47. Carducci, interview.

48. Carducci, Joe. Quoted in Parker, *Turned On*, 124.

49. Roessler, Kira. Interview with Ryan Leach. *Razorcake* #26, June/July 2005.

50. Stevenson, interview.

51. Mugger, interview.

52. Rollins, *Get in the Van*, 115.

53. Ginn, Greg. Interview with Lisa Mitchell and Alex Gordon, Radio Tokyo, July 11, 1984.

54. Watt, Mike. Interview with Michael T. Fournier. *Double Nickels on the Dime* (New York: Bloomsbury, 2007), 10.

55. Watt, Mike. Interview with Michael T. Fournier. Hootpage.com, January 3, 2006. Note, this was the interview that Fournier conducted for his 2007 book *Double Nickels on the Dime*. The interview took place on the date indicated and was posted sometime after that.

56. Watt, Mike. Interview with Michael T. Fournier. Hootpage.com.

57. While touring with Black Flag in March 1983, Watt went with Rollins to visit the singer's mother and plucked Richard Ellmann's study of the novel from her bookshelf. Watt read the book and wrote positively about the experience in his journal.

58. Lau, Andrew K. "Mike Watt Spiels about James Joyce." *No Recess!*, June 15, 2018.

59. Fournier, *Double Nickels on the Dime*, 40.

60. Bostrom, interview.

61. Loder, Kurt. Review of *Meat Puppets II*. *Rolling Stone*, August 24, 1984.

62. Sasfy, Joe. "Black Flag Flags, Meat Puppets Mature." *Washington Post*, April 6, 1984.

63. Sasfy, "Black Flag Flags, Meat Puppets Mature."

64. Rollins, Henry. Quoted in Prato, *Too High to Die*, 76.

65. Rollins, *Get in the Van*, 118.

66. Bostrom, interview.

67. Bostrom, interview.

68. Kirkwood, Curt. Quoted in Prato, *Too High to Die*, 88.

69. Troccoli, Tom. Interview with Mark Prindle. MarkPrindle.com, 2006.

70. Grad, "Fade to Black."

71. Four of SST's groundbreaking albums of 1984—*My War*, *Meat Puppets II*, *Zen Arcade*, and *Double Nickels on the Dime*—were recorded by a trio. Do you think Kurt Cobain was paying attention?

72. Arm, Mark. Quoted in McMurray, *Taking Punk to the Masses*, 79.

73. Thayil, Kim. Interview by Jim Ruland. March 31, 2021.

74. Pavitt, Bruce. Interview by Jim Ruland. February 24, 2021.

75. Bostrom, interview.

76. Stevenson, interview.

77. Bostrom, interview.

Chapter 7: SST vs. College Radio

1. Britt, Russ. "Van Flips; S.P. Musician Dies." *News-Pilot*, December 28, 1985.
2. Roessler, Kira. Interview with Anthony Allen Begnal. *No Echo*, January 17, 2020.
3. Travis, Dave. Interview by Jim Ruland. January 29, 2021.
4. Stevenson, interview.
5. O'Donoghue and Rollins would remain friends, and when he became the host of his own radio show at KCRW in 2009, he credited O'Donoghue as an influence and muse.
6. Mould, Bob. *Zen Arcade*. SST Records, 1984.
7. Mould, Bob, with Michael Azerrad. *See a Little Light: The Trail of Rage and Melody* (New York: Little, Brown, 2011), 95.
8. Riley, Dave. "Will These Guys Be the Year's Top Pop Wimps?" *Matter*, July/August 1984.
9. Hart, Grant. Interview. *Hard Times* #1, August 1984.
10. Riley, "Will These Guys Be the Year's Top Pop Wimps?"
11. Mould with Azerrad, *See a Little Light*, 95.
12. Lee, Craig. "Hüsker Dü a Product of Minneapolis' Rock Scene." *Los Angeles Times*, December 15, 1984.
13. Gates made his occupation of South Central permanent, sowing the seeds for LAPD's Operation Hammer in 1987 and the LA Uprising in 1992.
14. Grad, "Fade to Black."
15. Carducci, interview.
16. Carducci, interview.
17. Baiza, Joe. Interview with David Lang. *Perfect Sound Forever*, July 2004.
18. Bostrom, interview.
19. Rose, Andy. "SST Bands Charged Through 'the Tour.'" *There's Something Hard in There*, August 8, 2012.
20. In the essay, Felton is spelled "Phelton," presumably to prevent fans from finding it. The 7-Eleven is still there.
21. Hart, Grant. Interview with Tom Novak. *Non*Stop Banter*, September/October 1985.
22. Collins, Cyn. *Complicated Fun: The Birth of Minneapolis Punk and Indie Rock, 1974–1984* (St. Paul: Minnesota Historical Society Press, 2017), 280.
23. Mould, Bob. Interview with Jack Rabid. *Rockpool Newsletter*. April 8, 1985.
24. Gill, Andy. "The Thrash Aesthetic." *New Musical Express*, June 8, 1985.
25. Norton, Greg. Interview. *Alternative Focus* #3, 1985.
26. Berg, Karin. Quoted in "A Tale of Twin Cities."
27. Mould, Bob. Interview with Jack Rabid.
28. Carducci, Joe, and Grant Hart. Quoted in "A Tale of Twin Cities."
29. Interview with Ray Farrell by *Dagger Zine*, January 19, 2020.
30. Cadena, Dez. Interview with Tony Rettman. "Dez Cadena of Black Flag, Misfits, and More on the Fight for His Life." *Vice*, September 3, 2015.
31. Turner, Gregg. Review of the Meat Puppets' *Up on the Sun*. *Creem*, July 1985. Romilar was a popular over-the-counter cough suppressant.
32. Farrell, Ray. Interview by Jim Ruland. January–February 2021.

33. Farrell, interview.

34. Farrell, interview.

35. Stevenson, interview.

36. Grad, "Everything Went Black."

37. Cameron, Greg. Interview with Brant Palko and Ryan Rodier. *You Don't Know Mojack* #157, December 18, 2020.

38. Cameron, Greg. Interview with Palko and Rodier.

39. Baiza, Joe. Interview with Amy Kelly. Ultimate Guitar.com, July 16, 2009.

40. Harrington, Richard. *Washington Post*, March 23, 1987.

Chapter 8: SST vs. Death

1. The gratitude went both ways. In the early days of SST, a cash order might mean the difference between whether whoever was fulfilling orders ate lunch that day.

2. To put this number in perspective, that's more copies than *Zen Arcade* and *Double Nickels on the Dime* combined sold in 1984.

3. Goldberg, Michael. "Punk Lives." *Rolling Stone*, July/August 1985.

4. Carducci, Joe. Interview with Andrew Katsikas. *High Hat*, Fall 2006.

5. Goldberg, "Punk Lives."

6. Leviton, Mark. *BAM*, March 29, 1985.

7. Kite, Linda. Interview by Jim Ruland. November 18, 2020.

8. Kite, interview.

9. Goldberg, "Punk Lives."

10. Dukowski, Chuck. Interview with Eric Davidson.

11. Cameron, interview.

12. Cameron, interview.

13. Carducci, interview.

14. SWA. *Your Future If You Have One*. SST Records. 1985.

15. Cameron, interview.

16. Farrell, interview.

17. Roessler, Kira. Interview with Greg Cameron, n.d., SoundGirls.org.

18. Mugger, interview.

19. Cameron, interview. A second sticker had to be created for Ginn's liner notes on the back cover. These issues were fixed in subsequent versions.

20. Mugger, interview.

21. Parker, *Turned On*, 233.

22. Carducci, Joe. Interview with Brad Cohan. *Village Voice*, October 12, 2012.

23. Ginn, Greg. Interview with Jarrod Dicker. *Stay Thirsty*, March 2010.

24. Ginn, Greg. Interview with Hank Shteamer.

25. Stevenson, interview.

26. Black Flag. *The Process of Weeding Out*. SST Records. 1985.

27. Mugger, interview.

28. Watt, Mike. Interview with Jeff Schwier. Varmintcong.com, April 1988.

29. Kite, interview.

30. Kite, interview.

31. Rollins, *Get in the Van*, 258.

32. Watt, *Spiels of a Minuteman*, 30.

33. Carducci, *Enter Naomi*, 199.

34. Watt, *Spiels of a Minuteman*, 24.

35. Watt, *Spiels of a Minuteman*, 22.

36. Kite, interview.

37. Roessler, Kira. Interview with Ryan Leach.

38. Watt, *Spiels of a Minuteman*, 12.

39. Nicks, Kara. Interview with Stacy Russo. *We Were Going to Change the World* (Solano Beach, CA: Santa Monica Press, 2017), 140.

40. Nicks, Kara. Interview with Stacy Russo, 141.

41. Cain, Sim. Interview with Amy Yates Wuelfing and Steven DiLodovico. *No Slam Dancing, No Stage Diving, No Spikes*, 164.

42. Cain, Sim. Interview with Amy Yates Wuelfing and Steven DiLodovico, 164.

43. When Markey was sixteen, he directed *The Omenous*, a horror parody with his friends Jordan and Jennifer Schwartz and kids from the neighborhood. This marked the film debut of Peter Ivers of *New Wave Theatre*.

44. SST released the soundtracks for both films in 1986.

45. Markey, Dave. Interview by Jim Ruland. January 4, 2021.

46. Rollins, *Get in the Van*, 269.

47. Cain, Sim. Interview with Amy Yates Wuelfing and Steven DiLodovico, 164.

48. Ginn, Greg. Interview with Amy Yates Wuelfing and Steven DiLodovico. *No Slam Dancing, No Stage Diving, No Spikes*, 164.

49. Cain, Sim. Interview with Amy Yates Wuelfing and Steven DiLodovico, 164.

50. Rollins, *Get in the Van*, 266.

51. Markey, Dave. "The Painted Willie Experience." WeGotPowerFilms.com. Accessed July 30, 2021.

52. Carducci, interview.

53. Carducci, interview.

54. The notes were finally reprinted, along with the artwork, in Joe Carducci's reissue of *Rock and the Pop Narcotic*.

55. Cameron, interview.

56. Markey, "The Painted Willie Experience."

Chapter 9: SST vs. New York

1. Jenifer, Darryl. Interview with Andrew Sacher. *Brooklyn Vegan*, March 2, 2021.

2. Andersen, Mark, and Mark Jenkins. *Dance of Days: Two Decades of Punk in the National Capital* (New York: Akashic Books, 2009), 40.

3. Andersen and Jenkins, *Dance of Days*, 56.

4. In interviews over the years, members of Bad Brains have expressed regret over their intolerance, which they attributed to their overzealous adherence to Rastafarianism, which could be even more homophobic than fundamental Christianity.

5. While Williams was out on tour with Bad Brains, Parsons used the studio to record the Beastie Boys' *Polly Wog Stew*.

6. Countey, Anthony. Interview by Jim Ruland. February 20, 2021.

7. Countey, interview.

8. Countey, interview.

9. Countey, interview.

10. Countey, interview.

11. Abrams, Howie, and James Lathos. *Finding Joseph I: An Oral History of H.R. from Bad Brains* (New York: Post Hill Press, 2019), 25.

12. H.R. originally wanted to call the label Jah Youth Records.

13. H.R. Interview with Jimi Riley. *WDC Period* #9, May 1985.

14. H.R. Interview with Jimi Riley.

15. Countey, interview.

16. Countey, interview.

17. Countey recalled the figure was approximately $7,500. Abrams and Lathos, *Finding Joseph I*, 155.

18. Farrell, interview.

19. Foege, Alec. *Confusion Is Next: The Sonic Youth Story* (New York: St. Martin's Press, 1994), 71.

20. Foege, *Confusion Is Next*, 50.

21. Tiers, Wharton. Interview with Brant Palko and Ryan Rodier. *You Don't Know Mojack* #155, December 4, 2020.

22. Ranaldo, Lee. *jrnls80s* (New York: Soft Skull Press, 1998), 164.

23. Browne, David. *Goodbye 20th Century: A Biography of Sonic Youth* (Philadelphia: Da Capo, 2008), 113–14.

24. Cotner, David. "Musicians Remember the Late Michael Sheppard, L.A.'s Champion of the Weird." *L.A. Weekly*, March 22, 2016.

25. Noble, Peter L. "Tales from Death Valley." *Melody Maker*, May 11, 1985.

26. Lunch, Lydia. Quoted in Foege, *Confusion Is Next*, 135–36.

27. Swezey, interview.

28. Bien-Kahn, Joseph. "How a 20-Year-Old Punk Kid and the Minutemen Pioneered Mainstream Music Festival Culture." *Vice*, September 12, 2015.

29. Browne, *Goodbye 20th Century*, 144.

30. Although the latter two tracks were recorded in March 1986 by Bisi, "Burnin' Up" was recorded by Mike Watt, Greg Ginn, and Ethan James at Radio Tokyo a few months later. These songs would be released on New Alliance Records with sleeve art that was credited to Kim Gordon and marketing by SST Records. However, the art was actually a screen print of a *New York Post* cover that Andy Warhol created as a wedding gift for Madonna and Sean Penn. Regarded as a novelty in the United States, "Into the Groove(y)" was a surprise dance club hit in the UK.

31. For instance, finding a photograph of the band from this period where at least one member isn't wearing sunglasses indoors is next to impossible.

32. The song ends with Moore uttering a line about a meter man that will sound familiar to Minutemen fans.

33. This song would eventually be released as a single (SST 080) backed with a cover of "Bubble Gum," by Kim Fowley and features a guest appearance by Watt. Although "Bubblegum" wasn't included on the album, it was added as a bonus track to the CD.

34. Gordon, Kim. "Boys Are Smelly: Sonic Youth Tour Diary, '87." *Village Voice*, September 1, 1988.

35. Moore, Thurston. Quoted in *Goodbye 20th Century*, 147.

36. This was the catalog number that originally had been assigned to Henry Rollins and Lydia Lunch's project.

Chapter 10: SST vs. MTV

1. Countey insists that on the master tapes of Jenifer's bass tracks, those cows can be heard mooing in the background.

2. Andersen and Jenkins, *Dance of Days*, 187.

3. Farrell, interview.

4. Farrell, interview.

5. Crawford, Ed. Interview with Glenn BurnSilver. *Phoenix New Times*, April 10, 2012.

6. Roessler, Kira. Interview with Ryan Leach.

7. Ciccone Youth. *The Whitey Album*. Enigma Records. 1989.

8. The actress, whose real name is Elisabeth Carr, also makes a brief appearance in Kern's videos for "Death Valley '69" and the Butthole Surfers' "Concubine."

9. Demos from these recordings would be released in 2016 as *Spinhead Sessions*.

10. Watt, Mike. Interview with Amy Yates Wuelfing and Steven DiLodovico. *No Slam Dancing, No Stage Diving, No Spikes*, 172–173.

11. Ranaldo, *jrnls80s*, 82.

12. Ranaldo, *jrnls80s*, 57.

13. Dukowski, Chuck. Interview with Al Flipside. *Flipside #50*, July 1986.

14. True then, even more true today.

15. Hein, Bill. Interview by Jim Ruland. March 26, 2021.

16. Dinsmore, Clifford. Interview. *Double Cross*, February 9, 2010.

17. Much of this footage would find its way into Rachman's 2006 documentary *American Hardcore* based on the book by Steven Blush.

18. Rachman, Paul. Interview by Jim Ruland. January 20, 2021.

19. Rachman, interview.

20. Rachman, interview.

21. Rachman, interview.

22. Long, Brian. Interview by Jim Ruland. January 30, 2021.

23. Farrell, interview.

24. Long, interview.

25. Dick attended high school with another legendary figure in science fiction: Ursula K. Le Guin. Although they both graduated from Berkeley High School in 1947, the two didn't know one another.

26. Unfortunately, Dick didn't live to see it; he died a few months before the film was released.

27. Gordon, Kim. Interview with Byron Coley. Sonic Youth *Sister* Interview Disc. 1987.

28. Ranaldo, Lee. Interview with Byron Coley. Sonic Youth *Sister* Interview Disc. 1987.

29. Long, interview.

30. Countey, interview.

31. *HR Tapes '84–'86*, which combines these two reissues, was released the following year on CD and cassette, yet it was given an earlier catalog number of SST 171.
32. Thomson, Jim. Interview by Jim Ruland. May 19, 2020.
33. Mugger, interview.
34. Mataré, interview.
35. Mataré, interview.
36. Weasel, Ben. *Maximum Rocknroll*, November 1987.
37. Farrell, interview.
38. Weasel, *Maximum Rocknroll*.

Chapter 11: SST vs. the Northwest

1. Farrell, interview.
2. Farrell, interview.
3. Farrell, interview.
4. Farrell, interview.
5. Frith would also release *The Technology of Tears* (SST 172), a double album of experimental music for dance and theater commissioned by various arts organizations and remastered for SST.
6. Lewis, interview.
7. Fisk, Steve. Interview by Jim Ruland. April 6, 2021.
8. Fisk, interview.
9. Pickerel, Mark. Interview by Jim Ruland. March 31, 2021.
10. Farrell, interview. Incidentally, Ray and Susan Farrell aren't related.
11. Lanegan, Mark. Interview by Jim Ruland. January 8, 2021.
12. Lanegan, interview.
13. The music festival, whose name was inspired by the Charlie Manson song the Beach Boys included under a different name on its 1969 album *20/20*, was originally scheduled for LA as part of a series of festivals but had to be rescheduled when its permit was pulled. SST attempted to sue the city but to no avail.
14. Long, interview.
15. The CD single "Rocket Machine" (SST 255) was schedule for release in 1991, seemingly to capitalize on the Capitol's signing of Mazzy Star in 1990, but it was never issued.
16. Pickerel, interview.
17. Lanegan, interview.
18. Mascis, J. Interview with Dan Whiteley. *Thrasher*, 2015.
19. Attfield, Nick. *You're Living All Over Me* (New York: Bloomsbury, 2007), 41.
20. Long, interview.
21. O'Bryan, Ed. Interview by Jim Ruland. February 23, 2021.
22. Ibarra, Craig. Interview by Jim Ruland. April–May 2021.
23. Ibarra, interview.
24. Farrell, interview.
25. Eddy, Chuck. *Village Voice*, September 22, 1987.
26. Negativland. *Helter Stupid*. SST Records. 1989.
27. Negativland. *JamCon'84*. SST Records. 1988.

28. Initially released by Seeland Records in 1985, *JamCon'84* (SST 233) was reissued by SST on cassette in 1988.

29. Long, interview.

30. Long, interview.

31. Long, interview.

32. Thomson, interview.

33. Pickerel, interview.

34. Lanegan, interview.

35. Lanegan, interview.

36. Lanegan, interview.

37. Lanegan, interview.

38. Mould with Azerrad, *See a Little Light*, 98.

39. Anderson, Dawn. Review of *Deep Six*. *Rocket*, March 1986.

40. Thayil, interview.

41. Long, interview.

42. Thayil, interview.

43. Thayil, interview.

44. Thayil, interview.

45. Thayil, interview.

46. Thayil, interview.

Chapter 12: SST vs. Negativland

1. Whittaker, Michael. Interview with Brant Palko and Ryan Rodier. *You Don't Know Mojack* #80, April 12, 2019.

2. O'Bryan, interview.

3. Bostrom, interview.

4. Bostrom, interview.

5. Farrell, interview.

6. Long, interview.

7. Ranaldo, Lee. Quoted in Prato, *Too High to Die*, 180.

8. Farrell, interview.

9. Chick, Stevie. *Psychic Confusion: The Sonic Youth Story* (London: Omnibus Press, 2009), 141.

10. Long, interview.

11. Mugger, interview.

12. O'Bryan, interview.

13. Ibarra, interview.

14. Spector, Daniel. Interview by Jim Ruland. October 7, 2021.

15. Spector, interview.

16. Long, interview.

17. Ibarra, interview.

18. When Soundgarden finally got around to remixing *Ultramega OK* in 2017, the band turned to Endino. Incidentally, Endino was also a member of the band Skin Yard, who put out three albums on Ginn's Cruz Records between 1990 and 1993.

19. Fisk, interview.
20. Anderson, Steve. Interview with Dave Lang. *Perfect Sound Forever*, April 2019.
21. Long, interview.
22. Long, interview.
23. Bostrom, Derrick. Quoted in Prato, *Too High to Die*, 179.
24. Kirkwood, Curt. Quoted in Prato, *Too High to Die*, 179.
25. Kirkwood, Curt. Quoted in Prato, *Too High to Die*, 179.
26. Lanegan, interview.
27. Spector, interview.
28. Spector, interview. Nevertheless, on H.R.'s *Charge* the name "Daniel" appears as executive producer. Spector wasn't the only employee who operated under this edict. Spector estimates Richard Ford was an uncredited producer on at least fifty SST releases.
29. Negativland, *Helter Stupid*.
30. Nicks, Kara. Interview with Stacy Russo, 143.
31. Ibarra, Nicks's former boyfriend, would last another five years at SST.
32. SST also reissued the Descendents LP *Enjoy!* (SST 242).
33. Lanegan, interview.
34. Spector, interview.
35. Spector, interview.
36. Negativland. *Fair Use: The Story of the Letter U and the Numeral 2*. (Concord: Seeland Records, 1995), Preface.
37. Negativland, *Fair Use*, 5.
38. Negativland, *Fair Use*, 6.
39. Negativland, *Fair Use*, 22.
40. Negativland, *Fair Use*, 23.
41. Negativland, *Fair Use*, 32.
42. Negativland. *Guns*. SST Records. 1992.
43. Negativland, *Fair Use*, 41.
44. Negativland, *Fair Use*, 41.
45. Incredibly, at the time of publication, this T-shirt was still on sale at the SST Superstore.
46. Negativland, *Fair Use*, 50.
47. Negativland, *Fair Use*, 50.
48. This number is only accurate if one includes releases by Cruz Records and New Alliance Records in the tally. Ginn states at the end of the release that he is the sole owner of all three labels. Negativland, *Fair Use*, 51.
49. Negativland, *Fair Use*, 52.
50. Bostrom, interview.
51. Negativland, *Fair Use*, 94.
52. Fletcher, Tony. "The Letter U, The Numeral 2 and a Fistful of Lawsuits." *Creem*, April 1993.
53. He brought Pell Mell into the fold because he believed in the band but also because he could.
54. Ginn, Greg. Interview with Eric Olsen. Blogcritics.org, November 21, 2003. This interview occurred in late 1992 but wasn't published until 2003.

55. Thayil, interview.

56. According to Thayil, SST was so consistent in its payments that when it came time to renew the contract after the initial period expired, Soundgarden reupped with SST. Then, when Soundgarden broke up, problems with SST started.

57. Negativland, *Fair Use*, 73.

58. "Et U2, SST?" *Village Voice*, December 22, 1992.

59. Fletcher, "The Letter U, The Numeral 2 and a Fistful of Lawsuits."

Chapter 13: SST vs. Techno

1. Batwinas, Andy. Interview by Jim Ruland. March 20, 2021.

2. Batwinas, interview.

3. Moore would eventually embrace the moniker "Drummer" but for clarity he will be referred to by his surname here.

4. Cameron, Greg. Interview with Palko and Rodier.

5. Batwinas, interview.

6. Batwinas, interview.

7. Screw Radio. *The Best of Screw Radio*. SST Records. 1997.

8. Boehm, Mike. "SST Plugs into Irreverence on 'Screw Radio.'" *Los Angeles Times*, August 7, 1993.

9. *The Best of Screw Radio*.

10. Beaugez, Jim. Review of Meat Puppets' *Dusty Notes*. *Rolling Stone*, March 7, 2019.

11. Appleford, Steve. "Littlest Music 'Superstore' Thrives in Shadow of Giants." *Los Angeles Times*, July 18, 1993.

12. Bostrom, interview.

13. Negativland, *Fair Use*, 151.

14. Negativland, *Fair Use*, 179.

15. Neither the CD nor the booklet ever appeared.

16. Batwinas, interview.

17. Batwinas, interview.

18. Batwinas, interview.

19. Ginn, Greg. Interview with Mark Prindle. MarkPrindle.com, 2003.

20. Batwinas, interview.

21. Batwinas, interview.

22. Batwinas, interview.

23. Benson, David. Interview by Jim Ruland. September 27, 2021.

24. Robinson, Eugene. Interview by Jim Ruland. March 19, 2021.

25. Robinson, interview.

26. Robinson, interview.

27. Robinson, interview.

28. OXBOW. *The Thin Black Book* (San Francisco: Hydrahead Records, 2017), 9.

29. Wenner, Niko. Interview by Jim Ruland. March 19, 2021.

30. Robinson, interview.

31. Adams, Dan. Interview by Jim Ruland. March 19, 2021.

32. Wenner, interview.

33. Robinson, interview.

34. Robinson, interview.

35. "Insylum" also appears on a picture disc released by Crippled Dick Hot Wax! The flip side features "The Stabbing Hand," a track from *Let Me Be a Woman*, with additional vocals by Kathy Acker.

36. Robinson, interview.

37. Robinson, interview.

38. Gone. *Country Dumb*. SST Records. 1998.

39. Batwinas, interview.

40. Batwinas, interview.

41. Batwinas, interview.

Chapter 14: SST vs. History

1. Ginn, Greg. Interview with Mark Prindle.

2. Greene, James, Jr. "Did Black Flag Reunite in 2003 with a Robot Playing Bass?" JGTWO.com, September 21, 2009.

3. Greene, "Did Black Flag Reunite in 2003 with a Robot Playing Bass?"

4. Rachman, interview.

5. Seki, Don. Review of Black Flag Benefit for Cats. *Razorcake*, September 17, 2003.

6. Ginn, Greg. Interview with Mark Prindle.

7. Bruno, Anthony. "SST to Offer Catalog through the Orchard." *Billboard*, January 11, 2006.

8. During the writing of this book, SST released deeper cuts from its catalog, including some—but not all—of the recordings by Slovenly, Transition, and several others.

9. McNeil, Legs. "Black Flag: Anatomy of a Lawsuit." *Vice*, August 15, 2013. Also, Morris's arithmetic doesn't add up. He says there were "four of us" but lists five people. Since Cadena wasn't there because he was added later, it was indeed four.

10. McNeil, "Black Flag: Anatomy of a Lawsuit."

11. Gitter, Mike. "FLAG vs. Black Flag." Noisecreep.com, February 19, 2013.

12. Ginn, Greg. Interview with Mark Prindle.

13. Colver, interview.

14. Colver, interview.

15. Fancher, interview.

16. When I moved out of the South Bay, I was horrified to discover all of the zines I'd stashed in my closet were covered in a thin layer of mold.

17. Pickerel, interview.

18. Lanegan, interview.

19. Lanegan, interview.

20. Holzman, interview.

21. Gurewitz, Brett. Interview by Jim Ruland. March 5, 2021.

22. Gurewitz, interview.

23. Pavitt, interview.

24. Gurewitz, interview.

25. Gurewitz, interview.
26. Bostrom, interview.
27. Pavitt, interview.
28. Bostrom, interview.
29. Wenner, interview.
30. Long, interview.
31. Carducci, Joe. Interview by Jim Ruland. December 23, 2020.
32. Fisk, interview.
33. Rodier, Ryan. Interview by Jim Ruland. May 1, 2021.
34. Palko, Brant. Interview by Jim Ruland. May 1, 2021.
35. Palko, interview.
36. Rodier, interview.
37. Mugger, interview.

BIBLIOGRAPHY

Our Band Could Be Your Life: Scenes from the American Indie Underground, by Michael Azerrad (2001); *Enter Naomi: SST, LA and All That*, by Joe Carducci (2007); and *Spray Paint the Walls: The Story of Black Flag*, by Stevie Chick (2011) form the foundation for any serious consideration of SST Records. If this book is your introduction to SST Records and its many sagas, they are required reading.

Any account of the early days of LA punk's weird and wonderful history owes a debt to Brendan Mullen's extensive documentation of the scene he helped create, and mine is no exception.

Details about the Stains, who were all but written out of the history of LA punk, are derived, except when noted in interviews, from Jimmy Alvarado's two-part "An Oral History of East Los Angeles's First Punk Band," which ran in *Razorcake* #67 and #68 in April and June 2011. Full disclosure: I've been a contributor to *Razorcake*, America's only nonprofit independent music magazine, since 2001. Before that I wrote (very poorly) for *Flipside* as well as for several other LA-based zines. Zines are the lifeblood of punk rock, and I'm grateful to the "kids" who cranked out interviews for *Big Takeover*, *Capitol Crisis*, *Conflict*, *Dagger Zine*, *Damage*, *Last Rites*, *Maximum Rocknroll*, *NO MAG*, *No Recess!*, *Outcry*, *Punk Planet*, *Ripper*, *Search and Destroy*, *Skitzoid*, *Slash*, *Smash!*, *Suburban Relapse*, *WDC Period*, *We Got Power*, and many, many more. Support the zines in your scene.

What follows is a list of books that helped inform my understanding of

SST Records, the artists who contributed to the label, and the times in which they lived. If there are multiple editions of a book, I note the version that I read, referred to, or in some cases, obsessed over.

Dance of Days: Two Decades of Punk in the Nation's Capital, by Mark Andersen and Mark Jenkins. Akashic Books, 2009.

You're Living All Over Me, by Nick Attfield. Bloomsbury, 2011.

Hardcore California: A History of Punk and New Wave, edited by Peter Belsito and Bob Davis. Last Gasp, 1989.

I'm Just the Drummer, by Bob Bert. HoZac Books 2019.

Texas Is the Reason: The Mavericks of Lone Star Punk, by Pat Blashill. Bazillion Points, 2020.

Goodbye 20th Century: A Biography of Sonic Youth, by David Browne. Da Capo Press, 2008.

Rock and the Pop Narcotic: Testament for the Electric Church, volume 1, by Joe Carducci. Redoubt Press, 1990.

Enter Naomi: SST, LA, and All That..., by Joe Carducci. Redoubt Press, 2007.

Life Against Dementia: Essays, Reviews, Interviews, 1975–2011, by Joe Carducci. Redoubt Press, 2012.

Psychic Confusion: The Sonic Youth Story, by Stevie Chick. Omnibus Press, 2009.

Planet Joe, by Joe Cole. 2.13.61 Publications, 2011.

Complicated Fun: The Birth of Minneapolis Punk and Indie Rock, 1974–1984, by Cyn Collins. Minnesota Historical Society Press, 2017.

Blight at the End of the Funnel, by Edward Colver. Last Gasp, 2015.

Coloring Outside the Lines: A Punk Rock Memoir, by Aimee Cooper. Rowdy's Press, 2003.

Barred for Life: How Black Flag's Iconic Logo Became Punk Rock's Secret Handshake, by Stewart Dean Ebersole. PM Press, 2013.

Hüsker Dü: The Story of the Noise-Pop Pioneers Who Launched Modern Rock, by Andrew Earles. Voyageur Press, 2010.

Gimme Indie Rock: 500 Essential American Underground Rock Albums 1981–1996, by Andrew Earles. Voyageur Press, 2014.

Rock and Roll Always Forgets: A Quarter Century of Music Criticism, by Chuck Eddy. Duke University Press, 2011.

Los Angeles Flipside Fanzine #54: Ten-Year Anniversary Issue, compiled by Hudley Flipside. Independently published, 2019.

Please Bee Nice: My Life Up 'til Now, by Gary Floyd with David Ensminger. CreateSpace, 2014.

Confusion Is Next: The Sonic Youth Story, by Alec Foege. St. Martin's Press, 1994.

Double Nickels on the Dime, by Michael T. Fournier. Bloomsbury, 2007.

Punk Diary: The Ultimate Trainspotter's Guide to Underground Rock 1970–1982, by George Gimarc. Backbeat Books, 2005.

Tyger! Tyger!, by R. C. K. Ginn. Macmillan, 1968.

Babylon's Burning: From Punk to Grunge, by Clinton Heylin. Viking, 2007.

A Wailing of a Town: An Oral History of Early San Pedro Punks and More 1977–1985, by Craig Ibarra. END FWY Press, 2015.

Sing Backwards and Weep, by Mark Lanegan, edited by Mishka Shubaly. Hachette Books, 2020.

Punk Elegies: True Tales of Death Trip Kids, Wrongful Sex, and Trial by Angel Dust, by Allan MacDonell. Rare Bird Books, 2015.

Kids of the Black Hole: Punk Rock in Postsuburban California, by Dewar MacLeod. University of Oklahoma Press, 2010.

In the Fascist Bathroom: Punk in Pop Music 1977–1992, by Greil Marcus. Harvard University Press, 1993.

We Got Power: Hardcore Punk Scenes from 1980s Southern California, edited by David Markey and Jordan Schwartz. Bazillion Points, 2012.

Louie Louie, by Dave Marsh. Hyperion, 1995.

Taking Punk to the Masses: From Nowhere to Nevermind, edited by Jacob McMurray. Fantagraphics Books, 2011.

See a Little Light: The Trail of Rage and Melody, by Bob Mould with Michael Azerrad. Little, Brown, 2011.

My War, by Kurt Morris. Self-published, 2020.

Lexicon Devil: The Fast Times and Short Life of Darby Crash and the Germs, by Brendan Mullen with Don Bolles and Adam Parfrey. Feral House, 2002.

Fair Use: The Story of the Letter U and the Numeral 2, by Negativland. Seeland Records, 1995.

Savage Young Dü, by Erin Osmon. Numero Group, 2017.

The Thin Black Blook, by OXBOW. Hydrahead Records, 2017.

Turned On: A Biography of Henry Rollins, by James Parker. Cooper Square Press, 2000.

Too High to Die: Meet the Meat Puppets, by Greg Prato. CreateSpace, 2012.

jrnls80s, by Lee Ranaldo. Soft Skull Press, 1998.

High Adventures in the Great Outdoors: Writing 1982–1985, by Henry Rollins. 2.13.61 Publications, 1993 (second printing).

Art to Choke Hearts & Pissing in the Gene Pool: Collected Writing 1985–1987, by Henry Rollins. 2.13.61 Publications, 1992.

Get in the Van: On the Road with Black Flag, by Henry Rollins. 2.13.61 Publications, 1994.

Total F*cking Godhead: The Biography of Chris Cornell, by Corbin Reif. Post Hill Press, 2020.

Panic!, curated by Ryan Richardson. Ryebread Rodeo, 2018.

Rip It Up and Start Again: Postpunk 1978–1984, by Simon Reynolds. Faber and Faber, 2005.

We're Going to Change the World: Interviews with Women from the 1970s & 1980s Southern California Punk Rock Scene, by Stacy Russo. Santa Monica Press, 2017.

We Owe You Nothing: Punk Planet, the Collected Interviews, edited by Daniel Sinker. Punk Planet Books, 2008 (expanded edition).

Forming: The Early Days of LA Punk. Smart Art Press, 2000.

Make the Music Go Bang: The Early LA Punk Scene, by Don Snowden and Gary Leonard. St. Martin's Press, 1997.

Anti–Punk Rock: A History, by Spot. No Auditions, 2017.

Spiels of a Minuteman, by Mike Watt. L'Oie de Cravan, 2003.

Everybody Loves Our Town: An Oral History of Grunge, by Mark Yarm. Three Rivers Press, 2011.

No Slam Dancing, No Stage Diving, No Spikes, by Amy Yates Wuelfing and Steven DiLodovico. DiWulf, 2014.

INDEX